THE MIGHTY AND THE ALMIGHTY

Also by Madeleine Albright

Madam Secretary: A Memoir (2003)

THE MIGHTY AND THE ALMIGHTY

Reflections on

America, God, and

World Affairs

MADELEINE ALBRIGHT
with Bill Woodward

HarperCollins*Publishers*

FIRST EDITION

Designed by Joseph Rutt

Printed on acid-free paper

Library of Congress Cataloging-in-Publication Data

Albright, Madeleine Korbel.
The mighty and the Almighty : reflections on America, God, and world affairs / Madeleine Albright.—1st ed.
p. cm.
Includes index.
ISBN-10: 0-06-089257-9
ISBN-13: 978-0-06-089257-9
1. Religion and international affairs.   2. United States—Foreign relations.   I. Title.

BL65.I55A53 2006
261.8'7—dc22   2005055002

06 07 08 09 10 NMSG/RRD 10 9 8 7 6 5 4 3 2 1

Dedicated to those of every nation and faith who defend liberty, build peace, dispel ignorance, fight poverty, and seek justice.

Contents

Part Two

Cross, Crescent, Star

Part Three

Final Reflections

Introduction

by William J. Clinton
Forty-second President of the United States

During the time she was secretary of state, the world learned what I already knew: Madeleine Albright is unafraid to take on hard issues or to speak her mind. In *The Mighty and the Almighty*, she writes with uncommon frankness and good sense about America's international role, religion, ethics, and the current divided and anxious state of the world. To my knowledge, no former secretary of state has written anything similar. It is an unexpected book, drafted against the advice of friends who worried that these topics could not be discussed without stepping on toes. In my experience, the only way to avoid stepping on toes is to stand still. Madeleine Albright is the embodiment of forward movement.

After our initial conversation about this project, I called Madeleine to discuss it further, not knowing at the time where she was. It turned out that she was in Gdánsk, Poland, commemorating the twenty-fifth anniversary of Solidarity, the democracy movement that ended the cold war and brought freedom to Central and East Europe. When I rang, Madeleine was standing in a crowd that included the former Czech president Václav Havel and the current presidents of Ukraine and Poland. She passed the phone around, and I had an unforeseen but welcome chance to catch up with some old friends. Meanwhile, Madeleine placed a bouquet of flowers as a memorial to Solidarity and attended a three-hour open-air mass in celebration of freedom. I had caught her at a moment and in a place where God and democracy were together at center stage. One theme of this book, and a source of continuing controversy in public life, concerns the relationship between the two.

"The core of democracy," wrote Walt Whitman, "is the religious element. All the religions, old and new, are there." I expect we have all come across people who would embrace the first of Whitman's sentences while ignoring the second, rendering both without meaning. At their best, religion and democracy each respect the equality and value of every human being: all of us stamped with the Creator's image, each endowed with certain inalienable rights. These doctrines sit next to one another comfortably; they are unifying and inclusive. Problems arise when we try to place our own interpretation ahead of Whitman's, arguing that those sharing our particular understanding of the universe are more worthy than others. To have faith is to believe in the existence of absolute truth. It is quite another thing to assert that imperfect human beings can be in full possession of this truth, or that we have a political ideology that is fully true and allows us to penalize, coerce, or abuse those who believe differently.

The Constitution of the United States created something truly new: a system of government in which the highest trust is placed not in the top officials, who are hemmed in by an ingenious system of checks and balances, but in the people as a whole. Among the limitations our founders placed on those in government was that they could not establish an official state religion, or abridge the right of anyone to worship freely. The founders understood from history that the concentration of political and religious authority in the same hands could be toxic.

We know, of course, that the power of faith is often exploited by those seeking to enhance their own power at the expense of others. In the Balkans, Slobodan Milošević talked much about defending Christian Europe, but his real interest was in using religion and extreme divisiveness to fortify his hold on power. Osama bin Laden poses as a defender of Islam, but his willingness to murder innocents, including other Muslims, is not a fair reading of the Quran and is disloyal to the tenets of that faith. In the wrong hands, religion becomes a lever used to pry one group of people away from another not because of some profound spiritual insight, but because it helps whoever is doing the prying.

Does this mean that policy-makers should try to keep religion walled off from public life? As Madeleine Albright argues, the answer to that question is a resounding no. Not only shouldn't we do that; we couldn't succeed if we tried. Religious convictions, if they are convictions, can't be pulled on and off like a pair of boots. We walk with them wherever we go, the skeptics and atheists side by side with the devout. A president or secretary of state must make decisions with regard both to his or her own religious convictions and to the impact of those decisions on people of different faiths. However, as Madeleine points out, assessing that impact is no easy task.

During my visit to India in 2000, some Hindu militants decided to vent their outrage by murdering thirty-eight Sikhs in cold blood. If I hadn't made the trip, the victims would probably still be alive. If I hadn't made the trip because I feared what religious extremists might do, I couldn't have done my job as president of the United States. The nature of America is such that many people define themselves—or a part of themselves—in relation to it, for or against. This is part of the reality in which our leaders must operate.

When radical imams try to subvert the thinking of alienated, disaffected young people, not all of whom are poor or lacking in education, by offering a supposed quick trip to paradise in return for the believers' willingness to kill civilians by blowing themselves up, how should we respond? We can try to kill and capture them, but we can't get them all. We can try to persuade them to abandon violence, but if our arguments have no basis in their own experience, we can't fully succeed. Our best chance is to work cooperatively with those in the Muslim world who are trying to reach the same minds as the radicals by preaching a more complete Islam, not a distorted, jagged shard.

I truly believe that this can be done, not by diluting spiritual beliefs but by probing their depths. The three Abrahamic faiths have more similarities than differences. Each calls for reverence, charity, humility, and love. None is fully revealed. The challenge for our leaders is to use what we have in common as a basis for defeating the most extreme elements and draining support for terror. Once people acknowledge their common humanity, it becomes more difficult for them to demonize and destroy each other. It is far easier to find principled compromise with one of "us" than with one of "them." Our religious convictions can help us erase the age-old dividing line. No job is more important, but as this book by Madeleine Albright makes clear, it is a job that—four and a half years after 9/11—we have barely begun.

—*New York, February 2006*

Part One

God, Liberty, Country

One

The Mighty and the Almighty

———— ❧ ————

I had watched previous inaugural addresses, but the first one I truly took in was John Kennedy's in 1961. My brother John, who was in junior high school, played the trumpet in the Denver police band and had been invited to Washington to march in the inaugural parade. It seems that everyone remembers the snow on the ground and how the glare of sunshine made it impossible for Robert Frost to read the poem he had composed for the occasion. The new president, hatless in the crystal-cold air, his breath visible, asked us to "ask not." It was the speech about "passing the torch" to another generation. I saw it on television—that is how I experienced all the inaugural addresses until 1993. Then, and again four years later, I watched President Clinton deliver his speeches from the balcony of the U.S. Capitol. The words combined with the crowds and the view of the Washington Monument brought out the sense of history and pride in the United States that has done so much to shape my view of the world.

•　　•　　•

The inaugural address provides an American president with a matchless opportunity to speak directly to 6 billion fellow human beings, including some 300 million fellow citizens. By defining his country's purpose, a commander in chief can make history and carve out a special place for himself (or perhaps, one day, herself) within it. On January 20, 2005, facing an audience assembled in the shadow of the Capitol, President George W. Bush addressed America and the world. From the first words, it was evident that both he and his speechwriters had aimed high. "It is the policy of the United States," he declared, "to seek and support the growth of democratic movements and institutions in every nation and culture, with the ultimate goal of ending tyranny in our world." He continued, "History has an ebb and flow of justice, but history also has a visible direction, set by liberty and the Author of Liberty." The president concluded that "America, in this young century, proclaims liberty throughout the world and to all the inhabitants thereof." He might have added that, in the Bible, God had assigned that same job, in the same words, to Moses.

The speech was vintage George W. Bush, one that his admirers would hail as inspirational and his detractors would dismiss as self-exalting. It was of a piece with the president's first term, during which he had responded to history's deadliest strike on U.S. soil, led America into two wars, roused passions among both liberals and conservatives, set America apart from longtime allies, aggravated relations with Arab and Muslim societies, and conveyed a sense of U.S. intentions that millions found exhilarating, many others ill-advised.

Within the United States, there are those who see the president as a radical presiding over a foreign policy that is, in the words of one commentator, "more than preemptive, it is theologically presumptuous; not only unilateral, but dangerously messianic; not just arrogant, but rather bordering on the idolatrous and blasphemous." The president's supporters suggest the contrary, that his leadership is ideally, even heroically, suited to the perils of this era and in keeping with the best traditions of America.

My own initial instinct, particularly when the president is trumpeting the merits of freedom, is to applaud. I firmly believe that democracy is one of humankind's best inventions: a form of government superior to any other and a powerful source of hope. I believe just as firmly in the necessity of American leadership. Why wouldn't I? When I was a little girl, U.S. soldiers crossed the ocean to help save Europe from the menace of Adolf Hitler. When I was barely in my teens, the American people welcomed my family after the communists had seized power in my native Czechoslovakia. Unlike most in my generation who were born in Central Europe, I had the chance to grow up in a democracy, a privilege for which I will forever be grateful. I take seriously the welcoming words at the base of the Statue of Liberty; and I love to think of America as an inspiration to people everywhere—especially to those who have been denied freedom in their own lands.

As appealing as President Bush's rhetoric may sometimes be, however, I also know that proclaiming liberty is far simpler than building genuine democracy. Political liberty is not a magic pill people can swallow at night and awaken with all problems solved, nor can it be imposed from the outside. According to the president, "Freedom is God's gift to everybody in the world." He told Bob Woodward, "As a matter of fact, I was the person who wrote the line, or said it. I didn't write it, I just said it in a speech. And it became part of the jargon. And I believe that. And I believe we have a duty to free people. I would hope we wouldn't have to do it militarily, but we have a duty."

These are uplifting sentiments, undoubtedly, but what exactly do they mean? The president says that liberty is a gift to everybody, but is he also implying that God appointed America to deliver that gift? Even to raise that question is to invite others. Does the United States believe it has a special relationship with God? Does it have a divinely inspired mission to promote liberty? What role, if any, should religious convictions play in the decisions of those responsible for U.S. foreign policy? But perhaps we should begin by asking why we are even thinking about these questions, given America's constitutional separation between church and state. And haven't we long since concluded that it is a mistake, in any case, to mix religion and foreign policy? I had certainly thought so.

Although—as I learned late in life—my heritage is Jewish,* I was raised a Roman Catholic. As a child, I studied the catechism, prayed regularly to the Virgin Mary, and fantasized about becoming a priest (even a Catholic girl can dream). As I was growing up, my sense of morality was molded by what I learned in church and by the example and instruction of my parents. The message was drilled into me to work hard, do my best at all times, and respect the rights of others. As a sophomore at Wellesley College, I was required to study the Bible as history, learning the saga of ancient Israel in the same way as that of Greece or Rome.†

As an immigrant and the daughter of a former Czechoslovak diplomat, I was primarily interested in world affairs. I did not,

---

* A full discussion of the discovery of my Jewish heritage, including the shock of learning that three of my grandparents and a number of other family members had died in the Holocaust, is included in my autobiography, *Madam Secretary: A Memoir*, Miramax, New York, 2003, 235–249.

† Wellesley is a college for women. The school's motto is "Non ministrari sed ministrare": "Not to be ministered unto but to minister." My classmates and I used to joke that it really meant "Not to be ministers, but to be ministers' wives."

however, view the great issues of the day through the prism of religion—either my own or that of others. Nor did I ever feel secure enough about the depth of my religious knowledge to think I was in a position to lecture acquaintances about what they should believe. I did not consider spiritual faith a subject to talk about in public. For the generation that came of age when and where I did, this was typical. I am sure there were parts of America where attitudes were different, but the scholar Michael Novak got it right when he asserted in the early 1960s, "As matters now stand, the one word [that could not be used] in serious conversation without upsetting someone is 'God.' "

The star most of us navigated by in those years was modernization, which many took as a synonym for secularization. The wonders we celebrated were less biblical than technological: the space race, breakthroughs in medicine, the birth of nuclear power, the introduction of color television, and the dawn of the computer age. In the United States, the play and movie *Inherit the Wind* dramatized the triumph of science (the theory of evolution) over creationism (a literal interpretation of Genesis).* When we thought of Moses, the image that came to mind was Charlton Heston, in technicolor. Religious values endured, but excitement came from anticipating what our laboratories and researchers might come up with next. We Americans were not alone in our pragmatic preoccupations. Abroad, the ris-

---

* This "triumph of science" did not arrive all at once and may not be permanent. Not until 1968 did it become legal to teach evolution in every part of the United States. More recently, there has been pressure from some church groups to teach "intelligent design" as an alternative to the theory of evolution. The idea behind intelligent design, as I understand it, is that the complexity of life proves that the world must have been created by an all-knowing supernatural force. I do not consider myself an expert on everything that should be taught in classrooms, but I do believe a clear distinction should be drawn between concepts that are derived from the scientific method and those that are not.

ing political tides were socialism and nationalism, as Africans and Asians freed themselves from their colonial overseers and began the task of building countries that could stand on their own.

In the early 1980s, I became a professor at Georgetown University. My specialty was foreign policy, about which such icons as Hans Morgenthau, George Kennan, and Dean Acheson theorized in almost exclusively secular terms. In their view, individuals and groups could be identified by the nations to which they belonged. Countries had governments. Governments acted to protect their nations' interests. Diplomacy consisted of reconciling different interests, at least to the point where wars did not break out and the world did not blow up. Foreign policy was commonly compared to a game of chess: cerebral, with both sides knowing the rules. This was a contest governed by logic; its players spoke in the manner of lawyers, not preachers. During my adult years, western leaders gained political advantage by deriding "godless communism"; otherwise, I cannot remember any leading American diplomat (even the born-again Christian Jimmy Carter) speaking in depth about the role of religion in shaping the world. Religion was not a respecter of national borders; it was above and beyond reason; it evoked the deepest passions; and historically, it was the cause of much bloodshed. Diplomats in my era were taught not to invite trouble, and no subject seemed more inherently treacherous than religion.

This was the understanding that guided me while I was serving as President Clinton's ambassador to the United Nations and secretary of state. My colleagues felt the same. When, in 1993, Professor Samuel Huntington of Harvard predicted that the era following the end of the cold war might well witness an interreligious "clash of civilizations," we did all we could to distance ourselves from that theory. We had in mind a future in which nations and regions would draw closer as democratic bonds grew stronger, not a world splitting apart along historic fault lines of culture and creed.

When fighting broke out in the Balkans, we urged each side to focus on the rights of the individual, not the competing prerogatives of religious groups. In 1998, after U.S. embassies in Kenya and Tanzania were bombed by terrorists, we published posters seeking information and offering a reward; these posters had the heading, "This is not about religion. This is not about politics. This is about murder, plain and simple." During the administration's marathon effort to find a basis for peace in the Middle East, President Clinton and I were fully aware of the religious significance of Jerusalem's holy places. We hoped, nevertheless, to devise a legal formula clever enough to quiet the emotions generated by the past. We asked and expected both sides to be realistic and settle for the best deal they could get.

We were living, after all, in modern times. The wars between Catholics and Protestants that had claimed the lives of one-third the population of Christian Europe had been brought to a close in 1648 by the Peace of Westphalia. Large-scale fighting between Christians and Muslims had ceased when, in 1683, the advance of the Ottoman Turks was halted at the gates of Vienna. I found it incredible, as the twenty-first century approached, that Catholics and Protestants were still quarreling in Northern Ireland and that Hindus and Muslims were still squaring off against each other in south Asia; surely, I thought, these rivalries were the echoes of earlier, less enlightened times, not a sign of battles still to come.

Since the terror attacks of 9/11, I have come to realize that it may have been I who was stuck in an earlier time. Like many other foreign policy professionals, I have had to adjust the lens through which I view the world, comprehending something that seemed to be a new reality but that had actually been evident for some time. The 1990s had been a decade of globalization and spectacular technological gains; the information revolution altered our lifestyle, transformed the workplace, and fostered the development of a whole new vocabulary. There was, however, another force at work. Almost everywhere, religious movements are thriving.

In many parts of Central and South America, Protestant evangelicals are contesting the centuries-old dominance of the Catholic Church. In China, authorities saddled with an obsolete ideology of their own are struggling to prevent burgeoning religious and spiritual movements from becoming a political threat. India's identity as a secular society is under challenge by Hindu nationalists. Throughout the former Soviet Union, long-repressed religious institutions have been reinvigorated. In Israel, Orthodox religious parties are seeking more influence over laws and society. Secular Arab nationalism, once thought to embody the future, has been supplanted by a resurgent Islam extending beyond Arab lands to Iran, Pakistan, central and southeast Asia, and parts of Africa. Christianity, too, is making remarkable inroads in Asia and Africa; ten of the world's eleven largest congregations are in South Korea, and the other is in Nigeria. A reawakening of Christian activism is also altering how we think about politics and culture here in the United States. In contrast to Michael Novak's observation four decades ago, people now talk (and argue) about God all the time. Even in Europe, which seems otherwise exempt from the trend toward religious growth, the number of observant Muslims is rising quickly, and a new pope—named for Benedict of Nursia, the continent's patron saint—is determined to re-evangelize its Christian population.

What does one make of this phenomenon? For those who design and implement U.S. foreign policy, what does it mean? How can we best manage events in a world in which there are many religions, with belief systems that flatly contradict one another at key points? How do we deal with the threat posed by extremists who, acting in the name of God, try to impose their will on others? We know that the nature of this test extends back to pagan times and is therefore nothing new; what is new is the extent of damage violence can inflict. This is where technology has truly made a difference. A religious war fought with swords, chain mail, catapults, and battering rams is one thing. A war fought with high explosives against civilian targets is quite another. And the prospect of a nuclear bomb detonated by terrorists in purported service to the Almighty is a nightmare that may one day come true.

Leaving government service in 2001, I returned to an earlier love, the university classroom. At Georgetown, I teach one course a semester, alternating between graduates and undergraduates. At the beginning of each course, I explain to my students that the main purpose of foreign policy is to persuade other countries to do what we want. To that end, a president or secretary of state has tools ranging from the blunt instrument of military force to the hard work of back-and-forth negotiations to the simple use of logical argument. The art of statecraft consists of finding the combination that produces the best results. That, in turn, requires a clear grasp of what matters most to those we are trying to influence. For businesspeople, this translates into "knowing your customer." In world affairs, it means learning about foreign countries and cultures; at a time when religious passions are embroiling the globe, that cannot be done without taking religious tenets and motivations fully into account.

Increasingly, in the classes I teach and in discussions with friends and colleagues, I have solicited thoughts about the impact of religion on current events. At first most people are surprised, as if uncertain what to think; then they open up.

My request leads not to one set of debates, but to many. It is a Rorschach test, revealing much about the preoccupations and anxieties of those who respond.

My students tend to equate religion with ethics and so frame their responses in moral terms. They want to know why the world is not doing more to alleviate poverty and disease, prevent genocide, and help developing countries compete in the global economy. After 9/11, quite a number were eager to join the military or the CIA, feeling a powerful urge to volunteer; but in most cases the feeling did not last. The war in Iraq created confusion about the wisdom of U.S. policy, and about whether America's goal was to lead the world or try to dominate it. The foreign students I teach are an eclectic group and therefore offer a mixed bag of opinions. They are most divided, not surprisingly, by questions of right and wrong in the Middle East.

My friends who are experts on foreign policy—a somewhat older group—are focused on the threat posed by religious extremists, including the possibility that terrorists will gain access to weapons of mass murder. They are alarmed, as well, about the gap in understanding that has opened between predominately Islamic societies and the West.

Arab leaders to whom I have spoken share this concern. They are upset, too, by the spread of what they consider to be false and damaging generalizations about Islam.

The religious scholars I have consulted are passionate about the need for political leaders to educate themselves in the varieties of faith and to see religion more as a potential means for reconciliation than as a source of conflict.

Political activists, not just Democrats, are agitated about the influence of the religious right on the White House and Congress; this is a subject also weighing on the minds of foreign diplomats.

My own reactions are grounded in my various identities,

as a daughter of Czechoslovakia, an American who is intensely proud of her adopted country, and a former secretary of state. My hero when I was growing up was Tomáš Garrigue Masaryk, who founded modern Czechoslovakia in 1918. Masaryk was a major influence on the thinking of my father and—through him—on me. Unlike many religious people, who see humanism as an alternative to faith in God, Masaryk saw the two as linked. To him, religious faith meant showing respect for every person and being willing to help others. Masaryk did not think it was necessary to believe in God to be moral, but he did argue that religious faith, properly understood, did much to encourage and strengthen right behavior. I have similar views. It is a perversion of faith to turn religion into a source of conflict and hate; it also creates severe problems for America and for the world.

Growing up in the United States transformed me, despite having witnessed much turbulence at a tender age, into a confirmed optimist. As a young woman, I took my theme—but without irony—from Leonard Bernstein's adaptation of *Candide*: "Everything is for the best in this best of all possible worlds." All through my years of government service, I maintained a positive outlook. In the Clinton administration, we talked a lot about the twenty-first century and, characteristically, felt sure that America, with others, could find a solution to most problems. I still feel that way, but I worry that we have been making some serious and avoidable mistakes.

There are days now when it is hard to pick up a newspaper. I think the U.S. government has thoroughly botched its response to international terror, damaged America's reputation, and substituted slogans for strategy in promoting freedom. I willingly concede, however, the difficulty and complexity of the problems the Bush administration is facing. I have often said that those who have never held the highest jobs in government do not know how hard these jobs can be, and that those who retire from them tend to forget quickly. Critics have an obligation to be fair and to offer constructive ideas. That is the purpose of this book. Part One deals with America's position in the world and the role played by religion and morality in shaping U.S. foreign policy, both now and in the past. Part Two concentrates on troubled relationships between Islamic communities and the West. Part Three offers my thoughts about how U.S. foreign policy and religion can best intersect. In keeping with my nature, the chapters are aimed primarily at practical policy-making—doing what works best. In keeping with the nature of religion, they are sometimes dominated by a parallel theme—doing what is right. Locating the convergence of the two is my ultimate goal, as it should be for the policy-makers of a nation that has, from its earliest days, sought to be judged both by its prowess and by its ideals.

Two

"The Eyes of All People Are upon Us"

———— ❧ ————

A s a junior in high school, six years after my family arrived in this country, I took my first full course in U.S. history. In that simpler time, my classmates and I were taught a more uniformly positive view of America's past than many students learn now: a saga of freedom-loving men and women overcoming obstacles in which every crisis was capped by a happy ending. It was, to me, an amazing tale made more real by the place where we lived—Colorado. Out west, the states were bigger than many European countries; the mountains so high that we marveled at how the first settlers had ever been able to cross them. The history hooked me; it was one of the reasons I wanted so much to be accepted as an American. Looking back, I do not remember devoting many hours to the study of religion in the United States, but we did of course begin with the story of the earliest arrivals from Europe, the intrepid people who made a long and uncomfortable voyage in search of a place to practice their faith freely, without interference from the government.

•   •   •

Writing in his shipboard diary in 1630, John Winthrop, governor of the Massachusetts Bay Colony, imagined that the community he and his fellow Puritans were about to establish would be "as a Citty upon a Hill, [with] the eies of all people . . . uppon us."* The Puritans believed that, if God so willed, the new colony would become a model for how to live a righteous life. They came to the New World in order to escape God's judgment on the corrupt churches of Europe, find refuge from the poverty and overpopulation of England, and obey the divine command to spread the gospel.

Theirs was a society based on a certain understanding of God's will, dependent on God's favor, eager to enjoy the fruits of the earth, but careful not to become too attached to worldly goods. To protect their virtue, they excluded from their community those whose thinking did not conform to their own rigid ideas. Among those made unwelcome was Roger Williams, an advocate of what he called "soul-liberty," the right of everyone to practice religion in the way he or she saw fit. This doctrine offended the Puritans, who viewed tolerance as a sin and saw themselves as right thinkers, not freethinkers. Banished by Massachusetts, Williams started his own colony in Rhode Island under the twin banners of religious freedom and separation between church and state. Another exile was the Reverend Thomas Hooker, founder of Connecticut. Hooker was famous as a preacher and a minister to "wounded souls." He is of particular interest for his role in promulgating the world's first written constitution based on democratic prin-

---

* Winthrop's phrase is derived from Matthew 5:14: "Ye are the light of the world. A city that is set on an hill cannot be hid." The passage was copied from a sermon, "A Model of Christian Charity," delivered by Winthrop on board ship before the Puritans' departure from England. Once in Massachusetts, Winthrop was considered something of a moderate. He opposed, for example, the suggestion of some Puritans that their women be required to wear veils.

ciples, the Fundamental Orders of Connecticut. Hooker argued that people have a God-given right to choose their own leaders, as well as a responsibility to place limits on the powers granted to civil authority. He found support for this concept in the Old Testament, declaring in a sermon, "God has given us liberty; let us take it."*

By the time of the American Revolution, the direct descendants of the Puritans were a small minority. Dutch Protestants had settled New York. William Penn had established his Society of Friends in Pennsylvania. Maryland had been founded by Catholics who were eventually overthrown by Protestants—a distant mirror of the English civil war. Virginia was led by planters who were well-versed—ironically, given that they owned slaves—in the latest European theories about the universal nature of human rights. America, already a magnet for immigrants, was populated by followers of many faiths and sects. Mindful of what religious strife had done to Europe and seeing echoes of it in their own colonial history, the founders followed the example of Williams and embraced religious liberty. The new American Constitution provided, in Article VI, that "No religious Test shall ever be required as a Qualification to any Office or public Trust under the United States." The Bill of Rights went further, to prohibit both the official establishment of a religion and any abridgement of the right to worship. In this design, neither state nor church would be able to control or harm the other.

---

* The Fundamental Orders of Connecticut did not separate religion and state. Indeed, one purpose of the constitution was to "maintain and preserve the liberty and purity of the Gospel." In his sermon, Hooker referred to Deuteronomy 1:13, "Take ye wise men, and understanding, and known among your tribes, and I will make them rulers over you." He interpreted this to mean that God intended for people to choose their own leaders.

It is common in our day to assume that the separation of church and state was intended to keep religion out of government, but the objective was more the other way around: the primary goal of the founders was to protect religion from the heavy hand of politicians. However, to accomplish that, they thought it necessary to keep each from interfering with the other. James Madison, for instance, was consistent in supporting a distinct separation between church and state in the face of efforts by others to blur it. In Congress, he voted against creating the office of congressional chaplain. As president, he vetoed one bill to grant federal incorporation to the Episcopal Church, and another to give public land to an assemblage of Baptists. In retirement, he wrote, "Every new and successful example of a perfect separation between ecclesiastical and civil matters is of importance . . . in shewing that religion & Government will both exist in greater purity, the less they are mixed together."

Until I began researching this book, I did not give much thought to the religious philosophy of our nation's founders; I considered them to be primarily political—not spiritual— theorists. They did, however, think deeply about religion. The early American presidents, for example, were firm believers in a divine being, but not wedded to the finer points of church doctrine. George Washington, in his first inaugural address, acknowledged a debt to the divine by saying that America's every step "seems to have been distinguished by some token of providential agency." He pledged to repay that debt by ensuring that "the foundation of our national policy will be laid in the pure and immutable principles of private morality." More important, he set the pattern for future administrations through his scrupulous support for religious tolerance. Washington disclaimed any interest in whether people were "Mohametans, Jews or Christians of any sect, or Atheists." His sole concern was that they should have the right to exercise freedom of worship, expression, and thought. In 1790, in a letter to the Hebrew congregation of Newport, Washington wrote reassuringly, "The government of the United States gives to bigotry no sanction, to persecution no assistance."

The second president, John Adams, had little use for the concept of the Trinity or other theological embellishments. He was a Unitarian. He also drew an important distinction between liberty and democracy: the former, he asserted, was a gift from God; the latter a creation of man. "Although the detail of the formation of the American government is at present little known or regarded either in Europe or in America," he wrote, "it may hereafter become an object of curiosity. It [should] never be pretended that any persons employed in that service had interviews with the gods, or were in any degree under the influence of heaven, more than those at work upon ships or houses, or laboring in merchandise or agriculture; it [should] forever be acknowledged that these governments were contrived merely by the use of reason and the senses."

Adams's successor, Thomas Jefferson, dismissed the Christian clergy as "the greatest obstacles to the advancement of the real doctrines of Jesus." A student of both science and ethics, he drafted his own version of the Gospels, omitting the miraculous parts, such as the Virgin Birth and the resurrection. It is hard to imagine a political leader in our time doing anything similar. Even then, Jefferson received a pummeling. During the presidential election of 1800, his opponents in the Federalist Party attacked his beliefs. As one hostile editorial writer put the question, "Shall I continue in my allegiance to GOD—AND A RELIGIOUS PRESIDENT; or impiously declare for Jefferson and no god!!!!"

America's founders were conscious that they were building something new and extraordinary—a system of govern-

ment based on the rights and responsibilities of the individual. This was a concept that would influence political thinking around the world. As Winthrop's early vision suggests,
Americans saw themselves as establishing a society superior
in organization and morality to the decaying aristocracies of
Europe. They compared themselves freely to the ancient
Israelites as a people selected by providence to participate in
the working out of a divine plan. Benjamin Franklin proposed that the great seal of the young country depict the
Israelites crossing between the parted waters of the Red Sea,
with Moses raising his staff and the pharaoh's troops about
to be drowned.* Thomas Jefferson thought the seal should
show the children of Israel in the wilderness, "led by a cloud
by day and a pillar of fire at night." To Americans of the
time, it seemed natural to associate their freedom with that
earned by Moses, their bountiful new land with that
promised to the Jews, and their commitment to the principle
that "all men are created equal" with man's creation in the
image of Abraham's God.

During the first decades of national independence,
Americans' belief that their country had been the special
recipient of God's favor grew apace. Despite periodic economic downturns and the sacking of the White House by
the British in the War of 1812, the United States was vigorous and dynamic, bursting at the seams. The Louisiana
Purchase, Lewis and Clark's expedition, the annexation of
Texas, the discovery of gold in California—all pushed
Americans relentlessly westward. As they moved, they built
democratic institutions thought to be those of a model

---

* Franklin was a particular champion of religious tolerance. In Philadelphia,
he raised money for a public hall that would be available to any preacher from
any faith. "Even if the Mufti of Constantinople were to send a missionary to
preach Mohammedanism to us," he said, "he would find a pulpit at his service."

republic. The qualities of self-reliance, free enterprise, and equal opportunity became the nation's creed. The spirit of the frontier may have been coarse, but it was also fired by energy and optimism. After observing Americans at work, worship, and play in the 1830s, Alexis de Tocqueville wrote, "America is a land of wonders, in which everything is in constant motion and every change seems an improvement. . . . No natural boundary seems to be set to the efforts of man; and in his eyes what is not yet done is only what he has not yet attempted to do." The historian George Bancroft, de Tocqueville's older contemporary, contended that the expression of popular will made possible by American democracy was intrinsically consistent with God's purpose. "Taming the frontier" meant extending the reach of civilization. The movement westward was ordained, in the words of the journalist John L. O'Sullivan, to fulfill America's "manifest destiny."*

Of course, not everyone interpreted the divine will in the same way. Some Native American religious leaders warned their followers not to expect any reward in the afterlife unless they rejected the immoral customs of the white man and returned to traditional ways. That meant forsaking alcohol and firearms, relying on the bow and arrow, and maintaining the spiritual beliefs of their ancestors. Among the traditionalists was Red Jacket, a Seneca chief who complained to a Christian missionary proselytizing among Indians: "Brother, you say there is but one way to worship and serve the Great Spirit. If there is but one religion, why do you white people

---

* According to O'Sullivan (in *Democracy Review*, July 1845), America's claim to Oregon at the time was justified "by right of our manifest destiny to overspread and possess the whole of the continent which Providence has given us for the great experiment of liberative and federative self-government entrusted to us."

differ so much about it? ... We also have a religion. ... It teaches us to be thankful for all the favors we receive, to love each other and to be united. We never quarrel about religion. Brother, we do not wish to destroy your religion or take it from you. We only want to enjoy our own."

The shameful treatment of Native Americans caused soul-searching among thoughtful people, but it was slavery that tore the country apart. Abolitionists and slave owners alike invoked God's name when pleading their cause. Southerners declared that slavery was sanctioned by the Bible; their opponents insisted that slavery was an abomination. In the Senate, the argument was taken up by John Calhoun, a slave-owning planter from South Carolina; and by Charles Sumner of Massachusetts, a liberal state then and now. Rather than try to reconcile slavery with the Declaration of Independence, Calhoun dared to denounce America's founding premise. "All men are not created," he insisted. "According to the Bible, only two, a man and a woman, ever were [created], and of these one was pronounced subordinate to the other. All others have come into the world by being born, and in no sense ... either free or equal." As for Sumner, he took to the Senate floor in May 1856 to deliver a speech that lasted two full days. Referring to a pro-slavery legislator he declared:

> How little that senator knows himself or the strength of the [abolitionist] cause which he persecutes! He is but a mortal man; against him is an immortal principle. With finite power he wrestles with the infinite, and he must fall. Against him are stronger battalions than any marshaled by mortal arm—the inborn, ineradicable, invincible sentiments of the human heart; against him is nature in all her subtle forces; against him is God. Let him try to subdue these!

Through the tumultuous decades of expansion, war, and economic booms and busts, there flowed the conviction that God was watchfully guiding America's course and fate. This belief remained widespread as the twentieth century approached and the country's energy and ambition moved beyond the now settled American frontier to the distant reaches of the Pacific. In 1898, explaining his administration's conquest of the Philippines, William McKinley told a group of Methodist clergymen:

> The truth is I didn't want the Philippines, and when they came to us, as a gift from the gods, I did not know what to do with them.... I walked the floor of the White House night after night until midnight; and I am not ashamed to tell you, gentlemen, that I went down on my knees and prayed Almighty God for light and guidance.... And one night it came to me.... There was nothing left for us to do but to take them all, and to educate the Filipinos, and uplift and civilize and Christianize them.

History would be far different if we did not tend to hear God most clearly when we think He is telling us exactly what it is we want to hear. McKinley liked to conceive of the expansion of American power as part of a divine plan, but although the war against Spain was successful and quick, consolidating control over the Philippines proved difficult and slow. Many Filipinos, even those long since "Christianized" by Catholic Spain, welcomed their liberators not with open arms but with arms of a deadlier kind. A rebellion against the U.S. occupation raged for four years, much to the puzzlement of many Americans. One leading newspaper said in an editorial, "It seems strange that the

Filipinos—or so many of them—are bitterly opposed to our sovereignty. They must know it is likely to be a great improvement over former conditions. . . . Nevertheless they fight on. The situation is a depressing one from every point of view." By the time the resistance was ended, more than 100,000 of the islanders had died.

Was this imperialism? Not according to those most responsible for the policy. While campaigning to become McKinley's vice president, Theodore Roosevelt told an audience in Utah, "There is not an imperialist in the country that I have met yet." A leading Republican senator, Henry Cabot Lodge, offered this explanation: "I do not think there is any such thing as 'imperialism,' but I am clearly of the opinion that there is such a thing as 'expansion,' and that the United States must control some distant dependencies."

Whatever it was called, the missionary impulse was mixed with more worldly considerations. At the turn of the twentieth century, a young senator from Indiana, Albert Jeremiah Beveridge, became famous for an oration, "The March of the Flag," that he gave repeatedly in public appearances and on the Senate floor. "The Philippines are ours forever," exulted the senator, "and just beyond them are China's illimitable markets. We will not retreat from either. . . . We will not abandon one opportunity in the Orient. We will not renounce our part in the mission of our race, trustee under God, of the civilization of the world." Whatever else may be said, Beveridge did not lack ambition for his country. "Most future wars," he said, "will be conflicts for commerce. The power that rules the Pacific, therefore, is the power that rules the world. And, with the Philippines, that power is and will forever be the American Republic."

Such attitudes were typical of the time and should not be surprising to us. It was, after all, an age of exploration, acquisition, and zeal. The British had taken on what Kipling referred to as the "white man's burden" to spread Christianity and educational uplift to the Indian subcontinent and Africa. The French were embarked on a *mission civilisatrice* to spread the benefits of their culture among Africans and Arabs. The Spanish, Belgians, Portugese, and Dutch all had overseas possessions. By taking the Philippines, the United States was in effect announcing its entry into the ranks of world powers.

Although most Americans welcomed their new status, some thought it hypocritical, based on a misreading of scripture and a misunderstanding of American ideals. William Jennings Bryan, the Democratic presidential nominee in 1900, had a rebuttal for Beveridge: "If true Christianity consists in carrying out in our daily lives the teachings of Christ, who will say that we are commanded to civilize with dynamite and proselyte with the sword? . . . Imperialism finds no warrant in the Bible. The command 'Go ye into all the world and preach the gospel to every creature' has no Gatling gun attachment."

The historian Charles Francis Adams, great-grandson of the second president, remarked contemptuously:

The clergymen have all got hold of the idea of Duty; we have a Mission; it is a distinct Call of the Almighty. They want to go out, and have this Great Nation [export] the blessings of Liberty and the Gospel to other Inferior Races, who wait for us, as for their Messiah;—only we must remember to take with us lots of shot-guns to keep those other Superior Races,—all wolves in sheep's clothing,—away from our flock. They would devour them;— but we won't. Oh no!—such ideas are "pessimistic"; you should have more faith in the American people!—Such cant!—It does make me tired.

Anti-imperialism leagues formed in many cities in the United States, but the American sense of mission still thrived, partly because it was embodied in more than gunboats and merchant ships. In increasing numbers, religious Americans found a calling to share their faith with those in distant lands. By the early 1900s, tens of thousands of American missionaries were established in foreign countries. They came from virtually every Christian denomination, with heavy representation from a movement that began in the United States, the Church of Jesus Christ of Latter-Day Saints, referred to commonly as the Mormons. The missionaries carried with them both the good news of the gospel and the democratizing influence of American values and culture. Missionaries were among the nation's first experts on foreign customs and the first to learn foreign languages. Their letters home heightened the interest of fellow parishioners in countries to which few Americans had previously given a thought. For the first time, people from places such as New York, Nebraska, and North Carolina began pressing Washington to recognize human rights (to protect the converted), support higher standards of commercial ethics (to prevent the exploitation of workers), and pursue a moral foreign policy (to protest the Chinese opium trade).

Missionaries brought with them the expertise and resources to establish schools, universities, clinics, and hospitals. To carry out their work safely, however, they needed the forbearance of foreign governments; and for this, they relied on their own government to help. American diplomats negotiated treaties with China, Japan, Siam, and the Ottoman Empire, providing missionaries with the right to take up residence, hold property, and seek converts. This had significance that went beyond the economic and the spiritual, for missionaries transmitted concepts not only about God but also about the proper relationship between governments and the governed.

An early, albeit stunted, example of this occurred in China in 1912, when the reform-minded Sun Yat-sen was elected president, bringing to an end 5,000 years of imperial rule. Sun, who had been educated by Christian missionaries, modeled his "Three Principles of the People" on a phrase in Lincoln's Gettysburg Address: "of the people, by the people, for the people." Although Sun ultimately failed in his dream to create a fully democratic China, his career dramatized the potential impact that the Bible and the ideals of human liberty together might have.

Separation of church and state rests on three "nos": no religious tests for public office, no established state religion, and no abridgement of the right to religious liberty. These principles are essential to our democracy and to our identity as a nation; let us hope they are never breached. In expressing that wish, however, we must recognize that such a separation does not require and has not led to the removal of God from the civic life, currency, coinage, patriotic songs, or public rhetoric of the United States. This reality reflects both the depth of America's religious roots and a universal rule of practical politics: religion may be separated from government, but it is intimately connected to how leaders are judged. As Machiavelli wrote in 1505, "A prince . . . should seem to be all mercy, faith, integrity, humanity and religion. And nothing is more necessary than to seem to have this last quality."*

From the original George W. to the current one, every president has seen fit during his inaugural address to mention God in one context or another. Most have expressed gratitude for the blessings America has received. Many have suggested that

---

* It says something about the state of the Catholic Church in Machiavelli's time that the writer was offering his advice to Prince Cesare Borgia, whose father was Pope Alexander VI.

God would continue to favor the United States as long as its policies were moral and just. Several have led the nation in prayer in time of national crisis. Some have found reason to discuss the nature of their religious faith in public settings. President Coolidge cited America's Christianity as proof of its good intentions ("The legions which she sends forth are armed, not with the sword, but with the cross") and proclaimed the Christianization of humanity as the country's national purpose ("The higher state to which she [America] seeks the allegiance of all mankind is not of human, but of divine origin").

Individuals, not nations, are said to be made in the image of God; but America's self-image has always been influenced by the feeling—faint at times and powerful at others—that it is the instrument of heaven. As President Ronald Reagan cautioned, "If you take away the belief in a greater future, you cannot explain America—that we're a people who believed there was a promised land; we were a people who believed we were chosen by God to create a greater world." Reagan did not specify how that world was to be created, but the answer most American leaders have given is "freedom."

In the Christian gospel, the kingdom of heaven is compared to a mustard seed and to yeast: little things that grow. Proponents of the American gospel have shown similar faith in democratic ideals. Shortly before his death, Jefferson wrote that the democratic system would spread across the globe "to some parts sooner, to others later, but finally to all." At first, Americans were confident that the merits of democracy were sufficiently obvious that others would adopt the system without any need for nudging by the United States. Through the nineteenth century, the country was in any case reluctant to involve itself very deeply in the affairs of others. After all, George Washington had warned against entering into permanent alliances, and John Quincy Adams had declared that America should be a well-wisher to freedom everywhere, but a defender only of her own. The twentieth century brought a new set of circumstances and imperatives. With first coal and then oil replacing wind as a source of power, transoceanic crossings became routine; next came airplanes. The world grew smaller, while America's interests expanded. In addition to the Philippines, the United States began to intervene closer to home, to protect economic interests and foster good governance in Cuba, Mexico, Haiti, Nicaragua, and the Dominican Republic. The country also found itself unable—despite strenuous efforts—to protect its security while remaining neutral in European conflicts. Confronted by the necessity of pulling Americans from their living rooms and dropping them into a cauldron of war thousands of miles across the sea, it was natural for U.S. leaders to define the stakes in the starkest terms.

"We shall fight for democracy," said Woodrow Wilson in his war message in 1917, "for the right of those who submit to authority to have a voice in their own governments, for the rights and liberties of small nations, for a universal dominion of right by such a concert of free peoples as shall bring peace and safety to all nations and make the world itself at last free." Following the war, he praised American troops for their victory: "These men were crusaders. They were not going forth to prove the might of the United States. They were going forth to prove the might of justice and right, and all the world accepted them as crusaders, and their transcendent achievement has made all the world believe in America as it believes in no other nation organized in the modern world."

Such claims may seem overblown from this distance, but to the people of many small nations at the time, they rang true. While European leaders were eagerly dividing postwar spoils in the Middle East and elsewhere, Wilson was championing democracy and the right of every nation to control its own fate. Largely because of his influence, an independent Czechoslovakia was born, with institutions patterned on America's. As a child, I was taught to think of Wilson as a hero who reflected the ideals of a country different from any other, a nation with immense power that nevertheless believed the world should be ruled not by the sword, but by law. Wilson was a stubborn man and not the best politician, but he did much to burnish America's reputation as a beacon of freedom and justice. It has become customary to mock his idealistic plan for a League of Nations, but his warning—that a second global war would be inevitable if America failed to join the League—proved sadly prescient.

That second war, fought heroically on two fronts, followed by the cold war against communism, secured America's standing as the world's foremost proponent of democracy. This role was memorably embodied in John Kennedy's inaugural promise to "pay any price, bear any burden, meet any hardship, support any friend, oppose any foe, to assure the survival and success of liberty." The poem that Robert Frost had prepared for the ceremony, but was unable to read, acknowledged the American mission:

> *We see how seriously the races swarm*
> *In their attempts at sovereignty and form.*
> *They are our wards we think to some extent*
> *For the time being and with their consent,*
> *To teach them how Democracy is meant.*
> *"New order of the ages" did we say?*
> *If it looks none too orderly today,*
> *'Tis a confusion it was ours to start*
> *So in it have to take courageous part.*

There are, of course, some who argue that any talk of an American mission on behalf of morality or democracy is dangerous nonsense. Overseas, it is well understood that America has high pretensions. It is not universally accepted, however, that the actions of the United States are based on calculations any more honorable than those of other nations. The leaders of every country boast; it is part of their job description. The difference with Americans, say the skeptics, is their tendency to believe their own rhetoric. In this opposing view, America is not an exception to anything; it is just another nation among many—albeit bigger and stronger. Americans may pretend or like to believe otherwise, so the argument runs, but our country responds to dangers and opportunities in the same manner and with the same degree of practical self-interest as others do. The purpose of any government's foreign policy is to protect its citizens' economic well-being and physical security; that our leaders have a tendency to camouflage narrow interests with rhetoric about universal values simply reflects their desire to appear better than they are, and to perpetuate the myth that America is special. Closer to home, George Kennan has warned that for Americans to see themselves "as the center of political enlightenment and as teachers to a great part of the rest of the world [is] unthought-through, vainglorious and undesirable."

My own inclination is to say "Bunk" to those who argue that America is not an exceptional country. I can point to the Declaration of Independence, the Constitution, the Bill of Rights, the Gettysburg Address, the role of the United States in two world wars, and the example of America's multiracial, multiethnic democracy and ask: what country can compare? A few are as big, some are as free, many have admirable qualities, but none has had the same overall positive influence on world history and none has been as clearly associated with opportunity and freedom.

Does this mean that I am among those who believe the United States has a mission to spread liberty across the globe? No. I am uncomfortable with such an idea, as if our country's purpose had been defined by some outside force—God, providence, nature, or history. I do, however, believe in the principle that much is expected from those to whom much has been given. Ours is a country of abundant resources, momentous accomplishments, and unique capabilities. We have a responsibility to lead, but as we fulfill that obligation we should bear in mind the distinction pointed out by John Adams. Liberty, at least in the sense of free will, is God's gift, not ours; it is also morally neutral. It may be used for any purpose, whether good or ill. Democracy, by contrast, is a human creation; its purpose is to see that liberty is directed into channels that respect the rights of all. As the world's most powerful democracy, America should help others who desire help to establish and strengthen free institutions. But, in so doing, we should remember that promoting democracy is a policy, not a mission, and policies must be tested on the hard ground of diplomacy, practical politics, and respect for international norms. Our cause will not be helped if we are so sure of our rightness that we forget our propensity, as humans, to make mistakes. Though America may be exceptional, we cannot demand that exceptions be made for us. We are not above the law; nor do we have a divine calling to spread democracy any more than we have a national mission to spread Christianity. We have, in short, the right to ask—but never to insist or blithely assume—that God bless America.

Three

Good Intentions
Gone Astray:
Vietnam and the Shah

─────── ⚜ ───────

I attended college in the late 1950s, a time (I tell my students now) somewhere between the discovery of fire and the invention of the handheld BlackBerry. For most Americans, it was a period of moral clarity. With my father writing books about the dangers of communism, I myself had little trouble separating the global good guys from the villains. There were few public quibbles, at least not in the United States, when Vice President Nixon asserted that "We are on God's side." A few weeks after I graduated, Nixon engaged the blustery premier of the Soviet Union, Nikita Khrushchev, in the so-called "kitchen debate" at an exhibit of modern housewares in Moscow. The vice president argued that the U.S. system was superior by pointing to the high quality of American home appliances. This technological divide was more than matched, in 1961, by concrete proof of a moral divide, the construction of the Berlin Wall (or, as East German authorities preferred to call it, the "Anti-Fascist Protection Wall"). Unlike the communists, the free world had no need to erect barriers to keep its people from escaping. The West, with the United States in the lead, was clearly winning the battle of ideas.

Then came Vietnam.

America's involvement in the war in southeast Asia, stretching from the early 1960s until the spring of 1973, muddied what had seemed so clear. This was a conflict in which no amount of courage on the part of American troops could produce victory. The containment of communism proved complicated in a region where nationalism and anti-imperial attitudes were readily exploited by charismatic leaders such as Ho Chi Minh of North Vietnam. The qualities of confidence and optimism that had contributed so much to America's rise to greatness steered its strategists wrong in Vietnam. Unused to failure, American leaders were unable to fathom how this tiny communist country could withstand the power they had unleashed against it. They misread the local culture; placed too much faith in corrupt, unpopular surrogates; and adopted a military strategy of gradual escalation that deepened our country's involvement without making a decisive difference on the battlefield. In the arena of world opinion, America's strength became a handicap; dramatic accounts of the massacre at My Lai and of Vietnamese children fleeing in terror from napalm made the United States appear more a bully than a champion of freedom.

It is startling how criticisms heard during the Vietnam era have a parallel in those uttered more recently about a different type of war, the invasion of Iraq by the United States. In 1965, Hans Morgenthau, whose classic writings on history and foreign policy I had studied at Wellesley, complained, "While normally foreign and military policy is based upon intelligence—that is, the objective assessment of the facts—the process is here reversed: a new policy has been decided upon, and intelligence must provide the facts to justify it." At Yale, twenty-two-year-old John Kerry warned his fellow graduates of the "serious danger of assuming the roles of policeman, prosecutor, judge and jury, all at one time, and then, rationalizing our way deeper and deeper into a hole of commitment that other nations neither understand nor support." The widely respected congress-man Morris Udall of Arizona summed up the opinion of many when he declared bluntly that Vietnam was "the wrong war in the wrong place at the wrong time."

Certainly, the conflict divided America. Although Richard Nixon claimed that the "silent majority" of U.S. citizens sup-ported the war, millions opposed it, often on moral grounds. Prominent religious leaders—such as Yale's William Sloane Coffin and Rabbi Abraham Joshua Heschel of the Jewish Theological Seminary—were among those raising their voices in opposition. Martin Luther King Jr. condemned the war for squandering resources needed to fight poverty, requiring African Americans to bear an unfair share of the risks, undermining the principle of nonviolence, and killing innocent Vietnamese. King also spoke of the damage done to America's standing overseas: "Each day the war goes on the hatred increases in the hearts of the Vietnamese and in the hearts of those of humanitarian instinct. The Americans are forcing even their friends into becoming their enemies. . . . The image of America will never again be the image of rev-olution, freedom and democracy, but the image of violence and militarism."

Opponents of the war had a partner in the movement for African American civil rights. Both causes were promoted with zeal from the pulpit, on college campuses, and in the streets. These movements soon spawned others: campaigns to advocate for women, protect the environment, combat world hunger, halt arms sales to repressive regimes, and increase respect for human rights. This activism constituted less a repudiation of the belief that America is an exceptional country than a demand that the nation live up to its ideals. Protesters charged that the true spirit of America was being subverted by leaders who relied too much on force, practiced a double standard regarding human rights, and paid too little heed to world opinion. The critics felt vindicated when the threadbare moral fiber of the Nixon administration was exposed, leading to the unprecedented resignations first of the vice president, then of Nixon himself. The protesters also applauded when congressional investigators exposed the complicity of the CIA in propping up authoritarian governments and in carrying out political assassinations.

The tragic experience in Vietnam did not diminish America's commitment to fighting communism, but it did raise questions about how best to engage the battle. It also created a demand for more honest leadership. When Jimmy Carter, the little-known governor of Georgia, announced his campaign for the presidency in the election of 1976, he promised never to lie to the American people and to give them a government as good as they were. It was the right message for the time and Carter was elected. To my delight, the new president chose as his national security adviser Zbigniew Brzezinski, who was a leading theorist on world affairs and had been a professor of mine at Columbia University, where I had attended graduate school. Although Columbia had been a center of antiwar protests, neither Brzezinski nor I had joined them. We agreed that the war had been mismanaged, but we did not share the casual attitude exhibited by some protest leaders toward the dangers of communism. We believed firmly in America's goals for the cold war and thought it possible to develop a better approach to achieving them. When Brzezinski offered me a job on his staff, I joined an administration that would try to find the right balance between two moral demands: fighting communism effectively and showing consistent support for democratic principles and human rights.

We inherited a debate that had simmered throughout the cold war about how to confront communism most wisely. One side in this debate argued that America would be justified in using almost any means to defeat the threat posed by the Soviet bloc. If those means included aiding anticommunist dictators, so be it; that was still morally preferable to allowing Marxist revolutionaries to seize power, strangle freedom, and leave no hope of eventual reform. The other side in the debate insisted that America could best defeat communism by consistently upholding humanitarian principles. In this view, America would have nothing to fear if it placed itself solidly on the side of people struggling to improve their lives. The Carter administration sought to combine the merits of each argument. This required coming to terms with some internal differences. Brzezinski had no illusions about our struggle with the Soviet Union. He did not trust the Kremlin, and he felt that we had to be tough in our actions and policies. Carter was more idealistic; he wanted America to present a morally untainted image to the world. Both could agree, however, that we would be more successful in countering communism if we made respect for human rights a fundamental tenet of our foreign policy.

Four months after taking office, in a commencement speech at Notre Dame, President Carter explained our new approach. Although rejecting "simplistic moral maxims," he said that America had so much faith in democratic methods that it would no longer be tempted to use improper tactics at home or overseas:

> Being confident of our own future, we are now free of that inordinate fear of Communism which once led us to embrace any dictator who joined us in that fear. For

too many years, we have been willing to adopt the flawed and erroneous principles and tactics of our adversaries, sometimes abandoning our own values for theirs. We have fought fire with fire, never thinking that fire is better quenched with water. This approach failed, with Vietnam the best example of its intellectual and moral poverty. But through failure, we have found our way back to our own principles and values, and we have regained our lost confidence.

The president's speech was welcomed as a breakthrough by the groups that had blossomed during the Vietnamese war as advocates of human rights and peace. They were further pleased when, for the first time, an assistant secretary of state for human rights was appointed. Pursuant to a congressional mandate, the administration began preparing annual reports chronicling the human rights practices of countries receiving assistance from the United States. New restrictions were placed on military training and arms sales to friendly but authoritarian governments in such countries as the Philippines, Argentina, El Salvador, Guatemala, and Nicaragua. One dictator, however, escaped all such sanctions: the shah of Iran.

The flamboyant Mohammad Reza Pahlavi had been America's ally since 1953, the year the CIA engineered a coup installing him as shah of Iran in place of an elected but antiwestern prime minister. Once enthroned, the shah proved himself both rigidly autocratic and an enthusiastic modernizer. His "white revolution" won plaudits from the West for reforming education, building roads, improving health care, and expanding opportunities for women. The Nixon administration had agreed to sell Iran virtually any nonnuclear weapon that its government was willing to buy, expecting in return a regime that would serve as a bulwark of anticommunist stability.

For President Carter, the shah was an early test. A foreign policy based on human rights alone would have shunned such a dictator, whose secret police were well practiced in torture. Instead, the administration embraced him. Iran, with its abundant oil reserves and its strategic location along the northern banks of the Persian Gulf, was viewed as too great a prize to risk. This was a case in which both the president and Brzezinski agreed that the United States should allow its realistic side to prevail over its more idealistic instincts. We were, after all, engaged in a zero-sum game with the highest possible stakes. Washington and Moscow sat across from each other with the global chessboard between them. The world at the time was divided in two, or so we thought. It took awhile for the superpowers to realize that a bearded man in a long robe had sat down beside them and was already making moves of his own.

No one had paid attention in the 1960s when an obscure Iranian cleric, Ayatollah Ruholla Khomeini, was thrown out of his country for protesting against the "decadence" of the shah's regime. Few noticed when the exiled ayatollah began communicating with the Iranian population, using cassette tapes smuggled in from France. Nor was much concern expressed when, in November 1977, Khomeini's son was murdered by the shah's security forces. The following year, after the shah declared martial law, his troops opened fire on a crowd of unarmed demonstrators, killing 900. Alarmed at last, the United States assured the shah of its continuing support while urging him, in vain, to adopt reforms that might appease his opponents and restore calm.

Years later, in my classes, I was able to cite the next events as an example of what happens when our government is divided. The key decision-makers at the White House, the National Security Council, the State Department, and the U.S. embassy in Tehran all had different sources of information, different understandings of what was going on, and different ideas about what to do. Until almost the end, the ambassador was convinced the shah could hold on to power. The State Department in Washington was preoccupied with finding a way to ease the monarch out and install, in his stead, a coalition of moderates. Brzezinski thought that the shah should use military force, if necessary, to put down the protests. Meanwhile, the CIA had little to contribute. At one crucial meeting, Stansfield Turner, then the agency's director, was asked for his assessment of the Iranians protesting against the shah. He replied that he did not have one: the shah had prohibited the CIA from talking to any political opponents of the regime. As a result, no overtures sponsored by the United States were ever made to Khomeini, and efforts by Khomeini's aides to contact U.S. officials were rebuffed. To the highest levels of American government, the Iranian insurgents were virtually anonymous—a band of religious reactionaries, whose membership and intentions were a mystery.

We were caught off guard by the revolution in Iran for the simple reason that we had never seen anything like it. As a political force, Islam was thought to be waning, not rising. Everyone in the region was presumed to be preoccupied with the practical problems of economics and modernization. A revolution in Iran based on a religious backlash against America and the West? Other than a few fanatics, who would support such a thing?

Our experts failed to grasp either the depth of hostility toward the shah or the loyal following that the Muslim clerics could muster, even amid the rampant materialism of the late twentieth century. The policy-makers compounded their error by assuming that the revolutionaries would be satisfied with getting rid of the shah and installing a democratic government. We learned soon enough that the Iranian uprising was not just a coup, a "regime change," or even a civil war, but a true political earthquake, like the revolutions of France or Russia. After the shah finally departed in January 1979, Ayatollah Khomeini seized power and the old security structures crumbled. Prisoners and jailers exchanged roles. A new view of the world was established as the official truth and, amazingly, that truth had nothing to do with either communism or democracy. It was a truth indifferent to both the economic needs of society and the political rights of the individual; a truth based instead on a narrow and inflexible interpretation of divine will.

The United States was not the only superpower at the time to undervalue the importance of religion. The leaders of the Soviet Union viewed the rupture in relations between Washington and Tehran as a strategic opportunity. Concerned since the time of the czars about the fractious populations along their southern border, they now saw a chance to invade Afghanistan (which they did in December 1979) without worry that Iran would provide a base from which America could respond. Although the Soviet leaders had little trouble establishing a puppet government, they failed to anticipate the anger their invasion would generate among Muslims not only in Afghanistan but throughout south Asia and the Arabian Peninsula. This hostility generated, in turn, a strategic opportunity for the United States. With Iran now off-limits, we turned to another of Afghanistan's neighbors, Pakistan. Following the logic of rivalries everywhere (the enemy of my enemy is my friend), we funneled large quantities of assistance through Pakistan to Muslim fighters who were determined to wage war against the Soviet infidels. Brzezinski felt it essential to make the Russians pay a high price for the invasion, which he saw as crossing a dangerous line in the way the cold war was conducted. Visiting Pakistan's border region, he declared to the Muslim warriors assembled there, "God is on your side." It took a decade, but the Afghans, with their allies, eventually pushed the invaders out and reclaimed their country. In contrast to Iran, the struggle in Afghanistan seemed an unqualified victory for the United States. Of course, we did not know then that many of the Muslim militants who fought so effectively against our shared enemy would one day redirect their anger—against us.

The experiences of the United States in Vietnam and Iran during the 1970s offer lessons that we would do well to recall today. The first is that we tend to think of ourselves more highly than others think of us. We were able over time to understand why so many Vietnamese fought the American presence in their country. But when we switched on our televisions in 1979 and 1980 and saw mobs of Iranians chanting, "Death to the United States," we encountered a level of hatred we could not comprehend. After all, Iran was not southeast Asia. We had sent no troops, nor had we dropped any bombs. We thought of ourselves as the defenders of freedom, the good guys, who had never meant this distant country any harm. The Iranians' frenzied outburst of anger seemed irrational; it had to be madness. How could people in their right mind refer to Uncle Sam as the "great Satan"?

That question leads directly to the second lesson: religion counts. To Muslims in Iran, the United States was intimately associated with a dictator who also shunned Islamic values. Thus the religious revolution was directed against both the shah and America. Because we underestimated the importance of tradition and faith to Iranian Muslims, we made enemies that we did not intend to make. Even the Vietnam War, primarily a struggle over political ideology and nationalism, had a religious component. From the outset, the anticommunist cause was undermined because the government in Saigon repressed Buddhism, the largest noncommunist institution in the country. Denied the right to display religious banners in celebration of the Buddha's birthday, worshippers rioted, prompting troops to shoot, a reaction that in turn provoked more riots. Several yellow-robed monks set themselves on fire in front of international news photographers, helping to turn local and world opinion against American policy. President Diem, whose government we were propping up, declared martial law and began arresting Buddhist leaders. Diem's sister-in-law made the disaster complete by publicly referring to the immolations as "a barbecue." This was hardly the way to win the hearts and minds of the Vietnamese people.

In 1977, a scholar of the Middle East, Bernard Lewis, wrote, "Westerners, with few exceptions, have ceased to give religion a central place among their concerns, and therefore have been unwilling to concede that anyone else could do so. For the progressive modern mind, it is simply not admissible that people would fight and die over mere differences of religion." For the Carter administration, this was a lesson learned the hard way. After the Iranian revolution, the president ordered a series of White House briefings by experts and scholars regarding the tenets and politics of Islam. The effort intensified after our embassy in Tehran was stormed and American diplomats were taken hostage. The briefings made little difference, however, because by then the popularity of the administration had dropped so low that it was defeated for reelection.

The third lesson is that even smart and well-meaning people can make moral assumptions that turn out wrong. The involvement of the United States in Vietnam began with noble intentions and little self-doubt; we would save the grateful South Vietnamese from the slavery of communism. When the war became a quagmire, the feeling grew that the moral course was to withdraw. Once that happened, activists celebrated. But the best of them grew somber when the corrupt, pro-western governments in South Vietnam and neighboring Cambodia were overthrown by regimes that imposed totalitarian rule in the former and created the killing fields of Pol Pot in the latter. America *in* Vietnam was a nightmare of body counts, search-and-destroy missions, napalm, and endless predictions of a victory that never came. America *out* of Vietnam was a nightmare of a million boat people and a mountain of skulls.

In Iran, a comparable scenario has unfolded. The shah was a cruel and insecure leader who brutally repressed his opponents. When his hold on power began to slip, human rights activists accused the Carter administration of hypocrisy for continuing to support him. Many rejoiced when the monarch was brought down, but from any objective standpoint, the practices of Iran's successor governments with regard to human rights have been far worse than the shah's. In the first few years alone, thousands of people were executed for political dissent and "moral crimes." The shah's secret police were replaced by religious "guardians of the faith," who were even more ruthless. Hundreds of thousands of Iranians, including longtime opponents of the shah, had little choice but to follow him into exile. Today, more than a quarter century after the revolution, power in Iran remains in the hands of a small group of unelected mullahs.

Jimmy Carter, as much as any president before or since, thought that morality should be at the center of U.S. foreign policy. His commitment to human rights made me proud to serve in his administration. It also contributed mightily to the credibility of American leadership and to the eventual expansion of democracy in Latin America, Asia, Africa, and Central Europe. The president's convictions made the question of democratic values part of every deliberation on foreign policy, even though the final decisions sometimes gave more weight to other factors, as was the case in Iran. Our experience there showed how complex decisions about foreign policy can be. To maintain a hard line against one source of villainy (the communism of the Soviet Union) we stood too close to a second source (the repressive shah), thereby helping to open the way for the rise of a third (Ayatollah Khomeini).

Although I was not a senior policy-maker at the time, I recall the sense of frustration we all felt as our assumptions proved wrong, our options narrowed, and the situation drifted out of control. Some critics said that we should have placed democratic values first and abandoned the shah much earlier. Others contended that we should have placed security interests first and backed the shah, with military force if necessary. In hindsight, it is always easy to identify mistakes whether of omission or commission. It is much harder to see clearly before the decisions are made, when the outcome is still in doubt and the players involved have yet to reveal their hands. In those circumstances, we need guidance; but for that, to whom—or to what—should we turn?

Four

The Question of Conscience

The opposition of Martin Luther King Jr. to the Vietnam War was but a minor part of his career and legacy. Fixed in his commitment to justice and nonviolence, he demanded a thorough reexamination of the moral foundation of American society and of its policies both at home and abroad. In countless appearances in crowded churches and assembly halls, his soaring voice thundered the challenge:

> On some positions, cowardice asks the question, Is it expedient?
> And then expedience comes along and asks the question, Is it politic?
> Vanity asks the question, Is it popular?
> Conscience asks the question, Is it right?
> There comes a time when one must take the position that is neither safe, nor politic, nor popular; but he must do it because conscience tells him it is right.

Dr. King's rhetoric is compelling; it does, however, leave the impression that when decision-makers gather around the table, they have in front of them a set of containers in which the options are clearly labeled "safe," "politic," "popular," or "right"—like individual dishes at a restaurant buffet.

As the examples of Vietnam and Iran suggest, this is rarely the case. To make smart decisions, our leaders must begin with good information. When I was secretary of state, I started each day in my kitchen reading newspapers over a cup of coffee. By the time I arrived in my office on the seventh floor of the State Department, a packet of information from the department's Bureau of Intelligence and Research would be on my desk. The bureau's analysis was especially good on the history and diplomatic context of particular situations: who was doing what to whom, why, and since when. I read next a copy of the President's Daily Brief (PDB). This was a highly classified document but on most days less than riveting. While I read, a representative of the CIA would stand by and watch, in case I had any questions or special requests.

The PDB was quite short; I studied it so that I would be sure what the president was being told. Then I waded through a longer version of the same material called the National Intelligence Daily, and after that I received a briefing on potential terrorist threats. Amid this wealth of data, one ingredient was almost always missing: certainty. If intelligence were a television set, it would be an early black-and-white model with poor reception, so that much of the picture was gray and the figures on the screen were snowy and indistinct. You could fiddle with the knobs all you wanted, but unless you were careful, what you would see often depended more on what you expected or hoped to see than on what was really there.

Still, the Clinton administration's foreign policy team had to make decisions; whether we were confident about how much we knew or not, events would not wait. Even relatively small decisions mattered, because once we began moving in a certain direction, it would be difficult to turn back. Decisions tended to build one upon another. We were conscious of this and so weighed our options carefully. Our first obligation was to protect the best interests of the American people. We had each also taken an oath to defend the Constitution and to execute faithfully the duties of our respective offices. But when—if ever—did our consciences come into play? Did we have a moral responsibility as well?

Dean Acheson was a brilliant but distinctly unsentimental man who had served as President Truman's secretary of state. In 1965, he wrote that "a good deal of trouble comes from the anthropomorphic urge to regard nations as individuals and apply to our own national conduct, for instance, the Golden Rule—even though in practice individuals rarely adopt it. The fact is that nations are not individuals; the cause and effect of their actions are wholly different."

Twenty years later, George Kennan argued, "The interests of a national society for which a government has to concern itself are basically those of its military security, the integrity of its political life, and the well-being of its people. These needs have no moral quality. . . . They are the unavoidable necessities of a national existence and therefore not subject to classification as either 'good' or 'bad.' "

The statements by Acheson and Kennan are classic expressions of a school of thought in foreign policy commonly referred to by academics as "realism." Realists caution against paying heed to moral considerations because such considerations may cause us to lose sight of how governments actually behave. When I studied this school of thought in college, I was also taught to consider nations as "rational actors" that could be counted on to behave solely in accordance with their interests. This mode of thinking, once considered persuasive, has lost popularity. Certainly, in an imperfect world, a completely altruistic foreign policy is not feasible; but to argue that the cause and effect of actions by states are "wholly different" from those of individuals is to lean too far in the other direction. After all, the policies of nations result from the decisions and actions of individuals.

As for Kennan's assertions, one might just as well say that our individual interests are to obtain food, shelter, and protection against external threats. These, too, are "unavoidable necessities" of existence and have no moral quality. But to secure those interests we must act, and when we do act, we leave ourselves open to moral judgment. Our needs do not automatically validate our means. This is true for individuals and for nations. It is one matter for me to protect myself from my neighbor by installing an alarm in my house, but quite another to knock him on the head with a crowbar. It is one thing for a government to raise an army to patrol its borders, quite another to dispatch that army to annihilate a neighboring population. A similar test applies to how we respond to the needs of others. The failure of the West to admit more Jewish refugees during World War II can hardly be classified as morally neutral.

When I was in government, I thought of myself neither as strictly a realist nor as strictly an idealist, but as a hybrid of the two. I saw government as a practical enterprise that had to operate in a messy and dangerous world, although the realist approach struck me as cold-blooded. I did not understand how we could possibly steer a steady course without moral principles to help guide us. What does this mean? To me, morality is measured by the impact of actions on lives. That is why I insisted as secretary of state on moving beyond the normal routine of diplomatic meetings. I wanted to see and hear from the people most affected by the decisions governments make.

To this end, I visited refugees, persons living with HIV/AIDS, families whose breadwinners had had limbs blown off by land mines, people struggling to recover from wounds inflicted by terrorist bombs, widows whose loved ones had been put to death because of their ethnicity, and mothers who lacked the means to feed their children. I remember, especially, holding a three-year-old girl in Sierra Leone. Her name was Mamuna; she wore a red jumper and played happily with a toy car using her one arm. A soldier had chopped the other arm off with a machete. I had, at the time, a grandchild about the same age. I could not comprehend how anyone could have taken a machete to that girl. Whom exactly did she threaten? Whose enemy was she?

At each stop, I wished I could have brought all of America with me. Given the opportunity to see the wretched conditions in which so many people must live, I was sure we would respond with urgency and generosity. I could not, of course, fit all of America into my plane, nor did I want to sound like a bleeding heart in describing the basis of our foreign policy. So as soon as I returned home, I would enumerate all the practical reasons Americans should care: because we had an interest in stability, in prosperous overseas markets, in strengthening the rule of law, in extending our influence, and in burnishing our reputation. But even as I presented these arguments, I felt that they should have been superfluous.

To illustrate why, I offer my favorite story about Abraham Lincoln: One day, when he was still a young lawyer riding from courthouse to courthouse in search of clients, he came across a pig struggling in vain to free itself from a bog. Lincoln paused for a moment, torn between sympathy for the pig and concern about what the mud might do to his new suit. He rode on. After about two miles, he turned back, unable to stop thinking about the animal and its plight. Arriving at the scene, he laid out some wood planks on which he descended into the bog, reaching the pig and hauling it out at great cost to his clothing. When asked why he had done all that for a pig, Lincoln replied, in essence, "I didn't do it for the pig; I did it for me—to take a pain out of my mind."

If Lincoln could recognize his self-interest in rescuing a pig at the cost of his suit, America should be able to see its stake in helping people to escape their own desperate circumstances. One of my father's deepest beliefs was that it is possible to ascribe characteristics to nations. Much of America's history has been driven by its sense of moral purpose. This is an essential part of our national identity. When that purpose is blurred, as it was in Vietnam, we grow divided and lose our capacity to inspire others. This had been the thinking behind Jimmy Carter's decision to emphasize human rights. It wasn't only a question of trying to do good; it was a way of reminding Americans of their true self-interest and of putting our country in a position of leadership on a matter vital to people everywhere.

More than a decade ago, Professor Joseph Nye of Harvard offered the theory that a country's moral reputation is a tangible asset; it can help the government to win friends, expand the nation's influence, and secure support in times of crisis. His argument makes sense. Even at the community level, we are more likely to respond favorably to requests from those we like and respect. Nye argued that America's historic reputation as a fighter for freedom and law has long been a source of "soft power," enhancing our security and strengthening our global position. As secretary of state, I liked the premise but not the phrase. I often spoke about what I saw as the goodness of American power, but politically "soft power" sounded, well—soft. Americans prefer to think of themselves as flying with eagles.

To accept the principle that questions of morality should enter into judgments about foreign policy is to settle one question only to confront two others. How do we determine what is moral? And how much weight should we attach to morality in proportion to more obviously self-interested considerations?

To help answer these questions, Professor Michael Walzer, of Princeton, has identified four obligations, in order of descending importance. A country's first priority, according to Walzer, is to protect the life and liberty of its own citizens; if it fails to do that, it cannot put itself into a position to help others. A country's second duty is not to inflict harm. Its third is, when possible, to help people avoid man-made and natural disasters. Its fourth is to assist those who want aid in building better and less repressive political systems.

Another way to apply roughly the same concept is to define as moral those actions that produce a net increase in what we associate with good: life, liberty, justice, prosperity, health, and peace of mind—as opposed to death, repression, lawlessness, poverty, illness, and fear. Even with this simple formula, trade-offs will be required. For example, to end a civil war, amnesty might be offered to members of an outlaw militia in return for its demobilization and surrender of arms. Under this arrangement, the need for peace receives precedence over the ideal of justice. This is pragmatism. The test of whether an action is moral is not whether it conforms to some rigid principle, but whether it achieves (as best as we can assess) a moral result.

On some issues, the right path is clear, but on many, perhaps most, the relative morality of various options can be extremely hard to pin down.

Often, decisions must be made not only with incomplete information but also in the face of contradictory claims, bewildering uncertainties, and reassuring "truths" that shrink into half-truths the moment they are seriously tested. Although good and evil both exist, they tend to be mixed together, not separately packaged. This reality, a central theme of philosophy, drama, literature, art, and my childhood catechism,* is often ignored in the sweeping rhetoric of political leaders. It has a habit of showing itself, however, when the talking stops and actions begin. That is when the gap between what we intend and what we actually accomplish can become painfully evident, clouding the distinction between wrong and right. For example, in 1991, after the Persian Gulf War, the administration of the first President Bush expected Saddam Hussein to be driven from power by his own people. That did not happen. As a result, "temporary" economic sanctions were put in place and then were extended every six months for more than a decade. The sanctions did not apply to medicine or food, but the Iraqi economy still suffered and innocent civilians were harmed. Hussein milked the suffering for all the propaganda it was worth. Though shedding crocodile tears in public, he worked behind the scenes to delay and later to corrupt international efforts to help his people through a program that exchanged oil for food. If the sanctions had been lifted, Hussein would surely have rebuilt his military and become once again a genuine regional threat.

During my years in office, Iraq always involved a choice between two evils; we tried our best to mitigate the harm caused by the alternative we chose. Unfortunately, in the process of attempting to explain our policy, I said something that will cause many to wonder how I could possibly presume to write this book. A reporter had asked whether maintaining sanctions was important enough to justify the many deaths of

---

* According to the catechism (paragraph 1707), "Man is divided in himself. As a result, the whole life of men, both individual and social, shows itself to be a struggle, and a dramatic one, between good and evil, between light and darkness."

Iraqi children that were alleged to have occurred as a result. I hesitated, then replied, "That is a very hard choice, but the price—we think the price is worth it." I should have said, "Of course not—that is precisely why we are doing everything we can to see that Iraq has the money it needs to buy medicine and food." Because my mouth worked faster than my mind, I came across as cold-blooded and cruel. I will leave it for others to judge whether, on the basis of my career as a whole, those adjectives fit. I plead guilty, however, to temporary brain-lock and a terrible choice of words.

A second moral dilemma involved genocide in Rwanda, a country torn by strife between two ethnic groups—the Hutus and Tutsis. In August 1993, the United Nations assigned a peacekeeping mission to monitor a cease-fire between the two sides. All such missions face problems; this was an extreme case. The end of the cold war had produced a rise in the number of UN peacekeepers from approximately 18,000 to almost 80,000 in less than two years, badly overextending the system. More than a dozen operations—including four others in Africa—were already under way. The UN commander for Rwanda was able to recruit only about half the desired number of troops, and many of those he did recruit had little enthusiasm for the job. Further, the mission's mandate was designed at precisely the time a UN mission in Somalia was ending in disaster. The lesson the UN drew from that calamity was to avoid ever again taking sides in a civil war. Thus the operation in Rwanda was ordered to remain strictly neutral. That meant its success would depend entirely on the willingness of the local parties to cooperate in fulfilling their obligations. In fact, the Hutu side was planning a war of annihilation.

When that war broke out, the European powers and the United States intervened immediately—to rescue their own citizens. Much too little was done until much too late to help innocent Rwandans, who were slaughtered in the course of two months of nonstop killing. In my memoir, I discuss in some detail why and how this occurred, but the outcome is both undeniable and indefensible. The major powers failed to act; the result was mass murder. The moral challenge, however, did not end there. As the killing wound down, the United States decided to lead a "humanitarian" effort to save refugees who had fled from Rwanda into neighboring countries. The plight of the refugees was depicted vividly on CNN. Onward they trudged, mile after mile, with fear in their faces, belongings on their backs, and children in their arms. The dramatic images tugged at the heartstrings and aroused sympathy; less well reported was the fact that among the refugees were many who had participated in the genocide—people fleeing the vengeance their own crimes had provoked. The office of the UN High Commissioner for Refugees did its job in caring for the transients. Many lives were saved. But the presence of killers in the camps later led to further violence, contributing to a disastrous war in the neighboring Democratic Republic of Congo. Not even refugee relief is morally pure.

That same year, closer to home, Democratic leaders in Congress criticized President Clinton for his policy of sending back to Haiti would-be migrants who had been apprehended at sea while trying to reach the United States. These well-meaning critics said it was immoral, even racist, to return such defenseless people to a country then governed by a ruthless and illegitimate military government. Reluctantly, the president yielded and the policy was changed. The result was an immediate upward spike in the number of Haitians trying to flee their island on leaky rafts and unseaworthy boats. Inevitably, some of the overcrowded vessels capsized; hundreds of people drowned.

As these cases illustrate, efforts to pursue an ethical course in foreign policy are frequently undermined by unintended consequences. To achieve moral results, a policy-maker must both want to do what is right and be able to predict what that might be. Ideally, he or she would have the conscience of a saint, the wisdom of a philosopher, and the prescience of a prophet. In reality, we stumble along as best we can despite shortages in all three qualities.

By far the toughest policy decisions are those governing the use of force. While in office, I visited American troops serving at home and in more than a dozen foreign lands. On each of these visits, I tried to do more than just thank our soldiers, sailors, and aviators. I sat down and ate with them, listened to their stories, tried to answer their questions, and studied their faces. I knew that any misjudgments on my part could lead to the destruction of their lives and, for their loved ones, to irreparable loss.

Back at the State Department, I could see through the window of my office the rows of white stone markers in Arlington National Cemetery and the crowds of visitors to the memorials of our wars in Korea and Vietnam. I could not help asking myself: when is it really necessary to go to war? Under what circumstances is there no other choice? How would I feel if I were a soldier? I believed that, if younger, I would have been prepared to serve, and also that I would have been terrified. It is a cliché, but true: ordering the military into combat is the hardest decision a president can make or a secretary of state can recommend. Fortunately, the use of force is not easily justified. Tragically, there are times it cannot be avoided.

Imagine the world's reaction if, on the evening of September 11, 2001, President George W. Bush had gone before the American people and said, "Resist not evil: but whosoever shall smite thee on thy right cheek, turn to him the other also." Yet what could have been more natural for a devout Christian president than to refer for guidance at a moment of crisis to the Sermon on the Mount? What would have been more logical than for America's chief executive to ask his fellow citizens to heed the advice of his favorite political philosopher—Jesus of Nazareth—and to suggest forgiving those who had trespassed against the United States? Instead, President Bush did the opposite, vowing to strike back hard and hold the terrorists accountable for their deeds. Was this hypocrisy? Does a government, in fighting back against evil, and in using military force that results in the death of innocents, commit a sin? Or are governments exempt from the injunctions of the Bible?

To summarize centuries of scholarship in a single sentence, most would agree that governments cannot realistically be held to the scriptural norm, but that does not mean there are no standards. Tian Rangju, ancient China's foremost military scholar, declared nearly 2,500 years ago, "If you attack a country out of love for the people of that country, your attack is justified; if you wage war to end a war, that war is also justified." In the fifth century, Saint Augustine pondered the question whether a Christian could justify going to war. Observing the horrors then being inflicted on Roman citizens by barbarian invaders, he answered "yes." War was justified to "defend the vulnerable other." Later scholars (most notably Saint Thomas Aquinas and Hugo Grotius, the founding architect of international law) developed over time a set of criteria commonly referred to as the doctrine of the "just war," much of which is now reflected in the Geneva Conventions and other secular international legal documents. The criteria seek to define what is morally necessary both before a war and while it is being waged.

Generally speaking, a "just war" is one carried out by a competent authority with moral intentions for a cause that is right. The effort must have a reasonable chance of success, with the expectation that it will result in no greater harm than the injury that produced it. Those who order military actions must discriminate between combatants and noncombatants and should seek to avoid unnecessary damage. Before going to war, a government should explore thoroughly and in good faith all other options.

Countries also have the right to defend themselves. The charter of the United Nations calls on every member state to attempt to settle disputes peacefully and, failing that, to refer matters to the Security Council for appropriate action. Article 51 provides that nothing in the charter "shall impair the inherent right of individual or collective self-defense if an armed attack occurs against a Member of the United Nations, until the Security Council has taken measures necessary to maintain international peace and security." In practice, countries have frequently taken military action outside these guidelines, sometimes provoking censure by the UN, sometimes not. Despite such violations, the standards in the charter remain relevant, just as laws against murder remain relevant even though murders are still committed.

Although most rules limiting the use of force have their origins in religious tradition, those rules are not sufficiently strict to satisfy all who profess religious faith. In the spring of 2004, I delivered a speech on religion and American foreign policy to an audience at Yale Divinity School. Editors of the school's journal invited experts to respond and received a letter from Stanley Hauerwas, who was once hailed by *Time* magazine as "America's best theologian."

Hauerwas wrote to protest not so much the substance of my speech as the notion—preposterous to him—that I might have something of interest to say to students of religion. He wrote that my record in government had been "anything but honorable," and that "being a Christian . . . made it difficult, difficult but not impossible, to be the American Secretary of State." To Hauerwas, pacifism is a fundamental part of being Christian. He suggests that Americans who fight or support military action have no rightful claim to be Christians at all. I understand his logic, but do not accept it. No story is more uplifting than Christ's example in dying while forgiving at the same time. But the whole point of the doctrine of "just war" is that military actions are sometimes necessary for moral reasons. Hauerwas rejects the doctrine because, he says, it has been used to justify too many wars, and he is right about that. However, a sound doctrine does not become discredited because it is, on occasion, misused. Hauerwas may feel it is irrelevant who wins battles here on Earth because, in the end, we are all in God's hands; but it is due to past American military actions that he is able to take his own freedom for granted.

Attending church while in office, every time I heard "Blessed are the peacemakers," I took the words deeply to heart. I cherish peace and admire Gandhi, the Quakers, and other proponents of nonviolent resistance; but when I consider Hitler and the many episodes of ethnic cleansing and genocide, I cannot agree that nonviolence is always the best moral course. In some circumstances, the results are unacceptable. Here again, my views are a reflection of my heritage. The pros and cons of armed resistance were intensely debated in the Czechoslovak republic between the two world wars. President Masaryk declared passionately that the meaning of Czechoslovakia's history and democracy could be found in the life of Jesus, not Caesar. He wrote also, however, that "war is not the greatest evil. To live dishonestly, to be a slave, to enslave, many other things are much worse." At age eighty, he told the novelist John Galsworthy, "Old as I am, if someone attacked me, I would seize a brick with these old hands and throw it at him." Sometimes the only way to achieve peace is to fight for it.

This is not to imply that a decision to initiate the use of force should ever be entered into without deep reflection. Violence wreaks damage on those who use it as well as those against whom it is used. It is also likely to result, sometimes disastrously, in consequences that were not foreseen. As Mark Twain's harrowing *War Prayer* reminds us, even to pray for victory in war is tantamount to asking that horrors be visited upon the innocent of the opposing side. The duty of leadership, however, is inescapable: to try to make moral choices despite the immense difficulty of doing so, and at the risk of being wrong.

In recent years, the United States has had to confront the question of "just war" in Afghanistan and Iraq. As secretary of state, I faced a similar challenge in the Balkans. Early in the 1990s, the Serbian dictator Slobodan Milošević had initiated three unsuccessful wars: against Slovenia, Croatia, and Bosnia. In 1999, he directed his wrath toward the ethnic Albanian majority in Kosovo, a province of Serbia. For a year, I explored every possible avenue to secure a diplomatic settlement that would have respected the rights of both sides. The Albanians ultimately accepted our proposal; Milošević refused, instead unleashing his security forces against the civilian population. His intent was to drive the Albanians from Kosovo by killing their leaders, burning their villages, and spreading terror. His goal was to "solve" the problem of Kosovo once and for all.

Since the province was part of Serbia, Milošević's crimes could not be characterized as international aggression. No member of NATO was under attack, so the alliance could not claim the right of self-defense. Serbia had not threatened to invade another country, so there was no rationale for a preventive strike. We did, however, have a duty "to defend the vulnerable other." The UN Security Council approved a resolution demanding the withdrawal of the marauding Serb troops; but Russian diplomats, historically sympathetic to their fellow Slavs, promised to veto any measure authorizing force to stop them.

This left the Clinton administration and NATO with a difficult choice. We could allow Russia's threatened veto to stop us from acting, or we could use force to save the people of Kosovo even without the UN's explicit permission. I pushed hard and successfully for the second option. My reasons were partly strategic: Europe was never going to be fully at peace as long as the Balkans were unstable, and the Balkans were never going to be stable as long as Milošević was in power. My primary motive, however, was moral: I did not want to see innocent people murdered. NATO's presence in Europe gave us the means to stop ethnic cleansing on that continent, and I hoped that by doing so we could help prevent similar atrocities elsewhere. This was indeed one of those times when, to echo the words of Martin Luther King Jr., our position should be based not on what was safe, but on what was right.

Because we lacked a specific UN mandate for military action, we worked particularly hard to demonstrate the justness of our cause. First, the Clinton administration secured the unanimous support of NATO. Second, I remained in constant touch with UN Secretary General Kofi Annan, who agreed publicly with us that the Serbs' actions were morally unacceptable. Third, during the war itself, NATO targets were vetted by military lawyers who compared each with the standards spelled out in the Geneva Conventions. In every instance a judgment was made as to whether the value of the target outweighed the potential risks to civilians.

As the war progressed, we increased the military pressure on Belgrade, while still exercising care to minimize unnecessary casualties. Three civilian targets (the Chinese embassy, a passenger train, and a refugee convoy) were struck by mistake. Estimates of the number of civilians killed by the bombing range from 500 to 2,000. The Serbs, before they were stopped, killed an estimated 10,000 Albanians in Kosovo and drove hundreds of thousands more from their homes. Throughout the war, we continued our diplomatic efforts to bring peace. Ultimately, these efforts succeeded. Milošević capitulated; the Serbs withdrew their security forces from Kosovo; refugees were allowed to return; a peacekeeping force, led by NATO, was introduced; and the UN organized a reconstruction effort that has since produced several rounds of democratic elections.

The seeds of conflict in Kosovo, as in earlier wars that stemmed from the dissolution of Yugoslavia, were planted in the religious history of the region. Pleading Serbia's cause, Milošević told me that his people had spent centuries defending "Christian Europe." Serbia's epic national story is a recounting of the battle of Kosovo, fought against the Ottoman Turks on the Field of Blackbirds in 1389. According to legend, the prophet Elijah appeared to Serbia's Prince Lazar on the fateful day. Elijah offered the prince a choice between victory in battle (and an earthly empire) and defeat (compensated by a place in heaven.) The prince chose the lasting victory of heaven. It is an inspiring story, one that played a role in Serbia's brave decision to resist the Nazis during World War II.* The problem is that some Serbs have

---

* When Serbia's civilian leaders chose collaboration, they were overthrown by their own military. In a radio broadcast, the Serbian Orthodox patriarch explained the decision to resist: "Before our nation in these days the question of our fate again presents itself. This morning at dawn the question received its answer. We chose the heavenly kingdom—the kingdom of truth, justice, national strength, and freedom. That eternal idea is carried in the hearts of all Serbs, preserved in the shrines of our churches, and written on our banners." In response to this brave choice, the Nazis invaded—but faced indomitable fighting from Serb partisans.

remained intent on avenging the defeat in Kosovo for more than 600 years, motivated by a fierce sense of nationalism and a belief in their own special relationship with God.

While the war in Kosovo was under way, Václav Havel characterized it in these terms:

> If one can say that any war is ethical, or that it is being waged for ethical reasons, then it is true of this war. Kosovo [unlike Kuwait] has no oil fields to be coveted; no member nation in the alliance has any territorial demands; Milošević does not threaten the territorial integrity of any member of the alliance. And yet the alliance is at war. It is fighting out of concern for the fate of others. It is fighting because no decent person can stand by and watch the systematic government-directed murder of other people.... This war places human rights above the rights of states.

Most of us would agree that morality, though often hard to define, is essential if we are to get along with one another. We would feel more secure in a world where the conscience served as the primary guide to the actions of both nations and individuals. But what about religion? Religion is perhaps the single largest influence in shaping the human conscience, and yet it is also a source of conflict and hate. After what we have witnessed in the Balkans and other regions ripped apart by faith-based strife, is religion also something we should want in greater abundance?

Five

Faith and Diplomacy

━━━━━━✧━━━━━━

This would be the best of all possible worlds if there were no religion in it!!" So wrote John Adams to Thomas Jefferson. The quotation, well known to proselytizing atheists, appears differently when placed in context. The full passage reads:

> Twenty times in the course of my late reading have I been on the point of breaking out, "This would be the best of all possible worlds if there were no religion in it!!" But in this exclamation I would have been ... fanatical. ... Without religion this world would be something not fit to be mentioned in polite company, I mean hell.

In his song "Imagine," John Lennon urged us to dream of a world free of religious doctrines. For many nonbelievers, religion is not the solution to anything. For centuries, they argue, people have been making each other miserable in the name of God. Studies indicate that wars with a religious component last longer and are fought more savagely than other conflicts. As the acerbic liberal columnist I. F. Stone observed, "Too many throats have been cut in God's name through the ages, and God has enlisted in too many wars. War for sport or plunder has never been as bad as war waged because one man's belief was theoretically 'irreconcilable' with another."

The fault in such logic is that, although we know what a globe plagued by religious strife is like, we do not know what it would be like to live in a world where religious faith is absent. We have, however, had clues from Lenin, Stalin, Mao Zedong, and, I would also argue, the Nazis, who conjured up a soulless Christianity that denied and defamed the Jewish roots of that faith. It is easy to blame religion—or, more fairly, what some people do in the name of religion—for all our troubles, but that is too simple. Religion is a powerful force, but its impact depends entirely on what it inspires people to do. The challenge for policy-makers is to harness the unifying potential of faith, while containing its capacity to divide. This requires, at a minimum, that we see spiritual matters as a subject worth studying. Too often, as the Catholic theologian Bryan Hehir notes, "there is an assumption that you do not have to understand religion in order to understand the world. You need to understand politics, strategy, economics and law, but you do not need to understand religion. If you look at standard textbooks of international relations or the way we organize our foreign ministry, there's no place where a sophisticated understanding of religion as a public force in the world is dealt with."

To anticipate events rather than merely respond to them, American diplomats will need to take Hehir's advice and think more expansively about the role of religion in foreign policy and about their own need for expertise. They should develop the ability to recognize where and how religious beliefs contribute to conflicts and when religious principles might be invoked to ease strife. They should also reorient our foreign policy institutions to take fully into account the immense power of religion to influence how people think, feel, and act. The signs of such influence are all around us in the lives of people of many different faiths. By way of illustration, I offer three stories.

In 1981, I visited Poland; it was during the second year of the uprising by the Solidarity movement against the communist government. I had long studied central and eastern Europe, where, for decades, very little had changed. Now the entire region was awakening, as from a deep slumber. A large part of the reason was that Pope John Paul II had earlier returned for the first time to Poland, his native land. Formerly Karol Wojtyla, a teacher, priest, and bishop of Kraków, the pope exemplified the pervasive role that religion had played in the history of Poland. While communist leaders in Warsaw dictated what Poles could do, parish priests in every corner of the country still spoke to what Poles believed. The government, alarmed by the prospect of the pope's pilgrimage, sent a memorandum to schoolteachers identifying John Paul II as "our enemy" and warning of the dangers posed by "his uncommon skills and great sense of humor." The authorities nevertheless made a tactical mistake by allowing church officials to organize the visit, giving them a chance to schedule a series of direct contacts between the "people's pope" and the pope's people.

One of the titles of the bishop of Rome is pontifex maximus, or "greatest bridge-builder." In Poland, John Paul II helped construct a bridge that would ultimately restore the connection between Europe's East and West. For bricks, he used words carefully chosen to expose the void at the heart of the communist system, arguing that if people were to fulfill their responsibility to live according to moral principles, they must first have the right to do so. He made plain his conviction that the totalitarian regime could not survive if Poles had the courage to withhold their cooperation. Above all, he urged his countrymen not to be afraid—a simple request with enormous impact. Slowly at first, but with gathering momentum, the pope's listeners drew strength from one another. No longer were they separated into small, controllable groups; the communists' obsession with isolating dangerous ideas had met its match. Standing amid huge crowds, the listeners recognized in each other once again the qualities that made them proud to be Polish—faith in God and a willingness to run risks for freedom. The pope's visits—for he made more than one—sparked a revolution of the spirit that liberated Poland, brought down the Berlin Wall, reunited Europe, and transformed the face of the world.

The pope helped the people of Poland to overcome their fear. Bob Seiple, who served with me in the State Department as the first American ambassador-at-large for international religious freedom, tells a second story, this one about overcoming hate. It concerns Mary, a young Lebanese woman he encountered while working as the head of World Vision, a Christian relief and development agency. In the 1980s, Lebanon had been the scene of a destructive and multisided civil war. Mary lived in a mostly Christian village; and when a Muslim militia invaded it, everyone fled. Mary tripped on a root, plunging face-first to the ground. As she scrambled to her knees, a young man of no more than twenty pressed the barrel of a pistol into the side of her head and demanded, "Renounce the cross or die." Mary did not flinch. "I was born a Christian," she said. "I will die a Christian." The pistol fired, propelling a bullet through Mary's neck and spine. Remorselessly, the mili-

tiaman carved a cross on her chest with his bayonet, then left
her to die.

The following day, the militia returned and prepared to
occupy the village. As they carted off the dead, a few of
them came across Mary, still alive but unable to move; she
was paralyzed. Instead of finishing her off, the militiamen
improvised a stretcher out of wood and cloth and took her to
a hospital. Seiple continues:

> And I'm talking to Mary, sitting across from her, and I
> said, "Mary, this makes absolutely no sense. These are
> people who tried to kill you. Why in the world would
> they take you to the hospital the next day?"
>
> She says, "You know, sometimes bad people are
> taught to do good things."
>
> And I said, "Mary, how do you feel about the person
> who pulled the trigger? Here you are, an Arab woman
> in a land twice occupied at that time—the Israelis in
> the south, the Syrians every place else—strapped to a
> wheelchair, held hostage by your own body, a ward of
> the state for the rest of your life. How do you feel about
> the guy who pulled the trigger?"
>
> She said, "I have forgiven him."
>
> "Mary, how in the world could you forgive him?"
>
> "Well, I forgave him because my God forgave me. It's
> as simple as that."

In Seiple's view, there are two lessons in this story. The
first is that there are people who are willing to die—and
kill—for their faith. This was true thousands of years ago
and is no less true today. The second lesson is that religion at
its best teaches forgiveness and reconciliation, not only when
those acts are relatively easy but also when they are almost

unbelievably difficult. (Mary, I need hardly add, is a more forgiving person than most—including me.)

The third story involves a boy with haunted eyes whom I met on a blisteringly hot afternoon in December 1997 during my first trip to Africa as secretary of state. The youngster looked about five years old and spoke softly, in a voice drained of emotion. He told me that, two weeks earlier, the small village where his family lived had been attacked. His mother had thrown him to the ground, shielding him with her body. When it was quiet, he wriggled his way out from under her and looked. His mother was dead. The bodies of other women were nearby, more than a dozen, drenched in blood. The boy then heard an infant crying; it was his sister, lying among the corpses. He gathered the baby into his arms and started walking. For hours, as the youngster stumbled along over hills and rocks, the infant wailed. Eventually they came to a place where the boy knew from experience that they would be welcomed and kept safe.

That place was Gulu, a town in a remote part of northern Uganda. World Vision ran the camp and hospital there—a haven for local villagers, who were being terrorized by an outlaw militia group. During the previous decade, an estimated 8,000 children had been kidnapped; most were presumed dead. Boys who survived and did not escape were impressed into rebel units; girls were taken as servants or "wives."

Camp officials blamed rebel leaders who had twisted religion into something grotesque. The tragedy had begun in 1986, when a change in government threatened the privileges of a previously dominant tribe, the Acholi. Fear is a powerful motivator, and the Acholi feared retribution for the many abuses they had committed while in power. A potential savior arrived in the unlikely form of a thirty-year-old woman, Alice Auma, who said that she was able to commune with spirits—a rare but by no means unique claim in her culture. She told her companions that she had been possessed by a deceased Italian military officer who had instructed her to organize an army and retake Kampala, the Ugandan capital. Once victory was achieved, commanded the spirit, the Acholi should cleanse themselves by seeking forgiveness. Auma's sacred campaign was launched but lacked the military clout to match its supernatural inspiration. After some initial successes, the movement—armed only with sticks, stones, and voodoo dolls—was crushed. Auma, her mind no longer host to the Italian officer, found refuge across the border in Kenya.

That would have ended the story had not Joseph Kony, Auma's nephew, decided to take up the cause of holy war. Piecing together a small force from various rebel groups, he assembled what came to be known as the Lord's Resistance Army (LRA). From 1987 on, the LRA has attacked villagers throughout the region, also targeting local governments and aid workers. Because Kony finds adults hard to control and reluctant to enlist, he kidnaps children as a means of procuring troops. Once captured, the children are forced to obey or be put to death; and obedience demands a willingness to kill anyone, including one another. Discipline is administered in the form of beatings, lashings, and amputations predicated on their leader's reading of the Old Testament. The LRA's professed goal is to overthrow the Ugandan government and replace it with one based on the Ten Commandments—or actually ten plus one. The eleventh, added by Kony to restrict the movements of adversaries, is "Thou shalt not ride a bicycle."

Itself a product of fear, the LRA has survived twenty years by instilling fear in others. The Ugandan government has veered between efforts to make peace with the LRA and efforts to destroy it, but officials lack the resources to protect those living in the vicinity of the rebel force. That task has been left to World Vision and similar groups whose resources are also limited, as I saw during my tour of the camp in Gulu. The surroundings reminded me of pictures I had seen of the Crimean War. The camp hospital smelled of disinfectant and human waste. Ancient IVs dripped. Mosquitoes were buzzing everywhere. There were hundreds of patients, most of them children, many covered with welts and scars, some missing a limb. I met a group of teenage girls sitting on mattresses, braiding each other's hair. They looked as if they belonged in junior high school, yet several were already mothers, their babies sired by LRA rapists. "Even if you are a very young girl," said one, who was wearing a Mickey Mouse T-shirt, "you would be given to a man who was the age of my father."

As I started to leave, a young man came up to me holding an infant. "This is the girl that little boy brought to us, his little sister. Her name is Charity." As I cradled the tiny orphan, I was told that the girl had been named for one of the volunteers at the mission. There were many such volunteers. It was a place filled with terrible suffering but also a resilient joy. Patients and volunteers laughed, sang, played games, and cared for each other. The Italian doctor who ran the facility had been in Gulu for more than twenty years. What a contrast between the faith that manifests itself in such love and the twisted fantasies pursued by the LRA.*

One insight that is present in these stories and often in religious faith more generally is that we share a kinship with one

---

* In October 2005, the International Criminal Court issued arrest warrants for Joseph Kony and four other LRA leaders on the charge of crimes against humanity. The court does not, however, have any independent capacity to enforce those warrants.

another, however distant it may sometimes seem; we are all created in the image of God. This in turn places upon us a responsibility to our neighbors. That principle provides both a solid foundation for religion and a respectable basis for organizing the affairs of secular society. What complicates matters is that religion can be interpreted in ways that exclude large numbers of people from any claim to kinship. Those truly imbued with religious faith—such as Pope John Paul II, Bob Seiple's Mary, and the volunteers in Gulu—may affirm "We are all God's children"; but others may follow their convictions to a more argumentative conclusion—"I am right, you are wrong, go to hell!"

When I appeared on a panel with the Jewish writer and thinker Elie Wiesel, a survivor of the Holocaust, he recalled how a group of scholars had once been asked to name the unhappiest character in the Bible. Some said Job, because of the trials he endured. Some said Moses, because he was denied entry to the promised land. Some said the Virgin Mary, because she witnessed the death of her son. The best answer, Wiesel suggested, might in fact be God, because of the sorrow caused by people fighting, killing, and abusing each other in His name.

This is why so many practitioners of foreign policy—including me—have sought to separate religion from world politics, to liberate logic from beliefs that transcend logic. It is, after all, hard enough to divide land between two groups on the basis of legal or economic equity; it is far harder if one or both claim that the land in question was given to them by God. But religious motivations do not disappear simply because they are not mentioned; more often they lie dormant only to rise up again at the least convenient moment. As our experience in Iran reflected, the United States has not always understood this well enough. To lead internationally, American policy-makers must learn as much as possible about religion, and then incorporate that knowledge in their strategies. Bryan Hehir has compared this challenge to brain surgery—a necessary task, but fatal if not done well.

In any conflict, reconciliation becomes possible when the antagonists cease dehumanizing each other and begin instead to see a bit of themselves in their enemy. That is why it is a standard negotiating technique to ask each side to stand in the shoes of the other. Often this is not as difficult as it might seem. The very fact that adversaries have been fighting over the same issue or prize can furnish a common ground. For centuries, Protestants and Catholics competed for religious ascendancy in Europe. That was a point of similarity: wanting to be number one. For even longer, Christians, Muslims, and Jews have pursued rival claims in Jerusalem; that, too, is a point of similarity—wanting to occupy the same space. In parts of Asia and Africa, Christians and Muslims are fighting, but they share a desire to worship freely and without fear. When people are pursuing the same goal, each side should be able to understand what motivates the other. To settle their differences, they need only find a formula for sharing what both want—a tricky task, but one that can at least be addressed through an appeal to reason.

Not all conflicts lend themselves to this sort of negotiation. During World War II, the Axis and the Allies were fighting for two entirely different visions of the future. Today, Al Qaeda's lust for a war of vengeance fought with the tools of terror cannot be accommodated. Some differences are too great to be reconciled. In most situations, however, reconciliation will be eminently preferable to continued stalemate or war. But how is reconciliation achieved?

When participants in a conflict claim to be people of faith, a negotiator who has the credentials and the credibility to do so might wish to call their bluff. If the combatants argue the morality of their cause, how is that morality reflected in their actions? Are they allowing their religion to guide them or using it as a debating point to advance their interests? Has their faith instilled in them a sense of responsibility toward others or a sense of entitlement causing them to disregard the rights and views of everyone else?

If I were secretary of state today, I would not seek to mediate disputes on the basis of religious principles any more than I would try to negotiate alone the more intricate details of a trade agreement or a pact on arms control. In each case, I would ask people more expert than I to begin the process of identifying key issues, exploring the possibilities, and suggesting a course of action. It might well be that my involvement, or the president's, would be necessary to close a deal, but the outlines would be drawn by those who know every nuance of the issues at hand. When I was secretary of state, I had an entire bureau of economic experts I could turn to, and a cadre of experts on nonproliferation and arms control whose mastery of technical jargon earned them a nickname, "the priesthood." With the notable exception of Ambassador Seiple, I did not have similar expertise available for integrating religious principles into our efforts at diplomacy. Given the nature of today's world, knowledge of this type is essential.

If diplomacy is the art of persuading others to act as we would wish, effective foreign policy requires that we comprehend why others act as they do. Fortunately, the constitutional requirement that separates state from church in the United States does not also insist that the state be ignorant of the church, mosque, synagogue, pagoda, and temple. In the future, no American ambassador should be assigned to a country where religious feelings are strong unless he or she has a deep understanding of the faiths commonly practiced there. Ambassadors and their representatives, wherever they are assigned, should establish relationships with local religious leaders. The State Department should hire or train a core of specialists in religion to be deployed both in Washington and in key embassies overseas.

In 1994, the Center for Strategic and International Studies published *Religion, the Missing Dimension of Statecraft.* The book makes a compelling case for recognizing the role of religion in affecting political behavior and for using spiritual tools to help resolve conflicts. Douglas Johnston, the book's coauthor, subsequently formed the International Center for Religion and Diplomacy (ICRD), which has continued to study what it calls "faith-based diplomacy" while also playing an important mediating role in Sudan and establishing useful relationships in Kashmir, Pakistan, and Iran. Johnston, a former naval officer and senior official in the Defense Department, believes that, ordinarily, everyone of influence in a given situation is not necessarily bad, and those who are bad aren't bad all the time. He argues that a faith-based mediator has means that a conventional diplomat lacks, including prayers, fasting, forgiveness, repentance, and the inspiration of scripture.

The ICRD is not alone in its efforts. After leaving the State Department, Bob Seiple founded the Institute for Global Engagement, which is working to improve the climate for religious liberty in such volatile nations as Uzbekistan and Laos. The institute's mantra is, "Know your faith at its deepest and richest best, and enough about your neighbor's faith to respect it."

While in office, I had occasion to work closely with the Community of Sant'Egidio, a lay movement that began in Rome in the 1960s, inspired by the Second Vatican Council of Pope John XXIII. Over a period of years, Sant'Egidio successfully brokered negotiations ending a long and bloody civil war in Mozambique. It has also played a constructive role in, among other places, Kosovo, Algeria, Burundi, and Congo. The community sees prayer, service to the poor, ecumenism, and dialogue as the building blocks of interreligious cooperation and problem solving.

Numerous other faith-based organizations, representing every major religion, are in operation. They are most effective when they function cooperatively, pooling their resources and finding areas in which to specialize. Some are most skilled at mediation; others are best at helping former combatants readjust to civilian life. Still others emphasize prevention, addressing a problem before it can explode into violence. Many are experts in economic development or building democracy, both insurance policies against war. Together, these activists have more resources, more skilled personnel, a longer attention span, more experience, more dedication, and more success in fostering reconciliation than any government.

The most famous example of faith-based peacemaking was orchestrated by President Jimmy Carter at Camp David in 1978. Most observers acknowledge that the peace agreement between Egypt and Israel would never have come about if not for Carter's ability to understand and appeal to the deep religious convictions of President Sadat and Prime Minister Begin. I recently asked the former president how policy-makers should think about religion as part of the foreign policy puzzle. He told me that it is not possible to separate what people feel and believe in the spiritual realm from what they will do as a matter of public policy. "This is an opportunity," he argued, "because the basic elements of the major religious faiths are so similar—humility, justice, and peace." He said that in the unofficial diplomacy he is often asked to conduct through the Carter Center, one of the first aspects he investigates is whether the parties to a dispute represent the same faith. He said it is often simpler to deal with people of completely different faiths than with those who share a religion but disagree about how it should be interpreted. As a moderate Baptist, Carter said he found it less complicated to have a conversation with a Catholic than with a Baptist fundamentalist; with the Catholic it was easier simply to accept the differences and not feel obliged to argue about them.

When I broached this same subject with Bill Clinton, he stressed two points. First, religious leaders can help to validate a peace process before, during, and after negotiations; through dialogue and public statements, they can make peace easier to achieve and sustain. Second, persuading people of different faiths to work cooperatively requires separating what is debatable in scripture from what is not. "If you're dealing with people who profess faith," he said, "they must believe there is a Creator; if they believe that, they should agree that God created everyone. This takes them from the specific to the universal. Once they acknowledge their common humanity, it becomes harder to kill each other; then compromise becomes easier because they've admitted that they are dealing with people like themselves, not some kind of Satan or subhuman species."

Faith-based diplomacy can be a useful tool of foreign policy. I am not arguing, however, that it can replace traditional diplomacy. Often the protagonists in a political drama are immune to, or deeply suspicious of, appeals made on religious or moral grounds. But if we do not expect miracles, little is lost in making the attempt. The resurgence of religious feeling will continue to influence world events. American policy-makers cannot afford to ignore this; on balance they should welcome it. Religion at its best can reinforce the core values necessary for people from different cultures to live in some degree of harmony; we should make the most of that possibility.

Six

The Devil and Madeleine Albright

———— ⚓ ————

Between 1981 and 1993, I was out of government, pursuing a career as a university professor and, when called on, advising Democratic presidential candidates—who, until Bill Clinton came along, were uniformly trounced. At the end of that period, I returned to government service to find a world transformed by the breakup of the Soviet Union, the reunification of Europe, and the victory of the coalition in Operation Desert Storm. It was an extraordinary moment. Events around the globe were in flux; the Berlin Wall was no more; millions of people were newly free. It appeared to me the right time to try to restore bipartisanship to American foreign policy. After all, conservatives and liberals had quarreled about how best to fight communism; with that threat gone, what cause did we have to disagree?

The answer, it turned out, was plenty. As I set to work in New York in my new post as U.S. ambassador to the United Nations, I found quickly that our policy toward that institution was at the heart of a new divide. On one side were the advocates of using the UN to attack global problems; on the other was a conservative Christian movement of growing power. I knew, of course, that there was an extensive network of right-wing Christian radio and television stations stretched across the country. What surprised me was the degree to which this movement had become politically organized in response to a perceived assault on traditional family values. During the preceding quarter century, the Supreme Court had interpreted the Constitution as protecting a woman's right to have an abortion; sex education had been introduced into classrooms; prayers in public schools had been prohibited; feminists had campaigned for an Equal Rights Amendment; gays and lesbians had become markedly more open about their lifestyles; and Hollywood had been producing "entertainment" containing ever larger doses of sex and gore. As for popular music, parents who had once been upset by Elvis's swaying hips and the Beatles' Liverpool haircuts now had to deal with androgynous creatures setting fire to guitars while screaming indecipherable lyrics to nonexistent melodies.

Some of these trends concerned individual rights, others the direction of popular culture; these are different categories, but the trends all appeared threatening to the Christian right. My own reaction was to embrace some of the changes while doing my best to ignore others. I oppose discrimination against gays and lesbians and am convinced that heterosexual adultery is a greater danger to the institution of marriage than homosexuality will ever be. I believe sex education prevents many more problems than it creates. I am a supporter of *Roe v. Wade* because I think women should have the right to choose and because illegal abortions too often put the life of the woman at risk. President Clinton's formulation seems on target to me: abortions should be safe, legal, and rare, and we should do everything possible to encourage adoption as an alternative to abortion and to reduce unwanted pregnancies through counseling and improved social conditions. As for television, movies, and radio, I oppose any kind of "thought police," but I am also appalled by vulgarity and violence. I am mortified that the image America presents to people overseas is influenced so heavily by dumbed-down television shows and garish action films. As a mother and grandmother, I am tempted to apply a bar of soap to the mouths of many performers; I am all for V-chips and rating systems and think no punishment is severe enough for offensive spammers. I don't mind being called a hopeless prude.

Despite all the mind-polluting background noise, my daughters turned out magnificently, and overall I have coped. If something disgusts me, I change the channel or look the other way. Members of the Christian right are evidently far more alarmed. Like the religious conservatives in prerevolutionary Iran, they believe that their core values are under assault and that they are being compelled to raise their children in surroundings hostile to their deepest beliefs. Many are receptive to the argument that evil forces conspire against them and that they need to unite and fight back. One conservative Christian leader, James Dobson, describes such people as "just ordinary folks . . . trying to raise their kids . . . do a good job and . . . cope with the pressures that are on them. They're worried about what their kids are being taught in safe-sex classes. They're worried about the spiraling drug problem in this country. They're worried about the epidemic of sexually-transmitted diseases. They're especially worried about a culture that is at war with what they believe."

Senator Jesse Helms of North Carolina has addressed the same general issues but more bluntly. "Especially in the past twenty-five years," he wrote, "the federal government has not even tried to conceal its hostility to religion; now, with many of our churches in disarray, the attack is being waged against the family as the last bastion of those opposing the totalitarian state. Militant atheists and socialists have gone very far in imposing their view of life and man on almost every American institution." The result of all this, Helms declared, has been "atheistic schools, rampaging crime, God-forsaken homes, drugs, abortion, pornography, permissiveness and a sense of cynicism and spiritual desolation absolutely unprecedented in our country's history."

By the time I took up my duties at the UN, the Christian right was a rising political power. Senator Helms was the vice chairman of the Senate Committee on Foreign Relations. Reverend Pat Robertson's Christian Coalition had become a major force within the Republican Party. The country's largest women's organization was not the secular National Organization for Women but Concerned Women for America (CWA), made up of socially conservative Christians. This movement had developed a list of items to oppose internationally that mirrored its domestic concerns: abortion, threats to American sovereignty, and "betrayal" of family values. To the Christian right, within the United States "big government" was the enemy of all that was good; in the international arena, world government (in the form of the United Nations) played the villain's role.

In 1991, Pat Robertson had written a best-seller, *The New World Order*, in which he described a plot to place a "satanic dictator" in charge of us all.* Once in power, the dictator would control every aspect of our lives. All human activity

---

* According to Robertson, the conspiracy was hatched in Bavaria in 1776 and has been unfolding ever since. The list of conspirators, either as knowing participants or as unwitting dupes, includes the ancient order of Freemasons, the leaders of the French Revolution, Karl Marx, Margaret Sanger (the first president of Planned Parenthood), Adolf Hitler, the Rockefellers, Henry Kissinger, the

would be monitored by satellites. Every man, woman, and child would have to carry an international identity card. Freedom of religion would be abolished and the right to own guns terminated. Anyone uttering a politically incorrect statement could be prosecuted in a world court, possibly under Islamic law. Nothing could be bought or sold without the permission of global authorities. Children would be indoctrinated from birth to obey their wicked masters and the American military could be ordered by the UN Security Council to invade Israel. "For the past two hundred years," Robertson declared, "the term 'new world order' has been the code phrase of those who desired to destroy the Christian faith. . . . They wish to replace it with an occult-inspired world socialist dictatorship." Naturally, in Robertson's account, the headquarters of this global dictatorship would be the United Nations.

I had assumed, as ambassador to the UN, that I could best silence domestic critics by striving to make the organization more effective. I did not understand that a significant portion of those critics had no interest in a more efficient UN. To them, I was less a diplomat striving to protect American interests than I was—quite literally—the devil's advocate. Traveling around the country to explain my plans to reform the UN, I often found myself on the defensive, trying to dispel the misapprehensions of alarmed questioners. No, I said, the UN is not about to impose a global income tax; it does not have the authority to order us into war; it is not planning to confiscate our handguns; it is not conspiring to abolish the concept of private property; it does not operate a fleet of black helicopters that fly over American cities at night; it is not plotting to take over the world.

Trilateral Commission, the authors of New Age literature, the administrators of global financial institutions, the designers of the American dollar bill, Zbigniew Brzezinski, and members of the Council on Foreign Relations (on whose board of directors I serve.)

The notion that the UN has or ever will have the ability to dominate the United States is laughable. The authority of the UN flows entirely from its members; it is servant, not master. It has no armed forces of its own, no authority to arrest, no right to tax, no mandate to regulate, and no capacity to override treaties. Its General Assembly has little power. The Security Council, which at least theoretically has the authority to command action, cannot do so without our agreement; the United States has the power to veto any action contrary to our national interests. So where is the danger?

Meanwhile, the UN's World Food Program feeds 90 million people each year; the UN High Commissioner for Refugees maintains a lifeline for the international homeless; the UN Children's Fund has launched a campaign to end forced childhood marriage; the UNAIDS initiative remains a focal point for global efforts to defeat HIV/AIDS; and the UN Population Fund helps families plan, mothers survive, and children grow up healthy in the most impoverished places on earth. All this, I used to say in my speeches, for a cost to the average American each year that was less than the price of a movie ticket.*

The UN does, however, occasionally provide its critics with damaging ammunition. Like most international institutions, it maintains a list of unofficial organizations that are allowed to send representatives to observe its meetings and conferences. One such group, I learned from the press, was the National Man/Boy Love Association (NAMBLA). The next thing I knew, I was sitting in my apartment watching a news

---

* Anti-UN sentiment within the political right has not receded. This is an excerpt from the official platform of Texas Republicans in 2004: "The Party believes it is in the best interest of the citizens of the United States that we immediately rescind our membership, as well as financial and military contributions to, the United Nations.... The Party urges Congress to evict the United Nations from U.S. soil."

broadcast about NAMBLA's link to the UN; the picture then changed to show me in the Security Council with my hand raised on some routine measure as if I were instead voting in favor of sex between men and boys. A skilled satirist could not have cooked up a more embarrassing juxtaposition. It took me months of painstaking effort, amid gloating from the right-wing press, to purge NAMBLA from the UN's list.

Most often, it was the excesses of the UN General Assembly that attracted criticism from conservatives, but if ever there was an occasion tailored to arouse the passions of the Christian right, it was the Fourth World Conference on Women, held in Beijing in 1995. Here was a UN conference, convened to advance the status of women, hosted by Communist China, and attended by First Lady Hillary Clinton and Ambassador Madeleine Albright.

In the weeks preceding the gathering, columnists and talk-show hosts claimed that the American delegation was intent on redefining motherhood, fatherhood, family, and gender; that we sought statistical parity between men and women in every office and on every work floor; and that the conference would demand that fathers and mothers record equal hours tending their children. A report by the conservative Independent Women's Forum alleged that our plan was to sell the world on the international legal equality of "five genders" (male and female heterosexuals, male and female homosexuals, and trans-bisexuals); we were also said to be contemplating support for a sixth gender, referred to ominously as "omnisexuality." The result, declared the report, is that "our understanding of marriage and the particular legitimacy accorded to children born in marriage is to be overturned by radical feminist moral dictate." James Dobson, whose radio ministry reaches millions of listeners in dozens of countries, called the conference "the biggest threat to the family that's ever occurred in the history of the world."

According to Concerned Women for America, "Hillary Rodham Clinton flew to the 'Women's Conference' with a planeload of lesbians and radical feminists." Actually I flew with her. Moreover, the priorities that mattered most to us and to the vast majority of delegates were not the ones that so excited the passions of our conservative critics—or, to be honest, the most liberal of our colleagues. We sought and obtained support for the rights of women and girls to have equal access to education and health care, to participate in the economic life of their societies, and to live free from the threat of violence. To establish a consensus behind these goals, we assured Catholic and Muslim representatives that we were not asking them to consent to policies contrary to their ethical or religious beliefs—such as claiming that abortion is an international legal right. The Beijing conference was just a conference, but it addressed the status and treatment of more than half of the world's people, many of whom face abuse and discrimination that remain all too real. I am proud to have led the United States' delegation. James Dobson was less enthusiastic, describing the Platform for Action as "Satan's trump card."

Before serving at the UN, I thought that morality in world affairs revolved around issues of war and peace, liberty and despotism, development and poverty. In the 1990s, matters that had once been considered primarily personal—abortion, contraception, gender roles, the rights of children, and sexual orientation—found a prominent place on the international stage. As if on cue, American activists from the left and the right began accusing each other of trying to impose their own moral values on everyone else and of tarnishing the country's international reputation in the process. As is generally the case in politics, the more extreme advocates from one side helped to validate the arguments of extremists on the other. Hence, the political right warned of secular socialist feminism run amok; the left warned of fundamentalist Christians making it impossible to deal with real world problems.

Both the right and the left have sought to recruit international allies. Conservatives have joined forces at times with Muslims and the Vatican, liberals with like-minded Europeans and activists in the developing world. For each group, there have been surprises. Conservatives eager to enlist Muslims in condemning abortion and homosexuality have had to work around their differences concerning arranged marriages and polygamy. Liberals eager to denounce such objectionable practices as female genital mutilation have sometimes found their expected allies from developing countries uninterested, preferring instead to concentrate on economic justice.

The debate between right and left has often been heated, with name-calling, exaggerations, and scare tactics. I personally disagree with much of the conservative position. When I was in government, I fought for more generous funding for comprehensive HIV/AIDS education, child and maternal health programs, and international family planning. I oppose the restrictions the Bush administration has since placed on those programs, and also efforts by religious conservatives—whether Catholic, Protestant, or Muslim— to discourage the distribution of condoms. I do not, however, fault members of the Christian right for expressing and fighting for a moral view, since many others engaged in public policy—including me—do the same. Articulating moral principles is what movements to establish international norms are in business to do. That is precisely how military aggression, slavery, piracy, torture, religious persecution, and racial discrimination have come to be outlawed.

It is also how abuses against women, including domestic violence, "dowry murders," "honor crimes," trafficking, and female infanticide may one day be further reduced. This is a question not of imposing our views on others, but of convincing enough people in enough places that we are right. That is persuasion, not imposition.

Both the political left and the Christian right agree that "moral values" should be near the center of U.S. foreign policy. Each is patriotic and has high aspirations for America; and both would probably agree, although for opposite reasons, with the conclusion of Oliver Wendell Holmes's whimsical rhyme:

> *God's plan made a hopeful beginning;*
> *But man spoiled his chances by sinning;*
> *We trust that the story will end in God's glory;*
> *Though, at present, the other side's winning.*

The right tends to see the United States, at least ideally, as distinct from and morally superior to the rest of the world. In the view of Richard Land, a thoughtful and widely quoted executive of the Southern Baptist Convention, "We are not, and never have been, a nation in the ordinary sense of the word. We are in many ways unique. This does not mean that the United States is God's chosen nation or the successor of Israel. It does not mean that God has a special relationship with the American people. It does mean, however, that our nation still has the heart and soul of our Puritan ancestors and still sees itself as 'a city on the hill.' "

To those on the right, America's shortcomings are primarily in the realm of personal behavior: pornography, homosexuality, and a falling away from traditional values and the church. They tend to see criticism of America's global role, especially under a favored president like George W. Bush, as providing aid to the enemy and comfort to the forces of evil. There is a parallel, I think, between religious fundamentalism and the unquestioning jingoism that views all of history through a narrowly American lens. Both traits are fed by a desire for certainty, a hunger for solid answers on which to build a comforting and coherent picture of the world.

A similar thirst for certainty may be found at the other end of the spectrum among people who focus primarily on the blemishes in American history. In their worldview, the cold war was less a morally essential struggle to defeat communism than an ethically ambiguous competition for power characterized on both sides by hypocrisy, militarism, and heavy-handed interventions in the affairs of others. Perhaps because I am from a country that was taken over by communists, I find the tendency to fault American policies during the cold war to be overdone. Mistakes were certainly made, but the moral superiority of the West compared with the Soviet Union cannot be seriously questioned. Similarly, I see much that is simplistic in the stance of the left on globalization and the use of force. I do, however, sympathize with the concern of the religious left about the huge gap between rich and poor. I think there is some truth in their perception of America less as a city on a hill than as a gated community that has tried to avert its eyes from those in need.

Especially since the bitterly contested national elections of 2000 and 2004, commentators have made much of the role of religion in widening political and cultural divisions within America. Conventional wisdom suggests that those divisions will continue to grow. If that happens, the America I grew up in and fell in love with will become harder to recognize. I am already angered by the facile discussion of a split between so-called "red" states and "blue" states, as if we did not all pledge allegiance to the same tricolor flag. I regret that we have fostered a political culture that rewards the extremes, a culture in which dogmatic belief is deemed a virtue and open-mindedness a weakness, and sarcasm and slanderous attacks frequently drown out intelligent discussion. Haven't we had enough of this? We need a dose of unity. Perhaps we should indeed begin by recalling John Winthrop's prediction that "the eyes of the world will be upon us," and by asking ourselves, "What kind of America do we want the world to see?"

Seven

"Because It Is Right"

———— ༒ ————

W e Americans think of ourselves as generous, and it is true that a host of international charitable organizations rely upon us for the donations they need to carry out their work. But the U.S. government is stingy, ranking next to last among the twenty-two most industrialized countries in the proportion of wealth devoted to international development. In 2002, at the summit on global poverty, President Bush endorsed the Monterrey Consensus, committing wealthy nations to allocate 0.7 percent of their income to helping others. Five European countries already give that much; half a dozen more have established a timetable for doing so.* Despite some recent increases, the percentage given by the United States remains stuck at 0.16, a shortfall of some $40 billion a year.

————————

* The five countries that are over 0.7 percent are Sweden, Norway, Denmark, the Netherlands, and Luxembourg. Britain, France, Finland, Spain, Ireland, and Belgium are committed to reach that level on specific timetables. Economist Jeffrey Sachs points out, "Some have claimed that while the U.S. government budget provides relatively little assistance to the poorest countries, the private sector makes up the gap. In fact, the Organization for Economic Cooperation and

It wasn't always so. Following World War II, America changed history by helping war-torn Europe to rebuild. The Marshall Plan was a classic example of "doing well by doing good"; Europe was revitalized, and the United States benefited from a strong and prosperous West European partner. That was only a start. In 1949, President Truman created a program to assist needy countries everywhere. "Our aim," he said, "should be to help the free peoples of the world, through their own efforts, to produce more food, clothing, housing, and power. Only by helping the least fortunate of its members to help themselves can the human family achieve the decent, satisfying life that is the right of all people."

Truman's initiative was expanded by John Kennedy, who established the U.S. Agency for International Development, the Peace Corps, and the Alliance for Progress. In his inaugural address, Kennedy pledged America's commitment "to those peoples in the huts and villages across the globe struggling to break the bonds of mass misery . . . our best efforts to help them help themselves, for whatever period is required—not because the Communists may be doing it, not because we seek their votes, but because it is right."

Foreign aid was supported at first by leaders from both major political parties, but critics soon began to speak out. The concept of "giveaway" programs ran contrary to the American ethos of self-reliance. Charity, it was widely thought, should go only to the deserving poor, and not all the poor were deserving. In any case, charity rightly began at home. Why devote money to helping people overseas when

---

Development has estimated that private foundations and nongovernmental organizations give roughly $6 billion a year in international assistance, or 0.05 percent of U.S. gross national product (GNP). In that case, total U.S. international aid is around 0.21 percent of GNP—still among the lowest ratios of all donor nations."

those same dollars could be used to address America's own social needs? No politician capitalized on these misgivings more creatively than Ronald Reagan. In 1964, in a speech that was to begin his career as a conservative icon, Reagan claimed that American aid had "bought a two-million-dollar yacht for [the Ethiopian leader] Haile Selassie . . . dress suits for Greek undertakers, extra wives for Kenyan government officials, [and] . . . a thousand TV sets for a place where they have no electricity." Reagan insisted that American assistance expanded foreign bureaucracies, and that "a government bureau is the nearest thing to eternal life we'll ever see on this earth." The "great communicator" did not always have a firm grip on the facts, but no one was better at turning half-truths into enduring myths. As president, he actually increased foreign aid but did nothing publicly to dispel the impressions he had popularized. By then the stereotype was well established: these programs accomplished nothing, encouraged dependence, and wasted the hard-earned dollars of American taxpayers.

It is true that some aid projects were badly designed, and that some others were aimed more at luring governments to the right side of the competition between East and West than at improving the lives of the disadvantaged. The actual record of assistance, however, was better than advertised. Between 1960 and the mid-1990s, the average person's life expectancy in poor countries increased by twenty years. The rate of infant mortality was cut in half. The introduction of low-cost vaccines saved tens of millions of lives. Smallpox was wiped out, and polio was brought to the edge of extinction. Foreign assistance helped many nations in Asia, Latin America, and Africa to become more prosperous, with hundreds of millions of people climbing out of poverty.

These accomplishments should have impressed, but did not. During my years in government, I found that foreign aid was about as popular as fleas. It didn't help that the term "foreign aid" sounded vaguely treasonous. I removed the phrase from my own vocabulary, referring instead to "national security support." This may have eased resistance a bit, but not much. With a lingering budget deficit and no further threat from the Soviet Union, members of Congress were reluctant to allocate money for projects overseas. The chairman of the congressional subcommittee responsible for funding the program informed me with relish that not once had he voted for a foreign aid bill, implying that he never would. Leading Republicans bragged that they had no interest in even visiting foreign countries. Many of their constituents were convinced that foreign "giveaways" already swallowed up 20 percent of the federal budget, instead of nibbling away at less than 1 percent. As secretary of state, I was frankly embarrassed at times when visiting clinics, refugee camps, and impoverished neighborhoods in distant lands, because I knew that, even though the American economy was booming, the only immediate help I could offer was in the form of coloring books and crayons.

By the late 1990s, the Republican arguments had become so predictable I never expected to hear anything different. Then suddenly I did. Among the usual questions I received at hearings, there were some with a fresh slant—accusing us not of trying to do too much to help people abroad, but of doing too little. I had grown accustomed to hearing liberals express horror about the devastation caused by HIV/AIDS, while conservatives implied that the victims had only themselves to blame. But during my final years in office, and ever since, much of the Christian right has come to agree that halting the pandemic is a moral imperative. A few years ago even Jesse Helms came around, admitting, "It had been my feeling that AIDS was a disease largely spread by reckless and voluntary sexual and drug-abusing behavior, and that it would probably be confined to those in high-risk populations. I was wrong."

What is going on? The answer is that religion is becoming entwined with U.S. foreign policy in a new way. When I was in office, partisan Republicans often delighted in calling me "naive" or a "do-gooder." One disgruntled academic even sneered that the Clinton administration was conducting "foreign policy as social work." Now, the Republican senator Sam Brownback of Kansas, as conservative a man as you will find, argues that the United States "must move humbly and wisely, not just for our own economic and strategic interests but for what is morally right."

The ideological right and left have long stood at opposite poles on almost every international issue; that is no longer true. Especially on humanitarian matters, in which religious conservatives have expressed a special interest, the two extremes overlap. Both sides recognize not only a practical interest but also a moral obligation to help those in direst need. Both believe that the story of the Good Samaritan, cited by President Bush in his first inaugural address, should find at least an echo in American foreign policy. This is not just interesting; it is a potentially historic opportunity.

We have heard much in recent years about the "axis of evil." Those searching for evil will find it in the suffering caused by poverty, ignorance, and disease, compass points on a circle of misery in which between 2 and 3 billion human beings are trapped. An estimated 30,000 children die each day from preventable disease and hunger: that is—for purposes of comparison—almost the equivalent of ten 9/11 attacks every twenty-four hours. Billions of people still live under governments that fail to recognize or protect basic human rights. The plight of the poor and repressed should be reason enough for Americans to close ranks, if not always in common cause then at least in separate causes that come together at key points. The list of potential cooperative projects is long, but let me suggest three to start.

The first is support for the principle and practice of religious liberty.

About a decade ago, a coalition of Christian and Jewish activists in the United States began a campaign against religious persecution overseas. In response, Congress approved legislation—the International Religious Freedom Act of 1998—that was signed into law by President Clinton. The statute created an independent United States Commission on International Religious Freedom and required the State Department to prepare an annual report on the status of religious liberty around the world. This landmark law has made identifying and condemning all forms of religious persecution an integral part of U.S. foreign policy and has caused American diplomats to become more comfortable and practiced at raising the issue.

It is natural for Americans to care about religious liberty. Not only is this principle at the center of our own democracy; it provides a reliable litmus test for judging other governments. If a government does not respect the dignity of its own citizens, it is unlikely to honor the rights of anybody else. The countries where religious persecution is widespread (such as North Korea, Burma, Iran, and Sudan) are also—and not coincidentally—a source of broader dangers, including terrorism and the proliferation of weapons of mass destruction. The decision by the Taliban in 2001 to destroy two ancient stone Buddhas in central Afghanistan displayed the same contempt for world opinion as its willingness to host Al Qaeda. China is another country whose government fails to observe religious freedom, but that nation, because of its size and influence, presents some unique complications for American policy-makers.

Members of Congress frequently complained to me during my years in office that Chinese Christians could worship legally only in churches registered with the government. I promised to raise the issue with officials in Beijing, and I did so both in meetings and by making a point of attending church services in China myself.* My to-do list, however, did not end there. I also presented my concerns about the mistreatment of Tibetan Buddhists and members of the Falun Gong, a spiritual health organization. I urged China to allow its citizens to organize politically and to have independent labor unions; expressed my interest in the fate of political prisoners; asked for clarification of China's controversial population control policies; and explored a series of political and military issues with a moral dimension—North Korea's nuclear programs, peaceful relations with Taiwan, Burma's military dictatorship, the treaty on global climate change, and international peacekeeping. Years later, these issues and more remain on the agenda for the United States and China. With a list this long, there is always a chance that questions of religious liberty, whether affecting Christians or others, will get lost. They shouldn't. In fact, I would not be surprised if the growth of religion in China turns out to be among the most significant developments of the next quarter century and—for China's authoritarian leaders—the most difficult to manage.

Those eager to promote religious liberty must also recognize that there is a right and a wrong way to go about it. Lasting change is more likely to come through persuasion than by making blunt demands. In Laos, Bob Seiple's Institute for Global Engagement has adopted a step-by-step

---

* In February 1998, President Clinton sent a delegation of American religious leaders to China to emphasize the importance of religious liberty. The delegation consisted of Rabbi Arthur Schneier of New York; Roman Catholic Archbishop Theodore McCarrick; and Donald Argue, a minister of the Assemblies of God and president of the National Association of Evangelicals.

approach in a desperately poor country with a Soviet-style government, a Buddhist majority, and no democratic tradition. Stressing the importance of religious freedom in a nation mired in economic and social troubles is a dicey proposition. Still, there is steady, visible progress. Prisoners of conscience have been released. Officials are being trained to respect freedom of worship. Study centers have opened to encourage interreligious cooperation. In one village, a government official who had forced more than a thousand Christians to renounce their faith later apologized; before his death, he received hospice care from a church he had previously tried to shut down.

A second area for cooperation across the American political spectrum should be the struggle to alleviate global poverty. In the late 1990s, many segments of the religious community joined with the Clinton administration in supporting a plan to write off much of the debt of the world's poorest countries. Although falling short of its most ambitious goals, the gains made were precedent-shattering—a watershed. Liberal organizations that had long campaigned for debt relief suddenly found themselves working in partnership with powerful politicians from the Christian right who, in turn, found themselves sharing a stage with Bono, the activist and rock star. Advocates of debt relief were clever enough to package their initiatives around a biblical reference to the semicentennial "jubilee year," during which the ancient Israelites were instructed by God to forgive debts and "return every man unto his possession." This initial step was followed by another, a decision in 2005 to write off the debts owed by the eighteen poorest countries to the International Monetary Fund and World Bank.

Notwithstanding the progress in reducing debt, the drive to defeat poverty still lacks momentum. One reason is that the old myths are hard to kill. Many self-described experts continue to argue that foreign assistance will be wasted; that "big government" solutions don't work; and that poverty is a permanent part of the human condition. To an extent, this line of thinking is understandable. Decades of aid have not eliminated poverty, and in sub-Saharan Africa the situation has worsened considerably in recent years. Why? Among the culprits cited are ethnic conflicts; flawed economic models; and demographic factors such as population growth, disease, and the exhaustion of natural resources. Some people point to the lack of truly democratic governments, Robert Mugabe's corrupt regime in Zimbabwe being one blatant example. Those on the left tend to blame economic and trade policies that stack the deck against poor countries (and against the poor within countries) in favor of large corporations and the rich. In my judgment, each factor plays a role and must be taken into account.

Fighting poverty is not, of course, just a matter of shoveling money in the direction of the poor. Historically, the left has put too much faith in aid administered through foreign governments while the right has preached discredited ideas of trickle-down economics. Both sides have grown more sophisticated. Specialists in the field have also learned more about how to make effective use of aid dollars by channeling the majority of funds through nongovernmental institutions, emphasizing opportunities for women, stressing low-tech solutions, heeding environmental considerations, and finding ways to let even the poorest participate economically. It is essential, as well, for developed countries to end the hypocrisy of advocating free markets while spending tens of billions of dollars in agricultural subsidies for their own farmers that make it impossible for those from poor countries to compete.

Another way to help the poor is to extend to them the protections of law. The High-Level Commission on Legal Empowerment of the Poor, which I cochair with the

Peruvian economist Hernando de Soto, is looking at ways to do this. Many poor people who have property in the form of land, housing, and livestock are unable to make the most of it because they lack any legal title. In some countries, as much as 90 percent of property is owned outside the law. This means that people are vulnerable to exploitation and theft and are barred from using their assets to obtain credit, make investments, or start saving. This hurts them and their societies, for it leaves their governments without the tax base necessary to provide basic services. The result is a social fabric that remains unwoven, causing economic stagnation and civil strife. I like the approach of extending legal protections to the poor in part because it defies any particular ideological label. It is a hybrid—a blend of the "ownership society" and "power to the people."

President Bush has declared, "We fight against poverty because hope is an answer to terrorism." In July 2005, he joined the other G-8 leaders in pledging to double total assistance to Africa over the next five years from $25 billion to $50 billion annually. Two months later, the U.S. trumpet sounded a less certain note. America's ambassador to the UN, John Bolton, caused a commotion by distancing his government from the international goal of halving the rate of extreme poverty by 2015. After a week of confusion and mixed signals, President Bush said that the United States did indeed support the goal and would work to meet it. We should keep that pledge and more, not only because we hope it will make us safer, but because—as John Kennedy said— it is right.

A third item I would place near the top of any agenda for bipartisan cooperation is preventing the mass killing of human beings. Over time, the world has become reasonably adept at delivering food, water, and medicine to places that don't have them, provided that people with guns are not standing in the way. It has not, however, developed a reliable means for preventing genocide.

Ever since the massacres in Rwanda in 1994, there has been much talk about how we must never allow something similar to happen again. Meanwhile, something similar has happened again. Over the past decade, a sporadic, pointless, and inconclusive war in the Democratic Republic of Congo has led to the deaths of more than 3 million people. In the Darfur region of Sudan, as many as 300,000 people have died in genocidal violence. The outbreak of killing in these countries—unlike Rwanda—was gradual rather than volcanic, giving the international community ample time to respond. It has responded, however, only slowly and feebly. The problem is not a lack of moral indignation—the violence in Darfur was widely publicized—but a failure to use force effectively.

One possible solution in such cases is for the Security Council to deputize an appropriate major power to organize a coalition that can enforce the world's will. The intervention in Haiti, led by the United States in 1994; the rescue of East Timor, led by Australia in 1999; and the British action in Sierra Leone in 2000 were largely successful. The problem with relying on "coalitions of the willing," however, is that there are sure to be times when no one steps forward. This is less because world leaders are callous than because international peacemaking is an expensive, hard, dangerous, and often thankless task.

To deter people with guns, well-equipped and adequately trained forces are needed; but finding them is not easy. Expecting a soldier to risk everything in defense of his or her homeland is one thing; expecting that same soldier to travel thousands of miles to intervene in, and perhaps die because of, somebody else's quarrel is another. Most people are not that altruistic, especially when, as is typical, they see an international force more blamed for its failures than credited for what it has achieved. As a result, we are left with a system of responding to crises that will occasionally work well, usually not so well, and sometimes not at all.

In September 2005, the UN General Assembly for the first time acknowledged a collective international responsibility to protect populations from genocide, war crimes, ethnic cleansing, and crimes against humanity. Accepting the existence of this responsibility, however, will not help anyone unless there is also both a capacity to protect people and a willingness to do so. The UN was created sixty years ago with the expectation that it would develop its own army. The rivalry between the superpowers put a quick end to that idea, and there is little support for reviving it. The logical role of the UN in a crisis is to authorize an intervention by some combination of national military forces. The logical role for the United States is to take the lead in ensuring that such a combination of forces will be available when needed and successful when deployed. To do that, we must work hard to allay suspicions about our intentions. We must also be clear about what is required.

A force intended to prevent genocide must be a serious military enterprise; it cannot be cobbled together from the bits and pieces of underfunded armies, detailed for brief periods, and assembled at the last minute. Countries must be asked to identify capable personnel who will be dedicated to the job of humanitarian response and prepared over a period of years to excel in that function. Ideally, these forces would train together long enough to develop complementary skills and maintain their readiness for deployment at short notice. They would be equipped with the latest communications, transportation, and weapons and would be supported by real-time intelligence provided by countries with the necessary equipment and know-how. Their military and paramilitary components would be accompanied by civilian administrators and prosecutors affiliated with international legal authorities. When a force is dispatched, the job of the military would be to restore order; the job of the civilians to jump-start reconstruction; and the job of the prosecutors to give those responsible for war crimes their day in court.

Once again, this would *not* be a standing UN army. It would be the international equivalent of a cavalry that leaders could call on to ride to the rescue in emergencies. There are many details (including financing) that would have to be worked out,* but in concept it is a better way to prevent future Darfurs than anything we have now. Before the United States could design or even participate in such an effort, however, conservatives and liberals would have to shed some traditional prejudices. A reliable mechanism for preventing genocide could not be created without unprecedented levels of international military cooperation. The UN might not be in charge, but it would surely have to be involved. Is the Christian right ready to explore such concepts with an open mind, or does it remain shackled by its long-standing suspicion, even paranoia, regarding the UN? Meanwhile, the political left would have to agree to spend substantial amounts of money to improve international military capabilities, even at the expense of pressing social needs.

If the past is truly prologue, there is no hope. But if the past is past, perhaps it is worth a try. After all, people who once opposed foreign aid, nation-building, and combating HIV/AIDS now endorse all three. And Ronald Reagan,

---

* One such detail would be a more favorable attitude by the United States toward the International Criminal Court. Even if we continue to refrain from participating in that tribunal, we should want it to succeed.

after retiring from the presidency, told the Oxford Union in 1992, "We should rely more on multilateral institutions. . . . What I propose is nothing less than a humanitarian velvet glove backed by the mailed fist of military power."

Widespread cooperation between the Christian right and other American activists on international humanitarian issues is no pipe dream; Senator Brownback and I cohosted a well-attended conference devoted to the topic in November 2005. Cooperation matters not only because of what it can help us accomplish overseas, but also because of the extent to which it can help Americans understand each other. We are not, I am convinced, as divided as we sometimes seem. Most of us do not want our leaders confusing their own will with God's, but neither do we want them to ignore religious and moral principles. We support the separation of church and state but not the enforced separation of religion from the public life of our nation. Many of us pray regularly that God will guide our leaders. We hope that those who make decisions in our name will think hard about questions of right and wrong. We want them to protect us but also to make us proud.

Bipartisan cooperation on humanitarian issues can also help to influence for the better how America is perceived in the world. I suspect that most of us would like our country to be seen as confident, caring, principled, honest, and strong. We learned long ago, however, in Vietnam and Iran, that we are not always seen as we would like. Some may think that the views of others do not matter, that we are so powerful we need no longer exhibit, as our Declaration of Independence once urged, a "decent respect for the opinions of mankind." To indulge such arrogance would be a fatal mistake and a disappointment to America's true friends everywhere. The standing of the United States would be crucial at any point in history; it is especially vital now, as we seek the key to victory in two wars simultaneously. That search begins with the knowledge that we cannot lead in the world unless we first understand those whom we most need to influence, including especially the followers of Islam.

Part Two

Cross, Crescent, Star

Eight

Learning about Islam

⌾

Christians and Muslims first met in battle in 636 near the Yarmūk River, a tributary of the Jordan; the fierce fighting ended with the massacre of 70,000 Christians and the inauguration of Islamic control in Jerusalem, previously a western outpost of the Byzantine Empire. In 1099, crusaders retook the holy city in the name of the cross; this time the result was the massacre of 70,000 Muslims and the killing of every Jew the triumphant Christians could track down. In 1187, Jerusalem was claimed once again for Islam under the generalship of Saladin the Great, a triumph followed by more crusades and tens of thousands of additional deaths. Through much of the world there echoed the call for holy war.

Civilization has since marched boldly into the twenty-first century; yet the same cry is heard again. Jews and Arabs are contesting the very lands and holy places fought over one thousand years ago. A gang of terrorists, acting in the name of Islam, inflicted the deadliest single attack ever on American soil. The Bush administration's response has stirred intense anger among many Muslims. Anxiety is growing in Europe, where Muslim immigration has expanded and acts of terror and examples of bigotry are on the increase. In Africa, resurgent Islam is colliding with resurgent Christianity. In Asia, from Chechnya to the Philippines, the divide between the followers of Islam and those of other faiths is causing bloodshed. Like a family torn apart by a disputed will, the children of Abraham are too often inspired less by feelings of kinship than by jealousy, insecurity, and hate.

When I raised my hand to take the oath of office as secretary of state, I had in mind a list of priorities; prominent among them was a desire to strengthen America's ties with the Muslim world. This seemed essential. The United States had long-standing interests to protect in the Middle East and south Asia. The end of the cold war had created an opportunity to forge partnerships with the newly independent and strategically located countries of central Asia. The surprise election of a moderate to the presidency of Iran would soon offer the prospect of a warming in our long-frozen relationship with that country. Democratic openings beckoned in Indonesia and Nigeria, each a regional giant where the influence of Islam was widely felt. Throughout the 1990s, foreign policy journals featured articles about "Islamic extremists." In meeting after meeting, I found myself scrawling on a notepad, "Learn more about Islam."

I did, of course, already know something of the subject. When I was ten, my father had served as chairman of a UN commission on India and Pakistan charged with resolving the status of Kashmir. Even at that age, I understood the basic facts. Because of religion, the Indian subcontinent was splitting apart. The leaders of India wanted a secular, multiethnic state. The leaders of Pakistan wanted a country for

Muslims. Kashmir was caught between the two; it had a Muslim majority, but a large Hindu minority and a Hindu ruler. The job for diplomats was to find a solution that would leave all sides satisfied. That was almost sixty years ago; now my father is dead and I am old, both countries have nuclear weapons, and the problem is little nearer to being solved.

There were not many Muslims in Denver, where I spent my teenage years. My father had made contacts while at the UN, however, and some of his acquaintances came to visit. One I remember particularly was Sir Zafrullah Khan, a former foreign minister of Pakistan. I liked him because he was dignified, erudite, and charming. When he took me to breakfast one day, my envious classmates jokingly pointed out that he could choose a second wife while keeping his first. What impressed me in talking to him about Kashmir, however, was how complicated life could be when a dispute is fueled by both religion and nationalism and each side is convinced that it has sole possession of the truth.

Sitting in the State Department many years later, I thought of Sir Zafrullah and how out of place he had seemed in Denver. The truth is that he would have seemed almost as anomalous in the State Department in 1997: we had no Muslims serving in senior positions and just a few in midlevel jobs. I decided that we had to improve communications. To that end, we reviewed everything from personnel recruitment and training to the listing of Islamic holidays alongside Jewish and Christian ones on our official calendar. We began a series of discussions with representatives of American Muslims, inviting them during Ramadan to the first *iftaar** dinners hosted by a secretary of state. We also

---

* *Iftaar* refers to the daily breaking of the fast after sunset by Muslims during the holy month of Ramadan.

developed an introductory guide to Islam to be available to persons traveling on behalf of the United States to countries that had a Muslim majority. The publication contained information such as the following, which, though basic, is still novel to many Americans:

- Muslims worship the same God (in Arabic, Allah) as Christians and Jews.*

- "Islam" means submission to God. A person who surrenders to God and lives faithfully will find that life has harmony and purpose.

- Muslims believe in the day of judgment, in an afterlife, and in the ethical accountability of every individual. A Muslim's first responsibility is to care for the poor, the orphaned, the widowed, and the oppressed.

- The Muslim holy book, the Quran, contains the exact words believed to have been revealed by God and conveyed by the Archangel Gabriel to a Meccan merchant, Muhammad ibn Abdallah (the Prophet), over a twenty-two-year period beginning in 610.

- Sharia, or Islamic law, is based on the Quran, the deeds and words of the Prophet, and scholarly interpretations. The law governs virtually every aspect of personal, social, and civic life.

- The five pillars of Islam are: (1) profession of faith; (2) ritual prayer; (3) purification through charity; (4) fasting; and (5) pilgrimage to Mecca.

---

* *Ilah* in Arabic means "god"; Allah is a contraction of *al-ilah*, "the god." The same word for God is used by Arabic-speaking Christians and Jews. The term is similar in Aramaic, the language spoken by Jesus, who is said to have cried out on the cross, *Eili, Eili lama sabachtani?*—"My God, my God, why have you forsaken me?"

- Muhammad is considered by Muslims to have been the last in a series of prophets that began with Adam and Noah, continued through Abraham and Moses, and included King David and Jesus of Nazareth. The Quran stipulates that the revelation to Muhammad confirmed the teaching of earlier prophets. Muhammad (like Jesus) did not think of himself as the founder of a new religion; he considered himself, instead, a messenger calling his people back to the one true God.

- Arabs trace their lineage to Abraham through Ishmael, son of Hagar—just as Jews trace theirs through Isaac, son of Sarah. The issue matters because both Muslims and Jews (as well as Christians) believe God commanded Abraham to go into the Land of Canaan with the promise that his descendants would settle the land and become a great nation.

- Muslims believe that Jesus was a major prophet, but they do not accept the possibility that God could have a "son." They agree that Jesus was born of a virgin and that he ascended into heaven, but they do not believe that he was either crucified or resurrected.

- In Muslim tradition, the first altar to God was built in Mecca by Adam and later rebuilt by Abraham and Ishmael. The mosques in Mecca and Medina, two cities where the Prophet lived, are the two holiest sites in Islam. The third holiest is Al-Aqsa Mosque in Jerusalem, on a site the Prophet visited—whether in a dream or physically is debated—to pray with Jesus and earlier prophets and climb to the seventh heaven in the company of Gabriel.

- The Quran provides that Jews and Christians living in areas ruled by Muslims should have protected status—meaning that their property, laws, religious customs, and places of worship should be preserved. Through most of the second millennium, Islamic societies showed more flexibility toward other religions than did Christian Europe. Although free to practice their faith, Christians and Jews living in Muslim societies were ordinarily treated as political inferiors.

- The Islamic concept of jihad is often and somewhat simplistically equated—even by some Muslims—with holy war. *Jihad* is correctly translated as "effort" or "striving" for the sake of God. For most Muslims, "greater jihad" refers to the individual's attempts to remain virtuous (the personal struggle). "Lesser jihad" refers to the struggle for justice, including the defense of Islam against those who attack it.

- Muslims draw a distinction between wars that are justified and those that are not. A war fought in the cause of God— in self-defense or against tyranny—is just. A war fought for other motives, such as the conquest of territory belonging to another, is unacceptable. There are also rules concerning how wars are fought. Noncombatants are not to be attacked; nor are prisoners to be mistreated. According to Khaled Abou el Fadl, a leading expert on Islamic law who now lives in the United States, jurists "insist that even if the enemy tortured or murdered Muslim hostages, Muslims are forbidden from doing the same."

- Suicide is prohibited by Islam, but dying while in genuine service to God is martyrdom, guaranteeing a place in heaven.

- Although Islam originated in the Arabian Peninsula, today only about one Muslim in five is Arab (and about one Arab in five is non-Muslim). The largest Muslim populations are in Asia.

• Muslims have a duty to help other Muslims, especially those who are suffering or oppressed.

Islamic tradition discourages the depiction of Muhammad in pictures or art, even in mosques. In his lifetime, however, he was described as being of moderate height, with black eyes, a pale complexion, long thick hair, and a profuse beard that fell to his chest. His home city, Mecca, was a commercial cross-roads, where pilgrims came to worship and offer sacrifices to hundreds of tribal gods. Local businessmen profited by catering to the pilgrims and selling them objects, animate and inanimate, to use in their tributes. Muhammad's revelation, centering as it did on belief in a single all-powerful God, threatened to undermine this lucrative practice, causing local authorities to plot to kill him. Narrowly escaping death, he journeyed in secret to the nearby city of Medina, where he established himself as a political and spiritual leader. As soon as he had gathered sufficient support, he returned to Mecca in triumph, smashing the pagan idols, dedicating the holy shrine to Allah, and asserting authority over the entire Arabian Peninsula.

Shortly after he turned sixty years of age, Muhammad delivered a farewell sermon on the Mount of Mercy, located across the plain of Arafat, east of Mecca. He cautioned his people to "hurt no one so that no one may hurt you. Remember that you will indeed meet your Lord and that he will indeed reckon your deeds." He also spoke of racial equality, a decision that would help smooth Islam's acceptance as a global religion. "An Arab has no superiority over a non-Arab," he said, "nor a non-Arab over an Arab; also a white [person] has no superiority over a black [person] nor a black over a white—except by piety and good action."

Like the other monotheistic faiths, Islam is a "big tent,"

interpreted and practiced in diverse ways. The richness of thought is due to ethnic and national influences, differences among leading scholars, and sectarian splits. As a result, almost every generalization about Islam is partly wrong. The requirement in some societies, for example, that women cover themselves completely while in public is more a reflection of Arab culture—Arab men also dress with extreme modesty—than a mandate of Islam. The majority of Muslim women do not wear the veil. The Quran does include passages that discriminate against women (for example, language on polygamy, divorce, and inheritance), but in each case the verses are less discriminatory than Arab customs prevailing at the time. Muhammad told his followers, "It is true that you have certain rights with regard to your women, but they also have rights over you."

Queen Noor of Jordan has pointed out, "Few Westerners realize that seventh-century Islam granted women political, legal, and social rights then unheard of in the West, rights, in fact, that women in the U.S. and elsewhere still struggled for in the twentieth century. Early Islam based these new rights, such as the equal right to education, to own and inherit property, to conduct business, and not to be coerced into marriage, on the equality of men and women before God—this when the rest of the world considered women chattels." Nor is there anything in the Quran that would prevent women from voting in an election, driving a car, associating with males in public, or working outside the home (the Prophet's wife, Khadija, was a successful businesswoman). The countries with the largest number of Muslims—Indonesia, India, Pakistan, Bangladesh, and Turkey—have each elected a female head of government; this is a distinction that neither any Arab state nor the United States can claim.

Muhammad's death in 632 ignited a series of battles over who should succeed him as ruler, eventually leaving Islam divided into two broad camps. The larger faction, which later became the Sunnis, initially supported the Prophet's father-in-law. A second group, the Shia, favored the descendants of Ali, the Prophet's son-in-law. Almost 1,400 years later, this schism continues to influence regional and world politics. The Sunnis are the majority in most regions, but the Shia predominate in Iran, Iraq, Bahrain, and Lebanon and are influential in Syria, Azerbaijan, and south Asia. The split is far more than a polite difference of opinion. Shiite minorities in Sunni-dominated countries frequently and justifiably complain of intolerance and discrimination. To Sunni extremists, the Shia are not Muslims at all.

A second division, between modernizers and conservatives, affects both Shia and Sunnis. Modernizers draw on a mainstream strand of Islam that seeks to reconcile rationalism and religious belief. They tend to be more comfortable coexisting with secular governments; more convinced of the value of education in science, mathematics, history, and foreign languages; more liberal in their treatment of women; and more likely to embrace democratic institutions. Conservatives insist on a high degree of control in family matters, separation of the sexes, and resistance to foreign customs.

Heavily influenced by the eighteenth-century Wahhabi (or Salafist) religious movement, Saudi Arabia has long served as the center of conservative Sunni Islam. The revolution of 1979 in Iran marked the high point for conservative Shias. As the fervor generated by that event faded, Iran gradually became what it is today: a battleground between conservatives and modernizers.

Muslims agree that the Quran is the literal word of God, but differ among themselves about how particular verses should be explained and implemented. For several centuries, a practice known as *ijtihad* was used by Muslim intellectuals to interpret and apply the principles of law in new contexts as

Islam spread through much of the Byzantine and Persian empires and outward to Spain, North Africa, Turkey, India, central Asia, and beyond. This expansion was helped by the accessible nature of Islam combined with the decadent condition of the Christian church and other religious institutions of the period. Islam did not require its followers to accept or understand a complex theology such as the Trinity. All it demanded was submission to God, whom every person could address as directly as any other. In the words of one historian, Islam "opened the door wide in a world of uncertainty, treachery and intolerable divisions to a great and increasing brotherhood of trustworthy men on earth, and to a paradise ... of equal fellowship and simple and understandable delights."

At the center of the Muslim world was Baghdad, which by the end of the first millennium had become an educational, scientific, and cultural capital. Here, Muslims worked alongside Christians and Jews to translate and study the finest works of ancient China, India, Egypt, Israel, Greece, and Rome. At a time when the practice of medicine was forbidden by the church in Christian lands, Arabs were using anesthetics and performing complex operations. Muslims developed the numerical system still in use today and invented the pendulum, algebra, and trigonometry. After learning from the Chinese how to make paper, they kept administrative records, wrote books on a wide range of subjects, and designed the world's first system of international banking. During this golden age, Islam was modern and forward-looking, eager to embrace learning of all kinds.

Why doesn't Islam enjoy the same reputation today? In the thirteenth century, Mongol horsemen brought a new and fearsome style of warfare from the east, conquering Baghdad and much of the Islamic empire. The invaders extended themselves too far, however, and were soon supplanted in the Near East by the Turks. Under the Ottoman sultans, the perceived need for innovative interpretations of Islamic law declined. The emperors were more concerned about ensuring obedience and preserving traditions. Today, the majority of Muslims would agree that the interpretation of Islam remains open, but how open is a matter of fierce debate. Some scholars are calling for a revival of *ijtihad*, especially as it applies to the role of women, participation in the global economy, relations with non-Muslims, and the definition of an Islamic state. These reformers are often critical of the West, but are nevertheless sometimes accused by conservatives of acting on behalf of the West to dilute or destroy the real spirit of Islam. Since the Sunnis lack a centralized clerical hierarchy, allegations of blasphemy are frequently made and rarely resolved.

Christian Europe, scarred from its battles with Muslims through much of the Middle Ages, bequeathed to the United States a suspicion of Islam. Most Americans saw it as an alien and somewhat mystical faith, outside the Judeo-Christian tradition with which they were comfortable. In the 1960s, the Nation of Islam acquired notoriety within the United States for its disputes over leadership and for its angry, separatist rhetoric. Many Americans were surprised when widely admired athletes such as Cassius Clay (Muhammad Ali) and Lew Alcindor (Kareem Abdul-Jabbar) converted to Islam and proudly replaced their "slave names" with African or Islamic ones. This puzzlement was acknowledged in the challenging words of Muhammad Ali: "I am America. I am the part you won't recognize. But get used to me. Black, confident, cocky; my name, not yours; my religion, not yours; my goals, my own, get used to me." Internationally, the sense of unease about Islam was periodically reinforced by Arab oil embargos, the hostile rants of Iranian ayatollahs, and incidents of terror.

These issues did not, however, prevent the United States

from having cordial diplomatic relations with most Muslim-majority states. From the beginning, American policy has been consistent in rejecting any thought of a cultural war. During his first term, President Clinton told the Jordanian parliament, "There are those who insist that between America and the Middle East there are impassable religious and other obstacles to harmony; that our beliefs and our cultures must somehow inevitably clash. But I believe they are wrong. America refuses to accept that our civilizations must collide."

The Clinton administration stressed this theme because we wanted Arabs and Muslims to look to the future with practical concerns rather than religious rivalries foremost in mind. We also hoped to show that we were ourselves free of prejudice against Islam. This was entirely sincere. We viewed terrorism as an aberration. Just as there is nothing Christian about the violent bigotry of the Ku Klux Klan, there is nothing Islamic about terrorism. One billion three hundred million people can hardly be characterized by the violence of a tiny fraction. The Quran is explicit that the taking of a single innocent life is prohibited, even equating it with the killing of all humanity.

This has not stopped some people from portraying Islam as "wicked and evil," or calling Muhammad a "terrorist."* Reading selectively, critics cite passages in the Quran that

---

* Reverend Jerry Falwell has called Muhammad a "terrorist." Reverend Franklin Graham has called Islam "wicked and evil." Graham later added, "I respect the people of the Islamic faith that have come to this country. I have Muslim friends. But that doesn't stop me from wanting to help them. I certainly don't believe the way they believe, and they don't believe the way I believe either. That doesn't make me dislike them, and I love them very much. I want to do all I can to help them. . . . I want them to know about God's son, Jesus Christ. I want them to know, but I certainly don't want to force it on them. I would like some day for Muslims to know what Christians do."

instruct believers to use force against enemies of the faith, instructions that violent extremists—who tend to have the loudest voices—can exploit to justify their actions. But incendiary language is also present in the Hebrew Bible, what Christians call the Old Testament. The books of Joshua and Judges provide a catalog of holy wars, and Deuteronomy includes a virtual endorsement of genocide in God's name.* In the New Testament, Jesus warns, "Think not that I am come to send peace on Earth: I came not to send peace, but a sword." As for the Book of Revelation, it can be interpreted in many ways, but peaceful it is not.

The Quran was compiled over a period of more than two decades, the Hebrew Bible over centuries. The New Testament was assembled in about 100 years, amid much squabbling about whose testimonies to include and whose to dismiss. Within each book there are inconsistencies and frequent shifts of subject and tone. To construct a dogma out of a few quotations is sophistry. A reader trolling the scriptures for language sanctifying intolerance and war will find it whether the texts are sacred to Christians, Muslims, or Jews. To be understood fairly, each of the holy books must be read and studied both comprehensively and in the context of its place and time. That is why generations of scholars have labored to highlight core passages, explain contradictions, clear away discrepancies, correct mistranslations, and detect the significance of obscure phrasings.

I know from experience that those responsible for managing U.S. foreign policy will want religious doctrines interpreted in ways that minimize the dangers of international

---

* E.g., Deuteronomy 20:16–17: "Of the cities of these people, which the LORD thy God doth give thee for an inheritance, thou shalt save alive nothing that breatheth: But thou shalt utterly destroy them; namely, the Hittites, and the Amorites, the Canaanites, and the Perizzites, the Hivites, and the Jebusites."

conflict—possibly a vain hope. Two ideas have proved particularly troublesome. The first is the claim made by some extreme Zionists (and backed by many Christians) that God's gift of land to Israel provides a license to ignore Palestinians' rights. Set against this are provisions of the Quran that exhort believers to fight to regain any lost lands. Khaled el Fadl writes, "Some jurists argue that any territory that has ever been ruled by Muslims remains forever a part of the abode of Islam."

Doctrines such as this, if followed blindly and without regard to other teachings, are written in blood. History has left little emotional padding between and among the major religions. It does not take much to lead groups of people with extreme views to believe that their faith is under attack and that their duty is to defend it by every available means.

Nine

Holy Land, but Whose?

————— ✄ —————

November 2, 1917, marked the beginning of a new era in the Middle East; it was a day long awaited and prayed for by some; long feared and prayed against by others. A letter signed by the British foreign secretary, Arthur J. Balfour, conveyed the news:

> His Majesty's Government views with favour the establishment in Palestine of a national home for the Jewish people, and will use their best endeavours to facilitate the achievement of this object. It being clearly understood that nothing shall be done which may prejudice the civil and religious rights of existing non-Jewish communities in Palestine.

When, after World War I, the League of Nations granted the British a mandate to govern Palestine, political authority over the Holy Land passed out of Muslim hands for the first time since Saladin's victory in the twelfth century. The Balfour

Declaration became official policy, enlisting the strength of the West to encourage, legitimize, and protect Jewish immigration. This historic shift, the product of decades of lobbying by Zionists, had also been sought by influential Christians. In 1891, a petition—the Blackstone Memorial*—addressed to President Benjamin Harrison and other world leaders urged an international conference to establish a Jewish state. Hundreds of prominent Americans signed the appeal, including the chief justice of the United States, the Speaker of the House of Representatives, John D. Rockefeller, and J. P. Morgan. The petition pointed out that the major powers had already "wrested" Bulgaria, Serbia, Romania, Montenegro, and Greece "from the Turks" and returned them "to their rightful owners." Why not, it asked, give Palestine back to the Jews? "According to God's distribution of nations it is their home."

To the frustration of future generations of diplomats, neither the Blackstone Memorial nor the Balfour Declaration addressed a crucial question: how, exactly, could a Jewish state be created without prejudice to the "civil and religious rights of existing non-Jewish communities in Palestine"? Balfour, for one, did not consider the matter important. "Zionism," he said, "is rooted in age-long traditions, in present needs, in future hopes of far profounder import than the desires and prejudices of the 700,000 Arabs who now inhabit the ancient land." When a fellow diplomat cautioned, "Let us not, for heaven's sake, tell the Moslem what he ought to

---

* The memorial emerged from a conference of Christians and Jews held in Chicago and organized by William E. Blackstone, who was a businessman and lay evangelical minister. Blackstone, who referred to himself as "God's little errand boy," also wrote a best-selling pamphlet, *Jesus Is Coming*, that described the return by Jews to Israel as a prerequisite to the second coming of Christ.

think," Balfour replied tartly: "I am quite unable to see why heaven or any other power should object to our telling the Moslem what he ought to think."

A little less than three decades later, as World War II drew to a close, the United States was in the process of replacing Great Britain as the country whose influence mattered most. To promote stability in the postwar Middle East, Franklin Roosevelt met secretly with Ibn Saud, the king of Saudi Arabia, on a warship moored in the Suez Canal. The president tried to persuade Ibn Saud to support Jewish claims in Palestine. Although the king was impressed by Roosevelt's wheelchair, a device he had never before seen, he was little taken with the president's words. "Make the enemy and the oppressor pay," he reasoned. "Amends should be made by the criminal, not by the innocent bystander. What injury have Arabs done to the Jews of Europe? It is the Christian Germans who stole their homes and lives." Roosevelt, though disappointed by the rebuff, nevertheless assured the king, "I will take no action with respect to the Palestine Mandate without consulting the Arabs." He also gave Ibn Saud a wheelchair as a gift. Two months later, Roosevelt died. As I am reminded on every trip I take to the Middle East, Arab leaders have not forgotten his promise, which they insist was never honored. They are half right. The State Department did consult regularly about Jewish emigration from Europe to Palestine, but without arriving at a common position. The Arabs wanted to halt the emigration; President Truman felt a moral duty, in the aftermath of the Holocaust, to support it. In May 1948, when the British mandate officially expired, Israel declared independence, which the United States was the first to recognize. Arabs complained that they had not been consulted; Truman insisted that his decision should have been no surprise.

Israel's declaration of statehood did not pass quietly. Arab armies attacked the new nation. The fighting that ensued caused hundreds of thousands of Palestinians to leave their homes, many settling in refugee camps in present-day Jordan and Lebanon, where large numbers of their descendants still live. In 1967, a second war, lasting only six days, expanded the territory under Jewish control as Israeli troops routed Arab forces on all fronts. As word of the victory spread, Menachem Begin, chairman of Israel's conservative Herut Party, rushed to the site where the temple of Solomon had once stood. For the first time since the ancient era, the sacred soil was in Jewish hands. Accompanied by other party leaders, Begin gave thanks and prayed:

> There has arisen in our Homeland a new generation . . . of warriors and heroes. And when they went forth to engage the enemy there burst forth from their hearts the call which echoes throughout the generation, the call from the father of the Prophets, the redeemer of Israel from the bondage of Egypt: "Arise, O Lord, and let Thine enemies be scattered and let them that hate Thee be put to flight." And we scattered and defeated them and flee they did.

Begin's prayer reflects the deepest yearnings of a people who had spent nearly 2,000 years in suffering and exile, held together by their traditions, their faith, and their dreams of returning to their historic homeland. Like the Babylonian, Greek, Syrian, Roman, Muslim, and Christian conquerors who preceded him in Jerusalem, Begin spoke in triumph. But for one side to triumph, another must be defeated. The war of 1967 extended Jewish authority over lands long occupied by Arabs and led to Israel's annexation of Arab East

Jerusalem. In most places, but especially in the Middle East, the reaction of anyone who loses land is to start laying plans to recover it.

I first visited Jerusalem in the mid-1980s. Standing by the window of my hotel room, I could see one of the world's most dramatic vistas—the stately Dome of the Rock, surrounded by the walls of the Old City, the holiest place in a holy land. This was during a relatively quiet moment in Israel's history; the first Palestinian uprising, or intifada, had yet to begin. I was overwhelmed, nonetheless, by the intensity of noise, light, and emotion. I couldn't help reflecting that the history that mattered most had happened here, in the narrow streets, stately olive groves, and surrounding hills.

The Church of the Holy Sepulchre, rebuilt by crusaders almost 900 years earlier, marked the site where, according to tradition, Jesus' body had been taken from the cross. I placed my hand on the spot where I was told the base of the true cross had been laid. Though tempted to ask how anyone could be so sure of such a thing, I still trembled. The experience was sadly undermined, however, by the history of squabbling evident within the church itself, which was and remains literally a house divided. Christian groups have fought over the space since it was first dedicated; today, the building is split into areas controlled by six groups—Greeks, Franciscans, Armenians, Copts, Ethiopians, and Syrians. The main key is retained by Muslims, whom the various Christian sects trust more than they do one another.*

---

* Violence broke out at the Church of the Holy Sepulchre as recently as September 2004, when Greek Orthodox and Franciscan monks were captured on film dragging, kicking, and punching each other.

Not far from the church is the place where Solomon had built his temple and Begin had offered his prayer. That shrine was first restored after the Jewish exile in Babylonia, then restored again by King Herod. It was destroyed in the first century by Romans, who leveled the entire city except for its outer walls, leaving intact the western side of the temple. This structure, which still survives, is sacred to Judaism. I watched as bearded men with covered heads and prayer shawls chanted in front of it and left pieces of paper between its stones. Observant Jews pray daily for God "to restore worship to Thy Temple in Zion."* A significant portion of Jewish law is devoted to the sacrifices that for centuries were offered inside the temple. Among the treasures once housed there was a gold-covered chest containing the Ten Commandments and thought to embody God's promise to Israel: the Ark of the Covenant.†

From the base of the Western Wall, a path leads up to a thirty-five-acre area of fountains, gardens, and buildings that Jews call the Temple Mount and Muslims know as the Haram al-Sharif, or "noble sanctuary." After the noise of the city, I welcomed its tranquillity. The sound of the water was soothing, as those preparing to pray washed themselves. The inside of Al-Aqsa Mosque was cool, adorned with arches and pillars, and filled with light. The Haram had been built by Muslims in the late seventh century. Their shrines commemorate Muhammad's celebrated night journey from Mecca to Jerusalem (al-aqsa translates as "most distant.")

---

* This is from the Amidah, or standing prayer, a collection of blessings. People reciting a blessing face in the direction of Israel if they are outside Israel; in the direction of Jerusalem if they are in Israel but outside Jerusalem; or in the direction of the Temple Mount if they are in Jerusalem.

† The Ark was lost, stolen, or hidden when the Babylonians conquered Jerusalem c. 587 BCE. Notwithstanding the final scenes of the film Raiders of the Lost Ark, it has not been found.

According to Muslim tradition, Muhammad began his ascent to the heavens from the rock now encased beneath the golden dome. Various Jewish traditions hold that this rock was the foundation used by God to create the heavens and Earth, or the altar upon which Abraham offered to God the sacrifice of his son Isaac, or the resting place where Jacob lay dreaming of the ladder to heaven. Tragically, holy ground is also coveted ground. During the crusades, triumphant Christians placed a cross atop the dome, used the rock to support an altar, covered the Quranic inscriptions with Latin texts, and converted Al-Aqsa Mosque into a military headquarters. Today, the Palestinian grand mufti of Jerusalem claims that the Temple Mount and all its structures, including the Western Wall, are sacred places for Muslims only. Fervently committed Jewish groups seek support for rebuilding the temple and moving the Muslim shrines elsewhere.

Ordinarily, when diplomats sit down to negotiate a border, they come equipped with maps, and with suggestions for compromise. In the Middle East, this is not enough. Israelis and Palestinians care as deeply as anyone about economic and security issues. They argue vociferously about security arrangements, access to water, transportation routes, and control of airspace; but to a negotiator these are all matters that can—at least potentially—be resolved through a process of give-and-take. Productive conversation stops, however, when the parties argue for the rightness of their positions not on the basis of human laws and precedents, but on the basis of the promises and intentions of God.

As this is written, early in 2006, the dream of peace in the Middle East has rarely appeared more distant. The Palestinians are divided against themselves. The Israelis have concluded that they have no partner with whom to make peace. Many look back on the high-profile negotiations of the 1990s as a mistake, the result of a naive belief that Yasser Arafat and the Palestinian Liberation Organization (PLO) were sincere in pledging their willingness to accept Israel's existence. The truth, I believe, is more complex. To understand the possibilities for the future, it is worth reviewing how the present stalemate came to be.

Throughout 2000, our final year in office, President Clinton, special negotiator Dennis Ross, and I struggled along with Israeli and Palestinian representatives to find a way around the obstacles to a peace settlement. Of these obstacles, the most troublesome was Jerusalem. The Palestinians insisted that the city, known to them as Al Quds ("the holy"), should be the capital of their state. They also demanded full sovereignty over the "noble sanctuary." In our discussions, we explored a host of creative variations on the themes of jurisdiction and authority. We even asked the two sides whether they could accept what we thought was a novel idea: "divine sovereignty" for the holiest sites. Searching for inspiration, President Clinton took time in private to study sections of the Quran and the Torah. In the end, he proposed that "what is Arab in the city should be Palestinian and what is Jewish should be Israeli." This would have meant Palestinian sovereignty over the "noble sanctuary" and Arab neighborhoods—where the Palestinians could have their capital—and Israeli sovereignty over the rest of the city, including the Western Wall. The Israeli prime minister, Ehud Barak, accepted the president's ideas. In so doing, he agreed to redivide Jerusalem, something successive Israeli leaders, including Barak himself, had promised never to do. He consented, as well, to the establishment of a Palestinian state consisting of 97 percent of the West Bank, Gaza, and East Jerusalem.

We were not, of course, the first to search for a formula

that would bring peace to Jerusalem. In 1192, Saladin and Richard Coeur de Lion (Lionheart), both commanding armies that were weary of hardship and death, sought to negotiate an end to the Third Crusade. The terms proposed by Richard were uncannily similar to those considered by us (though affecting Christians, not Jews). Under Richard's plan, Muslims would have control over the Dome of the Rock and Al-Aqsa Mosque; Christians would have their holy sites; the rest of Jerusalem and the surrounding areas would be divided. In their exchange of letters, both leaders stressed the centrality of the holy city. "Jerusalem is for us an object of worship that we could not give up even if there were only one of us left," wrote Richard. Saladin responded, "Jerusalem . . . is even more sacred to us than it is to you, for it is the place from which our Prophet accomplished his nocturnal journey and the place where our community will gather on the Day of Judgment. Do not imagine that we can renounce it or vacillate on this point." In the end, the negotiations broke down amid political intrigue, military misadventures, and allegations of bad faith. Richard retreated, and the Christians were left in Jerusalem with only the rights of pilgrims.

Eight hundred and eight years later, our negotiations, too, collapsed. In contrast to Barak's flexibility, Arafat showed stubbornness, flatly rejecting the deal Clinton had put forward. In our last-ditch effort to persuade him, we solicited the support of Arab leaders in Egypt, Jordan, Morocco, and Saudi Arabia. We hoped that their backing would make it easier for Arafat to say yes. In retrospect, their support mattered little. The Egyptians and Saudis did not push Arafat hard, and in any case their governments did not have enough credibility among Arabs to persuade him to run the personal risks a settlement would entail. In explanation,

Arafat did not hesitate to offer his built-in excuse: he lacked the authority, he said, to make concessions related to Islam's holy sites. He could not compromise or "vacillate" on issues sacred to Muslims everywhere without inviting his own funeral. Worse, he fed us the lie—popular among Arab propagandists—that Jews have no claim to Jerusalem, because the first and second temples had actually been built elsewhere. Arafat could have been the first president of an internationally recognized Palestine; he chose instead the applause of supporters who praised him for refusing to sign away even a slice of "Arab land" or acknowledge the sovereignty of Israel over the Western Wall. Returning to the West Bank, he was greeted by banners hailing him as the "Palestinian Saladin."

The question for the future is whether any Palestinian leader will accept what Arafat rejected—even if it were offered. The answer is complicated by a Quranic injunction to Muslims: "Fight in the cause of God those who fight you. . . . Slay them wherever you find them and expel them from the lands from which they expelled you." It is made harder, as well, by Israel's long-standing policy of building settlements on territory occupied during the war of 1967.

The first settlements, established in the mid-1970s, were justified by the government based on specific security concerns, such as control of high ground. Then conservative governments headed by Menachem Begin and Yitzhak Shamir came to office intent on the idea of a "greater Israel," reestablishing the country's claim to the entire West Bank (all of biblical Judea and Samaria) and essentially ignoring the aspirations of millions of Palestinians. Under their leadership, Israelis were given financial incentives to establish communities in places historically lived in by Arabs. Begin referred to the conquered territories as "liberated Israeli land."* Shamir called the construction of settlements "holy work." As one rabbi explained, "the Redemption of the whole world depends on the Redemption of Israel. From this derives our moral, spiritual and cultural influence over the entire world. The blessing will come to all humanity from the people of Israel living in the whole of its land."

The rabbi may believe that the settlements have enhanced Israel's influence, but the evidence is sparse. As many Israelis have pointed out, the aggressive program of construction on disputed territory tarnished their country's moral standing, deepened Arab anger and contributed to Palestinian misery. The settlements also imposed an unsustainable burden on Israel's security forces, who were required to protect the settlers from their hostile, impoverished Palestinian neighbors. Much to his credit, Israeli Prime Minister Ariel Sharon recognized the need for retrenchment, ordering the withdrawal, in August 2005, of Israeli troops and settlers from the dusty, overcrowded Gaza Strip. The controversy over the West Bank, however, is still to be thrashed out. Looking back over the long decades of stalemate, I find myself in sad agreement with Leon Wieseltier, the literary editor of the *New Republic:* "The idea of Greater Israel . . . was always a foul idea, morally and strategically. It promoted the immediate ecstasy of the few above the eventual safety of the many; [and] introduced the toxins of messianism and mysticism into the politics of a great modern democracy."

The settlements imposed another cost as well. Yigal Amir, the nineteen-year-old Israeli who murdered Yitzhak Rabin

---

* Between 1977, when Begin took office, and 1992, when Shamir left office, the number of Israeli settlers in the West Bank, the Gaza Strip, the Golan Heights, and east Jerusalem rose from about 57,000 (of which 50,000 were in East Jerusalem) to more than 240,000.

in 1995, claimed religious sanction for his despicable crime. An ultra-radical rabbi had assured him that he had a duty under Jewish law to murder Rabin, because the prime minister's support for peace had compromised the rights of settlers. Asked if he had acted alone, Amir said no; he was sure that he had acted with God.

Although I have disagreed with some policies of the Israeli government, especially the more aggressive ones regarding settlements, I am fully committed to the preservation of Israel's existence and security. The majority of Americans feel the same way. Why? We know that Jewish communities have long been persecuted, from the days of bondage in Egypt to the pogroms of czarist Russia. We consider the Holocaust to be in its own category—a tragedy beyond comprehension, never to be forgotten or repeated. We saw in the creation of Israel not only the rehabilitation of a people, but also a gesture of decency by the entire human race. We accept the argument that it was not too much to ask of the Arabs, who have other holy cities and much land, to make room for tiny Israel in the only place it has ever truly had a home. We have also seen the kind of country—a thriving democracy—that the Israelis have built. Foreigners, especially Arabs, wonder why America is allied with Israel. Searching for an answer, some subscribe to conspiracy theories or else wildly overestimate the percentage of Jews in the United States—according to one study, guesses range from 10 percent to 85 percent, when the actual proportion is less than 2 percent. Another recent survey found that Arabs believe the "Zionist lobby" to be the single most influential determinant of U.S. foreign policy. It is more accurate to say that Americans from across the ideological spectrum support Israel because we see in that society qualities with which we identify and that we admire.

Of course, Americans also care about Israel because of shared religious traditions. The Holocaust may have been the tipping point in U.S. support for Israel's statehood, but American policy has its roots in the Balfour Declaration—that there is indeed a promised land and that Israelites were the recipients of the promise. For our diplomats, the challenge has been to reconcile this starting point with the legitimate rights of Palestinians. That would be a hard enough job under any circumstances. For some Americans, however, religious convictions transcend any consideration of fairness to the Palestinians. They are convinced, on the basis of numerous biblical passages, that Jesus will return to Earth only when Solomon's temple is rebuilt and the climactic war between good and evil, described in the Book of Revelation, is fought.

A best-selling series of novels imagines the story unfolding in this way. A general breakdown in civilization is followed by the "Rapture," during which faithful Christians are spirited to heaven, leaving everyone else behind.* There soon appears the Antichrist, masquerading as the secretary general of the United Nations. Lulled by his promises, Israel signs a peace treaty under which the temple in Jerusalem is rebuilt (though it is later defiled by the Antichrist). This sets in motion the "tribulation," during which God, to encourage the wayward to find faith, pelts Earth with plagues. Distant armies gather to attack Israel—a force 200 million

---

* This is Jerry Falwell's description of the Rapture: "You'll be riding along in an automobile. You'll be the driver perhaps. There'll be several people in the automobile with you, maybe someone who is not a Christian. When the trumpet sounds you and the other born-again believers in that automobile will be instantly caught away—you will disappear, leaving behind only your clothes and physical things that cannot inherit eternal life.... Other cars on the highway driven by believers will suddenly be out of control and stark pandemonium will occur ... on every highway in the world."

strong. The decisive battle takes place near the West Bank town of Megiddo, less than fifty miles from Jerusalem. It is there that Jesus reappears, descending from heaven to lead the Christian faithful and 144,000 Jewish converts (the only Jews who survive) to a bloody victory. This is followed by a thousand years of Christ's rule on Earth.

In 1999, a poll conducted by *Newsweek* found that 40 percent of Americans—more than 100 million people—"believe that the world will end, as the Bible predicts, in a battle between Jesus and the Antichrist." Nineteen percent of the respondents believed that the Antichrist is alive today. Thirteen percent believed in the "Rapture," including some who still display bumper stickers bearing the thoughtful warning: "Come the Rapture, this car will be without a driver."

Perhaps because I was raised in the Roman Catholic Church, which does not stress the Book of Revelation, I see the text less as an elaborately coded map to the millennium than as an apocalyptic vision shaped by the struggle of early Christians to survive the hostility of Rome. I am also wearied by sightings of the Antichrist. During the crusades, Richard the Lionheart was assured by his religious advisers that Saladin fit the description; not much good arose from that. Martin Luther, who began the Reformation, declared that the pope was the Antichrist; Europe was ripped apart by religious wars for the next hundred years. The Russian Orthodox Church pinned the label on Napoleon; further destruction and war ensued. The language of Revelation is so dramatic that it tempts one to cast friends and, particularly, enemies as specific characters. We are lured by the self-centered sense that if history is to have a climax it should occur during our lifetimes. Imagining a past without us is not difficult; imagining such a future is harder and less pleasant—so we look for reasons to imagine something else.

•   •   •

It may be that Armageddon will settle all our accounts. It would be inexcusable, however, if our leaders relied on that supposition to justify their own inaction, only to be proved wrong, leaving us with all the destruction and none of the paradise. Setting the stage for Armageddon is not a defensible foreign policy. Peace is. This has sometimes put policy-makers and preachers at cross-purposes. In January 1998, Bill Clinton invited the Israeli prime minister, Benjamin Netanyahu, and Yasser Arafat to the White House. His goal was to persuade them to revive the peace process, which had been interrupted by terrorist incidents and by a spike in settlement activity. On the eve of the meeting, Netanyahu conferred with leaders of the Christian right, who saluted him as the "Ronald Reagan of Israel" and encouraged him—irresponsibly, in my view—not to compromise. Right-wing Christian activists and other critics of the Clinton administration argued that U.S. engagement in the peace process put undue pressure on Israel. To their way of thinking, any policy that resulted in Israel's returning more land to the Palestinians was either contrary to the Bible or dangerous to the security of Israel, or both.

When President Bush took office, he was determined not to repeat what he argued were President Clinton's mistakes. He refused to deal with Arafat, refrained from appointing a full-time negotiator for the region, and did not involve himself in efforts to stem the violence between Israelis and Palestinians that killed more than 4,000 people. Bush's approach may have had the advantage of conserving America's diplomatic resources for other purposes, but it also had the clear disadvantage of causing a sharp deterioration in America's standing among Arabs and Muslims.

Unfortunately, the issues that must be settled before a permanent peace becomes feasible grew more, rather than less, difficult during President Bush's first term. The years of fighting enabled the radical group Hamas—historically an opponent of peace—to become stronger compared with its secular rival, Fatah, the largest component of the PLO. The Palestinian economy stalled, but its production of bombs, grenades, and rockets increased. The defensive barrier being built by Israel through much of the West Bank created a de facto border that Palestinians will not accept and that many Israelis have come to feel they cannot live securely without. Israeli leaders have consistently refused Palestinian demands to release Arabs from jail if, in Israel's judgment, the prisoners have "blood on their hands"; there are many more such prisoners now than there were in 2000.

Yasser Arafat's death in November 2004 did open the door to new leadership on the Palestinian side. Arafat's successor, Mahmoud Abbas, appeared to be a welcome change. During negotiations in the 1990s, he was the Palestinian we turned to most often for frank talk. He did not betray confidences, but neither did he grandstand. He insisted that the solution to Palestinian problems could be found through the give-and-take of negotiations. As president, Abbas challenged the old Palestinian consensus that violence was the most effective route to progress. Unlike Arafat, he did not promote fantasies about restoring Arab rule from the Jordan River all the way to the Mediterranean Sea. His goal was to build a viable Palestinian state, which he said could only be done by peaceful means.

The problem was that Abbas—though democratically elected—lacked a solid political base. Fatah, the organization he inherited from Arafat, had a well-earned reputation for corruption and was torn by generational, ideological, and personal rivalries. Abbas's dilemma was compounded by a failure on the part of the United States or Israel to recognize the urgency of helping him to succeed. Instead, demands were made of the Palestinian president that he did not have the capacity to fulfill. This left Abbas with the worst of both worlds. He was pilloried by Palestinian opponents for being the preferred candidate of Israel and the West. Yet he was not given the help required to meet the basic needs of the Palestinian people. To buy time, Abbas postponed parliamentary elections from July 2005 until January 2006. The tactic proved in vain as Fatah's popularity continued to plummet. When the elections finally did take place, Hamas found itself in the majority—to the amazement of Fatah, Israel, the United States, and perhaps Hamas itself.

The rise of Hamas has seemingly dragged the Middle East peace process back to the point where it began roughly fifteen years ago. Hamas, like the early PLO, does not accept the existence of Israel, nor is it willing to disarm or renounce violence. Until it does, a peace agreement will not be possible. The best that can be hoped for in the interim is a suspension of hostilities. This would enable each side to catch its breath. For Hamas, the challenge will be to deliver on its campaign promises of "change and reform." These pledges have little to do with Israel and much to do with improving Palestinian governance.

The Israelis, too, have much work to do. Before falling prey to a stroke in January 2006, Ariel Sharon had embarked on a plan to make Israelis secure by taking unilateral steps to separate them from Palestinians. This plan, never fully spelled out, was designed to ensure the survival of a predominately Jewish state by leaving as many Jews and as few Palestinians as possible on Israeli-held territory. It specifically ruled out the possibility of dividing Jerusalem or of full Israeli withdrawal to the 1967 borders. The steps already taken toward implementation include the construction of the security fence, the redeployment from Gaza, and the "thickening" of settlements in and around Jerusalem. The hardest measures, still to come, would require the closure of some Jewish settlements on the West Bank in order to safe-guard the future of others.

Faced by opposition from conservatives in his own Likud party, Sharon created Kadima, a coalition that attracted sup-port from a broad spectrum. It remains to be seen whether Sharon's successors will be able to pursue a consistent strat-egy. The prominence of Hamas, however, is sure to postpone indefinitely Israeli recognition of a Palestinian state, while Sharon's goal of separating Jews from Palestinians will likely remain the focus of Israeli policy.

The Middle East is a place where wounds rarely heal and grievances are not forgotten; time, thus, is not ordinarily a friend to peace. For the Palestinians, however, time will be essential for them to develop the institutions they need to govern themselves responsibly. Effective administration requires honesty, skill, and a willingness to compromise. Neither Hamas nor Fatah seems richly endowed with these qualities. The Palestinian people, however, have made clear through their ballots that they expect more from their lead-ers than they have been getting. It is encouraging that the elections themselves were free, fair, and competitive. That is the first step toward the creation of responsive and account-able government. Many more such steps are needed. Outside countries and organizations should assist, but only if they are able to do so without smoothing the way for Hamas and other extreme elements to retain the option of violence.

The most hopeful commentators have suggested that par-ticipating in government will make Hamas more moderate. I have my doubts. I do think that the organization's new political status will aggravate the divisions that exist within it. Pragmatists will compete with ideologues for the upper hand. The United States should do all it can to help the more moderate Palestinian forces prevail, but the lack of American engagement these past five years has left us with less leverage and credibility than we have had in the past.

The changes in leadership in both Israel and the Palestinian Authority have created new political dynamics while further dimming the short-term prospects for peace. But what about the long term? Is the possibility of peace truly dead? In the absence of fresh thinking, I fear the answer may be yes.

Many were the times I wanted to grab the Palestinian and Israeli negotiators by the ears and try to knock some sense into them. Ultimately, I placed my hopes in our ability to draft language smart and fair enough to enable leaders from both sides to defend a peace agreement to their constituencies. Despite the many setbacks, I would still like to think that devising such a formula remains a possibility. An arrangement along the lines suggested by Bill Clinton would give both parties as generous a set of terms as each could reasonably expect. The question is whether the logic of peace will ever be powerful enough to determine the future of the Middle East. Appeals to reason and self-interest may be the only practical way to proceed, but if designing a settlement were simply a real estate transaction, it would have been completed years ago. If negotiations do again become practical, traditional diplomacy will be indispensable, but something more may also be needed: a convergence in our appreciation of what God really wants.

Historically, the conventional wisdom among American negotiators for the Middle East has been that the less talk about God the better. That is understandable, given the volatility of the region; but it is not possible to isolate religion and the history that goes along with it from the peace process. Sharon referred to Jerusalem as "Israel's capital, united for all eternity." Divided as they are, the Palestinians are united in saying that they will not even consider a two-state solution without Jerusalem as their capital. The largest Israeli settlements on the West Bank are immovable; yet even the most forthcoming peace proposals by the Arabs include a demand for the return of all lands taken during the war of 1967. Sharon's relentlessness in fighting against the second intifada was intended to convince Palestinians that resistance was hopeless. During the withdrawal from Gaza, Palestinian T-shirts read "Today Gaza—Tomorrow the West Bank and Jerusalem." Beginning in the seventh century, Muslims controlled Jerusalem for most of 1,300 years; less than sixty years—a historical eyeblink—have elapsed since Israel became a state. What now do Palestinians want most—a long-shot chance (through an orgy of blood) to relive the victory of Saladin, or a real chance to raise their families in dignity and peace? Is their dream to be martyrs or builders?

Jimmy Carter was not afraid to talk about religion when he brought the Egyptian and Israeli leaders together at Camp David. Bill Clinton was able to make as much headway as he did because he understood the history of the situation and was comfortable talking about spiritual matters. Future negotiators will not achieve the breakthroughs required, however, unless they are truly able to confront and defuse the clashing senses of entitlement. Is this realistic? I do not know. I do like George Bernard Shaw's observation that "the reasonable man adapts himself to the world; the unreasonable one persists in trying to adapt the world to himself. Therefore, all progress depends on the unreasonable man."

If hard-liners can find in the Quran and the Bible justifications for endless conflict, I believe others can find overriding commandments to pursue the opposite. One encouraging initiative is the Alexandria Process, launched in 2002, and sponsored by the Mosaica Association's Center for Inter-Religious Cooperation. The premise of this project is that peace between nations and peoples cannot be achieved without reconciliation between religions and cultures; accordingly, the power of religion must be transformed from a source of hostility to a source of tolerance and understanding. The principles of the Alexandria Declaration—support for peace, nonviolence, and respect for holy places—were used to resolve one standoff in 2003, when Palestinian fighters took over the Church of the Nativity; and another in 2004, when Islamic religious authorities met to discuss the problem of incitement of anti-Semitism within Arab societies. On a more routine basis, the principles are applied by "Adam" centers, located in Israel and the Palestinian Authority. The founder of and moving force behind this effort is Rabbi Michael Melchior, a brave and eloquent fighter for peace; he is receiving strong support from Sheikh Imad Falouji, a founder of Hamas who left the organization because its attacks on civilians were a violation of Islam.

Those who are so certain that God's intention for the Middle East is Armageddon might at least reflect on the passage in Isaiah foretelling the time when God will be worshipped not only by the Israelis but also by Arabs in Egypt and Syria. "In that day," declared the prophet, "shall Israel be the third with Egypt and with Assyria, even a blessing in the midst of the land, Whom the LORD of hosts shall bless, saying, Blessed be Egypt my people, and Assyria the work of my hands, and Israel mine inheritance." Since the time of Muhammad, most Arabs and Jews have worshipped the same God. However distant it may now appear, perhaps the moment will arrive when the spirit of the Alexandria Process is finally able to carry the day. Then, in the words of Yitzhak Rabin, Israelis and Palestinians will "draw on the springs of our great spiritual resources to forgive the anguish we caused to each other, to clear the minefield that divided us for so many years, and to supplant it with fields of plenty." Perhaps the time will come when both sides will heed the guidance of the Quran: "If the enemy inclines towards peace, do thou (also) incline towards peace and trust in Allah."

Until that day, the dilemma inherent in the Balfour Declaration will remain; the character of Middle Eastern leaders will be regularly tested; the proper approach for the United States will be debated; the peoples of the region will continue to live in fear; and the ever-present tension among Muslims, Jews, and Christians will exacerbate a confrontation that extends far beyond the Middle East and threatens truly to shake the globe.

Ten

"The Greatest Jihad"

Driven by drought, the inhabitants of Israel gathered anxiously on the slopes of Mount Carmel to witness a contest. On one side were 450 priests of Baal, the Canaanite god of fertility. On the other stood Elijah, prophet of Jahweh, god of Abraham, Moses, and David. Among the onlookers was Ahab, Samaria's weak, wayward king. The question to be settled was whose god was the mightier. The proof demanded was a sign in the form of fire igniting an altar on which a bull had been sacrificed. The followers of Baal, going first, prayed, danced, chanted, and scourged themselves for hours, but their exertions were all in vain. Elijah taunted them: "Cry aloud: for he is a god; either he is talking, or he is pursuing, or he is in a journey, or peradventure he sleepeth and must be awaked." Then it was the prophet's turn. He constructed his altar, using twelve stones to symbolize the tribes of Israel; drenched his offering with water; appealed to the Lord; and stepped back. Within seconds, fire consumed the sacrifice. Those watching threw themselves to the ground and shouted, "The Lord is God; the Lord alone is God."

More than 2,800 years later, the relationship between humans and the divine has not changed much. We still look for signs and to events here on Earth for clues about God's nature and purpose.

On September 11, 2001, the twin towers of the World Trade Center were consumed by fire. Was this such a sign?

"God continues to lift the curtain and allow the enemies of America to give us probably what we deserve," said Jerry Falwell in a television broadcast two days after the tragedy. He continued, "I really believe that the pagans, and the abortionists, and the feminists, and the gays and the lesbians who are actively trying to make an alternative lifestyle, the ACLU, the People for the American Way—all of them who have tried to secularize America—I point the finger in their face and say, 'You've helped this happen.' "*

Falwell was not alone in seeing God's hand behind the terrorists' attacks. The leaders of Al Qaeda were certain that their success was evidence of God's blessing. A videotape shows Osama bin Laden and a Saudi sheikh celebrating in the aftermath of the strikes, crediting Allah with a "clear victory" and exchanging stories about the prophetic dreams of friends who had foreseen planes smashing into buildings. "It will be," exulted the sheikh, "the greatest jihad in the history of Islam."

In the tradition of the ancient Hebrews, triumphs and defeats are commonly attributed to God's will. "If thou shalt indeed obey," promises the Lord, "then I will be an enemy unto thine enemies and an adversary unto thine adversaries." Early Muslims credited Allah for the military triumphs that enabled the rapid expansion of their religion. Spanish

---

* Confronted by a storm of criticism, Falwell later apologized for these remarks.

Catholics were sure that their acquisition of an overseas empire in the fifteenth and sixteenth centuries was God's reward for persecuting Christian heretics, Muslims, and Jews. When the British and other European powers colonized Africa, they believed they were doing God's work. As we have seen, many Americans have associated their country's rise with God's favor. Julia Ward Howe's "Battle Hymn of the Republic," composed after a visit to an army encampment in the early days of the Civil War, stirringly equated God's cause with the Union's struggle against the Confederacy.

It is human nature to want to see God's work in our own doings, and God's purpose as our own purpose. As individuals, we can often indulge this impulse without causing harm; perhaps we may even do some good. As a practical matter, however, a nation (or group) that believes its success or failure is a direct consequence of the wishes of God is likely either to invite or create trouble. If victorious, the nation and its leaders may become self-righteous and filled with a sense of omnipotence. If defeated, they may descend into bitterness and division, with one faction blaming another for incurring divine displeasure. Either way, a nation that says to God, "It's all up to you," risks neglecting an obligation to act on its own behalf. As Emily Dickinson wrote in a far different context, " 'Faith' is a fine invention / When gentlemen can see / But microscopes are prudent / In an emergency."

Not long after the attacks of 9/11, I was invited to speak at the spacious House of Hope Presbyterian Church in Saint Paul, Minnesota. The pews were packed and emotions ran high. As I climbed the stairs to the pulpit, I could see that handkerchiefs and tissues were already out. In my memory, the only comparable moment of national unity in the face of trauma had been the assassination of John Kennedy. I was not qualified to deliver a sermon, but I did want to capture as precisely as I could what 9/11 did and did not mean:

I see no sign of God's hand in these crimes, nor any trace of religious faith or social conscience in their motivation. The perpetrators could not be loyal to Islam, for, by their acts, they have betrayed the teachings of that benevolent faith. The perpetrators of these outrages do not care about the Palestinians, whose leaders have expressed anger and sorrow at the attacks. They do not care about the poor, for they use their resources not to teach skills but to instill hate. They are not crazy, for they acted with frozen-hearted calculation. These were crimes of purest evil, wholly unjustified by any reason of politics, culture, or faith.

We often ask in the wake of tragedy why a God who is both almighty and good would allow such events to occur. Part of the answer is that we have been given the liberty to think and act for ourselves. Some of us use that freedom to build, heal, teach, or compose great works of art; others blow up buildings. These are our actions, not God's (and, though it may be convenient to blame him, not Satan's). When illness or an accident takes the life of a child, we can only express anguish at the cruelty and unfairness of fate. As for hurricanes, earthquakes, and tsunamis, I blame Father Nature. The rest of the answer is beyond what any of us can know for sure. As preachers are at pains to remind us, we walk in faith, not in sight. However we walk, we have a responsibility to look after ourselves and to safeguard one another. The attacks of 9/11 added a new dimension to what that responsibility will require.

In the weeks following the attacks, President Bush proved to doubters that he has the capacity for true leadership. Addressing a joint session of Congress, he fulfilled the promise he had made before his election to be a uniter. He noted that people around the world had responded to the hijackings with prayers in English, Hebrew, and Arabic; and he called attention to the astonishing fact that the victims of 9/11 included people from no fewer than eighty nations. He expressed gratitude to international organizations and to friends in Europe, Africa, Latin America, and Asia. The president vowed to use every tool of foreign policy to oppose "terrorist organizations of global reach"; and he explained that Al Qaeda represented "a fringe form of Islam that has been rejected by Muslim scholars and the vast majority of Muslim clerics—a fringe movement that perverts the peaceful teachings of Islam." The president's words of healing seemed designed to bring the world together in opposition to Al Qaeda and its supporters. This was clearly the right strategy. To defeat terror, America would need help from friends and allies everywhere, and especially from those in predominantly Arab and Muslim societies.

The climactic line in the president's speech offered a stark choice: "Every nation, in every region, now has a decision to make. Either you are with us, or you are with the terrorists."* In subsequent weeks, most countries did not hesitate to make that choice.

America's allies in NATO invoked for the first time the mutual defense provisions of the North Atlantic Treaty, declaring the attacks an act of aggression against the entire alliance. Aside from Iraq, every government in the Muslim world, including Iran and the Palestinian Authority, condemned the strikes. When American troops were deployed to Afghanistan to oust the Taliban and round up Al Qaeda, allies such as Canada, Japan, and Australia rushed to assist them. Pakistan,

---

* In issuing his challenge, President Bush may well have been thinking of Jesus' warning, "He that is not with me is against me" (Luke 11:23). It is less likely that he was trying to remind the world of Lenin's statement during the Russian Revolution: "He who is not with us is against us."

despite close ties to the radical Afghan leaders, agreed to help. China and Russia, themselves challenged by Muslim separatists, pledged solidarity. Even those Muslims who initially protested the U.S. assault against the Taliban fell silent when it became clear that the Afghan majority welcomed the overthrow of the extremists. In the United States, a group of sixty academics—including Christians, Jews, Muslims, and atheists—signed a letter in support of the military operation in Afghanistan, calling it a defense of "universal human morality" and "a just war." For months after 9/11, it appeared that the administration would succeed in uniting most Americans and foreign governments in opposition to a common threat.

As a Democrat, I was proud of the way members of my party rallied to support the White House. Members of Congress and officials who had served in the Clinton administration led the applause. At every opportunity, I offered my own backing for the president's policies. When the Taliban were overthrown, I cheered. While I was in government, I had met with Afghan women and girls at a refugee camp in Pakistan near the Khyber Pass, listening to their accounts of deprivation and oppression. I promised those refugees that America would not forget them. I hoped now that they would be able to return to their homes, live safely, and have their rights respected. I also backed the Pentagon's decision to round up and detain suspected terrorists, taking for granted that the detainees would be questioned and investigated so that timely decisions could be made about whether to prosecute them or let them go.

I was, in short, pro-war, a hawk. So when the World Council of Churches opposed the military strikes in Afghanistan, I disagreed. When Gore Vidal argued that the invasion was all about oil, I thought he was delusional. And when Alice Walker suggested that, with respect to Osama bin Laden, "the only punishment that works is love," I was grateful that she was a prizewinning author, not our commander in chief.

In the weeks following the attacks, many commentators drew a comparison between what had happened on 9/11 and Japan's strikes on Pearl Harbor in 1941. Both took America by surprise, caused destruction on U.S. soil, and signaled the start of a larger struggle. Still, the differences were plain. In Hawaii, U.S. troops, ships, and aircraft were bombed by the clearly marked airplanes of an enemy state, a state that had uniformed armed forces and defined borders. The perpetrators of 9/11 wore no uniforms, raised no flag, commanded no air force, and bore allegiance to no nation or alliance of nations. Their attacks were designed not to destroy military targets, but rather to murder as many people as possible.

In February 1998, bin Laden had issued a fatwa in which he and other terrorist leaders called on Muslims to kill Americans everywhere. The reasons he cited included America's backing of sanctions against Iraq, its support for Israel, and the presence of American armed forces in Saudi Arabia. He accused the United States of having declared war on Allah, the Prophet, and all Muslims. To provide a facade of scholarship, he cited clerical rulings regarding the religious obligation to repel assaults on the faith. He then called on all Muslims to join in attacking "Satan's U.S. troops."

Bin Laden's pretensions aside, he is hardly qualified to instruct Muslims in the duties of their faith. Even his host and sponsor in Afghanistan, Mullah Muhammad Omar, admitted, "Bin Laden is not entitled to issue fatwas, as he did not complete the mandatory twelve years of Quranic studies to qualify for the position of mufti. Only muftis can issue fatwas. Bin Laden is not a mufti and therefore any fatwas he may have issued are illegal and null and void." The mullah's statement has not stopped bin Laden from being taken seriously. By its nature, Sunni Islam has no single unifying leader. There is no one person or institution that can speak authoritatively on behalf of all the religion's adherents to discredit bin Laden's message in a way that would be convincing to those most conditioned to accept that message.

During my years as secretary of state, bin Laden was on the run and being hunted in one of the most remote places on earth. To our knowledge, no government outside Afghanistan supported his activities. He was a terrorist, a murderer of Muslims, who had been disowned by his native land (Saudi Arabia) and expelled from his adopted country (Sudan). I knew he was trying to capture the sympathies of the Muslim world, but he seemed to have little to entice his followers except the opportunity to vent their anger and be blown to bits as "martyrs." A demagogue is always dangerous when he is telling people what they want to hear, however; and it takes only a small number of determined terrorists to create a large problem.

It was, of course, nonsense to say that America had declared war on Islam. Under President Clinton, the United States had been at the forefront in defending Muslims in Bosnia and Kosovo, aiding democracy in heavily Muslim Indonesia, denouncing the Russians' violations of human rights in Chechnya, and trying to broker peace in the Caucasus and Middle East. Under Carter and Reagan, America had helped the mujahideen expel the Soviet Union's troops from Afghanistan.

Proving a negative is never simple, though, especially to a deeply skeptical audience; many Muslims who had no use for bin Laden still shared his opposition to some U.S. policies. They would at least listen when he talked about "purifying" the Holy Land of nonbelievers, restoring Muslim rule in Jerusalem, and reviving the warrior spirit that had existed in the early days of Islam. They might even nod their heads when told that Americans should be held collectively accountable for the objectionable policies of the U.S. government in the Middle East and the Persian Gulf. After the terrorist bombings at the U.S. embassies in Kenya and Tanzania in 1998, the State Department offered a $5 million reward for information leading to bin Laden's capture. This prompted a torrent of donations to bin Laden from wealthy Arabs. Although Muslim governments did not echo or embrace bin Laden's call for holy war, some of their citizens did.

Bin Laden seeks to generate support by appealing to a combination of resentment, envy, and guilt. He refers to events of long ago that few outside the Muslim world still think about, but that many Muslims cannot forget: the destruction of the Ottoman Empire, the parceling out of the Arab Middle East and North Africa among Christian powers, and even the ejection of Muslims (along with Jews) from Spain in the same year Columbus first set sail for the New World. The Muslims who claim that their faith is under attack may seem paranoid to westerners, but the boundaries of the Muslim world have been considerably reduced in recent centuries. When the French marched into Damascus in 1920, their commander, General Henri Gouraud, strode to the tomb of Islam's most revered warrior-hero. "Saladin," Gouraud declared, "we have returned. My presence here consecrates the victory of the Cross over the Crescent." In colonizing the Arab states, representatives of the western powers intentionally fostered the development of secular elites who usurped the authority of religious leaders. Meanwhile, the apparatchiks of the Soviet Union's politburo spent decades insisting to millions of Muslims that God did not exist. Pan-Arab nationalists such as Gamal Abdel Nasser of Egypt portrayed Islam as an enemy of progress. The Zionist dream was fulfilled with the help of western powers at the expense of Arabs.

Bin Laden's goal is to reap a harvest of bitterness by cultivating these and other, more recent grievances. He wants to create a great global divide with "right-thinking" Muslims on one side and the West on the other—precisely what we should seek to avoid. Bin Laden, and those who think like him, are focused on old injustices, not future opportunities. When they turn to the Quran, it is not to passages such as this: "It may be that God will grant love and friendship between you and those whom you now hold as enemies, for God has power over all things; and God is most forgiving, most merciful." Bin Laden and his followers prefer instead the more bloodcurdling Quranic commands about brandishing spears and slaying pagans. They do not offer ideas for improving or enriching the lives of people here on Earth; they are preoccupied with the glories they expect to encounter in the hereafter. For them, their own morality is taken for granted, and God's revelation is a mandate to kill.

The horrible events of 9/11 ended the lives of more than 3,000 human beings. That day also marked the full emergence of a new and complex challenge to the national security of the United States. Unlike the "godless" communists, this enemy claimed to be engaged in holy work. In responding, America would need to be inventive not only in devising the means by which further attacks might be prevented, but also in developing a message that would successfully erode the enemy's base of support.

Eleven

"God Wants Me to Be President"

———— ✧ ————

When, after 9/11, President Bush presented his dramatic choice to the world, his message was clear: the globe had changed and America would fight back. The military intervention that the United States led in Afghanistan reinforced that message, scattering Al Qaeda and toppling the Taliban. The next steps, it seemed to me, were obvious: first, *military* action to prevent Al Qaeda from finding sanctuary across the Afghan border in Pakistan; second, *political* action to build democratic institutions throughout Afghanistan and ensure that radical elements would not reestablish a foothold there; and third, *diplomatic* action enlisting the help of Afghanistan's neighbors—including Iran, Pakistan, and the Muslim countries of central Asia—to forge the most powerful possible coalition against Al Qaeda. The overriding goal would be to destroy as much of bin Laden's network as possible, isolate the rest, and prevent it from putting down new roots.

To these ends, I expected the president to continue highlighting the themes he had raised so effectively during the first weeks after 9/11: global unity, defeating the terrorists, working with allies, and reaching out to Arabs and Muslims. These expectations were not met. At a moment when continuity of direction was both logical and essential, the president shifted course.

Instead of sticking to the job of smashing Al Qaeda, he adopted an approach with precisely the opposite effect. In 2002, in his State of the Union address, he focused not on the terrorists and the nation-building barely begun in Afghanistan, but on the so-called "axis of evil"—Iraq, Iran, and North Korea. In public remarks later that year, he emphasized not the urgent need for a multinational antiterror coalition, but America's unilateral intention to maintain "military strength beyond challenge." In publishing his national security strategy, the president asserted the right to attack foreign nations, even in the absence of an imminent threat, if he suspected that they might one day take hostile action against the United States. This was the controversial "preemption doctrine," which asserted for America a right we would never recognize as legitimate if claimed by any other government. He also asked Congress to authorize a new generation of nuclear weapons to add to the already daunting arsenal of the United States.

These bursts of muscular rhetoric evoked cheers from the president's admirers but did nothing to make Americans safer. On the contrary, they complicated what should have been a simple choice. The president had asked every country to oppose Al Qaeda. Now he was asking them to oppose Al Qaeda while also endorsing an unrestricted view of U.S. power. Faced with this choice, many who loathed terrorism were nevertheless reluctant to be "with" the United States. By failing to heed Theodore Roosevelt's advice to talk softly, the administration began inadvertently to shift the world's attention away from what the terrorists had done to what America might do.

In September 2002, President Bush again commanded a vast audience when he traveled to Manhattan for his annual appearance before the UN General Assembly. If I had been in a position to advise him, I would have urged him to rally nations against Al Qaeda; thank governments that had helped to track down terrorist suspects; and appeal to clerics, scholars, and educators to confirm that there are no circumstances under which terrorism could be justified. The president chose instead to demand support for fighting Saddam Hussein. Throughout that autumn, when the president did discuss Al Qaeda, he portrayed the challenge less as a multinational struggle against a global threat than as a campaign to bring terrorists to "American justice," as if "justice" alone were not enough.

In January 2003, the president had another opportunity to make known his priorities through his State of the Union address. This time, he devoted four times as much attention to Iraq as to Al Qaeda—citing Saddam Hussein by name eighteen times, and bin Laden not at all. To support the decision he had already made to invade Iraq, the president simply lumped Al Qaeda and the government in Baghdad together, describing them as two aspects of the same threat. This tactic led many Americans to conclude, wrongly, that Hussein had been behind the attacks of 9/11—why else would we be going to war with him? It also enabled the administration to accuse those who raised questions about invading Iraq as being soft on fighting terror. Thus countries such as Germany and France were castigated by the secretary of defense, Donald Rumsfeld, and scorned as virtual traitors by some members of Congress. This was unfair. French soldiers have served continuously alongside Americans in Afghanistan, where Al Qaeda had been based, and Germany had led the international security forces there.

At times during the months preceding the war with Iraq,

a triumphal tone crept into the rhetoric of the Bush administration. Those planning the war boasted about the "shock and awe" that American military power would produce. Vice President Richard Cheney predicted that our troops would be welcomed as "liberators." Condoleezza Rice spoke of America's plan to transform the entire Middle East. The president responded to his failure to assemble a more impressive multinational coalition with the retort, "At some point, we may be the only ones left. That's OK with me. We are America."

During these months, the administration did succeed in mobilizing the support of many Americans, while persuading Tony Blair in Great Britain and a few other foreign leaders to contribute troops to the invasion force. But what did any of this have to do with winning the war on terror? That question was paramount because if America's proper goal was to isolate the terrorists, Al Qaeda had an aim, too. Its strategy was to lure to its side, or at least into a state of confused neutrality, every Muslim opposed to U.S. policies. Bin Laden sought to associate himself, in his words, with the Palestinians' quest to recover sacred land and the Arabs' struggle to resist the invasion and occupation of Iraq by Christian imperialists. This link between attacks on Islam and foreign occupation is critical because, research indicates, those behind suicide bombings are rarely motivated by religious beliefs alone. Organized terror campaigns are almost always designed to force a withdrawal from some disputed territory. American saber rattling made Al Qaeda's job far easier than it should have been.

In the weeks after 9/11, public opinion was overwhelmingly sympathetic to the United States. Within two years, a far different picture had emerged. In Indonesia, the most populous Muslim-majority state, the attitude toward America plunged from 75 percent favorable in 2000 to 83 percent negative by 2003. Majorities in many Muslim countries feared that the United States was planning to attack them. In pivotal Pakistan, backing for the U.S.-led war on terror fell to 16 percent. Levels of support in 2005 remained disturbingly low: 12 percent in Jordan, 17 percent in Turkey, 31 percent in Lebanon.

Further, the motives of the United States in fighting terror are not considered sincere. Many people, and not only in Muslim societies, believe that America's real aims are to control oil, defeat Muslims, advance the interests of Israel, and dominate the world—just as Al Qaeda has alleged. An advisory panel of the State Department reported that in many countries the United States is viewed as "less a beacon of hope than a dangerous force to be countered," and that large majorities in Egypt, Morocco, and Saudi Arabia see "George W. Bush as a greater threat to the world order than Osama bin Laden." Historians may someday scratch their heads at the ability of stateless, on-the-run terrorists to compete credibly with the world's most powerful leader in framing public perceptions and debate.

Like Bill Clinton before him, President Bush has said many times and with the utmost sincerity that the United States is not engaged in a clash of religions. He knows that it is bad diplomacy, especially in this tempestuous time, to imply that America has a unique relationship with God. He has a way of speaking, however, that sometimes undercuts his intentions. The president's rhetoric, though of a type used by some earlier chief executives, is nevertheless an extreme example, steeped in a sense of mission and full of religious imagery. It is no accident that Al Qaeda is listened to when it excoriates him as a modern-day crusader.

For instance, the president has said repeatedly that America's duty is to "rid the world of evil"—for mortals, an impossible job. He has declared that "America's purpose is more than to follow a process. It is to achieve a result: the end of terrible threats to the civilized world." During his famous "mission accomplished" speech in May 2003, after the invasion of Iraq, the president quoted Isaiah, "To the captives, come out; and to those in darkness, be free." This was just a rhetorical flourish, perhaps, but it was a telling one. The president was talking about the fruits of U.S. military action; Isaiah was speaking of God's gift of freedom from moral bondage. When Saddam Hussein was captured, the president argued that America was doing God's work in restoring liberty to the Iraqi people. On being asked by an interviewer whether his father would approve of the war against Iraq, he said, "You know, he is the wrong father to appeal to in terms of strength. There is a higher father I appeal to." Even before he announced his candidacy for the White House, he confided to evangelicals, "I believe God wants me to be president."*

The difficulty, of course, is not that the Bush administration has sought to exercise leadership on moral grounds; virtually every administration has tried to do that. The problem is that its rhetoric has come close to justifying U.S. policy in explicitly religious terms—and that this is like waving a red flag in front of a bull. These are precisely the grounds upon which Al Qaeda would prefer to fight. With

---

* Interviewed on NBC's *Meet the Press*, March 27, 2005, Richard Land of the Southern Baptist Convention was asked whether the quotation was accurate. He replied, "It is, but it's incomplete. And the media keeps insisting on making it incomplete, which changes the entire context. He said, and it was right after he had been to a worship service the morning he was inaugurated for his second term as governor, and the Methodist minister had made a very stirring sermon about 'God has a purpose for your life and a plan for your life,' and his mother reached over and said, 'George, he's talking about you.' And he came back to the governor's mansion and he met with several of us and he said, 'I believe God wants me to be president, but if that doesn't happen, that's OK.' "

strong leadership, the United States can bring the world together in opposition to the murder of innocent people. But we will never unite anyone around the proposition that to disagree with the president of the United States is to pick a quarrel with God.

While it may be second nature for President Bush to refer to the fight against terror as a battle between evil and good, is the contrast truly that stark? If Al Qaeda is not evil, nothing is. But who is completely good? As a proud American, even I must admit that in any strict sense the honest answer must be—not us. Our leaders may have the best of hearts; but whether we are battling terror or pursuing some other objective, often our motives are impure, our planning is imperfect, our information is incomplete, and our actions are marred by errors of omission and commission. This has been true at every stage in American history and to a greater or lesser extent in the experience of every other nation. Even Jesus of Nazareth, when addressed by a stranger as "good master;" replied, "Why callest thou me good? There is none good but one, that is, God." In battling terror, we might more accurately refer to a confrontation between evil and "pretty good," or between evil and "not bad," or between evil and "doing the best we can." Or perhaps we should adopt Abraham Lincoln's formulation—a fight between evil and "right as God gives us to see the right."

I made this point in a speech in the spring of 2004, adding, "I say this not to criticize the president, because I think he has generally tried to be careful with his words and because I am as prone to making prideful statements as anyone else. We all yearn to believe what we want to believe and what it makes us feel good to believe. But faith does not always lead to wisdom. And in today's tinderbox of a world, we had better find a way to start putting old fires out instead of lighting new ones."

My disclaimer failed to dissuade the president's media guardians from rushing to his rescue. The very next day, the talk show host Sean Hannity of Fox News labeled me "a shrill left-wing leader" and asked rhetorically, "Is it that liberals are so in love with getting their power back that they'll say anything at this point?" One of Hannity's colleagues suggested with a derisory smile that my plan for fighting terror would be to "sing *Kumbaya* in Arabic."

As we have seen, President Bush is hardly the first American leader to associate his agenda with God's. Supporters of the abolition of slavery, of the civil rights movement, and of efforts to fight poverty and disease have done the same. Especially in the present circumstances, however, it is a tactic to be used with caution, a quality not in much evidence at the Republican Convention in 2004. That is when the cochair of the Iowa state Republican Party declared that "GOP stands for 'God's official party.' " The Texas Republicans' platform affirmed that "the United States of America is a Christian nation." The College Republican National Committee solicited contributions to give the president "the shield of God." Vice President Cheney cited a historian who had written, "When America was created, the stars must have danced in the sky." And President Bush declared in his speech accepting the nomination, "Like governments before us, we have a calling from beyond the stars to stand for freedom."

President Bush is proud of the faith he puts in his own judgments about right and wrong, and in his perceptions about what God does and does not want. He sees this level of certainty as an essential quality in a president. "You better know what you believe or you risk being tossed to and fro by the flattery of friends or the chorus of the critics," he told an audience in the fall of 2004. "It is crucial for America's president to be consistent." He continued, "America's president must base decisions on principle, core convictions from which you will not waver."

Who could quarrel with that? Without question, leaders need to have confidence in themselves, but there is a fine line between confidence and self-righteousness. Confidence comes from the effort to learn all one can about a problem; self-righteousness comes from a tendency to believe that one has learned all there is to know. A confident leader will make firm judgments about what is best, but also accept the need to revisit issues should new information surface; a self-righteous leader will resist any information that is at odds with what he already thinks.

It is a responsibility of leadership to draw moral distinctions, and it is a part of human nature to think in terms of absolutes; but discretion is advised. Few, if any, of us have moral vision that is 20-20. If we are sure we are right, we may be less likely to explore alternatives or to develop a plan B should plan A go astray. We may be so convinced of the merits of our cause that we neglect the effort to convince others. We may be so insistent about achieving the right goals that we fail to select the right means. History is filled with enterprises that have failed despite the firm beliefs of those who launched them. President Bush's core convictions led America from 9/11 to the invasion and prolonged occupation of a country that had nothing to do with the 9/11 attacks. This move has widened the split between Muslims and the United States, given new life to Al Qaeda, and made far more difficult the challenge of defeating international terror.

Twelve

Iraq: Unintended Consequences

———— ⚓ ————

It makes a great difference," wrote Saint Augustine, "by which causes and under what authorities men undertake the wars that must be waged."

Roughly 1,600 years later, in March 2003, Cardinal Pio Laghi tried to persuade President Bush not to act on his plan to invade Iraq. The cardinal, a special envoy of the Vatican, warned of civilian casualties and damage to relations between Christians and Muslims; he insisted that it would be neither moral nor legal to attack a country even to oust a regime as repulsive as Saddam Hussein's. President Bush was unmoved. The war, he said, "will make things better."

In a speech that same week, I argued that "even if there were an adequate rationale for invading Iraq, it might not be wise for America to start a war under these circumstances and at this time." I worried that a conflagration would detract from efforts to capture Osama bin Laden and would be exploited by Al Qaeda to recruit more terrorists. I cautioned that internal divisions in Iraq would surely complicate the aftermath of the conflict. I was concerned, as well, by the lack of international support, saying that although the United States could win the war without much help, it would need a great deal of aid to establish a stable democracy. Though I suspect that some people in government, especially in the State Department and among our uniformed military, held similar views, my warnings and those of many others were in vain.

My doubts about the wisdom of war were not grounded in any illusions about Saddam Hussein. While in office, I had myself insisted that calibrated military strikes were justified to penalize Iraq's many failures, including its unwillingness to cooperate with the United Nations' weapons inspections. Now on the outside, I thought—on the basis of the intelligence data I had studied previously—that Iraq might possess chemical and biological arms, but not the means to deploy them effectively beyond its borders. There were no indications that the country had resumed trying to build nuclear weapons. Admittedly, there was also no reason to think that Hussein would not try to do so if given the chance. He was, however, effectively caged—a fox with no way to get into the chicken coop. Iraq's military was barred from purchasing heavy weapons and was surrounded by superior forces; even the greater part of its airspace was outside its control. Hussein had been warned, moreover, that he would be obliterated if he ever again tried to invade a country. As a rule, people who build statues to themselves are not suicidal. After more than a decade of containment, Iraq was not in a position to attack anyone.

In 2001, Colin Powell, who was then secretary of state, summarized the situation accurately. Referring to the sanctions, he said, "Frankly, they have worked." Powell noted that Hussein "has not developed any significant capability with respect to weapons of mass destruction. He is unable to project power against his neighbors. So, in effect, our policies have strengthened the security of the neighbors of Iraq, and these are the policies we are going to keep in place." Powell did not predict, however, how long those policies would continue. By early 2002, President Bush had decided to abandon them and instead prepared to invade.

The tradition of "just war" sets out a series of hurdles that must be cleared before a decision to initiate conflict may be judged legitimate. These include (1) just cause; (2) right intention; (3) right authority; (4) reasonable hope of success; and (5) a favorable balance between good achieved compared to harm caused. As the administration's intentions became clear, a chorus of religious authorities joined the Vatican in arguing that the prospective invasion fell short of these standards. The Methodist bishop of Chicago argued, "There is no way to read the criteria of the 'just war theory' that could justify this foolhardy adventure. This is not an act of self-defense. All other options have not been exhausted. The devastation envisioned is in no way proportional to the perceived original aggression of Saddam Hussein. Innocent civilians—particularly women and children—will not be protected."

Petros VII of Alexandria, the second-ranking patriarch of the Orthodox Christian Church, warned that invading Iraq "would be seen as an attack on Islam" and would have "unjust, far-reaching and long-lasting consequences." The executive committee of the World Conference on Religion and Peace called on Baghdad to comply with the resolutions of the UN Security Council, but expressed fear that "military action against Iraq has the potential to create a long-term humanitarian disaster, to further destabilize the region, and to fuel dangerous extremist tendencies." A Protestant network, Call to Renewal, proposed a six-point alternative to war, including Hussein's indictment by an international tribunal, coercive inspections, humanitarian relief, and a more intense focus on the threat posed by suicide bombers.

Supporters of the administration brushed such alternatives aside, countering that the attacks of 9/11 had made the conventional criteria for just war obsolete. They argued that the United States was vulnerable to surprise attack by an enemy that welcomed death and so could not be deterred. They raised the possibility that Saddam Hussein and Al Qaeda would team up (or perhaps already had teamed up), and that Hussein was in a position to supply the terrorists with formidable weapons. Even if the United States could not prove that Iraq was helping Al Qaeda, this did not mean that Iraq was not helping Al Qaeda. "Absence of evidence," said Donald Rumsfeld, "is not evidence of absence." These arguments were sufficient to win the support of conservative and some moderate Christian and Jewish groups.*

In making their case, administration officials referred to the "gathering danger" posed by the Iraqi regime. Condoleezza Rice even conjured up the image of a mushroom cloud, as a warning that a failure on our part to attack might lead to nuclear annihilation. I was impressed myself, in February 2003, by Secretary Powell's dramatic show-and-tell presentation before the UN Security Council. With the director of the CIA, George Tenet, at his side, Powell offered a litany of allegations, including the assertion—startling to me—that Iraq possessed a fleet of mobile biological weapons laboratories. It was powerful testimony; but, unbeknownst to Powell, the juicier tidbits—including the mobile labs—

---

* The National Association of Evangelicals, for example, called the proposed invasion an act of self-defense. The Union for Reform Judaism agreed to support military action, but only if all other options for resolving the problem of Iraq's "possession of nonconventional weapons" were explored first.

were lies. Iraqi exiles, most notably an informant with the code name Curveball, had manufactured the fictions for the express purpose of prodding America into war.* As we soon found out, the weapons of mass destruction (WMD) did not exist.

It is clear in retrospect that the Iraqi government was a diminishing danger to everyone except the Iraqi people. It certainly posed no imminent threat to America or to America's allies. There is no evidence that it was in league with Al Qaeda. There was no justification for the Bush administration, which had won a diplomatic victory by pressing successfully for the return of weapons inspectors to Iraq, to undo that victory by forcing a premature end to those inspections. The United States lacked the "right authority" to go to war in Iraq. It could hardly claim to have acted to enforce the will of the UN Security Council when a majority of the council opposed the president's plan. According to an official British account of conversations with American officials in the summer of 2002, "Bush wanted to remove Saddam through military action, justified by the conjunction of terrorism and WMD. But the intelligence and the facts were being fixed around the policy."

Early on, the war achieved one valuable purpose—the removal from power of Saddam Hussein. It rapidly became clear, however, that the price of this "mission accomplished" had been grossly underestimated. Administration officials expected the war and the subsequent transition to be easy,

---

* It appears, from all accounts, that Secretary Powell had made a diligent effort to ensure that the information he conveyed at the UN was accurate. He had asked the right questions; the problems arose from the answers he received. In September 2005, in an interview with Barbara Walters of ABC, Powell said, "There were some people in the intelligence community who knew at the time that some of these sources were not good, and shouldn't be relied upon, and they didn't speak up. That devastated me."

inexpensive, and risk-free. Failing to anticipate trouble, they neglected to plan for it. At a briefing shortly before the invasion, I sat patiently while the civilian leaders of the Defense Department pointed to their charts and outlined their expectations. Raising my hand, I asked, "All this is fine, but where is your postwar plan?" Instead of answering, the officials told me not to worry; everything had been thought of and would turn out right. They were all supremely confident. Given Hussein's record, I could at least accept that there were reasons to consider going to war. I could not understand the decision to do so at that particular time, without enough troops, without the right equipment, without a realistic strategy for restoring order, and without a serious analysis of the environment in which America's fighting men and women would be asked to risk their lives.

The American military has performed in Iraq with its characteristic skill and courage. The Pentagon's management of the occupation, however, has been a tragedy of errors. The security situation fell apart at the outset; economic reconstruction was stillborn; the contracting process reeked of cronyism; the administration's unilateral approach drove allies away; and the human and financial costs have skyrocketed. As this is being written, more than 2,400 coalition troops have been killed and another 16,000 wounded. Many of the latter have been permanently disabled. Tens of thousands of innocent Iraqi civilians have also died. In addition, more than $250 billion, which could have been used to fight Al Qaeda, to rebuild after natural disasters, or for other necessary purposes, has instead been swallowed up by Iraq. Meanwhile, America's military, including our National Guard and Reserve units, has been dangerously overextended.

One criterion for a just war is "right intention"; on this the administration is entitled to a passing grade. The president was undoubtedly sincere in telling the papal ambassador that he thought the war would "make things better." In fact, he had so much faith in the rightness of his opinions that he ignored the counsel of friends both at home and overseas. The chain of his logic, as evidenced by his statements, is as follows: (1) good and evil exist in the world; (2) Saddam Hussein is evil; (3) removing him will therefore be good; (4) the newly democratic Iraq will become a model for other Arabs. The main difficulty with this thinking is what it left out—the complexities created by history and religion.

The mandate establishing British authority in the Middle East after World War I was not limited to Palestine; it extended as well to three provinces of the newly dismantled Ottoman Empire: one consisting primarily of ethnic Kurds, the second of Sunni Arabs, and the third of Shia Arabs. The territories were situated along the Tigris and Euphrates rivers, whose valley formed the cradle of ancient Mesopotamia. For purposes of administration, the British combined the disparate provinces into a single country: Iraq.

Like American leaders eighty-some years later, the British expected to be greeted warmly by their new subjects; after all, Britain had just freed the people of the region from those who had long oppressed them. The British commander, Lieutenant General Sir Frederick Maude, met local officials with reassuring words: "Our armies do not come into your cities and lands as conquerors or enemies, but as liberators. . . . [It is our wish] that you should prosper even as in the past, when your lands were fertile, when your ancestors gave to the world literature, science and art, and when Baghdad was one of the wonders of the world."

The general's flowery words failed to soothe. The Iraqis

had no interest in substituting a Christian master for a Muslim one; they wanted to govern themselves. By the summer of 1920, rebellion was raging through much of the country. Insurgents cut railway lines, attacked towns, and killed British officers. The English responded harshly, with bombs and poison gas, slaughtering rebels and civilians alike. Iraq's Shia authorities, who had led the uprising, refused to submit. When the British were finally able to restore order, they installed a constitutional monarchy that favored the Sunni minority, leaving the Shiites marginalized and embittered. As for Iraq's oil, it was divided among British, French, Dutch, and American interests.

Although the British mandate officially expired in 1932, Iraq remained under the crown's protection until 1958, when a renegade group of military officers overthrew the monarchy. A subsequent coup brought Saddam Hussein, in 1979, to the presidency. Hussein—a secular Sunni who patterned his leadership style after Joseph Stalin—brutalized all who opposed or questioned him and was especially vicious toward the Shia and the Kurds.

This history meant that in the spring of 2003—when Baghdad fell—American troops would encounter a sharply divided population that was profoundly suspicious of the West and instinctively hostile to the sight of a largely Christian military force occupying a city that had served for centuries as the capital of Islam during its golden age. Little wonder that, once again, good intentions and flowery words would fail to soothe.

Although we must fervently hope otherwise, the invasion of Iraq—and its aftermath—may eventually rank among the worst foreign policy disasters in U.S. history. The decision to attack has already become a case study in unintended consequences. It is extraordinary, for example, that the success of the Bush administration's biggest gamble in world affairs depends on the continued forbearance of a seventy-five-year-old Iranian-born ayatollah with a heart condition. When the removal of Saddam Hussein turned Iraqi politics upside down, the long-dominant Sunni minority was supplanted by the long-repressed Shia majority, whose most influential leader is Grand Ayatollah Sistani.

Unlike the Shiite clerics in Iran, who insist on exercising political power, Sistani is a "quietist," part of a mainstream Shiite tradition in which the clergy remain aloof from the routine of public life, though reserving the right to assert themselves at critical moments. Since the fall of Baghdad, Sistani has fulfilled this role creatively. Rather than repeat the mistake of openly rebelling against a powerful western military force, Sistani has found a way to make the occupiers work for him. In 2003, when the United States unveiled a multistage plan for Iraq to select an assembly and draft a constitution, Sistani blocked it—not because it was democratic but because it wasn't democratic enough. The Americans wanted a carefully controlled process that would establish the rules before elections were held. Sistani said that a constitution drafted by unelected representatives would be illegitimate; elections, he insisted, must come at the beginning. After trying at first to ignore this demand, and then failing to broker a compromise, U.S. officials had no choice—given all their talk about democracy—but to yield. The ayatollah's subsequent support for the balloting ensured its success despite terrorists' threats; he even ruled that women were duty-bound to vote whether their husbands wanted them to or not. Sistani's preferred candidates easily defeated those more closely associated with the United States.

Ayatollah Sistani operates as his predecessors might have done centuries ago, except that he uses far more elaborate communications. He is ascetic, lives in a small house in the

Shia holy city of An Najaf, and refrains from speaking or preaching in public. He also refuses to meet directly with officials of the United States. His image is nurtured by a circle of skilled advisers; his clout is magnified by the network of social and charitable organizations that he controls. Sistani is not strong enough to dictate Iraq's national agenda; but no other faction can achieve its goals without his acquiescence. He will use this power to ensure that Islam plays a prominent role in shaping Iraq's society and law. Sistani's wisdom will be tested repeatedly as conservative Muslims, long suppressed, vie with moderates and advocates of women's rights to determine how tolerant and diverse the new Iraq will be.

Among the most controversial Shiite leaders, and a rival of sorts to Sistani, is Moqtada al-Sadr, a young cleric with an impressive family tree. Al-Sadr's great-grandfather earned renown leading the Shiites against the British in the 1920s. His father, assassinated by government thugs in 1999, was also a major religious figure. Al-Sadr is determined to uphold the family tradition of rebellion but is apparently undecided about how best to do so. He has pursued an erratic strategy, sometimes calling on his loosely organized Al Mahdi militia to attack coalition troops, at other times assuming a defensive stance, at still others promising to renounce violence and go into politics. His role is critical because his demagogic style makes him more popular than any other figure among Baghdad's dispossessed, Shia or Sunni. This standing puts Al-Sadr in a position to cast the "swing vote": choosing either to help bring the country together or to rip it apart. He is, therefore, a litmus test of Iraqi progress. If his name is linked to efforts at promoting national unity, there is reason for encouragement. If his name is connected to new outbreaks of fighting, the chances are that dangers are multiplying.

While the Shiites and Kurds gained power when Saddam Hussein was ousted, the Arab Sunnis lost power. After dominating the country's governing institutions for more than eight decades, the Sunnis were suddenly on the outside. In 2003, American officials disbanded the Iraqi military and barred members of the old governing party from holding public jobs. These ill-advised steps deprived the country of a security structure and put tens of thousands of Sunnis out of work at a time when few replacement jobs were available. Many Arab Sunnis were stunned by their reduced standing. Some genuinely believe, even now, that they constitute a majority of Iraq's population, though experts agree that the proportion is closer to 20 percent.

The Sunnis lack a leader of prestige comparable to Sistani. Some of their more prominent spokesmen have been assassinated; others are tarred by past association with Saddam Hussein; still others are former exiles with little public following. The most influential have called for resistance to the occupation although there are disagreements about how much violence can be justified. Meanwhile, an indeterminate number of terrorists recruited from Sunni Arab states have been drawn to Iraq by the prospect of waging war against the American (i.e., Christian or atheist), Iranian (i.e., Shia), and Jewish agents they allege are intent on plundering their country and attacking their faith. The best-known of these foreigners has been a Jordanian-born terrorist, Abu Musab al-Zarqawi, who acquired notoriety from kidnappings and gory executions broadcast over the Internet. Although Zarqawi is thought to have planned some of the more spectacular attacks in Iraq, dozens of gangs have claimed responsibility for suicide bombings, assaults on security forces, murders, and sabotage. Taken together, these groups constitute a hydra-headed insurgency whose estimated size keeps increasing while it drains the country's resources and threatens to plunge Iraq into ever-widening sectarian strife. In part because it is so decentralized, the insurgency has shown an alarming capacity to absorb losses without losing the ability to carry out its crimes. The rebels have no chance of reestablishing Sunni control over Iraq, but neither does it appear that they can be defeated militarily, unless they fall to quarreling among themselves and begin to fight each other. Their agenda seems to consist entirely of trying to drive the coalition out and kill everyone who has cooperated with it. As one Sunni suicide bomber in training told *Time* magazine, "The first step is to remove the Americans from Iraq. After we have achieved that, we can work out the other details."

American leaders describe the confrontation in Iraq as a battle between the forces of freedom and those of tyranny, seeking without much success to downplay the religious dimension. Not everyone in the country is religious, of course, and millions are so focused on day-to-day survival that they have little time for other concerns, but faith is central to the identity of most Iraqis. Since the fall of Baghdad, religious leaders have repeatedly shown their ability to bring large numbers of people into the streets on behalf of a favored cause. The American military presence was tolerated by the majority of Iraqis at the outset because toleration was what Sistani instructed. It has been resisted by many Arab Sunnis, in part because the Association of Muslim Scholars, a leading Sunni group, claims that opposition is a religious duty. Though most religious Iraqis are not fanatics, some are. It is possible to pick up a newspaper almost any day and find stories about people who say they are willing to die (or kill) if so commanded by their imam. Mustafa Jabbar, for example, is a twenty-three-year-old with a baby son, his first child. He and his wife told an interviewer that they would readily "put mines in the baby and blow him up" if asked to do so by Moqtada al-Sadr.

One of the many ironies of U.S. policy is that the Bush

administration, for all its faith-based initiatives, is far more comfortable working with secular leaders than with those Iraqis (and Iraqi political parties) for whom religion is central. This is true even when the religious leaders are moderate in orientation and generally accepting of U.S. goals.

Evidence for this surfaced during preparations for the first round of elections in January 2005. The National Democratic Institute (NDI), which I chair, worked directly with Iraqi political parties as they prepared for the historic event. Our programs were designed to help the parties to understand the mechanics of the electoral process, organize and publicize their ideas, compile lists of voters, and ensure opportunities for the participation of women. NDI's ability to function in a place as riddled with strife as Iraq depended (then and now) on its neutrality. It cannot be seen as supporting one faction over another.

For this reason, I was stunned when I learned of a controversy within the State Department about whether to funnel tens of millions of dollars in material assistance to favored secular parties. As soon as we found out about this dangerous idea, Ken Wollack (NDI's president) and Les Campbell (its director for the Middle East) lodged a protest. Along with representatives of other organizations promoting democracy, they reminded the administration that the fundamental goal of U.S. policy was to help the Iraqi people elect and put in place a legitimate government. If we played favorites, we would confirm every suspicion about our intentions, make our rhetoric about democracy look foolish, and raise new questions about our attitude toward Islam. NDI warned that if the administration went forward with such a scheme, the institute would have to consider suspending its own programs, because its credibility would be destroyed and the security situation—already tense—would become intolerable.

The proposal to aid particular candidates was debated seriously for months before the top officials at the State Department finally turned thumbs down. Similar ideas, however, have been raised in connection with subsequent elections. To my knowledge, no such plan has been carried out by the State Department or by any other federal agency. Given all that America has invested in Iraq, there is a temptation to try to arrange outcomes that are pleasing to us. But either we have faith in democracy or we do not. Sending Americans to fight and die in Iraq was a questionable idea under any circumstances. Asking them to make such a sacrifice while sabotaging democracy ourselves would be shameful.

The invasion of Iraq was intended as a demonstration of America's power; it has instead shown the limits of that power. President Bush went to war because he believed that doing so was necessary to keep Americans safe. He surely did not intend, in the process, to cause what is taking place: a historic shift in the relative power of Sunni and Shiite Muslims not only in Iraq but throughout the region. The installation of a permanent government in Iraq marks the first time in history that Shiites have governed a leading Arab state. Officials in the major Sunni capitals of Saudi Arabia, Jordan, and Egypt worry about the emergence of a Shia "crescent" running from Bahrain to Iran, Iraq, Syria, and Lebanon. In a meeting in Washington during the spring of 2005, King Abdullah of Jordan expressed to me his concern about the possibility that the clash between the Sunnis and Shiites could supplant the conflict between the Arabs and Israelis as the core problem in the Middle East. For a millennium, Sunnis have been preeminent within Islam. The balance in the future will be more even; and no one can be sure what that will mean. King Abdullah warned, however, against allowing Shiite radicals in Iran and Iraq to represent themselves as legitimate descendants of Muhammad. Although moderates on both sides will seek to restrain the extremes, we should be aware of the potential for conflict—from verbal jousting to assassinations to the instigation, eventually, of a nuclear arms race between Sunnis and Shiites.

A related consequence of the war, also unintended, is the rising regional influence of Iran, thousands of whose citizens live in the Iraqi holy cities of An Najaf and Karbala. Many leaders of the new Iraq earlier spent years in exile in Iran, establishing close ties. In contrast to relations between Iraq and Sunni Arab capitals, which have been frosty, friendly high-level visits have been exchanged between Tehran and Baghdad; promises of cooperation, even on defense and security, have been made. The Shiite militia forces, which control security throughout southern Iraq, are virtual allies of Iran, whose intelligence and security agencies enjoy free rein. The war has already removed Iran's bitterest enemy, Saddam Hussein. Now two more of its adversaries, the United States and Sunni extremists, are engaged in a bloody confrontation. Within Iran itself, a religious conservative with fiercely anti-Israeli views scored a surprising triumph in the presidential election of 2005. From the perspective of the mullahs in Tehran, it is hard to imagine a more favorable sequence of events.

If American planners had had their way, the Shiite militias—and the Kurdish militias in the north—would long ago have disbanded or become integrated into a national army. This does not appear likely to happen soon, if ever. Instead of coming together, Iraq is in danger of falling completely apart. Although the Kurds will settle, for the time being, for a clearly marked-out autonomy, their preference—and ultimate goal—is an independent Kurdistan. The southern Shiites waited two years to declare officially their own interest in establishing an autonomous region complete with oil fields, a port (Basra) on the Persian Gulf, and a government with powers and privileges separate from Baghdad. Although religious and ethnic politics play a big role in this sectarianism, so does money. By exercising control over borders, the various militias have ample opportunity for smuggling. By gaining jurisdiction over oil, regional leaders hope to land lucrative deals with foreign investors. If the middle of the country is left weak and poor, that is a payback for the decades during which the capital exploited the regions. For American policy-makers, however, an Iraq split into three unequal parts would be unacceptable because it would also divide the region, deepening tension between Sunni Arabs and Shiites and complicating relations between Turkey and the Kurds. A divided Iraq would almost certainly lack the qualities of stability and democracy that would enable U.S. troops to depart at an early date, confident that their mission had been accomplished. American advisers have been urging Shia and Kurdish leaders to stop talking about separation and concentrate on working with the Arab Sunnis to build a single, unified country. That project will succeed only if enough Iraqis believe it is both desirable and possible, given past divisions and present crimes.

Adding to the mix is the situation faced by Iraq's Christian minority, which is nearly a million strong and includes Assyrians, Chaldean Catholics, Armenians, and Syrians. Because the Christians are associated in the minds of Muslim militants with the United States, many of their churches have been bombed. Most Iraqi Christians are determined not to be intimidated, but thousands of others have fled. The problem faced by Christian communities has been aggravated by the missionaries who eagerly followed American soldiers into Iraq.

After the battle of Baghdad, the executive administrator of the National Association of Evangelicals predicted that "Iraq will become the center for spreading the gospel of Jesus Christ to Iran, Libya, [and] throughout the Middle East. President Bush said democracy will spread from Iraq to nearby countries. A free Iraq also allows us to spread Jesus Christ's teachings even in nations where the laws keep us out."

The Christian communities in Iraq are almost as old as Christianity itself, and they have survived by *not* trying to convert Muslims. According to the Roman Catholic bishop of Baghdad, "The way the preachers arrived here . . . with soldiers . . . was not a good thing. I think they had the intention that they could convert Muslims, though Christians didn't do it here for 2,000 years." No one has better intentions, and few have more courage, than missionaries willing to venture into potentially hostile areas. Given the current circumstances in Iraq, however, even the perception of Christian proselytizing is no help to U.S. policy, and proselytizing is no way to reduce the dangers faced by U.S. troops.

Despite the many unintended consequences of the U.S. invasion, the Bush administration insists it can nevertheless fulfill the president's promise to "make things better." To probe this, I attended a meeting at the White House on January 5, 2006, for all living former secretaries of state and defense. It was a distinguished group, and experienced enough to make me feel almost young. We assembled in the Roosevelt Room, where we received a determined talk from the president followed by a report via video from our ambassador in Baghdad. When the video proved partly inaudible, I was reminded of all the technical glitches that had interrupted meetings while I was in office. Even at the White House in the twenty-first century, we sometimes expect more of technology than it is able to deliver.

While we were sitting there, the president's staff distributed a brochure featuring an upbeat quotation on Iraq from Vice President Cheney and a collection of talking points about the political and military gains that were being made. After another briefing, this one from the U.S. military commander in Iraq, we were accorded the chance for a conversation with the president. The former secretaries of defense—and there are a lot of them, extending back to Robert McNamara—debated military tactics with the chief executive and expressed concern about the impact on our armed forces of their prolonged deployment overseas. When it was my turn, I thanked the president for the meeting and joined others in voicing the hope that our troops would be successful. I also shared with him my worry about the decline in America's global standing and about the extent to which Iraq is making it harder to deal with dangers elsewhere around the world. The president thanked me for my thoughts but also challenged my criticisms. We were then ushered into the Oval Office for a group photo. It had been a polite meeting but not, I fear, a productive one.

Although U.S. policy has suffered numerous setbacks in Iraq, the administration still talks of "victory." In truth, the chance for the kind of clear-cut triumph achieved during the first Gulf War probably never existed. More than three years after the invasion, Iraq's future remains murky. Both in that country and in America, there is a sense that the coalition military—by its very presence—may be doing as much to unite and sustain the insurgency as to defeat it. Even training the Iraqi military and police could backfire if those forces do not give their loyalty to leaders who represent the whole country. There is a fine line, but a significant one, between creating a true national army and just teaching a lot of people who don't like each other how to use guns.

By invading, the United States assumed a moral responsibility to help Iraq become peaceful and reasonably democratic. An Iraq that is in one piece, has legitimate leadership, and is able on its own to provide security to its people would be considered—at this point—quite an accomplishment. That outcome is still feasible if the insurgency begins to break apart, torn by differences over tactics and targets. There is promise, as well, in the fact that many Iraqis, from all parts of the nation, are for the first time openly engaged in political activity, organizing, and debating what kind of society they want their country to be. Democracy is a powerful means for mobilizing hope. Respecting the rights of political opponents, however, can be viewed as too risky by those whose lives are dominated by fear. For decades, the people of Iraq have lived in fear—of Saddam Hussein and now the disruptions and uncertainty that have followed him. What remains of an American strategy is to reinforce hope through the workings of a representative government and the promise—eventually—of a prosperous economy. The question still to be answered is whether that strategy can succeed in the face of so many political and security challenges, and in light of the dread that many Iraqis feel both toward outsiders and each other.

Ignoring the advice of experts, President Bush gambled that invading Iraq would succeed despite the complications created by religion and history, the absence of a convincing "just war" rationale, and the consequent lack of international support. To justify the wager, he exaggerated both the dangers that Iraq's government posed and the benefits that ousting Saddam Hussein would bring. Most seriously, he promised U.S. troops that "the terrorist threat to America and the world will be diminished the moment that Saddam Hussein is disarmed." In fact, the invasion and occupation have heightened that danger.

Thirteen

Confronting Al Qaeda

———— ⚭ ————

I spent much of the first half of my adult life studying communist governments. During their heyday between the 1950s and early 1980s, they ruled half the world. The ideas behind communism, when cleverly packaged, held a powerful appeal. To the many people who were poor, they promised relief from the insecurities of daily life: the right to a job, education, decent health care, a place to live, and basic nutrition, all financed by efficient economies based on centralized planning.

To secure converts, communist propagandists needed a villain against which to set their own vision; they created one by holding up a fun-house mirror to the West—portraying a civilization notable not for its relative prosperity and freedom but for its racism, crime, drugs, unemployment, and exploitation. In world affairs, the West was denounced as imperialistic and aggressive, preying on less developed countries to reap profits for multinational corporations. To many in distant parts of the globe, these distortions were readily accepted. After all, most of Africa, Asia, and the

Middle East had long been subject to colonial domination; the natural resources of these regions had been pumped, mined, and harvested with little benefit to local populations. Communism failed, nevertheless, because its ideas, when put into practice, did not work. By the late 1980s, not even communist leaders could claim to be fashioning egalitarian societies or creating economic powerhouses that would "bury" the West. When the system started to collapse, it did so rapidly.

Unlike the Marxists, the leaders of Al Qaeda and its allies do not pretend to articulate a coherent economic philosophy; nor do they promise their followers better jobs, health care, or homes—though some terrorist operatives have quarreled about such items. Al Qaeda doesn't purport to be all things to all people; its goal is to seize control of a religion. Unlike communism after the Russian Revolution of 1917, Al Qaeda administers no government or defined territory; but like communism, it has been able to attract support for a reason: it explains suffering and directs anger at targets that, at least to some people, seem to deserve it.

Al Qaeda's most potent argument is that Muslims everywhere are under assault and that good Muslims are duty-bound to fight back. The terrorists compare U.S. troops in Afghanistan and Iraq to the Mongol hordes who stormed through those regions in the thirteenth century, wreaking havoc among the population, looting Muslim treasures, and destroying mosques. This thesis—that Islam is under attack—is believed not by extremists alone; on the contrary, it has become something close to conventional wisdom in Arab and Muslim-majority states. Muslims are threatened, it is thought, not only by American troops but by Zionists armed by the United States in the Middle East and by complicit regimes in the Caucasus, central Asia, Kashmir, China, the Balkans, Indonesia, the Philippines, Thailand, and parts of Africa. More humiliating still, it is alleged that much of the Arab world is ruled by apostate governments that have sold their souls to America or that have embraced atheist ideologies such as the Baathists of Syria or secularists in Turkey—ideologies at odds with the Islamic version of the "city on the hill" or "one nation under God." Islamic cultural values are also seen as endangered by the pervasive influence of the West, which is viewed as materialistic, pornographic, and superficial. This picture of the world is especially prevalent among the restless, unemployed, embittered young.

President Bush is fond of saying that Al Qaeda commits terrorist acts because it "hates freedom." Osama bin Laden has disputed this, asking why, if that were so, it has not attacked "Sweden, for example." Like President Bush, he portrays a clash between the good defender and the evil aggressor, but with the roles reversed. In 2004, one of the Defense Department's own advisory boards concluded that "Muslims do not 'hate our freedom,' but rather they hate our policies." "American actions and the flow of events," reported the panel, "have elevated the authority of the jihadi insurgents and tended to ratify their legitimacy among Muslims. What was a marginal network is now a community-wide movement." Just as communism once appealed to the world's poor as a means of defying the West, so Al Qaeda is being judged by many people based less on what it is than against whom it fights.

To lend emotional intensity to their cause, terrorist leaders hark back to the time of Muhammad, when Islamic warriors first proclaimed their faith, sweeping aside heretics and non-believers. The events of 9/11 were a psychological breakthrough, celebrated as "the holy attack that demolished the foolish infidel Americans and caused many young men to awaken from their deep sleep." In the time that has passed since that day, the frequency of suicide bombings has greatly increased; and the number of groups engaged in that loathsome practice has risen from half a dozen to more than thirty.

Now, say the terrorists, is the moment for true Muslims to define themselves through their actions and to secure their place in paradise by taking part in a sacred struggle. The prospective warriors are lured by the promise of fleshly delights and the expectation that they will be allowed to choose seventy friends and family members to join them in heaven. This highly credulous mind-set is made far more dangerous by twenty-first-century technology. Thousands of websites glorify the exploits of "martyrs," bewail the victimization of Muslims, and solicit new recruits. "Oh Mujahid brother, in order to join the great training camps, you don't have to travel to other lands," declares one online magazine. "Alone, in your home or with a group of your brothers, you too can begin to execute the training program." Like football fans, coin collectors, and quilters, jihadists congregate in multinational virtual communities to share the enthusiasms they have in common. For some, curiosity will grow into a commitment to act. Connections may be made to the shadowy network of terrorist recruiters who operate in parts of the Middle East, south and central Asia, North Africa, Europe, and, almost certainly, America.

Since 9/11, counterterrorism efforts led by the United States have seriously damaged Al Qaeda's network. Dozens of leaders have been killed or arrested, training camps have been dismantled, cells have been closed down, and planned attacks have been foiled. Communications are now more difficult; ringleaders must operate with extreme caution. As President Bush has said, "When terrorists spend their days and nights struggling to avoid death or capture, they are less capable of arming and training and planning new attacks." It is alarmingly apparent, however, that volunteers are stepping up to take the place of those who have been taken down or forced to lie low. In November 2005, for example, insurgents for the first time left Iraq to carry out a strike, this one in Jordan, where they killed fifty-seven people gathered at a hotel for a wedding celebration. According to an assessment by the CIA, Iraq may prove to be a more effective training ground for terrorists than Afghanistan was in the 1980s, because Iraq is serving as a real-world laboratory for urban combat. Experts fear that cadres of terrorists drawn from a score of countries are being trained in assassination, kidnapping, making bombs, and attacking fortified targets. "What we are now awaiting," says Claude Moniquet, director general of the European Strategic Intelligence and Security Center, "is the emergence of a new generation of terrorists; kids who were 12–15 years old on September 11, 2001, and who have taken a year to two to make the same ideological progress that leads to violence, and which took their elders around ten years or more."

If Al Qaeda and its allies are to be defeated, then plainly this assembly line must be shut down. That will require a political victory as decisive as the victory achieved by democracy over communism.

It should be an advantage that no government on Earth openly embraces Al Qaeda. One reason is that Al Qaeda would like to replace the current system of national states with a single religious government—a caliphate—that would command the loyalty of all Muslims. It is a rare regime that supports its own dissolution. This advantage, however, is offset by Al Qaeda's elusiveness and resilience. During the cold war, we could measure our progress on a map showing which countries belonged to the Soviet bloc, which were part of the free world, and which were aligned with neither. Gauging progress today is not as simple as making a list of bad guys and checking them off as each is captured or killed. The new recruits are joining a network that is becoming larger and more diffuse, as groups form that are inspired by Al Qaeda but not dependent on it for direction or resources. As Donald Rumsfeld complained, "We lack metrics to know if we are winning or losing the global war on terror. Are we capturing, killing or deterring and dissuading more terrorists every day than the *madrassas* and the radical clerics are recruiting, training and deploying against us?" Rumsfeld's question reminds me of "snakes and ladders," a game I played as a child and now play with my grandchildren; just when you think you're ahead, you land on a snake, slide back down, and have to begin climbing all over again.*

During the past decade, the United States has invested billions of dollars to restructure intelligence agencies, train security forces, improve surveillance capabilities overseas, and bolster homeland defense. All this is necessary; in fact, much more should be done. The truth, however, is that we have not yet figured out the best way to counter the terrorist threat. Conventional law enforcement is insufficient, and military theories about low-intensity conflict and asymmetrical fighting do not fit. Spokesmen for the administration have sought to reassure us by noting how many of Al Qaeda's leaders have been killed or captured. But as Rumsfeld's memo asks, how meaningful is this? Al Qaeda is not a criminal gang that can be rounded up on the streets or an army that can be crushed on the field of battle. It is like a virus that spreads from one infected person to another, becoming more

---

* Snakes and ladders originated centuries ago in India. In this Hindu game, each of the snakes was associated with a vice (such as theft or lying) and each ladder with a virtue (patience, sobriety). Reaching the end symbolized the quest for paradise, or nirvana. The newer, renamed version, "chutes and ladders," lacks this moral dimension.

virulent with every "sin"—real or alleged—committed by the United States.

It follows from this that America's leaders should minimize actions which terrorists can exploit to gain converts, but we have a hard time doing this. The attacks of 9/11 got our collective blood up; the spectacle of atrocities committed against U.S. servicemen and Iraqi civilians add to the emotions we feel. The terrorists want to provoke us, and they are succeeding. Consider the sentiments expressed by a retired colonel of the U.S. Army, who was speaking at the Forum on Religion and Security in Washington in the fall of 2004:

> On one front, we need to . . . capture and kill as many of the enemy as possible, show them we're the biggest, baddest, most fearsome force in the world who will stop at nothing to accomplish our mission. . . . On the other front, we need to target leaders indirectly. We need to . . . separate them from the people that follow them, and cause their internal support base to collapse. [And] we must take this two-front war on the offensive . . . all around the world. We must fight militant, radical Islam . . . from Africa to Southeast Asia, Central and South America, and Eastern Europe.

I expect that many Americans would agree with these words. I have participated in dozens of meetings about terrorism since 9/11 and have yet to hear anyone say that we should be anything other than tough in our response; and surely, the twin goals identified by the colonel—military success and isolating the bad guys—are exactly right. Separating hard-core terrorists from their base of support is essential. But how to do this? By fighting "militant radical Islam" wherever it exists? That is a recipe for exhausting our military, further alienating world opinion, and reviving the allegation that we want to refight the crusades. Surely this is too broad a target.

There are millions of politically active Muslims who believe in a narrow interpretation of Islam. Though otherwise diverse, most of these people may be antiwestern, undemocratic in their thinking, horrified by the American presence in Iraq, hostile to Israel, and eager to impose their own moral views on others; but they are terrorists only if they commit or facilitate terrorist acts. We should want to debate ideological adversaries with all the arguments at our command; but our government has no call, based simply on people's beliefs, to attack them militarily. Just as we did not shoot communists simply for being communist, we will never know peace if we fall into the trap of considering every Muslim with unwelcome political opinions a mortal foe. Our enemy isn't Islam or any variation of Islam; the enemy is Al Qaeda and its variations. As for the macho mantra that the U.S. military is big, bad, and fearsome and will "stop at nothing," that is hardly the way to persuade the Islamic silent majority to take a stand against terrorism. On the contrary, such boasting may lend support to the terrorists' assertion that they, too, are entitled to "stop at nothing."

Al Qaeda's style of terrorism will be defeated when its central arguments are understood to be lies by those most inclined to believe they are true. We cannot expect those who see themselves as defenders of Islam to abandon that self-image. We can, however, hope to persuade more of them that attacking the innocent on buses, trains, and planes is not the way to defend Islam. This message should not be hard to put across. Killing civilians, children, and fellow Muslims in the name of Islam is as rich a blend of hypocrisy and heresy as one could imagine. Communications across the cultural divide, however, are wretched. According to a study sponsored by the Defense Department, "The critical problem in American public diplomacy directed toward the Muslim world is not one of 'dissemination of information' or even one of crafting and delivering the 'right' message. Rather it is a fundamental problem of credibility. Simply, there is none—the United States today is without a working channel of communication to the world of Muslims and of Islam."

What has caused this breakdown? When the colonel talked about attacking "militant, radical Islam," he had in mind the human monsters in Iraq and elsewhere who are beheading or blowing up the innocent. His rage is understandable; we all share it. Responsible Muslim leaders around the world have condemned the killing of civilians in this or any other manner. But many Muslims are focused, as well, on the faces of noncombatants, including women and children, accidentally killed in the course of American military operations. The estimated number of civilians killed by coalition forces in Iraq ranges from 30,000 to as high as 100,000. If we also take into account the thousands more who have been wounded, whose houses have been destroyed or whose lives have been disrupted by U.S. military operations, we should not marvel at the bitter attitudes that have come to exist.

Muslims also have in mind the mistreatment of prisoners in Iraq, Afghanistan, and Guantánamo. The abuses at Abu Ghraib and other American detention facilities are inexcusable. Some will argue that they do not register heavily on the scale of human atrocities committed through the ages, nor compare to the many outrages committed by Al Qaeda and by Iraqi insurgents. There is, however, a reason why the Vatican's foreign minister called the prison scandal "an offense to God," and "a more serious blow to the U.S. than 9/11."

The issue of torture is simpler to think about in principle than in practice. Those of us who remember Vietnam also remember the demands by American authorities that North Vietnam be made to adhere to the Geneva Conventions regarding the treatment of prisoners of war. Ever since Jimmy Carter made human rights a priority for the United States, the State Department has regularly chastised foreign governments for holding prisoners in secret, denying them due process, or refusing to let them have access to humanitarian organizations. According to President Bush, mistreating prisoners is not the way we do things in America. But the reality is more complex. Especially after 9/11, U.S. officials were in no mood to observe legal niceties, and the American public did little to hold them accountable. Our anger at seeing the twin towers crumble produced an implicit question: why shouldn't we inflict pain on enemies who are out to destroy us, especially if by so doing we might obtain information that could save innocent lives? After all, a decade ago authorities in the Philippines reportedly used torture to make suspects talk, thereby foiling a plot to hijack airplanes. American popular culture, moreover, has long worshipped the kind of character typically portrayed by John Wayne or Clint Eastwood: the tough guy who makes villains pay regardless of the rules.

In 2005, the hero of the popular television drama *24* used torture repeatedly to obtain information in order to protect America from terror attacks. In this drama, when the president refused to authorize torture, he was portrayed as weak. When a human rights lawyer protested, he was shown to be a dupe of the evildoers. The deck was stacked in favor of torture: the person being abused was obviously a villain; the information being withheld was vital; time was of the essence; and the torturer, handsome and manly, was "only doing his job." The manipulations of television aside, many of us—if we are honest with ourselves—can at least imag-

ine real-life circumstances in which the use of coercive measures to extract information would seem justified.

Since 9/11, this question has attracted much attention
from experts on ethics and law. Professor Alan Dershowitz
of Harvard caused a ruckus by calling for a system in which
torture, like a wiretap, could be authorized by a judge when
presented with due cause.* Such an idea is not likely to go
far. America, like most countries, is on record as denouncing
torture. In 2003 and 2004, memos of the Justice Department
surfaced that seemed to legitimize torture; but the Bush
administration quickly distanced itself from that interpretation. As a matter of principle, we will remain firmly
opposed to torture. As a matter of fact, we may still have
mixed feelings.

This is not good enough. We need to think the issue
through. First of all, real life is not like *24*. It is an illusion to
believe that torture is a generally effective means of obtaining accurate information. Torture may work sometimes but
usually it does not. Napoleon, no bleeding heart, observed
more than two centuries ago, "The barbarous custom of having men beaten who are suspected of having important
secrets to reveal must be abolished. It has always been recognized that this way of interrogating men, by putting them to
torture, produces nothing worthwhile."

Second, as John McCain has argued, this debate is not
about what our enemies are like; it is about us. If we ratio-
nalize torture or make exceptions for special circumstances,

---

* Dershowitz does not advocate torture. He argues instead that authorities are
likely to engage in the practice in extreme cases and that it is better for them to
do so within the legal system than outside it. "If we are to have torture," he
wrote in the *Los Angeles Times* on November 8, 2001, "it should be authorized by
the law."

so will everybody else. Governments that routinely abuse prisoners will point to the United States for justification. Our standing to insist on the humane treatment of Americans in foreign prisons will be diminished. America will be known as the kind of country that tortures people or that arranges for others to do so. For what purpose? To defeat the terrorists? The effect will be just the opposite. Guantánamo has presumably kept some members of the terrorist class of 2002 out of action, but at the cost of significantly enlarging the class of 2006. The detention center there should have been shut down long ago. As for Abu Ghraib, it was the biggest gift Al Qaeda's propagandists could have received.

What has been singularly appalling is that so many of those who were abused appear to have been either innocent or not in a position to know much. There is profound ugliness in the spectacle of American guards doing their best to humiliate and hurt Arab men simply because they have the power to do so and were in need of entertainment. While most U.S. soldiers were seeking to build bridges of understanding and friendship to Muslims, the guards and interrogators—and those who gave them their instructions—were showing contempt for Arab culture and basic human rights. Their actions seemed designed to aggravate the feeling of many Muslims that they are victims who are under attack.

It is hard for those of us who believe in America's goodness to admit mistakes, but these abuses were serious and cannot be ameliorated by a few light punishments for those near the bottom of the chain of command. There must be accountability at the top. Otherwise, it will be virtually impossible for us to soften the harshly negative perception of the United States that so many Muslims have developed. In the time since the first photos from Abu Ghraib appeared, pamphlets have circulated in Arab communities showing those shameful images along with pictures of dead Palestinian and Iraqi children. "Where Are the Men?" reads the headline above the pictures, "Who Will Avenge Our Dignity?" In a region of long memories, I fear these images will be fueling anti-American violence for generations to come.

I know from experience that our military goes to extraordinary lengths to avoid civilian casualties. At the same time, political leaders can put our armed forces into situations where significant civilian casualties are virtually inevitable. The result can turn military success into political defeat. As in Vietnam, the battles may be won, but the war is not. Without an effective political strategy, the United States cannot defeat Al Qaeda.

That strategy should begin with confidence. Bin Laden and his cohorts have nothing real to offer anybody. The attacks of 9/11 gave them a visibility and a following that they do not deserve and that they will not be able to maintain in the absence of further mistakes on our part. Our job is to keep the spotlight on their nihilism, cruelty, and lies. If we do that, we will ultimately attract the support we need. Being confident, however, does not excuse complacency. We must argue our case before even the toughest audiences.

The U.S. National Commission on the 9/11 attacks concluded:

> Bin Laden and Islamist terrorists mean exactly what they say: to them America is the font of all evil, the "head of the snake," and it must be converted or destroyed. It is not a position with which Americans can bargain or negotiate. With it there is no common

ground—not even respect for life—on which to begin a dialogue. It can only be destroyed or utterly isolated.

The commission is unquestionably right to identify bin Laden and his ilk as irredeemable, and yet the commission also tells us that the decision to launch the attacks of 9/11 was far from unanimous. Mullah Omar, the Taliban leader, was reported to have opposed striking the United States, fearing retaliation. Al Qaeda's chief financial manager sided with Omar. Al Qaeda's leading theologian said that the attacks were contrary to the Quran. The longtime spiritual mentor of Abu Musab al-Zarqawi, the leader of the foreign insurgents in Iraq, has broken with him over the issue of suicide bombings against civilians. These differences of opinion do not mean that the West should seek to "negotiate" with Al Qaeda; it does mean that within the terrorist networks there is a diversity of views, which we should do our utmost to exploit.

Many, perhaps most, of the people who are recruited as terrorists are beyond the reach of logical argument or appeals to conscience, but some may still be what I learned in college to describe as "rational actors." It may be possible to convince them that killing noncombatants offends, rather than defends, Islam; or they may find it harder than others to leave family and friends behind; or they may be motivated primarily by local goals and have little interest in taking on the United States or the entire West. Some may even be susceptible to offers of jobs or other material benefits. It helps us not at all to treat terror networks as a monolith. Like other groups, they comprise individuals who should not be abandoned without a fight. In Yemen since 2002, Islamic scholars have challenged imprisoned members of Al Qaeda to debate their tactics in light of the Quran, convincing more than 350 to renounce violence and cooperate with the authorities. Judge Hamoud al-Hitar, who conceived this effort, explains, "If you study terrorism in the world, you will see that it has an intellectual theory behind it, and any kind of intellectual idea can be defeated by intellect." In other words, the best way to defeat a bad idea is with a good idea.

It matters that Islam places such an enormous emphasis on law. In Amman in 2005, 180 Muslim scholars from forty-five countries (including the United States) representing eight schools of Islamic thought convened a conference on "True Islam." Their purpose was to discredit self-promoting zealots who issue fatwas without being qualified to do so, and who seek to justify violence against other Muslims by dismissing the victims as apostates. The scholars sought to turn the excesses committed by terrorists against them and to apply Islamic law in a manner that exposes the yawning gap between the terrorists' holy pretensions and their unholy actions. Ultimately, this is how terrorism will be defeated, by real Muslims uniting to protect Islam from the murderers who are trying to steal it.

Confronting Al Qaeda will require the full range of our foreign policy tools, including our intelligence assets and our military. There are certain to be times when terrorist targets of opportunity are exposed and deadly force should be used. It would be a mistake, however, to believe that terrorism is primarily a military threat. If it were, it would have been defeated long ago. It is primarily a political and psychological challenge and must be opposed in political and psychological terms. Nothing the United States does will alleviate the hatred that some Arabs and Muslims feel, but it is not necessary to change the thinking of everyone.

According to Václav Havel, "Communism was not defeated by military force, but by life, by the human spirit, by conscience, by the resistance of Being and man to manipulation." It was defeated, in other words, because those who opposed it were able to summon the better aspects of human nature to expose its lies and wear it down. Terrorists may still succeed on occasion in penetrating barriers designed to keep them out. But they can never succeed, unless we let them, in separating us from the values that, over the long term, hold the key to their downfall and our success.

The ending of the cold war was televised. Sitting in my study, I saw students dancing on the glorious wreck of the Berlin Wall and raucous crowds celebrating in the newly free capital cities of central and east Europe. I recall especially my joy at the spectacle in Wenceslas Square in Prague, where Václav Havel and other heroes of the "velvet revolution" accepted the call to lead Czechoslovakia into a time of independence and liberty. "This is it," I said to myself at the time. "Thank God."

How will our confrontation with terror end? Quite differently, one presumes. There may be spectacular events. Perhaps in the time it takes for this book to be published, we will have finally seen bin Laden's capture or demise. In Iraq, al-Zarqawi may already be yesterday's news. Certainly there will continue to be attacks, arrests, and takedowns. It seems unlikely, however, that we will ever see the equivalent of the celebration in Wenceslas Square. I doubt that we will be able to turn on our televisions one day and say, "This is it." In the worst case, we will see a constant drumbeat of attacks (some possibly involving biological or even nuclear weapons) against an expanding list of targets. We may see more areas, conceivably entire countries, become havens for violent extremism. We could see Islam further divided between the followers of a peaceful faith and those whose minds have been poisoned by hate.

In the best case, we will see the opposite: a reduction in the number of attacks, a shrinkage of areas where terrorists have support, a closing of the ranks within Islam. If that should happen, our confrontation will end with a nonevent: bin Laden, or his successor, will videotape a threat to incinerate us, and nobody will broadcast it, because the terrorists lack even a smidgen of public backing. Will we ever get to this point? The answer to that question will become clear only gradually and will be based on events in a broad area, extending from the Malay Archipelago to the mountains of the Caucasus to the coast of North Africa. Most important will be the Arab world, where Islam was born; and within that world, the country whose direction will be likely to matter most is the kingdom of Saudi Arabia.

Fourteen

The Saudi Dilemma

———— ✄ ————

I am scared," said one Saudi Arabian during the summer of 2004. "There is no clear vision to where my country is heading. We want to progress, but we also want to live like good Muslims did 1,400 years ago. We want to change, but we believe that change is the road to hell. We want the people to have a role in leading the country, but we don't want democracy. We want to have dialogue with the West, but our preachers are preaching every Friday that all Westerners or non-Muslims go to hell."

The founder and uniter of modern Saudi Arabia, King Ibn Saud, declared early in the twentieth century: "My kingdom will survive only insofar as it remains a country difficult of access, where the foreigner will have no other aim, with his task fulfilled, but to get out." A statement issued by the Saudi royal family early in the twenty-first century asserted the contrary: "We are part of this world and cannot be disconnected from it. We cannot be mere spectators while the rest of the world is progressing toward a new global system."

Since the attacks of 9/11, a small library's worth of books

and articles have appeared in the West suggesting that Saudi Arabia is, essentially, evil—the birthplace, breeder, and banker of terror committed in the name of Islam. As the quotations above suggest, a more apt term than "evil" might be "confused."

No country has tried to leap more suddenly into the modern age than Saudi Arabia. Few countries have been less well-equipped psychologically to make that leap. Saudi culture has been heavily influenced by Wahhabism, a puritanical Sunni movement that originated in the eighteenth century and became firmly established when the house of Saud conquered the Arabian Peninsula in the 1920s. Proponents of Wahhabi doctrine sought to return to what they considered pure, authentic Islam.* They imposed a sort of national uniform—white for men and black for women—banned music, and drained the country of much of its regional and cultural diversity. The result is a rigidly controlled society whose public places are monitored by religious police and where public displays of affection (even familial affection) between the sexes are forbidden, dancing is outlawed, and women in urban areas are not allowed to drive. The kingdom's very identity is centered on its status as custodian of the holy mosques in Mecca, where the Prophet Muhammad was born; and Medina, where he is entombed. This status inspires pride but also an emphasis on conformity. Worship is restricted for Shiite Muslims and prohibited for non-Muslims. Non-Muslim adults cannot even be buried in Saudi soil. Ninety percent of the books published in the kingdom deal with religious topics, and

---

* Because the term "Wahhabi" has developed negative connotations, many practitioners prefer to be known as "Salafists," followers who seek to model themselves after the first three generations of Muslims.

most university graduates receive their degrees in Islamic studies. The country has no written constitution other than the Quran.* Its ideal is to be an island of purity, separate from and untainted by the vulgarity of the West.

And yet Saudi Arabia also sits atop a quarter of the world's petroleum reserves, a mixed blessing that has brought the Saudis into intimate and highly materialistic contact with industrial nations. The oil has long provided a measure of wealth, and the price shocks of the 1970s multiplied those riches many times. Western entrepreneurs, eager to cash in, signed billions of dollars in construction, technology, and service contracts with the Saudis. As the petrodollars piled up, Saudi princes became familiar figures at international nightspots, dressed in the most stylish clothes, their wives in designer fashions. Two decades earlier, a prince might have lived in a modest mud house, with space set aside for receiving petitions from the public. In the new era, that same prince built palatial estates, filled them with expensive furniture and electronic gadgets, and surrounded them with high walls.

The Iranian revolution of 1979 threatened to spoil the party. Almost as soon as he took power, Ayatollah Khomeini called for an uprising against the Saudi government, which he described as "un-Islamic." The threat became real in November of that year, when militants staged a dramatic protest and took hostages at the Grand Mosque in Mecca. The rebels denounced the royal family as corrupt and demanded its overthrow. Following a three-week siege, Saudi security forces made a concentrated attack, killing some of the insurgents and capturing the rest, who were

---

* In 1992, the Saudis did, however, establish a "basic law of government" that is in some ways analogous to a constitution.

later beheaded. The government then sought to regain the loyalty of the religious establishment by giving it full control over education and granting it authority to police the behavior of citizens and visitors. The Saudi social code became more restrictive, further empowering the most conservative elements of society. These trends were reinforced by extremist scholars from Syria and Egypt, who, fleeing the hostility of their secular governments, brought with them a commitment to pan-Islamic radicalism that was more activist and political than the traditional agenda of the Wahhabis.

Meanwhile, the boom in oil prices transformed Saudi Arabia into the ultimate welfare state. By the late 1980s, every Saudi was entitled to free medical care and higher education. Any college graduate, male or female, was eligible for a $50,000 grant to start a small business. Upon reaching adulthood, each young man received a plot of land plus a construction loan of $80,000. Electricity and water were provided without charge. The Saudis and their advisers expected the good times to last. They did not. The country was brought low by its failure to plan ahead, its spendthrift ways—and a baby boom.

Between 1981 and 2001, the Saudi population more than doubled. If Saudi women continue to bear children at the present average rate (seven each), the population will double again by 2020. When all these young people go looking for jobs, many will be disappointed. Unemployment has risen to 20 percent while per capita production is lower than it was forty years ago. The country's oil revenues, equal to $22,000 per Saudi in 1980, dropped to $4,000 in 2004 despite record high prices. Once glistening Saudi cities have taken on the look of cities elsewhere, marred by dirty neighborhoods and overcrowded slums.

While the social pressures have mounted, the contrast

between western and Islamic lifestyles has been apparent to all. The newly widespread phenomenon of satellite television, combined with images of Arabs' and Muslims' suffering, have nurtured anti-Western sentiments. Through the 1990s, American military forces were stationed in the kingdom to deter Saddam Hussein from once again invading Kuwait. This perceived desecration of the Holy Land created a casus belli for Osama bin Laden and Al Qaeda.

The convergence of these factors acquired new meaning after 9/11. Suddenly, Saudi Arabia—where fifteen of the nineteen hijackers had been born—no longer fit the stereotype of a rich and orderly society. In the time since, the house of Saud has come under siege from all sides. While some in the West accuse the royal family of supporting terror, Al Qaeda condemns it for colluding with the West. Al Qaeda says that the monarchy is illegitimate; President Bush's rhetoric about transforming and democratizing the Middle East, if taken to its logical conclusion, raises the same question. Domestically, the regime is facing pressure for wider political openness from un-enfranchised women, reform-minded intellectuals, the Shia minority, and the frustrated young. Conservative religious elements are fighting against any change that would reduce their influence. Almost everyone seems to want a more prominent voice in how and for whose benefit the country is run.

The Saudi government has found itself in the middle of a minefield. To navigate its way out, it will have to isolate and discredit those among its clerics who provide a rationale for terrorism. It will have to modernize its economy, create hundreds of thousands of new jobs, and reassess its attitude toward women. It must provide effective answers to critics in the West without seeming to validate Al Qaeda's allegation that it is too close to the West. All this is a tall order for a society whose most powerful leaders are in their seventies and eighties and who were brought up to expect a life of relative isolation based on old customs and simple truths.

Was the Saudi government responsible for 9/11? No. Is it in league with Al Qaeda? Of course not. Is it sinister that groups of Saudi nationals departed the United States on charter flights a few days after 9/11? Not according to the independent 9/11 commission, which found that every passenger was screened by the FBI and that "no one with known links to terrorism departed on these flights." The Saudi leaders are preservationists, not radicals; above all else, they prize stability. The connection between Saudi culture and the rise of Al Qaeda, however, goes beyond the question whether the government itself is implicated in terrorism. One cause for alarm is the extent to which private Saudi money has helped to finance terrorist operations. A second is whether Saudi leaders have inadvertently assumed the role of Dr. Frankenstein, creating a monster they are unable to control.

In 1986, King Fahd of Saudi Arabia formally changed his title from "His Majesty" to "Custodian of the Two Holy Mosques." Fahd (who died in August 2005) was proud of precisely what makes me nervous—the support his government has given to Islamic institutions overseas, including some 210 Islamic centers, more than 1,500 mosques, 200 colleges, and almost 2,000 schools. The Saudis are confident that their faith is the true one and thus see no inconsistency in subsidizing their own religion abroad and at the same time prohibiting the practice of other religions at home. In our discussions, Saudi officials made much of the kingdom's status as the protector and defender of Islam. This reflects their own sense of exceptionalism and a duty, as they see it, to propagate their faith. Whether this is a proper reason for pride, however, will depend on how and by whom that faith is being interpreted. During my meetings before 9/11, the Saudis reacted indignantly to any suggestion that Muslim terror networks were gaining strength. They viewed such allegations as an attempt to discredit Islam.

In light of what has happened since, the Saudis have to look at their responsibilities from a different perspective. It is true that some writers in America, Europe, and Israel have distorted Islamic beliefs and Saudi policies while pontificating with scarcely concealed bigotry about Arab culture. The real damage to Islam, however, is coming from the murderers who masquerade as pious Muslims, creating an ugly distortion of the faith. If Saudi Arabia is to lead in defending Islam, these are the enemies it must first defeat.

In Riyadh, the capital of Saudi Arabia, the initial reaction to the attacks of 9/11 was denial. Despite Osama bin Laden's role and the nationality of the majority of hijackers, Saudi officials did not want to admit that Al Qaeda had a significant presence in their kingdom. They saw this as a matter of public relations, not security. Then, on May 12, 2003, three terrorist bombings killed thirty-five people in Riyadh. In November, terrorist explosions rocked a housing complex there. In May 2004, gunmen murdered twenty-two people in a residential compound for oil industry workers in Khobar. The following month, again in Riyadh, kidnappers seized and executed Paul Johnson, an American contractor. In December that same year, gunmen attacked the U.S. consulate in Jeddah, killing five employees.

Even the Saudi authorities could not ignore such acts of violence; the government arrested hundreds of suspected terrorists; engaged in bloody shoot-outs with cells linked to Al Qaeda; and seized caches of illicit travel documents, grenades, and guns. Saudi officials also finally recognized—

at least implicitly—the connection between what was happening in their streets and what was being taught in their mosques. More than 3,500 imams were required to attend programs of reeducation designed to promote tolerance within Islam. Clerics were encouraged to preach about the danger of exaggeration in religion. Passages promoting violence against non-Muslims were removed from school textbooks. Under pressure from the United States, the Saudis enacted laws to curb money laundering and track the flow of Saudi funds to suspect charities.

The Saudi press is far from free, but within limits it is host to an increasingly vigorous debate. Diatribes against Israel are mixed with introspective discussions about the meaning and obligations of Islam. The managing editor of one daily paper, a childhood friend of bin Laden, has written a denunciation of those who use the Quran to condemn all Christians and Jews. Numerous columnists have lambasted Al Qaeda for trying to portray Islam as a religion of war. Abdel Rahman al-Rashad, general manager of the satellite news channel Al Arabiya, has declared:

> It is a certain fact that not all Muslims are terrorists, but it is equally certain, and exceptionally painful, that almost all terrorists are Muslims. . . . We cannot tolerate in our midst those who abduct journalists, murder civilians, explode buses; we cannot accept them as related to us, whatever the sufferings they claim to justify their criminal deeds. These are the people who have smeared Islam and stained its image.

On the official level, Saudi leaders have been vehement in denouncing terrorism as "a global crime perpetrated by evil minds filled with hatred toward humanity." The kingdom's clerics appear regularly on television to denounce terror as contrary to Islam. These declarations are welcome, but the rest of us will not relax until we are satisfied that neither Saudi funds nor Saudi doctrines are being used to foster a future generation of Al Qaeda recruits. It is discouraging that Saudi officials insist on denying that violent extremists have much backing in their country; a poll conducted privately by the kingdom found that 49 percent of Saudis support bin Laden's ideas. Equally disturbing, more than two dozen prominent Saudi clerics, most of whom lecture at state-supported universities, issued a fatwa in November 2004 calling on Iraq "to defend itself, its honor, its land, its oil, its present, and its future against the imperialist coalition, just as it resisted British colonialism in the past." The signatories argued that "jihad against the occupier is the obligation of any able person."* It should be no surprise that many of the foreign suicide bombers in Iraq come from Saudi Arabia.

In February 2005, I took part in the Jeddah Economic Forum. The event was held in an enormous hotel ballroom; the audience was a sea of men in white robes. Along one side of the room was a wall of mirrors, adding to the impression of size. In my remarks, I congratulated the Saudis on their decision to hold competitive municipal elections (which were under way at the time) and said that I hoped women would be given the right to vote in Saudi Arabia more rapidly than they had been in the United States.

To my surprise, these words elicited a vigorous round of

---

* The communiqué, issued on November 5, 2004, was denounced by the Saudi ambassadors to the United States and Great Britain. Numerous Saudi columnists condemned the fatwa for seeming to encourage their country's youth to go to Iraq to fight. Supporters of the communiqué praised it for urging unity between the Sunnis and Shiites in Iraq and for discouraging violence against noncombatants, including foreigners such as journalists and aid workers.

applause. When I looked at the audience in front of me, however, nobody was clapping. The sea of men was not generating any waves. Instead, the applause was coming from behind the mirrors; that's where the Saudi women were congregated. Separated as always from the men, they were invisible—but, having access to microphones, far from inaudible. When the Saudi labor minister claimed that women liked the policy of gender separation in the workplace and had no interest in being allowed to drive, the women asked why he thought that; when he referred to all the e-mail he had received, they asked for his e-mail address. Women make up half of the Saudis' university population, but less than a tenth of the country's workforce. Sooner or later, these educated women—potentially an enormous national asset—will find broader expression outside the home.

During the discussion in Jeddah, one Saudi man rose to assure me that his country's policies toward women were based on a desire not to repress but rather to respect. "We believe women sit at the feet of the gates of heaven," he said. "Our only goals are to honor our women and to protect them." I said that I understood this and did not think the West had all the answers. I added, "I do, however, believe in the right of people to make basic choices. If women had alternatives, perhaps many would decide to live the way they do now. But women, as much as men, should have the chance to decide for themselves. They are adults, not children, and should be treated accordingly. What are you men afraid of anyway? No one is interested in starting a war of the sexes."

As a teenager, when I went on my first dates with boys who had automobiles, my father insisted on following along in our family's car. The Saudi system is similarly overprotective, except that the father is actually in the vehicle sitting next to the boy, with the girl in the back, behind a curtain.

I had a chance during my visit to renew my acquaintance with Crown Prince Abdullah; this was about six months before he succeeded King Fahd, who had been ill for a long time. Although Abdullah is in his early eighties, he remains physically strong and full of life. He has a thick mustache and a goatee, both still black; and a quiet, dignified way of speaking. When I told him I was writing this book, he smiled approvingly and pointed to the green-covered copy of the Quran that sits beside him in his office.

During our discussion, he made plain his horror at the distorted picture some people have created of Islam, which he characterized as a religion of peace and compassion. He said that Christianity, Judaism, and Islam all attract their share of extreme elements, and that there are some Christian conservatives who feel they need to create a crisis in order to bring about Armageddon. I wondered if the Quran prohibited Muslims from ceding land they had once ruled. He said that there was nothing so rigid, except for special areas and holy sites. I asked him, "In this highly religious society, what role do you think God plays in the administration of the kingdom?" He replied, "Faith is a constant, but you do not go to God before you consult with friends, advisers, the public, and foreign countries. Then you rely on God to help you make the right decisions, and pray that everything turns out well." When I questioned him about Iraq, he grimaced slightly and said, "Perhaps we should change the subject."

Throughout this latest visit to Saudi Arabia, I found a startling difference from earlier trips. The prevailing attitude had been that every important question was already decided. Now, everything is in flux; the political atmosphere, long stagnant, is alive with speculation and argument; Saudi politics have acquired the attributes of drama.

During the past several years, the house of Saud has responded to calls for reform without yielding to them, parceling out progress in the thinnest of slices. That pace may accelerate because of Abdullah's new role. While still crown prince, he sponsored a series of national meetings on the rights of religious minorities and women, created a federal center for dialogue, and authorized competitive municipal elections. As king, he ordered the Jeddah Trade and Industry Chamber to allow female candidates for election to its board, and two were chosen. He has allocated $3.3 billion to modernize the Saudi education system and curriculum. On the economic side, he has brought Saudi Arabia into the World Trade Organization, an accomplishment he can use to justify anticorruption measures, reorganization of the country's sleepy bureaucracy, and educational improvements in such secular subjects as engineering, science, and mathematics.

More dramatically, within days of becoming king, Abdullah pardoned three activists who had been jailed for eighteen months for advocating a new constitution. This was an obvious rebuff to the official who had ordered the arrests, Prince Nayef, the interior minister. Nayef has long made it his business to promote the agenda of religious conservatives. Abdullah is a cautious reformer in a country where any kind of reform can seem radical. He is restrained by powerful rivals and bound by his family's tradition of making decisions by consensus. His policies are likely to produce not a series of bold steps but rather a sideways shuffle, inching ahead in some areas—elections, more options for women, economic change—before pausing to see if lightning strikes.

The Saudi dilemma and the associated challenge for the West may well prove intractable, but it must be confronted nonetheless. The country's economic position as a source of oil and an arbiter of oil prices will continue long after the reserves of most other suppliers have been exhausted. The kingdom's religious leaders still have much to say about how young Sunni Muslims are taught to view the world.

American leaders will be pushed by Congress, the public, and the press to take a tough stance with the Saudis on issues related to terrorism. However, America has less leverage than it once had. The Saudis no longer depend on the United States for technological expertise; and the importance of America as a customer for oil is diminishing as other countries buy more. Unless present security concerns ease, fewer Saudis will want to experience the indignities required to gain entry to the United States, and fewer Americans will travel to Saudi Arabia. Military-to-military contacts will become less frequent. If the negative perceptions on both sides persist, U.S. and Saudi leaders will gain little politically from helping each other.

The Saudis do not, however, feel comfortable in the role in which some have cast them: "a sort of oily heart of darkness," suggested one writer, "the wellspring of a bleak, hostile value system." They would surely be pleased with a return to a more relaxed time, when our two countries were on the same side in the biggest battles and were able to work around our differences regarding the Middle East. We should encourage the Saudis to restore that kind of relationship by persevering in their efforts to purge Al Qaeda, by denying funds to terrorists, and by seizing every chance to remind their citizens and coreligionists abroad that killing unarmed people is contrary to Arab values and no way to earn a place in paradise.

The philosophical battle in Saudi Arabia revolves around the fundamental question of what kind of country its people wish it to be: an isolated bastion ruled by conservative traditions or a modern country (albeit a deeply religious one) that is open to, and part of, the world. While some Saudis are eager to explore the boundaries of what Islam permits, others are determined to enforce as many limits as possible. Not surprisingly, many Saudis find themselves unable to line up unambiguously on one side or the other. The need for modernization is widely acknowledged, but so is the fear of losing control. This debate and the accompanying hopes and fears are echoed throughout much of the Arab world and many other Muslim societies. The resulting turbulence is the product of a momentous and inherently complex encounter between two profound ideas: that all power comes from God, and that legitimate authority on Earth comes from the people.

Fifteen

Arab Democracy

In July 1957, John F. Kennedy, at the time the junior U.S. senator from Massachusetts, declared that "the most powerful force in the world today is neither communism nor capitalism, nor the guided missile—it is man's eternal desire to be free and independent.

"The great enemy of that tremendous force for freedom," he continued, "is called, for want of a more precise term, imperialism. Thus the single most important test of American foreign policy today is how we meet the challenge of imperialism, what we do to further man's desire to be free."

In the depths of the cold war, Kennedy—remarkably—identified not communism but imperialism as America's premier foreign policy test. He did so at a moment when Algerian freedom fighters were engaged in a life-and-death struggle for independence from France, causing French leaders to decry his "rash intervention" in their affairs. The elder statesman of the Democratic Party, Adlai Stevenson, agreed, calling Kennedy's speech "terrible," an "invitation to chaos," and a threat to NATO. But independence was an idea whose time had come; Algeria achieved it in 1962. By then Kennedy was president, intent on putting the United States firmly on the side of liberty for colonized peoples throughout the developing world, a significant part of which was Muslim. When Kennedy spoke of man's desire to be free, he meant the yearning of nations to escape foreign domination. But independence provides no guarantee that people will also be free from repression by their own governments; establishing that kind of freedom is a separate and sometimes an even harder challenge.

In November 2003, President Bush announced that the United States would pursue "a forward strategy for freedom in the Middle East." Speaking before an audience gathered to celebrate the twentieth anniversary of the National Endowment for Democracy, Bush argued that "stability cannot be purchased at the expense of liberty. As long as the Middle East remains a place where freedom does not flourish, it will remain a place of stagnation, resentment, and violence ready for export. And with the spread of weapons that can bring catastrophic harm to our country and to our friends, it would be reckless to accept the status quo."

Having championed democracy for as long as I can remember, I welcomed the president's speech and agreed with its premise. Many of the countries that gained their independence from colonial rule simply exchanged foreign despotism for the homegrown kind. The Middle East is the only region where heads of government (as opposed to heads of state) still derive authority from their bloodlines. If President Bush is serious about challenging that tradition, he could alter relations between the United States and Arab governments and peoples for decades to come.

Supporting democracy in the Middle East is, however, much simpler in word than in deed. The State Department's original plan for the democratization of the Arab world was disclosed to the press before governments in the region had even been consulted, a diplomatic faux pas that elicited protests and allegations of arrogance. In Morocco in December 2004, Arab and western governments convened a "Forum for the Future" to discuss the need for democratic change, but while U.S. officials talked about opening the political process, Arab leaders stressed the need to end the U.S. occupation of Iraq and resolve the Israeli-Palestinian dispute. The view taken by the United States, then and now, is that extremism results from political frustration and that people become terrorists because they are unable to achieve change by other means. Arab officials insist that terrorism is a product of anger at U.S. actions, not a result of the Arabs' own undemocratic practices—and that the way to achieve stability is to alter American policies. This opinion is not restricted to Arab princes and kings. In Dubai in December 2005, I met with a group of young Muslim women, most of whom were dressed head to toe in black and expressed views that were decidedly feminist. When I made the point that the status quo in the Middle East is dangerous, one woman stood and made a point of her own. "It wasn't dangerous until the United States made it so."

In a region where conspiracy theories flourish, there is widespread suspicion about the intentions of the Bush administration. The proposition that America would back democracy because it has the best interests of Arabs at heart is not widely believed. Each side accuses the other, justly, of trying to change the subject: American officials would rather talk about the need for Arab governments to reform than the plight of the Palestinians; Arab leaders would rather talk about almost anything except democracy.

The president is right to try to correct the impression that America stands for freedom everywhere except in Arab countries, not least because there has been some truth to it. For decades, Republican and Democratic administrations alike have had good reason to seek smooth relations with autocratic Arab leaders. The governments of strategically vital countries such as Saudi Arabia and Egypt valued stability; so did the United States. The Arabs produced oil; American consumers demanded it. The Arabs wanted advanced technology; U.S. companies were eager to sell it. During the cold war, America needed Arab support against the Soviet Union. In the 1990s, the Clinton administration sought the backing of Arab governments for the Middle East peace process. These Arab governments, imperfect though they were, seemed preferable to likely alternatives. After all, we had our hands full with Saddam Hussein in Iraq, Muammar Qaddafi in Libya, and a theocratic regime in Iran. Although many of these practical considerations remain, the time is ripe for a new approach. One of Al Qaeda's major arguments is that the United States is propping up governments that are corrupt, illegitimate, repressive, and heretical. One way to rebut that is by honoring our ideals and supporting democratic reforms in every country that lacks freedom.

This is not a matter of trying to impose our system on people who don't want it. Islam teaches its followers to take the best from other civilizations; democracy is a big part of what is best about the West. Surveys have found that Arab and Muslim populations generally favor such concepts as freedom of expression, multiparty systems, and equal treatment under the law. Most say it is more important for a leader to be democratic than strong. Perhaps that is why democracy is already making inroads. The tiny emirate of Qatar has a new constitution that provides for a consultative assembly and protects religious liberty, freedom of the press, and women's rights. Kuwait's parliament, after years of rejecting the proposal, has finally granted women the right to vote. In 2003, Jordan and Yemen conducted legislative elections that were, if flawed, still partly competitive and reasonably free. The Palestinian Authority has held elections for both president and parliament. Most Arab countries now have some kind of representative legislative or advisory body, though its powers are often modest. Throughout the region, there is a sense that the old ways are changing, to be replaced by something not yet fully defined, but new.

The Bush administration had hoped that Iraq would emerge as a democratic model that other Arabs would be eager to emulate. Perhaps one day they will. However, given the daily spectacle of political infighting and violence in the streets, it may be some time before most Arabs look at Iraq and think, "I wish my country could be like that." So as yet there is no fully satisfactory Arab model of democracy.* In 1992, King Fahd of Saudi Arabia explained that "the election system has no place in the Islamic creed, which calls for a government of advice and consultation and for the shepherd's openness to his flock." This argument—that democracy is un-Islamic—may be convenient for Arab monarchs, but it carries little weight. The Arab tradition of consultation, referred to by Fahd, can readily be stretched to encompass democratic principles provided the will exists to do so. Certainly, outside the Arabian Peninsula Islam has been no barrier to political freedom; half the world's Muslims live under elected governments—in places such as Indonesia, India, Bangladesh, Malaysia, and Turkey.

Islam is no barrier to liberty, but neither is it irrelevant to the prospects for actually achieving democratic change. In countries where Islam is interpreted conservatively, there is a risk that democracy—especially when promoted in a tri-

---

* Egypt between the two world wars developed a functioning multiparty system, but this vanished when the military seized power in 1952.

umphal way by the United States—will not be welcomed as a companion to Islam but feared as a proposed replacement. Confusion about the intent behind certain words adds to the problem. Some Muslims, like some Christians and Jews, tend to equate the term "secular" with "godless," not accepting that one can be religious and still approach many matters of state without specific reference to religion. "To be a secularist," one expert writes, "has meant to . . . reject altogether not only religious faith but also its attendant morality and the traditions and rules that operate within Muslim societies." This perception has undoubtedly been strengthened by the experience of Muslims under such heavy-handed secular leaders as Nasser in Egypt and the shah in Iran.

These and other issues create an opening for some Muslims to argue that democracy is being advanced for the express purpose of weakening Islam. In rebuttal, advocates of reform should make clear that backing democracy does not mean choosing the rule of humans over that of God. On the contrary; it means denying to despots the right to play God. Democracy gives a voice to every citizen, not just the privileged few. I heard one Muslim leader, a Nigerian, argue that Islam is the most democratic of faiths for just this reason. Everyone is considered equal before God.

Some commentators suggest that the importance of religion is overstated and that the only truly relevant issues are economic—that once Arabs are convinced democracy will allow them to live more prosperously, nothing else will matter. This reminds me of the moment in the movie *The Graduate* when Dustin Hoffman's character is assured that the key to his future happiness is a career in plastics. There is a certain mind-set in the West that assumes everyone wants to live like a westerner. According to this line of thinking, if Arabs and other Muslims are resentful, it can only be because they envy the material wealth and comfortable lifestyle of the West. The opposing possibility is not considered: that at least some Arabs believe the West is trying to lure them into superficial, decadent lives and thereby leave them forever damned. Material interests matter, but history tells us that strongly held ideas, whether enlightened or misguided, matter more. "If one were to ask if Muslims want freedom," wrote one leading Islamic scholar, "the answer would definitely be yes. But the vast majority of Muslims would add that, first of all, for them freedom does not mean freedom *from* God and religion; they would embrace other freedoms, provided they do not destroy their faith and what gives meaning to their lives."

Another school of thought suggests that the two halves of democratic reform—economic and political—can come only in sequence. According to this theory, Arabs are not ready for democracy. They must first become better educated, more broadly prosperous, more middle-class: in other words, more western. This is condescending; it also ignores the fact that economic and political reforms reinforce one another. Authoritarianism is a roadblock to development whereas democracy helps smooth the way. Some Arab leaders are nevertheless strongly attracted to the idea of putting economic reforms first, hoping that this will enable them to delay real political change indefinitely. President Hosni Mubarak of Egypt is a prime example.

Since he came to power in 1981, Mubarak has been a responsible international figure who has endorsed moderate positions in world affairs and has lent vital backing to the peace process in the Middle East. He is also a skillful politician who has implemented some necessary economic changes. He is not, however, a democrat. For almost a quarter century, he has kept a lid on political dissent by maintaining a permanent state of emergency. Any Egyptian who opposes him on any major matter risks arrest and detention, even torture. Mubarak claims that his policies are harsh out of necessity and that they have largely worked; in recent years, there have been few incidents of domestic terrorism. President Bush argues that "liberty is the solution to terror," and that the rise of Al Qaeda should push Arab regimes in the direction of democracy. Not long after 9/11, the prime minister of Egypt asserted just the opposite—that terrorism should push the United States in the direction of Egypt. "The U.S. and U.K., including human rights groups, have, in the past, been calling on us to give these terrorists their 'human rights,' " he said. "You can give them all the human rights they deserve until they kill you. After these horrible crimes committed in New York and Virginia, maybe Western countries should begin to think of Egypt's own fight against terror as their new model."

President Bush has called on Egypt to "lead the way" toward Arab democracy. Mubarak responded by agreeing to allow opposing candidates when he ran for reelection in September 2005. This produced the kind of spectacle we have seen all too often in marginally democratic countries: presidential balloting with all the trappings of democracy but little of the substance. The campaign was absurdly short, only nineteen days. The governing party controlled most of the media and campaign cash. Candidates had to meet a set of criteria that squeezed out any serious opposition to Mubarak, who, predictably, won by an overwhelming margin. As unsatisfactory as the whole charade was, there were encouraging aspects. For the first time in the country's long history, Egyptians were treated to the sight of their leader appearing at campaign rallies to ask for support. Voters were given the experience of marking ballots with more than one option. Crowds found themselves able to chant antigovernment slogans without getting clubbed, or at least not every time.

The population of Egypt is sophisticated and educated enough to support political parties across the ideological spectrum. If truly open elections were held, however, the most potent opposition to the governing party would be the Muslim Brotherhood, an Islamic group founded in 1928. Over time, the Muslim Brotherhood has periodically embraced and renounced violence, survived numerous crackdowns, and established chapters in countries throughout the Arab world. Its central tenet is that Sunni Islam provides the solution to all problems and that a return to the pure faith will cure social ills. In Egypt in recent years, it has adopted the language of democracy and has sought to collaborate with more secular reform groups. Although the organization is officially banned, its social influence remains substantial, and its members—running independently—scored impressive gains in the parliamentary elections of 2005. The Muslim Brotherhood might evolve, if permitted, into a moderate Islamist party of the type that has held power in Turkey, Indonesia, and Bosnia-Herzegovina, and now, potentially, in Iraq. Less rosy scenarios, however, are also plausible. The Egyptian government insists that the Muslim Brotherhood is preparing to use violence, and that this is why it will not allow the organization to compete for power through nonviolent means. Such is the logic of repression.

Mubarak's intention, no doubt, is to foster a managed opposition that would create a patina of democracy without threatening his own party's hold on power. A population once awakened, however, can prove difficult to control. The idea that Egyptians should have true alternatives to single-party rule is likely to gain strength between now and 2011, when the next presidential elections are scheduled. To minimize pressure for further change, Mubarak will continue to remind U.S. policy-makers of his usefulness in other arenas. With the Gaza Strip no longer under Israel's control and the Middle East situation fluid once again, he will be careful to arrange events that demonstrate his capacity to sway the Palestinians and his role as an elder statesman among Arabs.

Thirty-four years after John Kennedy's speech about freedom, independent Algeria finally held a national multiparty election. The year was 1991; the winning party was Islamist. Western policy-makers worried that the party, though empowered through a democratic process, would fail to honor democratic obligations—such as allowing a legal opposition, a free press, and an independent judiciary. When the Algerian army intervened, annulling the results, the first Bush administration was relieved. Former secretary of state James Baker explained:

> When I was at the Department of State, we pursued a policy of excluding the radical fundamentalists in Algeria, even as we recognized that this was somewhat at odds with our support of democracy. Generally speaking, when you support democracy, you take what democracy gives you. If it gives you a radical Islamic fundamentalist, you're supposed to live with it. We didn't live with it in Algeria because we felt the radical fundamentalists' views were so adverse to what we believe in . . . and to the national interests of the United States.

As history reflects, not all democratic elections are won by democrats. In most Arab societies, the largest community-based groups are organized around religion. If democracy were to blossom tomorrow, the election results would be determined more by Muslim leaders than by the small groups of academicians, businesspeople, and professionals who are the most vocal supporters of democratic change. This is certainly the case in the Palestinian Authority and Iraq.

In 2005, I cochaired a bipartisan task force on Arab democracy for the Council on Foreign Relations. My partner was the widely respected former congressman Vin Weber. The task force concluded that if Arabs are able to express their grievances freely and peacefully, they will be less likely to turn to extreme measures and more likely to build open, prosperous societies. That will benefit them and us. We argued further, however, that in promoting democratic institutions, we should bear in mind that sudden change is neither necessary nor desirable. Our goal should be to encourage democratic evolution, not revolution. This caution was not sufficient for one member of the task force, who wrote in dissent that the United States should not focus on elections in the Arab world at all. "Even the most moderate and nonviolent of Arab Islamist parties," he argued, "disagree with American goals on Arab-Israeli issues and would not be willing to accept the kind of influence the United States now exercises in the region." This analysis, based on realpolitik, strikes me as out-of-date. To believe that America can sustain its influence in Muslim countries without supporting free and fair elections is to believe that we can defeat terrorism by acting the way terrorist leaders have predicted. This would be like fighting a battle on ground that will give way beneath our feet; strategically, it does not make sense.

Some analysts fear that democracy would allow Islamist political movements to sweep into power across North Africa, through the Middle East and Gulf, and all the way to southeast Asia. The result would be a formidable bloc of states united in their hatred of Israel, their opposition to America, and their resistance to external pressure regarding terrorism and the production of nuclear arms. Although risk is inherent in democracy, such an outcome is extremely unlikely. Islam has more potential to bring these societies together than communism had, but no single movement is likely to bridge the vast cultural and theological differences within the faith.

The argument made by Mubarak and like-minded Arab leaders is that political parties organized around Islam are uniformly undemocratic and prone to violence. This was the assumption made by the United States after the Algerian election in 1991. It is a view that cannot simply be dismissed. We should, in fact, assume that free elections might result in militant Islamist regimes in some countries. Yet it would be untenable to bar the participation of broadly supported political parties on the basis of an assumption about what some might do. It is all too easy for a repressive government to label anyone who disagrees with its policies a "terrorist." The label can be self-fulfilling: persecution is more often a cause of violence than a solution to it. If democracy is to take root in the Middle East, Islamist parties cannot be excluded out of hand. Through history, many legitimate political parties had their origins outside the law; even movements once associated with terrorism should be encouraged to renounce violence and move into the mainstream.

Those worried about Islamists would be well advised to concern themselves less with trying to ban such parties and more with the challenge of competing against them at the ballot box. In his novel *Snow*, the Turkish writer Orhan Pamuk explained the success of their methods:

As for these Islamists, they go from door to door in groups, paying house visits; they give women pots and pans, and those machines that squeeze oranges, and boxes of soap, cracked wheat, and detergent. They concentrate on the poor neighborhoods; they ingratiate themselves with the women; they bring out hooked needles and sew golden thread onto the children's shoulders to protect them against evil. They say, "Give your vote to the Prosperity Party, the party of God; we've fallen into this destitution because we've wandered off the path of God. . . ." They win the trust of the angry and humiliated unemployed; they sit with their wives, who don't know where the next meal is coming from, and they give them hope; promising more gifts. . . . We're not just talking about the lowest of the low. Even people with jobs—even tradesmen— respect them, because these Islamists are more hardworking, more honest, more modest than anyone else.

The inclusion of Islamist parties will give them a stake in the democratic process, just as their exclusion would give them a stake in trying to destroy that process. Democracy is valuable because it offers the means to solve the hardest problems nonviolently, through reason, debate, and voting. The hardest problems in the Arab world today revolve around the very issues that most concern Islamist parties: What does Islam demand? How is terror defined? What should young people be taught? How do we balance modern demands with traditional values? It is better to hash these issues out through the give-and-take of democratic procedures than try to solve them through recurring cycles of violence and repression.

Some factions may indeed be determined to prevail by force and terror. Recognizing this, every political party should be required to abide by the rules of democracy, including nonviolence and respect for constitutional procedures, as many Islamist parties have already pledged they will do.* In the long run, however, the best way to marginalize violent extremists is to make room for as broad an array of nonviolent perspectives as possible. Nothing will push any political movement toward the center more quickly than the need to find policies that attract votes. President Bush, who knows something about winning elections, put the argument this way: "Maybe some will . . . say, 'Vote for me; I look forward to blowing up America,' but . . . I think people who generally run for office say, 'Vote for me; I'm looking forward to fixing your potholes or making sure you've got bread on the table.' " Tip O'Neill made the same point another way: "All politics is local."

Arab leaders should know that progress toward democracy will have favorable consequences for their relations with the United States and that the reverse is also true. Countries moving toward democracy should receive special consideration on such matters as trade, investment, and aid; and Washington should distance itself from governments that refuse over time to recognize the rights of their citizens.

The United States should support democracy in the Middle East, just as it does elsewhere around the world and for the same reasons. I hope, however, that we proceed with some degree of humility. Democracy is not a gift delivered either by God or by the United States; it is a system of government that each country may choose to develop at its own pace and in its own way. In his second inaugural address, President Bush declared, "From the day of our founding, we

---

* According to *Islamism in North Africa I: The Legacies of History* (April 2004), a report by the International Crisis Group, "Islamic political movements in North Africa no longer condemn democracy as un-Islamic or counterpose the idea of an Islamic state to the states which actually exist. In fact, they explicitly reject theocratic ideas and proclaim acceptance of democratic and pluralist principles and respect for the rules of the game as defined by existing constitutions."

have proclaimed that every man and woman on this earth has rights, and dignity and matchless value." He did not add that in the United States for the first 130 years or so, half of those people of matchless value did not have the right to vote; or that for the first seventy-five years, millions were held in chains; or that before the American civilization could be built, another civilization had to be pushed aside.

We should also be realistic about what we expect. To the administration, transforming the Middle East is necessary to keep Americans safe—not an argument the average Arab reformer is likely to use. Arab democracy, if it comes at all, will arrive with the purpose of fulfilling Arab aspirations. It will not change overnight how Arabs look at the world; nor will it spur reconciliation with Israel; nor will it ensure social liberalization. But elections are still a step in the right direction if they lead to genuine political debate. There is a big difference between a society in which opinions depend on "what everybody thinks" and a society in which citizens begin by saying, "Let me tell you what I think."

When I was in government, I often made a suggestion that my colleagues rejected at the time, only to embrace it later when they could claim it as their own. I have also often rejected someone else's suggestion only to accept it after the opportunity for additional thought. Arab leaders cannot be expected to embrace democracy overnight, or if it appears that they are being coerced into doing so. The world can hope, however, that at least some will promote a system resembling democracy, even if they call it something else. When that happens, it will not be as a favor to the West. It will happen because Arab leaders have learned, perhaps the hard way, that as John Kennedy said many years ago, the most powerful force in the world is man's desire to be free.

Sixteen

Islam in the West

—————— ⌖ ——————

S oon after I became secretary of state, I took a trip around
the world. The first five stops were in Europe. Only in
Germany was religion an issue, and the religion in question
was scientology. The Germans, claiming that scientology
was a moneymaking cult, had banned it; the United States
(for reasons *not* having to do with Tom Cruise) considered it
a valid faith. In 1997, this passed for religious controversy.

The period of such innocence is over. The attacks on the
twin towers, the bombings of trains in Madrid, and the
explosions on the subway in London have darkened our outlook. These acts of terror differed in scale but were similar
in the passions they evoked and in the images stamped on
our minds: smoke, blood-smeared faces, anxious rescue
workers, sobbing relatives, candlelight services, and forlorn
piles of flowers. As might be expected, the tragedies have
brought Europeans and Americans closer together, but in a
solidarity soured by bickering. Leaders agree on the goal of
preventing further attacks, but not on how best to achieve
that. In my travels, I have found many Europeans angry

about Iraq and convinced that President Bush's ambivalence about legal due process and his rhetoric of good versus evil do more to create terrorists than to defeat them. Europeans, having lived for a long time with the threat of terrorism from various sources, are also puzzled by the U.S. claim that 9/11 changed everything. For its part, the Bush administration has suggested that some people across the Atlantic do not take the threat seriously enough, pointing especially to the withdrawal of Spanish troops from Iraq shortly after the train bombings in Madrid—an ill-timed move that gave the terrorists precisely what they had sought.

My own experience with bombing in Europe dates back to my earliest years, when I huddled in shelters with my family and neighbors during the Battle of Britain. There was no doubt then who was to blame for the terror. The question of responsibility was fiercely debated, however, following the strikes in London in July 2005. Some, including the mayor of London (on the political left) and Tory politician Kenneth Clarke (on the right), attributed the attacks to Britain's involvement in Iraq; others blamed the hate-filled rhetoric of some British-based Muslim clerics. Neither explanation is fully persuasive. The invasion of Iraq certainly made it easier for radical imams to assert that all Muslims are under attack; but a sense of victimization provides no moral excuse for blowing up subway cars in London. Fiery preachers should be held accountable for stirring up a hornet's nest, but this doesn't mean that it was smart to give them a stick with which to hit the hive.

The quarreling has evolved into a running controversy about the definition of European values, the boundaries of free speech, and the growing problem of integrating Muslim immigrants. Since 1975, the European continent's Muslim population has tripled because of high birthrates and an influx of workers from North Africa, the Middle East, and south Asia. If these trends continue, Muslims will account for about 10 percent of the population of the European Union (EU) by 2020. Meanwhile, tens of millions of prospective migrants await their chance, restlessly biding their time on the overcrowded streets of Tunis, Rabat, Algiers, and Damascus. As anyone who has spent time recently navigating the sidewalks of such cities as London, Paris, and Berlin can attest, the dam separating Christian Europe from the Muslim East has sprung a leak, altering Europe's culture.

The arrival of immigrants in any society has an impact on the host country's sense of self. In the United States, each successive wave of immigration has generated worries that the American identity would become diluted or lost. The recent rise in Asian and Latino populations has set off just such a volatile reaction; but the adjustment is even harder in Europe, whose countries are less accustomed to absorbing foreigners. The expansion of the EU to the east, north, and south has given fresh flavor to the old query about what it means to be European. Is it solely a question of where you lay your head at night, or is the answer determined by values, customs, and beliefs? As one church leader in Germany has remarked, "The countries of Europe have the same basic culture. We know how to live together with Catholics and Protestants because we have a common belief in Christ and common convictions. But relations with Muslims are quite different. . . . The U.S. is a coming-together of people from many cultures. But traditionally the countries of Europe have had the same form and culture."

I was eleven years old when my family arrived in the United States. Although proud of my European heritage, I had only one ambition in my new home, and that was to fit in. Eager to be seen as a bona fide American teenager, I chewed bubble gum, devoured comic books, and imitated the way my more stylish classmates dressed and talked. It drove me crazy when my parents acted foreign, with my mother telling fortunes and my father so formal that he wore a coat and tie even when fishing. In Europe today, the generational breakdown in many Muslim families is just the reverse. The elders may be more committed to blending in than their children or grandchildren. Young people in Birmingham, Marseille, and Rotterdam, just as much as those in Cairo and Casablanca, feel called—or pressured by their peers—to assert their Islamic identity by speaking out politically and by wearing the badges of faith: the head scarf, veil, and beard.

The challenge of integration is especially acute in France, the scene of widespread rioting in the fall of 2005, following the accidental electrocution of two Muslim teenagers who were fleeing the police. Young people, many unemployed and living in projects, burned thousands of cars to protest discrimination, vent frustration about harassment, and, as some admitted, "have fun." French authorities responded by invoking a state of emergency for the first time since the Algerian war of independence half a century earlier. Those analyzing the protests blamed the French for acting as if their slogan "Liberty, Equality, and Fraternity" were the reality instead of an ideal. The French secular state does not recognize racial or religious distinctions; thus, there is no basis for policies that might seek to reduce high unemployment among citizens of North African extraction. Conducting a survey on the basis of color or creed is something the Americans or British might do, but not the French. This leaves the recent immigrants in a bind; they are told they are fully French, but they are often treated as second-class citizens when they apply for a job or shop for an apartment or house. To address this, the government has appointed a council to fight discrimination and has begun considering the possibility of some sort of affirmative action

program. That would be, for France, a step both revolution-
ary and sure to be resisted by the country's robust right wing.

Even before the riots in France, European leaders were
increasingly anxious about the inability or unwillingness of
recent migrants to integrate themselves into the life of their
adopted countries. For Muslims in Europe, it is not a question of Islam and the West; their lives reflect the dilemma
and opportunity of Islam *in* the West. The ability of Europe
to translate this reality into something positive is still being
measured.*

I had the opportunity to discuss this challenge in September
2005 at a conference hosted by former president Clinton in
New York. Among those participating was Mustafa Cerić, the
grand mufti of Bosnia. Cerić suggested that many Europeans
have given short shrift to the contributions made by Muslims
and Jews to European history. For centuries, Muslim families
have lived in Central Europe and the Balkans; in the West,
there are millions of second- and third-generation immigrants
who are full members of their communities. It is the large flow
of newcomers that has created an awkward mix. Cerić said
that Muslims need to accept that they cannot expect Islamic
law to govern in a place where they are a minority, but that
Europeans need to accept the right of Muslims to live in equality with others. He proposed a social contract in which
European Muslims would pledge their unequivocal commitment to democratic principles while also asserting their political, economic, and religious rights. Cerić argues that Muslims

---

* The issues of integration and identity that are addressed in this chapter are
also relevant in the United States, but to a lesser extent. Although exact numbers
are elusive, Muslims probably make up between 1 and 2 percent of the American
population. Of that number, at least one-third are African Americans born in the
United States. The shape and direction of "American Islam" are vibrant subjects
of study and discussion within the religious and academic communities.

should focus on their responsibilities in order to be worthy of freedom and that Europeans must realize that Islam is not alien to their culture but part of it.

Cerić's task is complicated by a combustible political environment in which charges of prejudice are tossed around at the slightest provocation by one side and allegations of radicalism by the other. In September 2005, a Danish newspaper printed a series of cartoons that caricatured the Prophet Muhammad and associated him with terrorism. A wave of protests, some violent, erupted when the offensive cartoons were reprinted elsewhere in Europe and made available on the Internet. The hysteria dramatized both the divide between secular Europe and Muslims, and the eagerness of extremists on all sides to turn hate to their advantage. The publication of the cartoons, though an exercise in free speech, was also an act of bigotry. The protests were equally an exercise in free speech, except for those that turned violent. The whole sad episode, a triumph of emotion over reason, was deeply regrettable. The attitudes that gave rise to it, however, were hardly new.

In 1991, I participated in a *Los Angeles Times* survey entitled "The Pulse of Europe." We were not surprised to find prejudice toward minority groups, but I was still stunned by the extent of ill feeling toward Muslims, especially those who had emigrated from North Africa. During the war in Bosnia, I was further shocked (and depressed) by the attitude of some of my European colleagues who seemed to consider the Bosniak Muslims less civilized than their Serb and Croat tormenters. It has been common in recent years to hear shrill cries of "Europe for the Europeans" and "Foreigners go home." Politicians routinely call for tighter restrictions on immigration while Muslims complain they are being discriminated against, the victims of "Islamaphobia." The recent crisis of the cartoons was preceded by other ugly events—the murders, in 2002, of a Dutch politician who had criticized Islam, and in October 2004, of a second Dutchman, this one a filmmaker, who had released what was perceived to be a virulently anti-Muslim film.

Meanwhile, the culture of tolerance, long a source of pride to many Europeans, is being questioned by those who say that too much live-and-let-live leads to a loss of control. Indeed, experts worry that Europe could become the next major breeding ground for terrorists: a place where conspirators can conceal themselves behind the protective wall of legal due process, relatively easy access to social benefits, the tradition of free speech, and the absence of capital punishment. Europe's mainstream Muslim leaders are worried about the same thing. They have tried diligently to grab the microphone away from ideologues whose angry pronouncements earn headlines but embarrass and even endanger the law-abiding Muslim majority.* The presence of extreme elements, however, is uncontested.

In April 2004, the British police uncovered a half-ton cache of ammonium nitrate fertilizer, an explosive ingredient used earlier in terrorist attacks in Bali and Turkey. This discovery led to the arrest of eight Muslim men. Later that year, the Spanish police apprehended a group of Pakistanis allegedly linked to Al Qaeda. Early in 2005, the German and French police broke up cells recruiting insurgents for Iraq.

---

* The bombings in London have also prompted American Muslim leaders to intensify their efforts to prevent violent extremism. According to Salam al-Marayati, executive director of the Muslim Public Affairs Council in Los Angeles: "Before, people thought, 'We have nothing to do with the terrorism; our religion is clear and it should be obvious to everyone else.' Now, we can't afford to be bystanders anymore, we have to be involved in constructive intervention. So we're doing it collectively, speaking out with one voice and now telling our children that they have to get it right, they can't be confused and can't give any credence to anybody who comes to them and says there is room for violence."

Operatives of Abu Musab al-Zarqawi's terrorist organization have been arrested in six European countries. British officials estimate that 10,000 to 15,000 Muslims in the United Kingdom are supporters of Al Qaeda and that as many as 600 have received training from violent groups in Afghanistan or elsewhere.

It is frustrating to authorities that the terror suspects do not fit neatly into any demographic profile. Though most are from immigrant families, the perpetrators of the subway bombings were all British-born; one was quite well off, and none had a history of violence. If there is a pattern, it is that recruits experience a sharp change in attitude toward religion. A Muslim who has been drifting through life giving little heed to his faith may suddenly find a new identity through devotion and militance. The British prime minister, Tony Blair, told me, "Part of the Muslim community is just not integrating. Jews, Hindus, Chinese, and the majority of Muslims have integrated, but there are pockets of Muslims dedicated to extremism." Because there is no central authority in Sunni Islam, one does not have to be a religious scholar to preach. "In these neighborhoods, you have someone get up and announce, 'I am an imam and here is a fatwa,' " says Blair. That is why the radical imams can be so dangerous. What they teach is not real Islam but rather a version distorted by politics and the kind of out-of-context Quranic quotations favored by bin Laden. Young Muslims looking for something meaningful to care about can be fooled into thinking they have found it in the call to holy war; they are born again as terrorists.

It doesn't help that prisons in Europe are filled disproportionately with Muslims. In France, they make up a majority of the imprisoned population. Experts in counterterrorism fear that the criminal population is prime territory for the kind of recruitment that Al Qaeda practices.* Few western prisons are equipped to offer sound moral guidance to large numbers of Muslim inmates. European governments are alert to the problem but uncertain how to respond. Some have tried dispersing Muslim prisoners; others argue that this only spreads the danger. In any case, prison space is limited. Another challenge is finding a way to prevent ethnic neighborhoods from degenerating into ghettos. The latter are home to the kind of economically deprived and socially out-of-joint populations that a century ago might have been attracted to the utopian promise of Marxism. People who have left one country only to find the new one inhospitable may feel robbed of any national loyalty and eager to pledge themselves to a more universal cause.

In the face of all this, European leaders have little choice but to reconsider their approach to the balancing act between the imperatives of security and the principles of democracy. The question being asked in both religious and secular circles is whether it is wiser to try to accommodate the customs and values of immigrants or to insist that they fully conform to European rules. Hard-liners suggest that dialogue is fruitless because it fails to reach the people most likely to cause trouble; terrorists don't attend ecumenical conferences, nor are they swayed by appeals to shared moral concerns. Safety should come first.

In that spirit, efforts are under way in many countries to

---

* Richard Reid, who boarded a Miami-bound airplane in December 2001 with a bomb in his shoe, converted to Islam in a British jail. Mohammed Bouyeri, the murderer of the Dutch filmmaker Theo van Gogh, became radicalized during a seven-month jail term. Late in 2004, Spanish officials arrested thirteen North African immigrants for planning to blow up the national court in Madrid. The men were small-time criminals who, after meeting in prison, decided to form their own terror group, Martyrs for Morocco.

expand the authority of the police to spy on and detain suspected terrorists. Several countries have made it easier to expel extremist preachers and have begun programs to train moderate ones, in the hope of nurturing the development of a European version of Islam. Some countries have begun to finance mosques in order to make them less dependent on sources (such as Saudi Arabia) that counsel Islamic separation rather than social integration. In the Netherlands, Muslim clerics are required to conduct their services in Dutch instead of Arabic. Blair's government has moved to ban groups that have a history of supporting terror and has created a blacklist to block alleged sympathizers from entering Britain and deport those already there. It has also taken steps to outlaw the kind of preaching, articles, and websites that foment terrorism.

Democracy is based on the premise of settling policy differences through a process of open debate. A democratic government that shuts down whole categories of speech will immediately find itself in alien territory, walking the same ground as tyrants. The communists who seized control of Czechoslovakia in the years following World War II would not tolerate dissent; that is why my family ended up in the United States. For centuries, dictators have filled their jails with people whose ideas were judged dangerous, provocative, or likely to incite violence against the prevailing order. More recently, despots in many countries have used the threat of terrorism as an excuse to silence violent and nonviolent opponents alike. The risk in today's Europe (and for that matter, the United States) is that the difference between advocating terrorism and criticizing policy will be blurred, turning the law into a means of stifling legitimate debate.

That risk, however, must be weighed against others, including the possibility that inflammatory words will lead to incendiary actions, a sequence for which there is also much precedent. The old saying about free speech is that it does not extend to yelling "Fire!" in a crowded theater. We are in a crowded theater now, and I think it fair to proscribe public speech that is clearly intended to promote terrorism. I also find myself in agreement with Blair's warning to those who arrive in Great Britain from other countries, whether in search of a political safe haven or economic opportunity. "Staying here carries with it a duty," he said. "That duty is to share and support the values that sustain the British way of life. Those who break that duty and try to incite hatred or engage in violence against our country and its people have no place here." The same caution would be appropriate in the United States.

In saying this, I am placing my faith in the vigor of American and European civil society, an independent judiciary, and democracy itself to protect against abuses of power. The balance we must seek on both sides of the Atlantic is really nothing more than the product of common sense: stopping those who would destroy our system, without ourselves undermining the basic principles that define that system.

The real victory over terrorism will come not through silencing anyone, but through the amplification of more reasoned voices such as that of Mustafa Cerić. In Europe, as elsewhere, the battle that counts most is the one that is being waged for the heart and soul of Islam at every level, within families, neighborhoods, communities, and nations. In this battle, every ally can make a difference and every potential ally should be sought out. For that reason, I worry about the possibility that Europe and the United States will turn their backs on the people and government of Turkey, longtime friends of the West who are in a unique position to help.

•   •   •

The victory of the Allies in World War I destroyed what remained of the Ottoman Empire; from its ashes there emerged something never before seen: a secular Muslim state. The republic of Turkey was created in the image of its first president, Kemal Atatürk, a man of boundless energy intent on building a country both modern and oriented toward the West. Atatürk brashly described religion as "a poisonous dagger directed at the heart of my people." Reacting against the crowd-pleasing dervishes and religious sheikhs of the time, he declared, "I flatly refuse to believe that today, in the luminous presence of science, knowledge, and civilization, . . . there exist, in the civilized community of Turkey, men so primitive as to seek their material and moral well-being from the guidance of . . . [a] sheikh."

Atatürk took a sledgehammer to the foundations of society, abolishing the Islamic caliphate and asserting control over religion on behalf of the state. At his direction, religious schools were closed, the Turkish language was latinized, a western-style constitution was adopted, and the practice of separating the sexes in the classroom and workplace was ended. "We will not catch up with the modern world," he proclaimed, "if we only modernize half the population." In the decades since then, the Turkish military has served as the guardian of Atatürk's legacy, preserving the secular nature of the government. Eager to cement its status as a western country, Turkey began in 1960 to apply for membership in the European Common Market, which later became the EU; it is still knocking on the door.

Like most exclusive clubs, the EU selects its own members. Meddling by American secretaries of state is not welcome. While in office, I nevertheless did my best to nudge my European colleagues in the direction of accepting Turkey. My view, reflected in U.S. policy, was that a prosperous, pro-western Turkey was needed to ensure stability in a sensitive region. I was pleased when, in 1999, the EU finally declared that Turkey was an official candidate. The Turkish government has since been checking the boxes on a long list of changes required for it to meet European norms. It has abolished the death penalty, reformed its judiciary, adopted a new penal code, changed its banking laws, and implemented stronger protections for human rights. Most of the reforms have been implemented under the leadership of the Islamist Peace and Development Party, which has confounded the Islamist stereotype by accepting Atatürk's secular model, moving toward the political center, and generally respecting the rights of Turkey's women and minorities.

Turkey is uniquely important because it is the only member of NATO included in the Organization of the Islamic Conference, representing the world's Muslim states; it is also one of the few Muslim countries to have diplomatic relations with Israel. In the words of the Turkish foreign minister, Abdullah Gül, "At a time when people are talking of a clash of civilizations, Turkey is a natural bridge of civilizations. All we are trying to do is to use our position to bring Islam and the West closer together." Joschka Fischer, at the time Germany's foreign minister, echoed this thought: "To modernize an Islamic country based on the shared values of Europe would be almost a D-Day for Europe in the war against terror." So it seemed a breakthrough when the EU decided in December 2004 to take the next step, declaring that Turkey had made enough progress to warrant the start of formal negotiations. The question is whether these negotiations will lead Europeans to embrace Turkish Muslims or to give them the diplomatic equivalent of a cold shoulder.

When, in June 2005, French and Dutch voters rejected a proposed new constitution for the EU, anti-Turkish sentiment received much of the blame. Although most European leaders have expressed support for Turkey's application, the majority of their constituents are unconvinced. The process of enlarging the EU is based on a vision of the continent as dynamic and outward-looking, but many Europeans would prefer—in the face of globalization—to hunker down. Enlargement has already enabled millions of new workers to compete for jobs. Europeans are reluctant to open their borders and markets further to Turkey, a country both big (with 70 million people) and poor (with a per capita income roughly half that of Poland.)

The difficulties go beyond dollars and euros, however, to a more fundamental question: whether Turkish culture is compatible with that of the rest of Europe. The disdain toward Muslims I had encountered during the Bosnian conflict was also directed toward Turkey. This reflects the realities that virtually all of Europe has waged war against Turks at some point; that the Greeks have clashed repeatedly with Turkey over Cyprus and certain islands in the Aegean; and that Christians have not forgotten the Turks' massacre of Armenians during World War I. This history, distant as some of it is, has instilled enduring prejudice. Prime Minister Silvio Berlusconi of Italy has boasted about the "superiority" of European civilization compared with that of the "Islamic countries." Valéry Giscard d'Estaing, a former president of France, has declared that "Turkey is not a European country"; its admission, he says, would mean "the end of the European Union." Before becoming Pope Benedict XVI, Cardinal Joseph Ratzinger expressed his opposition to Turkey's application, saying that "Turkey has always represented a different continent, in contrast with Europe."

The failure of the European constitution to pass muster with voters was a traumatic setback for advocates of a larger EU. There are many who would now like the question of Turkey's membership to be forgotten. It should not. To push Turkey away would be a monumental error. It would also be yet another gift to those seeking to stir up trouble between Muslims and the West.

Assuming that the negotiations do proceed, several principles should be kept in mind. First, the EU and Turkey have already reached an understanding. If Turkey continues its rapid progress toward European standards, it has a right to expect European leaders to endorse its membership. That is the whole rationale behind the negotiating process.

Second, Turkey's European identity should not be questioned. Although the Ottoman Empire was, at times, more than a European power, it was never less than a European power. Turkey still includes regions that are inward-looking, where day-to-day life has changed little in hundreds of years; but since Atatürk, there can be no question that Turkey's primary focus is toward the West.

Third, Turkey's religious identity should not be relevant to its application to join the EU. That principle appears basic, but is by no means clearly understood. Both Europe and Turkey have secular governments. Europe, like the United States, has evolved into a multidenominational society. Just as important, the EU is organized around the norms of western democracy, at the heart of which is religious liberty. It would betray Europe's own values to exclude a country on religious grounds.

Finally, it is unconvincing to argue, as some do, that Turkey's membership would disrupt the cultural harmony of Europe. That line of thinking might have made sense in the days of a Common Market with only half a dozen members, but today's EU, with twenty-five members, is a cultural kaleidoscope. Adding Turkey will not change that.

During the 1990s, the prospect of joining NATO provided a powerful incentive for democratic reform within the newly free countries of Central and Eastern Europe. Instead of resuming historic rivalries, they focused on democratic goals, such as respect for the rule of law, human rights, free enterprise, and civilian control of the military. NATO provided a magnet for positive change, a place where onetime rivals could work together on behalf of peace. The EU has been serving a similar function, but that will continue only if it leaves the door open to new applicants and keeps its mind open in judging those who apply. Says Tony Blair, "No doubt very few countries would vote yes if there were a referendum on Turkish membership today. That's why we have to work to change the perceptions. To qualify, Turkey has come a long way; it would be a mistake now for us to push it in the other direction."

The United States has its own obligations. The decision of the Bush administration to invade Iraq shocked the Turks, 40 percent of whom—according to a survey made in 2005—now see America as their biggest enemy. A best-selling Turkish novel, *Metal Storm*, predicts an American invasion of Turkey, prompting in retaliation the detonation of a nuclear bomb near the White House.

I have traveled to Turkey several times in recent years. The fact that the United States invaded Iraq—Turkey's neighbor—without taking Turkey's perspective into account will not soon be forgotten. That perspective is heavily influenced by the Turks' complicated and inglorious relationship with the Kurds. Turkey is worried that an autonomous Kurdistan inside Iraq will encourage nationalist ambitions within its own Kurdish minority; it is upset that Kurdish terrorists have retained a foothold inside northern Iraq; and it is worried that Iraqi Kurds will out-muscle Iraq's Turkish minority for control of the prized oil-rich city of Kirkuk. Future American policy does not have to mesh perfectly with Turkish policy on these issues, but it would be wise to tread lightly and cooperate where possible, while still insisting on respect for Kurdish rights.

Looking ahead ten years, it seems likely that the dominant power in the Persian Gulf will be Iran, allied with the Shiite majority in Iraq. It would be hard to overstate the importance of Turkey at that point, as a member of NATO, a leader within the organization of Muslim states, a friend to Israel, and a potentially unifying force throughout Europe and the Near East. It would be comparably difficult, therefore, to overestimate the value for Europe and the United States of treating Turkish interests seriously. If the West does not respect a Muslim country such as Turkey that has been so responsive to our concerns, it will be hard to make the case to any other Muslim country that friendship will be rewarded.

Small gestures can sometimes make a big difference. I made this observation to Turkish officials who didn't agree or disagree; they just waited for the subject to change. That subject was the status of the Halki Greek Orthodox seminary on the island of Heybeliada, about an hour's ride by boat from Istanbul. The seminary began operations in 1844 and has been described as "a splendid piece of mid-nineteenth-century architecture—airy, high-ceilinged and with views of the city in every direction." The facility was shut down in 1971, not because it was involved in anything subversive but because its very existence was deemed an affront to the secular rules of the Turkish state. If Muslim institutions were not allowed to operate outside the government's control, why should a Christian seminary be allowed to do so?—or so the thinking went. This policy falls into the category of what Emerson referred to as "a foolish consistency."

Speaking as a friend and also as an American official, I pressed the Turks repeatedly to reopen the seminary as a gesture of goodwill toward the world's 250 million Orthodox

Christians—a move made more meaningful by a curious fact of history: that the center of Orthodox Christianity is not in a Christian country but in Turkey. Not even the Ottoman conquest of Constantinople in 1453 could dislodge the patriarchate—the Orthodox equivalent of the Vatican—from its historic capital.

Along with President and Mrs. Clinton, I had an opportunity to meet with Ecumenical Patriarch Bartholomew at his headquarters in the middle of Istanbul's old city. Istanbul is beautiful, but also noisy and crowded. The patriarchate, by contrast, is serene, mystical, and unassuming. The patriarch himself is a Turkish citizen, an alumnus of both the Halki seminary and the Turkish army reserve. He looks as you might expect a patriarch to look, with a long white beard, medallions, and a cross draped around his neck, and cloaked in a magnificent black robe.

Since he entered office in 1991, Bartholomew has earned praise for his environmental activism and his efforts at interfaith reconciliation. He is an intellectual, speaks seven languages, and is a thoughtful man; but he seemed genuinely puzzled when talking about the Halki seminary. He did not understand who profited from leaving the institution empty, or how the seminary or indeed Turkey's tiny Christian minority could be considered a threat to anyone. On the contrary, the seminary's reopening would surely boost Turkey's prospects for joining the EU, a goal the patriarch fully supports. The government says that it wants to find a solution, but after thirty-five years, that quest should be completed. The fate of a single center of learning would not seem to matter much in the relationship between two civilizations; but in a world such as ours, we should never underestimate what can be accomplished through civilized acts.

Seventeen

Africa: A Race for Souls

W e are heading—you can see it—toward a clash," said a Muslim leader in Uganda. The United States "will never stop fighting you until you turn away from your religion." "There is a race," said another Ugandan, this one a Christian minister. "Islam is also racing for the soul and the mind of the African." Nowhere is the global religious revival more in evidence than in Africa, where two opposing tides are rising and the information revolution is bringing the exhortations of Christian preachers and Muslim clerics into living rooms and community halls. Muslim countries in the Middle East and North Africa (notably Saudi Arabia and Libya) are pouring money in to educate and indoctrinate Africa's young. New mosques and religious schools are proliferating; instruction in Arabic is increasing; Islam is finding a substantial foothold even in traditionally Christian countries such as Zambia, Rwanda, and Uganda.

Meanwhile, the number of Africans who call themselves evangelical Christians has risen in just three decades from 17 million to an estimated 125 million; overall, there are now more than 350 million African Christians. The region is awash in storefront churches, revival tents, and bumper stickers reading "Jesus Saves." The Bible and related texts have been translated into hundreds of local languages and dialects.* It is anticipated that within twenty years there will be more Christians in Africa than in Europe and North America combined. This expansion has been helped along by missionaries of many nationalities and financed by affiliated churches in the West.

Much of this is good. Faith can provide hope to people who, burdened by the hardships of daily life, might be tempted to despair. Financial contributions—whether from the Middle East or Middle America—can build much-needed schools, clinics, and community centers. The connection established between Africans and U.S. churches can deepen understanding and support for America's perspective on democracy and terrorism, while raising awareness about such abuses as domestic violence and female genital mutilation.

The simultaneous expansion of Islamic and Christian activism also poses risks. In countries where populations are evenly divided, tense rivalries have emerged. In countries where one faith is dominant, the minority often feels intimidated. Africa today is a religious battleground, just as it was an ideological battleground during the cold war. That contest, too, had its positive side. The United States, western

---

* Missionaries have grown skilled at adapting their message to local surroundings. A creed composed for the Masai tribe reads: "We believe that God made good his promise by sending his Son Jesus Christ, a man in the flesh, a Jew by tribe, born poor in a little village, who left his home and *was always on safari* doing good, curing people by the power of God and man, showing that the meaning of religion is love. He was rejected by his people, tortured and nailed hands and feet to a cross, and died. He lay buried in the grave but *the hyenas did not touch him*, and on the third day, he rose from the grave." Cited in Jaroslav Pelikan, *Whose Bible Is It?* Viking, New York, 2005, 215.

Europe, the Soviet Union, and China all financed development in Africa, and each was eager to educate and thereby lure into its camp the rising generation of African elites. Those pluses were outweighed, however, by the lives that were lost when local rivalries escalated into proxy fights in a long list of countries including Chad, Sudan, Ethiopia, Somalia, Angola, Mozambique, and Zaire. As surrogates for communism and the free world slugged it out, arms flooded the region; compliant but autocratic governments were propped up; and essential nation-building tasks, such as instilling a sense of citizenship and creating strong state institutions, were neglected.

Economically and socially, the paramount need in Africa remains what it has been for decades: to build cohesive societies with good governments that can spur development. That task is made harder in almost every case by the ethnic and linguistic diversity so characteristic of Africa. It is further complicated when individuals or groups feel called on to place their religious identity ahead of national loyalty.

The traditional African religions make no such demand. Animistic beliefs are universal and are based on a conviction that God is present in all creatures and objects, and that the spirits of ancestors are also present in the world. Unlike the newer faiths, animistic rites are blended with daily life; there is no enforced separation, as when Christians attend church or Muslims halt other activities to pray; nor are there symbolic confrontations between Bible and Quran, cross and crescent, Arabic and local tongues.

A government trying to organize an army or build a better public school system will find itself stymied if every move must be analyzed for its impact on the competition between Christians and Muslims. This rivalry can become especially bitter when proselytizers shift from celebrating their own faith to denigrating the other. Muslims may dismiss followers of Jesus as polytheists who worship three gods instead of one. Christians may characterize Muhammad as an unworthy figure, warlike, lecherous, and unimpressive compared to the miracle-working Jesus. Although such religious one-upmanship has been practiced since Muslim traders first visited Africa's coasts in the seventh century, in recent years the sniping has grown worse.

Problematic relations between Muslims and Christians may well be aggravated by outsiders—most well-intentioned, some not—who see themselves as having a stake in Africa's internal struggle. There is also a risk that savvy Africans will exploit this outside interest to attract financial and political support for "moral" causes that are actually quite the opposite. It wouldn't be the first time. Funds raised for Islamic charities have often been diverted for political or personal gain; and in the 1980s, the American Christian right backed murderous Mozambican and Angolan rebel groups who had religious pretensions but only selfish interests at heart.

Violence between Christians and Muslims is a problem in many parts of Africa, but it has created particular havoc in Sudan, the continent's largest country, and Nigeria, the most populous. Both countries have much to fight over, including oil. Both are influential—Sudan in Africa's north and east, Nigeria in the west—and each has engaged the interest of the United States.

Although U.S. policy-makers are often criticized for neglecting Africa, I visited the continent seven times while I was in government, stopping in almost two dozen nations, including, in the spring of 1994, Sudan. I was anxious because this was my first diplomatic mission to a government we considered hostile. Still, our party was received correctly enough by President Omar al-Bashir, a former military officer who had several years earlier come to power through a coup.

Bashir, in his early fifties, had a mustache and a well-trimmed short beard. He was tough-looking and wielded a wooden staff; he exuded seriousness. However, before getting down to business he presented me with a tall glass filled with a pink liquid that appeared to have the consistency of shampoo. I had often joked that my job as an ambassador was to eat and drink for my country, but this seemed beyond the call of duty. I noticed, moreover, that Bashir was not drinking anything, nor were any of the other Sudanese. Why? It occurred to me that they might actually be trying to poison me. With Bashir watching, I took what I hoped was a convincing sip of the stuff but barely swallowed anything. The taste was sweet, like Pepto-Bismol. To my relief, I didn't keel over.

The substance of my meeting with Bashir was no more satisfying than the refreshments. My purpose had been to convey a warning about Sudan's role in providing a safe haven for terrorists. The warning was not heeded. The following year the government was implicated in a failed attempt to assassinate the president of Egypt. At the time, Sudanese authorities were in the process of trying to turn their country into the regional vanguard of Islamic revolution. Among the terrorists to whom they played host was Osama bin Laden, whose construction company built highways that helped Sudan's military in its fight against southern separatists.

Sudan is one-fourth the size of the United States, stretching from the shores of the Red Sea to the continent's tropical center. The northern half is poor; its inhabitants are mostly Arab Muslim. The south is even poorer and is home to black African animists and Christians, as well as some Muslims.

The fertile land could easily feed all of Sudan and more; instead it is littered with land mines. Since achieving independence in 1956, Sudan has been the scene of almost nonstop civil war. Leaders in the capital, Khartoum, have for decades sought to consolidate political control over the south, in part because of its oil. In the 1980s, they sought religious control as well, through the imposition of sharia law. Southern rebel movements, though themselves divided, have fought for independence or autonomy. The result has been a permanent humanitarian crisis, made worse by dust storms and droughts, and marked by the brutal fighting, which has claimed some 2 million lives. Although all sides have been guilty of killing civilians, Bashir's government has been the primary abuser, blocking food supplies, attacking villages, and driving huge numbers of displaced people into areas where they could not survive.

Seeking ways to help, I met both in Africa and in Washington with those who bore witness to the war's carnage. Their stories of starvation, slavery, religious persecution, torture, and attacks on civilians infuriated me. I was moved by the young Sudanese who presented me with a carving of a black Christ and by groups of American schoolchildren who came to offer prayers. A Catholic bishop, who had been working in the Nuba Mountains, reported the death of more than a dozen first-graders whose school had been intentionally bombed. A spokesman for the government had responded to the tragedy outrageously, saying that the school was a legitimate military target. The bishop asked for my help in seeing that such atrocities did not recur. I was sitting there with all the power of the United States behind me, but had to say I was unsure what more we could do. We had long since imposed military and economic sanctions. We had also made clear to Sudan that if it wanted normal relations, it would have to curb its violations of human rights. In addition, we had provided more than $1 billion in humanitarian relief to the victims of the fighting, and appointed a special envoy to assist negotiations between the government and the south.

The commander of the southern rebels was John Garang. He was fifty-two years old when I first met with him in Uganda, a stocky man with a round bald head and a short salt-and-pepper beard framing his rotund chin. Educated in the United States, Garang had a reputation for beguiling everyone from communist theoreticians to Christian activists; and I was not surprised when he told me precisely what I wanted to hear: he supported peace, respected human rights, was willing to share power, and hoped Sudan would evolve into a democratic country. We knew that Garang's record was far from spotless, and we were not about to get the United States involved militarily in Sudan's civil war. We did, however, see Garang as the only person potentially able to unite the south and thereby put pressure on the government to mend its ways. Garang, a fighter since 1983, had the intelligence and charismatic style of a true leader, and was knowledgeable about economic and military matters alike. His portrait adorned banners and T-shirts all over the south.

The attacks of 9/11 may not have changed everything, but they did scare Sudan's government into seeking improved relations with Washington. Suddenly, Bashir started to be helpful on terrorism and also to negotiate productively, albeit unhurriedly, with Garang. The American envoy, John Danforth, an Episcopal minister and former senator, prodded the north and south relentlessly. Finally, in 2005, the two sides reached a settlement, pledging to merge their armies and share political power and oil revenues. The pact was met with jubilation. An estimated 1 million people jammed the central square in Khartoum to cheer when the pair of longtime enemies—Bashir and Garang—raised their clasped hands as partners in a new government. There was, literally, dancing in the streets.

The ceremony took place on July 9 and coincided with Garang's installation as vice president. This was the high point. Three weeks later, Garang was killed in a helicopter accident. Orators at his funeral compared him to Moses, a leader cut down after the merest glimpse of the promised land. Shocked but putting on his best face, Garang's successor, Salva Kir Mayardit, held hands with Bashir and promised to honor the legacy of his fallen leader by implementing peace.

I am hopeful but not optimistic. There are figures within the Sudanese military who profited under the old arrangements and have no interest in working as partners with the south. They can be counted on to pit various factions in the region against one another, a task that will be easier with Garang no longer around to quell fights. The former rebels will have to heal their own divisions and at the same time develop the administrative skills required to deliver public services. The UN will help, and so will the return from exile of many educated Sudanese, but the country's development needs are boundless. The religious divide will remain an obstacle to unity as Islamist activists seek to expand their influence in the face of resistance from Christians and animists. Even more seriously, the peace agreement does not provide for peace throughout Sudan. It does not extend to the Darfur region in western Sudan, where murderous militias backed by the government have sought to purge non-Arabs at the cost of hundreds of thousands of lives. The government has also continued to provide a safe haven for Uganda's loathsome Lord's Resistance Army. Despite efforts to rehabilitate himself internationally, Bashir still has much to answer for.

Under the peace agreement, national elections are scheduled for 2009. Two years later, the south will be entitled to hold a referendum on whether or not to secede. Although Garang was committed to keeping the country intact, the prospect of secession will entice many of his followers. The United States should do all it can to help the peace settlement take hold and to encourage a broader diplomatic solution that will finally bring an end to the genocide in Darfur and the grotesque violence in northern Uganda. Recognizing that religion cannot be ignored, we must continually make clear that our policies are aimed at helping all Sudanese. We should do what we can to prevent divisive outside forces, whether Christian or Muslim, from making matters worse by their meddling. Instead of trying to do everything ourselves, we should work in partnership with other countries and support the efforts of faith-based mediation groups to bind Sudan together across geographic, racial, and religious lines.

Experience tells us that roughly half the nations emerging from civil war are able to achieve lasting stability; the other half lapse into violence within five years. Reaching peace between the north and the south in Sudan took more than two decades; maintaining that peace—and preventing yet another cycle of suffering—will require an effort at least as concentrated and as long.

The oldest city in West Africa—Kano, Nigeria—is not a place to which American secretaries of state ordinarily venture; that is one reason I went. The world was changing, and U.S. diplomacy needed to make new connections. For almost a millennium, Kano—now a city of half a million people—had been a center of Islam. Since 1804, it had been home to a caliphate established after a series of holy wars. The caliphate's thirteenth leader, Emir Ado Bayero, had served since 1963. In 1999, he was my host.

I met him in his palace. After exchanging greetings, we went into an ornately decorated hall. He invited me to sit on his right, a gesture of respect, before seating himself on a bench covered with lambskin. The emir's elaborate headdress, with colors representing his village and family, circled his neck and was tied on top. For the benefit of reporters, he made welcoming remarks in the local language (Hausa); then I spoke, in English. We walked out into the courtyard under two huge purple umbrellas and marched through the crowd that had gathered; it parted in front of us like a human Red Sea. Everyone was chanting, though I had no idea what the people were saying. Old men waved rifles aloft; others waved spears. I waved my hand. The emir showed a clenched fist, which I learned was also a sign of respect. We ascended a reviewing stand, where I was treated to the unique spectacle of a durbar: a celebration commemorating the victorious jihad two centuries before and showcasing Kano's rich blend of African and Islamic culture.

The event began with local rulers approaching and paying homage to the emir, accompanied by singers, dancers, jugglers, and stilt walkers. Groups of men then rode by on horseback saluting and holding signs indicating the villages from which they had come. Warriors fired old-fashioned muskets into the air. Medicine men whipped daggers around, touching their eyes, lips, and ears in a routine that made them symbolically immune from harm. Proudly, the emir identified several of the most colorfully costumed horsemen as some of his seventeen sons. At the climax of the ceremony, the warriors lined their steeds up and charged at the reviewing stand. Fortunately, I had been told to expect this and had also been told that the horses would stop in time. They did, just. Impressed and eager to show appreciation, I rose to my feet, beginning to clap before remembering instead to raise my clenched fist.

The durbar festivities and other traditions associated with the caliphate reflect the cultural and religious pride of the Islamic community. The emir is both an embodiment of that pride and someone who transcends the distinction. Within his region and throughout Nigeria, he is respected by Muslims and Christians alike. Such figures must be cherished because Nigeria's population of 128 million is almost equally divided between adherents of the two faiths. As in Sudan, Muslims are dominant in the northern part of the country, Christians in the south. The ability of the two to live in harmony is essential to their nation's future.

Unfortunately, symptoms of trouble showed themselves soon after my visit. Nigerians had just elected as their president Olusegun Obasanjo, a politician who had, from the perspective of some northern Nigerians, three strikes against him. First, Obasanjo was a southerner; second, he was a born-again Christian; and third, he had campaigned on a pledge to purge the corrupt Nigerian military, most of whose senior officers were Muslims from the north. For these reasons, Obasanjo's victory stirred fear in the northern Nigerian states and led promptly to a reaction. In one of the states, a candidate for governor thought it would be smart to promise that he would protect Muslim interests, if elected, by decreeing Islamic law. The ploy was successful, and the promise quickly fulfilled. Other governors followed suit, and within weeks sharia law was in place in a dozen northern states, including Kano.

Previously, Muslims had been allowed to settle personal matters (such as divorce) in their own courts, whereas criminal matters were handled by civil authorities. The general imposition of Islamic law meant that its rules would be applied more broadly. Muslim leaders justified the action as necessary to prevent corruption, curb lewd behavior, and control crime. Christians, however, felt threatened. They objected to requirements that the Quran be studied and the Arabic language taught in their schools. They opposed the rigorous punishments prescribed (though rarely carried out) by the sharia code and the enforcement of prohibitions against dancing and alcohol. They pointed in vain to the Nigerian constitution, which prohibits any state or local government from adopting an official religion.

In the time since, sensitivities have been rubbed raw, and both Muslim and Christian mobs have been guilty of violence. In Kano itself, the house of a Christian preacher who had been accused of converting Muslims was set on fire, killing the entire family. Widespread fighting broke out in 2002, when a local news columnist suggested with ill-judged enthusiasm that a contestant in a beauty pageant was worthy of marriage to the Prophet Muhammad. There have been hundreds of incidents of mob violence directed against churches and mosques, often triggered by allegations that adherents of one faith had disrespected the other. An estimated 10,000 people have been killed, and thousands more have been displaced. Although the federal government discourages religious incitement, it lacks both the means and the moral authority to enforce its will. Christian leaders continue to accuse Muslims of wanting to drive them completely out of northern Nigeria; Muslims continue to resent Christian efforts to evangelize their population.

The roots of religious strife in Nigeria are, of course, not altogether religious. Like many African countries (including Sudan, and indeed also like Iraq), Nigeria was cobbled together by western powers out of an array of ethnic groups. From the first days of independence, Nigeria's federal government has struggled to assert control over its component regions. For decades, greedy dictators mismanaged Nigeria's economy and plundered its oil income, leaving the population poorer and more cynical. Wherever there are large numbers of impoverished and underemployed people, any spark can ignite a big fire. Further, in Nigeria's central highlands, seminomadic Muslim herders have battled with Christian farmers over grazing rights and access to water for their cattle. (A similar competition for resources caused bloodshed on the American frontier through much of the nineteenth century.) In Nigeria, the strains have been made worse by the combination of little rain and a high birthrate, which has left more people trying to survive on smaller parcels of productive land. While economic strains may be the primary source of the violence, religious differences make it simpler to pretend that the killing is being done for a higher purpose than the right to graze cows or plant corn.

In Sudan, in Nigeria, and elsewhere in Africa, there will continue to be a more general danger: alienated Muslim populations provide particularly favorable recruiting grounds for groups like Al Qaeda. Weak governments, porous borders, and civil conflict create openings for predatory organizations. Islam in Africa has traditionally been of the most moderate variety, but extremist pressures have been coming in from the outside; the radicals swoop in with money to operate mosques and social centers that cater to, and sway the allegiances of, the poor. Traditional Muslim leaders lack the resources to compete and their message is, in any case, less stirring to those in search of excitement. Already, a significant number of Africans have been found among the antigovernment insurgents doing battle in Iraq. The United States has responded by deploying troops to Djibouti as part of an antiterrorist task force for the Horn of Africa. It is also training various military entities in the region in counterterrorism techniques. There is value in this, but also considerable risk. We need to ensure that our strategy is both comprehensive and selective. During the cold war, we sometimes supported anticommunist governments that were in other respects disreputable and wretched to their own people. If we provide aid to military forces that cooperate in fighting Al Qaeda but that are also widely hated, we will strengthen Al Qaeda's appeal.

If we want Africans to help in fighting the kind of terrorism that Al Qaeda practices, we need to assist them in combating the forces that most terrorize them—including disease, a lack of clean water, inadequate schooling, and environmental devastation. If we are going to conduct military training, it should be aimed at helping African security forces to prevent civil strife and genocide, as well as to combat terror. We must also develop a new sophistication in our approach to matters of faith. I wrote earlier about the need for American diplomats to be well versed in the religious beliefs and practices of the countries to which they are assigned. In the past, officers in the foreign service who have been trained in Arabic and Islam have shown a decided preference for assignments in Arab, as opposed to African, capitals. We should have no doubt: highly qualified diplomats are needed in both places.

Songs of Enchantment, by Nigerian writer Ben Okri, begins: "We didn't see the chaos growing; and when its advancing waves found us we were unprepared for its feverish narratives and wild manifestations." Today we have no such excuse. We can see the chaos growing. God help us if we are not prepared.

Final Reflections

Eighteen

The Whole
Shooting Match

A
n eye for an eye," said Mahatma Gandhi, "makes the
whole world blind." In earlier chapters, we have looked at
the harm caused by a zero-sum approach to religion in the
Middle East, Iran, Iraq, Afghanistan, Europe, and parts of
Africa. We could—at the risk of belaboring the point—
explore similar issues in such countries as Indonesia, Thailand,
and the Philippines in southeast Asia, and the Caucasus and
Chechnya in central Asia. We could examine the complex balancing act inherent in U.S. policy toward Pakistan, or the outlook in Lebanon, where Shia and Sunni Muslims and
Christians strive for calm in a cauldron long-divided by political, doctrinal, and clan-related issues. Even in North America,
where Islam is the fastest-growing religion, there are troublesome questions of cultural acceptance and discrimination reinforced by fears about violent extremism; the terrorists of 9/11
may have been born elsewhere, but they lived and trained in
the United States for months preceding the strikes.

Some people might conclude from the ubiquity and intensity of these conflicts that the central challenge in the world

today is not how to avoid a clash of civilizations but how to manage a struggle already under way. That is too dark a picture. Al Qaeda and its imitators may want to stir up a global Islamic revolution, but that does not mean they will succeed.

Fear fuels terrorism. Only if fear is allowed to spread can Al Qaeda hope to win lasting support. Surveys have found that Arabs view religious fanaticism as a significant problem both within their own societies and in the West. There is little generalized desire on the part of Muslims to involve themselves in violence. If they agree about anything, it is about the peaceful nature of their faith. Even when the Taliban held power in most of Afghanistan, the movement was recognized diplomatically by only three of the fifty-three Muslim-majority countries. Terror attacks that have killed Muslims in Saudi Arabia, Jordan, Egypt, Turkey, Indonesia and Bangladesh have caused some Muslims who had been sympathetic to Al Qaeda to change their minds.

For its part, the Bush administration, despite major errors in judgment, is not engaged in a religious crusade. The president understands that the best way to defeat Al Qaeda is to deprive it of the sympathy and support it has managed to attract among some Muslims. Most Americans grasp this as well. Few, even among Christian evangelicals, would agree with Pat Robertson that confronting Al Qaeda is at bottom a "religious struggle."* A plurality think Islam is no more likely than other religions to encourage violence.

It is good that relatively healthy attitudes have survived despite a succession of events that have conspired to poison

---

* Robertson told an audience in Jerusalem in 2004: "Ladies and gentlemen, make no mistake—the entire world is being convulsed by a religious struggle. The fight is not about money or territory; it is not about poverty versus wealth; it is not about ancient customs versus modernity. No—the struggle is whether Hubal, the Moon God of Mecca, known as Allah, is supreme, or whether the Judeo-Christian Jehovah God of the Bible is Supreme."

them. The truth is that most Muslims have interests compatible with those of the West, and that Arabs and Americans would both gain from improved relations. Indeed, the United States cannot defeat terrorism without the help of the Arabs; and the Arabs cannot maintain economic health without investment from the West. There is nothing inevitable about holy war.

Even so, there exist dangerous differences of opinion about three emotion-laden issues: first, the composition of a fair and just settlement in the Middle East; second, the legitimacy of the American military presence in Iraq; and third, the overall nature of U.S. intentions. When these issues are seen in the best light, there are prospects for progress on each front.

After years of violence, the Palestinians and Israelis both have new leaders. With change comes turbulence but also opportunities. The Israelis, under Sharon, came to accept what many once denied—compromise on land is essential to the preservation of a democratic and predominately Jewish state. The Palestinians chose a president, Mahmoud Abbas, who genuinely believes that negotiation, not attempts at intimidation, is the way to fulfill his people's most basic needs and hopes. Although Hamas is now well placed to block progress toward peace, there remains a thirst on both sides to find a permanent solution. Nothing would do more than an Israeli-Palestinian peace settlement to put relations between Arabs and the West on solid ground.

As for Iraq, Arabs' expectations are so low that even modest gains could have a major impact. If the Arab Sunnis in Iraq fully embrace the democratic process, it will be difficult for Arabs elsewhere to continue complaining about American policies. If the insurgency dwindles, it will be easier and safer to withdraw our troops. If we can extricate ourselves voluntarily and within a reasonable period, and if the government we leave behind is legitimate and the country undivided, anger should dissipate and suspicions about our motives should become less intense.

This bundle of "ifs" shows how much has to go right for Arab perceptions to change. The current view in the region, according to one joint study by groups in the United States and Egypt, is that "Americans are arrogant, paternalistic, decadent, unfair, cruel, uncaring, and driven by lust for power and wealth." A second survey found that a majority of Muslims view America as greedy, immoral, and violent. These stereotypes cannot be blamed solely, or even primarily, on President Bush, but they did deepen significantly during his first term. This was not coincidental. In Iraq, particularly, the president knowingly sacrificed international support to pursue a goal he thought right, consciously disregarding the views of many Arabs and Muslims. To the frustration of the State Department, then under Colin Powell, efforts to smooth the way diplomatically were dismissed as unnecessary. The president had the power and the will to press his agenda, for better or worse; part of the worse was the alienation of world opinion.

On taking office in early 2005, Condoleezza Rice declared that "the time for diplomacy is now." Indeed, under her direction the State Department has been more visible in shaping foreign policy than it had been during Bush's first term, and the administration has seemed more interested in working cooperatively with allies and other countries. Even the president, seemingly intent on healing the wounds opened earlier, gave Karen Hughes, one of his most trusted assistants, the job of coordinating outreach to the Muslim world.

At Hughes's swearing-in ceremony, the president said he expected her to make sure that "every agency and department gives public diplomacy the same level of priority that I do." He then outlined a somewhat anemic three-point strategy: enlisting the help of the private sector; responding more quickly to terrorist propaganda; and urging Americans to "study the great history and traditions" of the Middle East. He added that every citizen who "welcomes an exchange student into their home is an ambassador for America." The problem with this rosy sentiment is that the Muslim students who once lined up to get into our universities are now heading elsewhere; for both sides, this is a lost opportunity from which it may take generations to recover. It would contribute much to public diplomacy if we were to find a better balance between legitimate security measures and policies that heighten misunderstanding. Today, many Arabs have the impression that the United States regards all of them as actual or potential terrorists. Some are actually convinced, for example, that to procure a visa for travel to America, Arabs must first agree to be photographed naked, proving that they are not concealing a bomb.

I might scoff at such exaggerated fears if not for the experience of an acquaintance whom I shall call Ahmed.

Ahmed had always felt at home in the United States. He graduated from an American university, served as an official of the American Chamber of Commerce in his country, and had traveled to and from the United States on many occasions. He is someone who knows and likes America and is, as such, an ally in opposing extremism. In August 2005, while en route from abroad to a conference at which I was among the participants, Ahmed was stopped at an airport in the northern United States. With no provocation, he was asked about the well-being of his "friend" Osama bin Laden. He was then kept waiting for hours while he was interrogated in classic good-cop/bad-cop fashion and his luggage and laptop were searched. During the ordeal, a photo of his six-year-old son produced allegations of pedophilia. A copy of Robert Kessler's best-selling book *The CIA War on Terror* led to a series of sarcastic questions about Ahmed's "interest in terror." The agenda for the conference he was scheduled to attend prompted questions about his association with other Arabs. Finally, a CNN transcript that he was carrying, of an old broadcast by Al Qaeda, caused the cancellation of his visa, leaving him no choice but to fly back home. The agents may have thought they were making America safer, but what this and similar incidents really do is make Karen Hughes's assignment that much tougher.

Public diplomacy can achieve little unless the policies it is designed to back up are viable and the audience it is intended to persuade is listening.* On both counts, the outlook will brighten if the best-case scenarios cited earlier in this chapter materialize; if they do not, current problems will worsen. Political and security setbacks in the Middle East, for example, could easily generate new rounds of violence. Iraq could break apart or fail to settle down, emboldening terrorists and causing our troops to either retreat in disarray or remain indefinitely with no promise of ultimate success. The rivalry between the Sunnis and the Shiites could evolve into a combustible regionwide competition. More broadly, the tensions within Islam and among Muslims, Christians, and Jews could escalate further, causing people of all three faiths to lose sight of common values.

The former German chancellor Konrad Adenauer once quipped, "History is the sum total of things that could have been avoided." A generalized confrontation between Islam

---

* One clear example of the connection between policy and popularity was President Bush's decision to order a large-scale American military and civilian relief effort following the tsunami of December 2004 in southeast Asia. The favorability ratings for the United States in Indonesia and India improved dramatically and have remained at a relatively high level.

and the West can and should be avoided; it will be if those with the power to shape events and attitudes keep their wits about them. I offer seven ideas that—if not pillars of wisdom—are at least cautions against foolish mistakes.

First, localize, don't globalize. Al Qaeda yearns for a worldwide stage; we should prevent it from claiming one. The specific issues stirring the pot in Chechnya, Nigeria, the Middle East, Iraq, and other trouble-prone areas vary widely; they should be dealt with separately. That will make each easier to solve, while hindering the terrorists' drive to portray every front as part of a single religious struggle.

Second, remember who the enemy is. There is a cottage industry of western commentators eager to identify "radical Islam" as the new communism. There are Arab leaders who reflexively exploit the fears of their citizens by saying that Islam is under attack by the West. This is nonsense. Neither the West nor Islam is under attack by the other. Both, however, are imperiled by Al Qaeda and the groups it has spawned. We must keep the terms of confrontation as narrow as possible.

Third, don't play with matches. The political climate is already overheated. Every miscalculation of word and deed drives the temperature higher. In theory, modern communications should tamp down emotions by creating a base of commonly accepted facts. In reality, the media often amplify passions by transmitting harmful rumors and shocking pictures (or offensive cartoons) to audiences all too eager to react to them. In the spring of 2005, deadly riots broke out in response to a single unsubstantiated report that American soldiers had desecrated the Quran. To avoid similar incidents, our leaders must exercise extraordinary discipline in what they do and say, while demanding similar caution from their subordinates. This is not, however, a one-way street. Making an insensitive statement or mishandling a holy book is to be condemned, but—as Muslim leaders should be pressed to agree—it does not provide an excuse for violence.

Every effort, in any case, should be made to improve communications. The Bush administration's hostility toward the independent Arab broadcasting network Al Jazeera, for example, is misplaced. Al Jazeera's audience is precisely the one officials of the United States most need to reach. Instead of attacking Al Jazeera, our government should be making its finest spokespersons available to appear regularly on the network's shows.

Fourth, we should develop a common understanding of what terrorism is. In politics, controlling the accepted meaning of words can be as vital as controlling the high ground in combat: hence the effort by some to label certain categories of terrorists as freedom fighters. This effort cannot be allowed to succeed. People who use terror in pursuit of national independence or to resist occupation may be freedom fighters in their own minds, but their motives do not excuse their methods; they are terrorists and should be treated accordingly. I often argued with Arab leaders about this. None of them explicitly justified violence toward civilians, but many considered terror attacks by Palestinians against Israelis to be legitimate elements of a struggle to recover lost lands. The Saudis, for example, sent payments to the families of Palestinian suicide bombers, even issuing press releases about it.* When I protested, they said that the funds were being provided "for humanitarian reasons."

---

* The Saudi embassy in Washington issued a press release in January 2001 claiming that the Saudi Committee for Support for the Al Quds Intifada, chaired and administered by Interior Minister Prince Nayef, distributed $33 million in support of wounded and handicapped Palestinians to the "families of 2,281 prisoners and 358 martyrs." The press release also reported that the committee "pledged a sum of SR 20,000 ($5,333) cash to each family that has suffered from martyrdom."

This view was taken recently by Sayd Mohammed al-Musawi, head of the mainstream Shia World Islamic League in London, who insisted that "there should be a clear distinction between the suicide bombing of those who are trying to defend themselves from occupiers, which is something different from those who kill civilians, which is a big crime." Whatever claim to our consideration this statement might have vanishes in light of the actual record of Palestinian suicide bombers. How is it self-defense to blow up a school bus, a pizza parlor, and a vegetable market?

Violence that is intentionally directed at noncombatants is wrong legally and morally. This principle applies to people who place bombs in public places; to all sides in Iraq and the Middle East; and to individuals, militias, and regular armed forces whether serving a dictatorship or a democracy. It applies, as well, to those who are sure they have God's permission to make an exception. The principle is universal.

This is not to say that the contrast between legitimate and illegitimate uses of force will always be clear. A painful balancing is often required—even in a just cause—between anticipated military gains and possible risks to civilians. Reasonable people may well differ in some situations about who is a combatant and who is not. So, too, the line between self-defense and aggression can become muddied when each side fears attack by the other. Faulty information may also lead to tragic mistakes or to accidents. Clausewitz was right when he wrote that events in war can take on "exaggerated dimensions and unnatural appearance," like the "effect of fog or moonshine."

We can, however, at least be clear about what is clear. There is no excuse for intentionally targeting noncombatants or for not taking into account the danger to noncombatants when military targets are struck. Countries and causes without access to conventional military power have no right to compensate by using unconventional means to spread terror among civilians. Countries with superior military power have no sanction to act with impunity, secure in the knowledge they can escape accountability for their actions. The rules for one apply to all. If Christians, Jews, and Muslims can agree on that, they will find it easier to agree on other matters.*

Fifth, we should talk about the treatment of women in a manner that leads to actual progress. I support the empowerment of women both as a matter of individual human rights and as an essential element of economic and social development. The cause is not helped, however, by ill-informed, smug, or simplistic criticism of Islam. Historically, few societies have cause for pride in their treatment of women. Even today, I am asked by some Muslims whether I would rather see a teenage girl in a burka or in a brothel. Islam neither mandates nor justifies the marginalization of women, but the Quranic distinctions that do exist cannot be ignored by Muslims of either gender, for to them the Quran comprises the actual words of God. Non-Muslims have no right to impose their own standards; nor is there any need to do so. In many Muslim societies, women can and do thrive, although others struggle against the sometimes brutal chauvinism that can be found to a degree in every culture. It is a mistake to disparage Islam or to assume that all is lost under sharia law; a better approach is to fight for the prerogatives that women should have under such law and to focus on the rights of women everywhere to define their roles for themselves.

Sixth, Christians, Muslims, and Jews should realize how

---

* In September 2005, world leaders considered but failed to agree on a definition of terrorism that had been proposed by Kofi Annan. The main issue was whether actions taken to resist occupation should be considered terrorism if they result in the death or injury of noncombatants.

much they have in common. The same forces of globalization and change that raise fears in conservative Muslim societies are also generating anxiety in the West. The same concern that God's role as a source of law and a guide for living will be lost is felt by the devout in Kansas as much as in Karachi, in the average Orthodox kibbutz as much as in Riyadh. Rick Warren, a popular evangelical preacher who is the author of *The Purpose-Driven Life,* has identified the peaceful modernization of Islam as a primary international goal for the next two decades. I agree, but with creationism once more in vogue in many American communities, I am uncertain who is qualified to lecture whom about the need for modernization. Conservative Muslims perceive a war against Islam; conservative Christians believe that they, too, are under siege. Religious families on the Arabian Peninsula and in south Asia do not want Washington telling them what to teach their children; the same is true of families in Florida, Alaska, and points in between. Those in many societies who are inclined toward a more secular outlook or who practice a minority faith worry that the moral views of the religious majority will be imposed upon them; in the United States, some fear that the constitutional barrier between church and state is breaking down. What is most striking about the relationship between Islam and the West is not how different we are but how similar. We ought to be able to understand each other better.

During a telephone interview, I asked Bill Clinton about this; he said that the question comes down to whether we are willing to admit that we are not in possession of the whole truth. That is, he said, "the whole shooting match, the whole shebang.

"It is OK," he added, "to say you believe your religion is true, even truer than other faiths, but not that you are in possession in this life of a hundred percent of the truth." He quoted the apostle Paul talking about the difference between life on Earth and in heaven: "For now I see through a glass darkly; but then face to face; now I know in part, but then I shall know even as I am known by God."

In a later discussion, at his home in Chappaqua, New York, Clinton told me, "If you accept that you may not know everything, it is harder to feel any kind of joy in hurting others. I guarantee that the people who fly airplanes into skyscrapers do not believe they are seeing through a glass darkly; those who burn down mosques or destroy sacred places do not think they know only in part; the guy who killed Yitzhak Rabin for being a 'bad Jew' was absolutely convinced he knew it all. You can't pretend if you're a person of faith that religion doesn't affect your politics; but if you believe you know all there is to know, then you'll think of others as less holy, less worthy, less deserving of respect. Not that there isn't truth; it's just that we don't know all of it. Most religions teach a lot of the same thing—a kind of spiritual integrity that is good for any society. We'd be a lot better off with an honest dialogue about our differences provided everyone 'fesses up about not knowing the absolute truth."

The Quran has passages that make a point similar to Clinton's quotation from Paul: "Compete with one another in good works; unto God you shall return altogether, and He will tell you the truth about what you have been disputing." Referring to David's killing of Goliath, the Quran advises that "if Allah did not check one set of people by means of another, the earth indeed would be full of mischief: but Allah is full of bounty to all the worlds."

It is no overstatement to suggest that if the future is to be "full of bounty" for any of us, people of different religions and cultures will need to get along. Here education is central. We must explore every means of developing and conveying a more fully shared understanding of the history of the Middle East, relations between Islam and the West, the belief systems of the three Abrahamic faiths, and the whole question of how to differentiate between truth and propaganda or myth. These are hugely contentious issues, requiring input from many sources, and with no single set of "right" answers. A thorough consensus would require so many departures from deeply held beliefs as to be beyond the bounds of reasonable hope. Yet even stormy and inconclusive discussions will build common ground as participants shed their weaker arguments in order to shore up more vital ones. Dialogue alone is no guarantee of peace, but it is better than a status quo in which the various sides are preoccupied with preserving age-old dogmas and chastising those who even suggest revisiting them.

It would be naive to put too much faith in projects that could be grouped under the heading, "Why can't we all just get along?" Ordinarily, the people who participate in such projects don't need persuading, and those responsible for the problems don't participate. The result can be intellectual cotton candy—sweet and pleasing to the eye, but lacking in nourishment. On this set of issues, however, especially at this time, a concentration of energy at every level has value. We may not be able to convert the extremes, but we can make the middle more active, cohesive, and confident.

I am encouraged, therefore, by the fact that intercultural and interfaith efforts have become growth industries at many think tanks and universities. Almost everywhere you look, Christians, Muslims, and Jews—and often people of other faiths—are conferring, signing declarations, strategizing. Among those leading the charge, not surprisingly, is Bill Clinton's Global Initiative, which is rounding up practical commitments for action in four areas, including religion.

The UN's Alliance of Civilizations High-Level Group, sponsored by Turkey and Spain, is striving to promote tolerance by drawing on some of the world's most accomplished minds. An organization called Meaden—whose name comes from the Arabic word for a town square—is fostering a series of online conversations. What, for example, would one ask the parents of a girl in Saudi Arabia, a college student in Pakistan, a Sunni shopkeeper in Iraq, or a teacher in Iran? What would we want them to know about us?

Others rely more on the power of faith. The Cordoba Initiative, which is based in New York and is headed by Feisal Abdul Rauf, a prolific author and imam of a mosque there, is a multifaith, multinational project dedicated to healing relations between Muslims and the United States. It is named for the Spanish city where in medieval times Muslims, Jews, and Christians lived and flourished together. Yale University has joined the National Association of Evangelicals and the government of Morocco in launching a Christian-Muslim dialogue. The Interfaith Youth Core, which is based in Chicago, was started by Dr. Eboo Patel to bring young people of different faiths and nations together to work for social justice. The Seeds of Peace organization continues to give young Arabs and Israelis an opportunity to learn about each other in an environment free from the tension of their homelands.

The hope driving such projects brings to mind a story that was included in an eighteenth-century German drama, *Nathan the Just*. The story is about a special ring that conveys to its owner both the respect of his peers on Earth and the favor of God. The ring was handed down from generation to generation, going always to the most virtuous son (this was, after all, the eighteenth century, so daughters did not figure in the story). The system worked well until in one generation there were three sons of equal virtue. The father solved the problem by arranging for an artisan to make two duplicate rings so perfect that no one could tell the difference between them and the original. As his life ebbed away, the father gave each son a ring and cautioned all three to act as if theirs were the true ring, as indeed it might be. The sons soon fell to quarreling about whose ring was genuine, and the matter was submitted to a judge. With the judge's guidance, they agreed that the only solution was for each son to believe in his own ring and to remain worthy through moral action, while admitting the existence of other possibilities.

In that spirit, we arrive at the seventh and last of my suggestions. Al Qaeda's leaders do not speak factually, but neither do they speak trivially. They concern themselves with transcendent issues of history, identity, and faith. To be heard, the rest of us must address matters equally profound. The three monotheistic religions provide a rich tradition of overlapping principles, ethics, and beliefs. Each places a high value on justice and compassion, points the way toward common ground, offers the opportunity for repentance, and is a religion of peace. Leaders should not hesitate to draw on such values to identify what might best be called the Judeo-Christian-Islamic tradition and to pursue shared objectives. These objectives might include an assault on global poverty as envisioned in the UN's Millennium Development Goals; or the "peace of the brave" that Yitzhak Rabin desired for the Middle East; or the fulfillment of the desire expressed by King Abdullah of Jordan, to see the world's 1.2 billion Muslims become "full partners in the development of human civilization, and in the progress of humanity in our age."

In Aesop's fable, a lion hunts a group of bulls without success, because he always finds them gathered together in a circle. Whichever way the lion approaches, he is met by horns. One day, the bulls quarrel and angrily stomp off to separate pastures. Caught alone, each is devoured. We should all be aware, irrespective of our faiths, that there is in the world today no shortage of prowling lions.

Nineteen

Summoning the
Better Angels

———— ৵৵ ————

I have long been wary of those who claim to be sure of the truth about the biggest questions. Certainty is not in itself an asset; that depends on whether what one is certain about is actually true. Religion in particular defies attempts at proof. I find it interesting, for example, that some Christian groups have tried to use the scientific method to show that prayer works. They do this by dividing a list of ill people into two halves, then praying for one and not the other. The results of such experiments have, to date, been inconclusive. Is this because God isn't listening or because the best Christians spoil the experiment by secretly praying for both groups? As C. S. Lewis, the chronicler of Narnia, has observed, "Christians and their opponents again and again expect that some new discovery will either turn matters of faith into matters of knowledge or else reduce them to patent absurdities. But it has never happened."

As I grow older, I am reminded of a good Catholic—the friend of a friend—whose chosen epitaph was "I leave the world as I entered it: bewildered." The years have not brought me certainty about religion. I am a hopeful Christian but also an inadequate one, with doubts. I respect other religions because I think they are reaching for the same truth, though from a different angle. The Protestant theologian Paul Tillich wrote, "Doubt is not the opposite of faith; it is an element of faith." I like the sound of that.

Having admitted uncertainty, I can hardly say that fundamentalists must be wrong, but I am fairly sure they are not wholly right. Evangelicals accord scripture a high degree of authority; fundamentalists go beyond that to insist that every word in the Bible is literally true. To believe that of the Bible or of any other holy book is to assume too much about the ability of human narrators to rise above the subjective influences of their time and place. The scriptures are full of politics. To me, that is why the core teachings, not the minutiae, carry the weight of what a religion is about. I am particularly impatient with those who, having cited a few quotations, conclude that women should not be allowed to lead in church or that homosexuality is an abomination to God—who, after all, created homosexuals. As a practical guide to moral life in ancient Israel, a book such as Leviticus may have served well enough; but a piece of writing that accepts slavery, authorizes the sale of one's daughter, prohibits the trimming of beards, and bans the wearing of garments made from two different kinds of thread is neither timeless nor flawless. Jesus was not a fundamentalist, either. He was condemned by Pharisees for working on the Sabbath, sharing meals with a tax collector, and coming to the aid of an adulteress. He broke cultural taboos by conversing with a woman he met at a well and by taking children seriously. He rejected explicitly the doctrine of "an eye for an eye."

If God has a plan, it will be carried out. That is heaven's jurisdiction, not ours. If, however, one believes that creation has given us both life and free will, we are left with the question of what to do with those gifts. That is both a practical challenge and a moral one, and it is what this book has been about.

Religion concerns itself with the hopes and fears of all the years; the terms of American presidents are not so expansive. The policies of the United States government have to be based on what we might hope to accomplish in a finite period on Earth, not on postmillennial expectations. At the same time, what we can accomplish on Earth is mixed up with the different understandings people have of God. As I travel around the world, I am often asked, "Why can't we just keep religion out of foreign policy?" My answer is that we can't and shouldn't. Religion is a large part of what motivates people and shapes their views of justice and right behavior. It must be taken into account. Nor can we expect our leaders to make decisions in isolation from their religious beliefs. There is a limit to how much the human mind can compartmentalize. In any case, why should world leaders who are religious act and speak as if they are not? We must live with our beliefs and also with our differences; it does no good to deny them.

This does not mean, however, that we should inflate the importance of those differences. It is human instinct to organize into groups. For most of us, this sorting process is largely passive. The groups to which we belong are part of our inheritance and culture—a consequence of where we were born and how we were raised. My family's heritage was Jewish, but I was raised a Roman Catholic. If, as a child, I had been sent to temple instead of to church, I would have grown to adulthood with a different group identity. I was born overseas. If not for the cold war, my family would have had no cause to emigrate to the United States and I would never have become an American.

Nature allows us to choose neither our parents nor our place of birth, limiting from the outset the groups with which we will ever after identify. True, some of us will weigh competing philosophies and convert from one religion to another out of spiritual enlightenment or intellectual and emotional conviction. Some will find reason to shift allegiance from one country to another. More often, we remain within the same general categories we dropped into at birth or, as in my case, the categories where events beyond our control have placed us. That is not much of an accomplishment.

Logically, then, our differences should not matter so much. People of diverse nations and faiths ought to be able to live in harmony. However, the gap between what ought to be and what actually is has been a recurring source of drama throughout human existence. Decades ago, Reinhold Niebuhr warned us that the brutality of nations and groups cannot be tamed no matter how hard we try. "Social conflict," he wrote, is "an inevitability in human history, probably to its very end." Good and wise people might seek to prevent catastrophe, he conceded, but they would likely be no match for the fears and ambitions that drive groups into confrontation. It is sobering that Niebuhr arrived at this grim judgment before World War II. He was not reacting to the war; he was predicting it.

If Niebuhr is right, the pursuit of peace will always be uphill. And yet, I cannot accept the view that because our characters are flawed there is nothing we can do to improve the human condition. Decision makers can usefully search for ways to minimize the inevitable social conflicts referred to by Niebuhr—not so much with the aspiration of finding Utopia than with the goal of saving us from even greater destruction. Our inherent shortcomings notwithstanding, we can still hope to create a better future. And we know that the right kind of leadership can do much to prevent wars, rebuild devastated societies, expand freedom, and assist the poor.

I wrote at the start of this book that I wanted to identify ways to bring people together in support of policies that reflect the unifying rather than the divisive aspects of religion. My purpose is not to create a spiritual melting pot in which competing religious claims are reduced to mush; my interest is in solving problems and in responding to a practical political imperative. Technology has made outrages more visible, borders more permeable, weapons more dangerous, and conflicts more costly. In the process of realizing our dreams, scientists have also brought some nightmares closer to reality. The job of our leaders is to foster an international environment in which we can live with as much security, freedom, and justice as possible; this, by its nature, requires communication and cooperation.

President Bush deserves credit for affirming America's place at the rhetorical forefront of promoting democracy. He should be praised for acknowledging political freedom as a potential source of global unity. He has, however, undermined his own capacity to lead through mistakes and omissions that have made many countries less eager to stand with America. Clearly, the narrow vision and heedless unilateralism of the president's first term must not be repeated. We must restore alliances, take every region seriously, and understand that if we want other countries to collaborate on dangers that threaten us, we will need to assist in tackling the perils that threaten them. We must once again become known as a country whose leaders listen, admit mistakes, and work hard at addressing global challenges.

It would help a great deal if Americans from across the political spectrum did indeed come together (as I envisioned in Chapter 7) to push our government to lead on human rights and humanitarian issues. This would do much to restore respect for America and to legitimize our positions on the core security issues of proliferation and terror.

More vital still is the question of how we Americans define our country's international role. Do we see ourselves as subject to the same rules as other nations; or do we see ourselves as entitled to act in any way we see fit? Do we have a responsibility to strengthen international institutions and law, or a duty to remain free from such restraints in "answer to a calling from beyond the stars"? Is our proper role to lead or to dominate?

William Kristol, the neoconservative writer, has asked, "What's wrong with dominance, in the service of sound principles and high ideals?" This is a question Americans asked a century ago when conquering the Philippines. The answer President McKinley claimed to have received from heaven was that we had a mandate to impose our will. Whether or not that was the right reply then, it is the wrong answer today. The policy of dominance is at odds with America's self-image and a poor way to protect our interests. Its application in service to what our leaders believed were "sound principles and high ideals"—applied most obviously in Iraq—has proved to be a deadly drain on American resources, military power, and prestige. Let this be a lesson. American exceptionalism owes its long life not to the power of the United States but to the wisdom and restraint with which that power has most often been exerted—including the use not of military might alone but of all the assets that can contribute to our security and good name.

Looking ahead, we would be well advised to recall the character of wartime leadership provided by Abraham Lincoln. He did not flinch from fighting in a just cause, but he never claimed a monopoly on virtue. He accepted that God's will would be done without professing to comprehend it. He rejected a suggestion that he pray for God to be on the side of the Union, praying instead for the Union to be on the side of God.

Lincoln led a divided country. We must lead in a divided world. To that end, we should blend realism with idealism, placing morality near the center of our foreign policy even while we debate different understandings of what morality means. We should organize ourselves better to comprehend a globe in which religious devotion is both a powerfully positive force and an intermittently destructive one. We should respond with determination and confidence to the danger posed by Al Qaeda and its ilk. And we should make clear not only what America stands against, but also what we stand for.

Half a century ago, in writing about the cold war, my father argued that, whether we are "American individualists or British laborists, conservatives or progressives, socializing democrats or democratic socialists, white, black or yellow—we can all accept that human dignity and respect for the individual" must be the focus of everything. I believe that, too.

Respect for the rights and well-being of each individual is the place where religious faith and a commitment to political liberty have their closest connection. A philosophy based on this principle has the most potential to bring people from opposing viewpoints together because it excludes no one and yet demands from everyone full consideration of the ideas and needs of others.*

Yet the question arises: how can we hope to unite people around a principle—respect for the individual—that is such

---

* Respect for the individual is not, as some say, the opposite of respect for the rights of groups. On the contrary, individuals bring their rights to the groups to which they belong. Thus, freedom from discrimination on the basis of race, gender, or religion is *both* an individual and a group right.

a uniquely western concept? The answer, of course, is that it is not. Hinduism demands that "no man do to another that which would be repugnant to himself." The Torah instructs us, "Thou shalt love thy neighbor as myself." Zoroaster observed, "What I hold good for myself, I should for all." Confucius said, "What you do not want done to yourself, do not do unto others." Buddha taught us to consider others as ourselves. The Stoics of ancient Greece argued that all men are "equal persons in the great court of liberty." The Christian gospel demands, "Do unto others as you would have done unto you." The Quran warns that a true believer must love for his brother what he loves for himself. Finally, the world's first known legal code had as its announced purpose "to cause justice to prevail and to ensure that the strong do not oppress the weak." This is, we might think, the kind of legal system the world should develop now as a gift to the people of Iraq. In fact, it is the law code of Hammurabi, a gift civilization received four thousand years ago from ancient Babylon, now known as Iraq.

In setting down his idea of the true religion, Benjamin Franklin argued that the "most acceptable service of God is doing good to man." We cannot, I suppose, be certain of that, but we can at least make an informed guess that we have been given a conscience for a reason.

According to the poem by Yeats, it is when the best lack all conviction and the worst are full of passionate intensity that things fall apart, the center cannot hold, and anarchy is loosed upon the world.

We live at a time when the worst are indeed full of passionate intensity. The question is whether the rest of us have the courage of our convictions and the wisdom to make the right choices. Wisdom comes from learning, which comes from education. The heart of education is the search for truth. But there are many kinds of truth.

In mathematics and science, knowledge accumulates. Theorems are built on top of theorems and laws on top of laws. We discover that the Earth is round and will never again think of it as flat. We learn that the square of the hypotenuse of a right triangle is equal to the sum of the squares of the other two sides. Through experiments and research, scientists steadily add to our store of knowledge. We are, in this sense, far wiser than earlier generations about how the world works.

In the arenas of global politics and interfaith understanding, however, I am not sure we are any smarter now than we have been in the past.

The twentieth century was the bloodiest in human history. When the new millennium came, we vowed to make a fresh start, but we have not begun well.

I am an optimist who worries a lot. Through almost seven decades of life, I have seen enough examples of altruism and sacrifice to live in astonishment at what humans are willing to do *for* one another; and enough examples of cruelty to despair at what we are capable of doing *to* each other. The contradictions within human nature are inescapable. Liberty is our gift and our burden, carrying with it both the responsibility to choose and accountability for the choices we make.

I cannot write a happy ending to this book. We remain in the midst of struggle. As Bill Clinton reminds us, none of us can claim full title to the truth. We may hope, however, for leadership at home and abroad that will inspire us to look for the best in ourselves and in others. Lincoln, again, coined the perfect phrase, appealing in the aftermath of war to "the better angels of our nature"—summoning our capacity to care for one another in ways that cannot fully be explained by self-interest, logic, or science.

This is why the principle matters so much: every individual counts. If we truly accept and act on it, we will have the basis for unity across every border. We will take and hold the high ground against terrorists, dictators, tyrants, and bigots. We will gain from the contributions of all people; and we will defend and enrich liberty rather than merely consume it. In so doing, we may hope to inch our way over time not toward a glistening and exclusive city on a hill, but toward a globe on which might and right are close companions and where dignity and freedom are shared by all.

Notes

ONE: THE MIGHTY AND THE ALMIGHTY

4   *"It is the policy of the United States,"* President George W. Bush, second inaugural address, Washington, D.C., January 20, 2005.

4   *"more than preemptive,"* Jim Wallis, *"God's Politics: Why the Right Gets It Wrong and the Left Doesn't Get It,"* Harper San Francisco, 2005, 149.

5   *"Freedom is God's gift."* President George W. Bush, quoted in *Plan of Attack* by Bob Woodward, Simon and Schuster, New York, 2004, 88–89.

7   *"As matters now stand,"* Michael Novak, *Belief and Unbelief: A Philosophy of Self-Knowledge,* Mentor-Omega/New American Library, New York and Toronto, 1965, 17.

8   *"clash of civilizations,"* Samuel Huntington, "The Clash of Civilizations?" *Foreign Affairs,* Summer 1993, 22–49.

TWO: "THE EYES OF ALL PEOPLE ARE UPON US"

17   *The Fundamental Orders of Connecticut* [footnote], I came across this information in "Americanism—and Its Enemies," by David Gelernter, *Commentary* magazine, January 2005.

18   *"Every new and successful example,"* James Madison, letter to Edward Livingston, July 10, 1822, in Saul K. Padover, ed., *The Complete Madison: His Basic Writings,* Harper, New York, 1953.

18   *"seems to have been distinguished,"* President George Washington, first inaugural address, New York City, April 30, 1789.

19   *"The government of the United States,"* letter from President George Washington, cited in Barry Kosmin and S. Lachman, *One Nation under God: Religion in Contemporary American Society,* Harmony, New York, 1993, 23.

19   *"Although the detail of the formation of the American government,"* John Adams, "A Defense of the Constitution of Government of the United States

of America," from Adrienne Koch, ed., *The American Enlightenment: The Shaping of the American Experiment and a Free Society*, George Braziller, New York, 1965, 258.

19 *"the greatest obstacles,"* Thomas Jefferson, letter to Samuel Kercheval, 1810.

19 *"Shall I continue in my allegiance,"* quoted in H. W. Brands, "Too Close to Call," *Washington Post Book World*, October 31, 2004, 3.

20 *Franklin was a particular champion* [footnote], "Benjamin Franklin's Gift of Tolerance," by Walter Isaacson in Akbar Ahmed and Brian Forst, eds., *After Terror: Promoting Dialogue Among Civilizations*, Polity Press, Malden, Mass., 2005, 36.

20 *"led by a cloud by day,"* Thomas Jefferson, cited in Robert N. Bellah, "Civil Religion in America," *Daedalus: Journal of the American Academy of Arts and Sciences*, Vol. 96, No. 1, Winter 1967, 1–21.

21 *"America is a land of wonders,"* Alexis de Tocqueville, *Democracy in America*, 1835. (Online.)

21 *"Brother, you say there is but one way,"* Red Jacket, quoted in *Lend Me Your Ears: Great Speeches in History*, selected and introduced by William Safire, Norton, New York, 1992, 431–433.

22 *"All men are not created,"* Senator John C. Calhoun, U.S. Senate, June 27, 1848. *Liberty and Union: the Political Philosophy of John C. Calhoun* (1811–1850), Speeches, Part III, Online Library of Liberty, Liberty Fund, 2004.oll.libertyfund.org/Home3/Book.php?recordID=007.

22 *"How little that senator knows himself,"* Senator Charles Sumner, U.S. Senate, May 20, 1856. Wikisource: Speeches. En.wikisource.org/wiki/wikisource: speeches.

23 *"The truth is,"* President William McKinley, cited in John W. Robbins, "The Messianic Character of American Foreign Policy," *Trinity Review*, September–October 1990.

23 *"It seems strange,"* *Public Opinion*, cited in Stuart Creighton Miller, *Benevolent Assimilation: The American Conquest of the Philippines, 1899–1903*, Yale University Press, New Haven, Conn., 1982.

24 *"There is not an imperialist in the country,"* Theodore Roosevelt, cited in Howard K. Beale, *Theodore Roosevelt and the Rise of America to World Power*, Johns Hopkins Press, Baltimore, Md., 1956; and Collier, 1972, 75.

24 *"I do not think there is any such thing,"* Henry Cabot Lodge, cited ibid.

24 *"The March of the Flag,"* quotations are from the version of Beveridge's speech delivered on the U.S. Senate floor on January 9, 1900. *Congressional Record*, 56th Congress, I Session, pp. 704–712.

25 *"If true Christianity,"* William Jennings Bryan, acceptance speech, Democratic National Convention, Indianapolis, Indiana, August 8, 1900. Viewed at http://etsv.edu/cas/history/docs/bryan.htm.

25 *"The clergymen have all got hold,"* Charles Francis Adams, cited in John W.

Robbins, "The Messianic Character of American Foreign Policy," *Trinity Review,* September–October, 1990.

27 *"A prince,"* Niccolò Machiavelli, *The Prince,* Mentor/New American Library of World Literature, 1952, 94.

28 *"The legions,"* President Calvin Coolidge, inaugural address, March 4, 1925.

28 *As President Ronald Reagan cautioned.* Cited in John W. Robbins, "The Messianic Character of American Foreign Policy," *Trinity Review,* September–October 1990.

28 *Jefferson wrote,* letter from Thomas Jefferson to Roger C. Weightman, June 24, 1826, cited in Wikipedia entry for Jefferson, 10.

29 *"We shall fight,"* President Woodrow Wilson, address to a Joint Session of the United States Congress, April 2, 1917.

29 *"These men were crusaders,"* President Woodrow Wilson, Pueblo, Colorado, September 25, 1919.

30 *"pay any price,"* President John F. Kennedy, inaugural address, January 20, 1961.

30 *"We see how seriously,"* Robert Frost, excerpt from "For John F. Kennedy His Inauguration," from *The Poetry of Robert Frost,* edited by Edward Connery Lathem. Copyright © 1969 by Henry Holt and Company. Copyright © 1961, 1962 by Robert Frost. Reprinted by permission of Henry Holt and Company, LLC.

31 *"as the center of political enlightenment,"* George Kennan to Richard Ullman, "The U.S. and the World: An Interview with George Kennan," *New York Review of Books,* August 12, 1999.

THREE: GOOD INTENTIONS GONE ASTRAY:
VIETNAM AND THE SHAH

34 *"While normally,"* Hans Morgenthau, "We Are Deluding Ourselves in Vietnam," *New York Times Magazine,* April 18, 1965.

35 *"serious danger,"* John Kerry, Class Day address, Yale University, New Haven, Conn., May 1966. (Copied from the original text.)

35 *"the wrong war,"* U.S. Representative Morris K. Udall, "Vietnam: This Nation Is Caught on a Treadmill," *Reveille* magazine, July 1967, 12.

35 *"Each day,"* Rev. Martin Luther King Jr., "Beyond Vietnam," address delivered to the Clergy and Laity Concerned about Vietnam, Riverside Church, New York, April 4, 1967. Reprinted by arrangement with the heirs to the Estate of Martin Luther King Jr., care of the Writers House, as agent for the proprietor, New York, New York.

37 *"Being confident,"* President Jimmy Carter, commencement address, University of Notre Dame, South Bend, Ind., May 22, 1977.

40 *As a result,* Gary Sick, *All Fall Down,* Random House, New York, 1985, 54–55.

43 *"Westerners, with few exceptions,"* Bernard Lewis, *From Babel to Dragomans: Interpreting the Middle East,* Oxford University Press, New York, 2004, 285.

43 *For the Carter administration,* telephone conversation between the author and Jimmy Carter, March 15, 2005.

FOUR: THE QUESTION OF CONSCIENCE

47 *"Cowardice asks the question,"* this quotation appears with slight variations in many places, including "Remaining Awake Through a Great Revolution," a sermon delivered by Dr. King at the National Cathedral in Washington, D.C., on March 31, 1968, less than a week before his assassination. It is reprinted by arrangement with the heirs to the Estate of Martin Luther King, Jr., care of Writers House, as agent for the proprietor, New York, New York.

49 *"a good deal of trouble,"* Dean Acheson, "Ethics in International Relations Today," *Amherst Alumni News,* Winter 1965; cited in "Morality in Foreign Policy," in Michael Cromartie, ed., *Might and Right after the Cold War: Can Foreign Policy Be Moral?* Ethics and Public Policy Center, Washington, D.C., 1993, 38.

49 *"The interests of a national society,"* George F. Kennan, "Morality and Foreign Policy," *Foreign Affairs,* Winter 1985–1986, 206.

51 *One day, when he was still a young lawyer,* J. G. Holland, *The Life of Abraham Lincoln,* Samuel Fowles & Company, Springfield, Mass., 1866, 78–79.

52 *More than a decade ago,* see three books by Joseph S. Nye, Jr.: *Bound to Lead: The Changing Nature of American Power* (Basic Books, 1990); *The Paradox of American Power: Why the World's Only Superpower Can't Go It Alone* (Oxford University Press, 2002); and *Soft Power: The Means to Success in World Politics* (Public Affairs, 2004).

53 *A country's first priority,* Michael Walzer, in "Religion and American Foreign Policy: Prophetic, Perilous, Inevitable," Brookings Institution, Washington, D.C., February 5, 2003. (Panel discussion.)

56 *In my memoir,* Madeleine Albright, *Madam Secretary: A Memoir,* Miramax, New York, 2003, 146–155.

59 *"anything but honorable,"* Stanley Hauerwas, "The Last Word: What Does Madeleine Albright's Address Say about the Character of Contemporary Christianity?" *Reflections* magazine, Yale Divinity School, Fall 2004, 53–54.

60 *President Masaryk declared passionately,* Tomás Garrigue Masaryk, quoted in Josef Korbel, *Twentieth-Century Czechoslovakia: The Meanings of Its History,* Columbia University Press, New York, 1977, 15.

63 *When Serbia's civilian leaders* [footnote], Tim Judah, *Kosovo: War and Revenge,* Yale University Press, New Haven, Conn., 2000, 26.

64   *Havel characterized it in these terms*, Václav Havel, "Kosovo and the End of the Nation-State," *New York Review of Books*, Vol. 46, No. 10, June 10, 1999.

FIVE: FAITH AND DIPLOMACY

65   *"Twenty times,"* John Adams, quoted from Charles Francis Adams, ed. *Works of John Adams*, Vol. 10, Little, Brown, Boston, Mass., 1856, 254.

66   *"Too many throats,"* I. F. Stone, *The Truman Era*, Random House, New York, 1953, 218.

66   *"there is an assumption,"* Bryan Hehir, responding to Terrorism Forum Series, John F. Kennedy Library and Foundation, Boston, Mass., October 22, 2001. (Transcript.)

67   *The government, alarmed*, quotations cited in David Remnick, "The Talk of the Town: Comment, John Paul II," *New Yorker*, April 4, 2005.

69   *"And I'm talking,"* "Religion and Security: The New Nexus," Pew Forum on Religion and Public Life, Washington, D.C., November 10, 2004. (Transcript of panel discussion.)

71   *The LRA's professed goal*, Richard Petraitis, "Joseph Kony's Spirit War." Viewed at http://www.infidels.org/library/modern/Richard_Petraitis/spirit_war.shtml, January 17, 2003.

77   *"This is an opportunity,"* telephone conversation between Jimmy Carter and the author, March 15, 2005.

78   *"If you're dealing,"* interview with Bill Clinton, Chappaqua, New York, September 27, 2005.

SIX: THE DEVIL AND MADELEINE ALBRIGHT

81   *"just ordinary folks,"* James Dobson on *Larry King Live*, CNN, May 6, 1998.

81   *"Especially in the past twenty-five,"* Jesse Helms, *When Free Men Shall Stand*, Potomac, 1976 (rev. ed. 1994), 16.

83   *"For the past two hundred years,"* Pat Robertson, *The New World Order*, Word, Dallas, 1991, 92.

85   *"our understanding of marriage,"* report of the Independent Women's Forum cited in "Women Riled by 'Gender' Agenda," *Washington Times*, July 24, 1995.

85   *"the biggest threat,"* James Dobson, quoted in Larry Stammer, "Religious Right Challenges 'Anti-Family' Beijing Agenda," *Chicago Sun-Times*, September 10, 1995.

86   *"Hillary Rodham Clinton,"* Concerned Women for America, "Feminism at the Helm of U.S. Foreign Policy," May 12, 1997. (Press release.)

86   *"Satan's trump card,"* James Dobson, quoted in Stammer, op. cit.

88   *"God's plan."* Cited in most collections of quotations by Oliver Wendell Holmes. This is the senior Holmes, father of the Supreme Court justice.

88   *"We are not,"* Richard D. Land, response to essay "Morality and Foreign Policy," by James Finn in Michael Cromartie, ed., *Might and Right after the Cold War: Can Foreign Policy Be Moral?* Ethics and Public Policy Center, Washington, D.C., 1993, 65.

SEVEN: "BECAUSE IT IS RIGHT"

91   *Economist Jeffrey Sachs points out* [footnote], cited in "Can Extreme Poverty Be Eliminated?" by Jeffrey Sachs, *Scientific American*, September 2005, 60.

92   *"Our aim,"* President Harry S Truman, inaugural address, Washington, D.C., January 20, 1949.

92   *"to those peoples,"* President John F. Kennedy, inaugural address, Washington, D.C., January 20, 1961.

93   *"bought a two-million-dollar yacht,"* Ronald W. Reagan, nationwide television broadcast, October 27, 1964. www.Reaganfoundation.org/reagan/speeches/rendezvous.asp.

94   *"It had been my feeling,"* Jesse Helms, quoted in Carl Hulse, "In Memoir, Jesse Helms Says He Was No Racist," *New York Times*, August 31, 2005.

95   *"foreign policy as social work,"* Michael Mandelbaum, "Foreign Policy as Social Work," *Foreign Affairs*, January–February 1996.

95   *"must move humbly and wisely,"* Senator Sam Brownback, cited in Peter Waldman, "Evangelicals Give U.S. Foreign Policy an Activist Tinge," *Wall Street Journal*, May 26, 2004.

98   *In one village,* Ambassador Robert A. Seiple, "Trip Notes," Laos, 2005.

98   *"return every man unto his possession,"* Leviticus 25:10.

100   *"We fight against poverty,"* President George W. Bush, cited in Robin Wright, "Aid to Poorest Nations Trails Global Goal," *Washington Post*, January 15, 2005, 18.

104   *"We should rely more,"* Ronald Reagan, remarks to the Oxford Union Society, London, December 4, 1992.

EIGHT: LEARNING ABOUT ISLAM

109   *massacre of 70,000 Christians,* Internet Medieval Source Book, Paul Halshall, Fordham University, 1996.

114   *"insist that even,"* Khaled Abou el Fadl, "Conflict Resolution as a Normative Value in Islamic Law," in Douglas Johnson, ed., *Faith-Based Diplomacy: Trumping Realpolitik*, Oxford University Press, New York, 2003, 192.

115   *"hurt no one,"* Prophet Muhammad, cited in Susan Tyler Hitchcock with John L. Esposito, *National Geographic Geography of Religion*, National Geographic, Washington, D.C., 2004, 346.

116   *"It is true,"* ibid.

116 *"Few Westerners,"* Queen Noor, "Security through Dialogue," in Akbar Ahmed and Brian Forst, eds., *After Terror: Promoting Dialogue among Civilizations,* Polity, Malden, Mass., 2005, 122.

118 *"opened the door wide,"* H. G. Wells, *The Outline of History,* Garden City Publishing, Garden City, N.Y., 1920, 581.

119 *Today, the majority of Muslims,* "Itjihad: Reinterpreting Islamic Principles for the Twenty-first Century," United States Institute of Peace, Special Report 125, August 2004.

119 *Some scholars,* "Revisiting the Arab Street: Research from Within," Center for Strategic Studies, University of Jordan, February 2005, 52.

119 *"I am America."* This quotation is widely attributed to Ali, including on websites maintained by Wikipedia, Brainyquote, and Infoplease.

120 *"There are those who insist,"* President William J. Clinton, address to the parliament of Jordan, October 26, 1994.

121 *"Think not,"* Matthew 10:34.

122 *"Some jurists,"* Khaled Abou el Fadl, op. cit., 194.

NINE: HOLY LAND, BUT WHOSE?

123 *A letter signed by the British foreign secretary,* letter from Arthur James Balfour to Lord Rothschild, November 2, 1917. Viewed at http://www. Yale.edu/lawweb /avalon/mideast/balfour.htm.

124 *"Zionism is rooted,"* David Balfour, cited in Margaret MacMillan, *Paris 1919,* Random House, New York, 2001, 422.

124 *"Let us not,"* ibid., 380.

125 *"Make the enemy,"* Ibn Saud, cited in Dennis Ross, *The Missing Peace: The Inside Story of the Fight for Middle East Peace,* Farrar, Straus, and Giroux, New York, 2004, 34. (Ambassador Ross's book provides an excellent history of the Arab-Israeli dispute, along with the definitive account of efforts to arrive at a negotiated solution.)

125 *"I will take no action,"* letter from President Roosevelt, cited in interview with Hermann F. Eilts, *Frontline,* PBS, June 23, 2003.

126 *Begin gave thanks and prayed,* prayer of Menachem Begin, June 1967, published in *Jerusalem Post* Internet edition, September 13, 1998.

131 *"Jerusalem is for us,"* Saladin and Richard the Lionheart are quoted in James Reston, Jr., in *Warriors of God: Richard the Lionheart and Saladin in the Third Crusade,* Doubleday, New York, 2001, 230–231.

132 *"Fight in the cause of God,"* Quran 2:190–191.

133 *"the Redemption of the whole world,"* Rabbi Eleazar Waldman, quoted in Karen Armstrong, *The Battle for God,* Knopf, New York, 2000, 286.

133 *"The idea of Greater Israel,"* Leon Wieseltier, "The Fall," *New Republic,* September 5, 2005.

134 *Asked if he had acted,* Sarah Coleman, "Incitement Campaign Fueled

Rabin's Assassin, Book Says," *Jewish Bulletin of Northern California,* August 20, 1999.

134 *wildly overestimate,* Craig R. Charney and Nicole Yakatan, "A New Beginning: Strategies for a More Fruitful Dialogue with the Muslim World," Council of Foreign Relations, May 2005. (Special report.)

134 *Another recent survey,* Center for Strategic Studies, University of Jordan, "Revisiting the Arab Street: Research from Within," February 2005, 63.

135 *A best-selling series,* "Left Behind": books by Jerry Jenkins and Tim LaHaye, published by Tyndale House.

142 *"the reasonable man,"* George Bernard Shaw, *Man and Superman: A Comedy and a Philosophy—Maxims for Revolutionists,* University Press, Cambridge, Mass., 1903; Bartleby, New York, 1999.

143 *"In that day,"* Isaiah 19:24–25. For a provocative essay on this passage, see Manfred T. Brauch, "Choosing Exclusion or Embrace: An Abrahamic Theological Perspective," in Robert A. Seiple and Dennis R. Hoover, eds., *Religion and Security: The New Nexus in International Relations,* Rowman and Littlefield, Lanham, Md., 2004.

143 *"draw on the springs,"* Yitzhak Rabin, Prime Minister of Israel, ceremony commemorating peace between Israel and Jordan, Aqaba, Jordan, October 27, 1994.

144 *"If the enemy inclines,"* Quran 8:61.

TEN: "THE GREATEST JIHAD"

145 *"Cry aloud,"* I Kings 18:27.

146 *"God continues,"* Jerry Falwell, quoted in John F. Harris, "God Gave U.S. 'What We Deserve,' " *Washington Post,* September 14, 2001.

146 *"clear victory,"* transcript of a videotaped meeting between Osama bin Laden and an unidentified Saudi sheikh, released by the Pentagon on December 13, 2001. The quotations cited are of those of the sheikh.

146 *"If thou shalt indeed obey,"* Exodus 23:22.

147 " *'Faith' is a fine,"* Emily Dickinson, "Faith Is a Fine Invention." Viewed at http://www.poetseers.org/themes/poems_about_faith.

148 *"I see no sign,"* Remarks of the author, House of Hope Presbyterian Church, Saint Paul, Minnesota, September 30, 2001.

150 *a group of sixty academics,* "What We're Fighting For: A Letter from America," February 2002.

150 *When Gore Vidal,* Gore Vidal, "The Enemy Within," *Observer* (London), October 27, 2002.

151 *"the only punishment,"* Alice Walker, quoted in the *Village Voice,* October 9, 2001.

151 *In February 1998,* "Jihad against Jews and Crusaders," statement issued by the World Islamic Front in the names of Shaykh Usamah Bin-Muhammad Bin-Ladin, Ayman al-Zawahiri, amir of the Jihad Group in Egypt; Abu-

Yasser Rifa'i Ahmad Taha, Egyptian Islamic Group; Shaykh Mir Hamzah, secretary of the Jamiat-ul-Ulema-e-Pakistan; and Fazlur Rahman, amir of the Jihad Movement in Bangladesh, February 23, 1998.

151   *"Bin Laden is not entitled,"* United Press International, "Taliban Annuls Bin Laden Fatwas against U.S.," June 17, 1999.

153   *a torrent of donations,* CBS News report, July 6, 1999.

153   *"Saladin,"* Henri Gouraud, cited in James Reston Jr., *Warriors of God: Richard the Lionheart and Saladin in the Third Crusade,* Doubleday, New York, 2005, xvii.

154   *"It may be,"* Quran 60:7–8.

ELEVEN: "GOD WANTS ME TO BE PRESIDENT"

158   *"At some point,"* President George W. Bush, cited in Bob Woodward, *Bush at War,* Simon and Schuster, New York, 2002, 81.

158   *research indicates,* Robert A. Pape, "Blowing Up an Assumption," *New York Times,* May 18, 2005.

158   *Within two years,* Pew Global Attitudes Project, Pew Research Center for the People and the Press, surveys released in June 2003 and June 2005.

159   *An advisory panel of the State Department,* Glenn Kessler and Robin Wright, "Report: U.S. Image in Bad Shape," *Washington Post,* September 25, 2005.

160   *"You know, he is the wrong father,"* quoted in Bob Woodward, *Plan of Attack,* Simon and Schuster, New York, 2004, 421.

160   *"I believe God,"* interview with Richard Land, director of the Southern Baptist Convention, "The Jesus Factor," *Frontline,* National Public Broadcasting, April 29, 2004.

161   *"Why callest thou,"* Mark 10:18.

161   *"right as God,"* President Abraham Lincoln, Second Inaugural Address, Washington, D.C., March 4, 1865.

161   *"I say this,"* remarks of the author at Yale Divinity School, March 30, 2004.

162   *"sing Kumbaya,"* Jed Babbin, former deputy undersecretary of defense, on Sean Hannity's show, "Is Albright Right That Iraq Is Making the World Hate Us?" March 31, 2004.

162   *"GOP stands for,"* Leon Mosley, quoted by Michelle Crowley, "Press the Flesh," *New Republic,* September 13–20, 2004, 11.

162   *"the shield of God,"* Thomas Edsall, "College Republicans' Fundraising Criticized," *Washington Post,* December 26, 2004, A5.

162   *"When America was created,"* Vice President Richard Cheney, speech to Republican National Convention, New York, September 1, 2004.

162   *"Like governments before us,"* President George W. Bush, speech to Republican National Convention, New York, September 2, 2004.

162   *"You better know what you believe,"* President George W. Bush, remarks in Westlake, Ohio, October 28, 2004.

TWELVE: IRAQ: UNINTENDED CONSEQUENCES

165 *"It makes a great difference,"* Augustine of Hippo, "Against Faustus the Manichaean XXII," in Michael W. Tkacz and Douglas Kries, trans., and Ernest L. Fortin and Douglas Kries, eds., *Augustine: Political Writings*, Hackett, Indianapolis, Ind., 1994.

165 *"will make things better,"* President Bush, quoted in Bob Woodward, *Plan of Attack*, Simon and Schuster, New York, 2004, 332.

165 *"even if there were an adequate rationale,"* remarks by the author at Columbia University, New York, March 4, 2003.

166 *"Frankly, they have worked,"* Secretary of State Colin Powell, press conference in Cairo, Egypt, February 24, 2001.

167 *The Methodist bishop,* quoted by Susan B. Thistlewaite, "Just and Unjust Wars in the Christian Tradition: What Does History Teach Us?" Sermon delivered at Saint Peter's United Church of Christ, Elmhurst, Ill., February 23, 2003.

167 *Petros VII,* Susan Sachs, "Petros VII, Top Patriarch Who Sought Religious Dialogue, Dies," *New York Times*, September 13, 2004.

167 *"military action,"* Executive Committee, World Conference on Religion and Peace, "The Crisis in Iraq: The Need for Common Security, Common Responsibility, and Common Action," February 14, 2003.

167 *A Protestant network,* Jim Wallis, *God's Politics: Why the Right Gets It Wrong and the Left Doesn't Get It*, Harper San Francisco, 2005, 45–55.

168 *"Absence of evidence,"* Donald Rumsfeld, U.S. secretary of defense, press briefing at the Pentagon, Washington, D.C., August 5, 2003.

169 *"Bush wanted,"* memo from Matthew Rycroft to Sir David Manning (both foreign policy advisers to Prime Minister Tony Blair) concerning a meeting with the prime minister on the subject of Iraq, July 23, 2002. The memo, labeled "Secret and Strictly Personnel," was made public by the *Sunday Times* of London in the spring of 2005.

171 *"Our armies,"* Sir Frederick Stanley Maude, Proclamation of Baghdad, March 19, 1917. www.lib.byu./rdh/wwi/1917/procbaghdad.html.

176 *"The first step,"* Aparisim Gosh, "Inside the Mind of an Iraqi Suicide Bomber," *Time* magazine, July 4, 2005.

176 *Mustafa Jabbar,* Somini Sengupta, "The Reach of War," *New York Times*, July 10, 2004.

177 *For this reason,* For a provocative article on this episode, see Seymour Hersh, "Did Washington Try to Manipulate Iraq's Election?" *New Yorker*, July 18, 2005.

178 *In a meeting,* meeting between the author and King Abdullah of Jordan, Washington, D.C., March 15, 2005.

180 *"Iraq will become the center,"* Kyle Fisk, quoted in Katharine T. Phan, "Evangelical Missionaries Rush to Win Iraq as Middle East Mission Base," *Christian Post*, June 2, 2004.

181 "*The way the preachers arrived,*" Bishop Jean Sleiman, quoted in Caryle Murphy, "Evangelicals Building a Base in Iraq," *Washington Post*, June 23, 2005.

183 "*the terrorist threat to America,*" President George W. Bush, address to the nation, Washington, D.C., March 17, 2003.

THIRTEEN: CONFRONTING AL QAEDA

187 *Islamic cultural values.* These conclusions are derived from a study conducted in Jordan, Syria, Egypt, Lebanon, and the Palestinian Authority: "Revisiting the Arab Street," Center for Strategic Studies, University of Jordan, February 2005.

187 "*Sweden, for example,*" Osama bin Laden, statement released by Al Jazeera television, October 29, 2004. English.aliazeera.net/NR/exeres/79CGAF22-98FB-4AIC-B21F-2BC36E87F61F.htm.

187 *In 2004, one of the Defense Department's own advisory boards,* report of Defense Science Board, cited in Michael Getler, "What Readers Saw and Didn't See," *Washington Post*, December 5, 2004, B6.

187 "*the holy attack,*" quotation from a jihadist website, cited in Susan B. Glasser, "'Martyrs' in Iraq Mostly Saudis," *Washington Post*, May 15, 2005, 1.

188 *the frequency of suicide bombings,* remarks of Dr. Bruce Hoffman, an expert on terrorism for the Rand Foundation at a panel discussion: "Suicide Terrorism: How Should the United States Combat This Growing Threat?" sponsored by the Center for American Progress, Washington, D.C., August 25, 2005.

188 "*Oh Mujahid brother,*" quotation from the inaugural issue of *Muaskas al-Battar* ("Camp of the Sword"), published by the Saudi Arabian branch of Al Qaeda, cited in Steve Coll and Susan B. Glasser, "Terrorists Turn to the Web as Base of Operations," *Washington Post*, August 7, 2005.

188 "*When terrorists spend their days and nights,*" President George W. Bush, speech to FBI Academy, Quantico, Va., July 11, 2005.

189 *According to an assessment by the CIA,* Douglas Jehl, "Iraq May Be Prime Place for Training of Militants, CIA Report Concludes," *New York Times*, June 22, 2005, A10.

189 "*What we are now awaiting,*" Claude Moniquet, quoted in Roula Kalaf and Jonathan Guthrie, "Europe's Radical Young Muslims Turn to Violence," *Financial Times*, July 11, 2005.

190 "*We lack metrics,*" Defense Secretary Donald Rumsfeld, "The Global War on Terrorism," October 16, 2003. (Memo to the senior Defense Department staff.) www.Foxnews.com/story/0,2933,100917,00.html.

191 "*On one front,*" Colonel Charles P. Borchini, USA (Ret.), forum transcript, "Religion and Security: The New Nexus in International Relations," Pew Forum on Religion and Public Life, Washington, D.C., November 10, 2004.

192 "*The critical problem,*" report of Defense Science Board, cited in Thom

Shanker, "U.S. Fails to Explain Policies to Muslim World, Panel Says," *New York Times,* November 24, 2004.

193 *"an offense to God,"* Archbishop Giovanni Lajolo, interview with Italian press, May 11, 2004, cited in "Abu Ghraib Torture and Prisoner Abuse," Wikipedia.

195 *"The barbarous custom,"* Napoleon Bonaparte, letter to Berthier, November 11, 1798. Viewed at http://www.military_quotes.com/Napoleon.htm.

197 *"Where Are the Men?"* Neil MacFarquhar, "Lebanese Would-Be Suicide Bomber Tells How Volunteers Are Waging Jihad in Iraq," *New York Times,* November 2, 2004, A10.

197 *"Bin Laden and Islamist terrorists,"* National Commission on Terrorist Attacks against the United States, *The 9/11 Commission Report,* Norton, New York, 2004, 362.

198 *Al Qaeda's leading,* ibid., 251–252.

198 *In Yemen since 2002,* Brian Michael Jenkins, "Strategy: Political Warfare Neglected," *San Diego Union-Tribune,* June 26, 2005.

199 *"If you study terrorism,"* Hamoud al-Hitar, quoted in James Brandon, "Koranic Duels Ease Terror," March 7, 2005, Interfaith Cooperation blog. Viewed at http://daga.dhs.org/icp/blog.html.

199 *"Communism was not defeated,"* Václav Havel, *The Art of the Impossible: Politics as Morality in Practice,* Knopf, Toronto and New York, 1997, 90.

FOURTEEN: THE SAUDI DILEMMA

203 *"I am scared,"* Mona Eltahawy, "The Wahhabi Threat to Islam," *Washington Post,* June 6, 2004, B7.

203 *"My kingdom will survive,"* Ibn Saud, quoted in Sandra MacKey, *The Saudis: Inside the Desert Kingdom,* Norton, 2002, 371. (Updated edition.)

203 *"We are part of this world,"* King Fahd, statement issued by government of Saudi Arabia, May 20, 2004. www.Saudiembassy.net/Reportlink/ Extremism-Report-January-2005.pdf.

205 *"un-Islamic,"* Ayatollah Khomeini, quoted in Fawaz A. Gerges, *America and Political Islam: Clash of Culture or Clash of Interests?* Cambridge University Press, Cambridge, 1999, 44.

206 *transformed Saudi Arabia into the ultimate welfare state.* Information drawn from remarks of Charles W. Freeman, former U.S. ambassador to Saudi Arabia, at a New Republic Symposium on Public Policy, "Political Reform in Saudi Arabia: Examining the Kingdom's Political Future," Washington, D.C., October 2, 2003.

206 *The country's oil revenues,* Jad Mouawad, "Saudis Shift toward Letting OPEC Aim Higher," *New York Times,* January 28, 2005, C1–2.

208 *"no one with known links,"* National Commission on Terrorist Attacks against the United States, *The 9/11 Commission Report,* Norton, New York, 2004, 330.

208   *some 210 Islamic Centers.* Statistics are from King Fahd's official website, www.kingfahdbinabdulaziz.com.

210   *The managing editor of one daily paper,* Khaled Batarfi, "The Problem Lies with Those Who Misinterpret History in Order to Serve Self-Interest," Middle East Research Institute, Special Dispatch Series, No. 830, December 17, 2004. (Dr. Batarfi is the managing editor of the Saudi Arabian daily *Al Madina.*)

210   *"It is a certain fact,"* Abdel Rahman al-Rashad, "A Wake-Up Call: Almost All Terrorists Are Muslims," *Arab News,* September 9, 2004.

210   *"a global crime perpetrated,"* Crown Prince Abdullah, International Conference on Counter-Terrorism, Riyadh, Saudi Arabia, February, 2005. www.Saudiembassy.net/2005news/statements/StateDetail.asp?cIndex=498.

211   *a poll conducted privately,* survey cited in Fareed Zakaria, "The Saudi Trap," *Newsweek,* June 28, 2004.

211   *It should be no surprise,* Susan B. Glasser, " 'Martyrs' in Iraq Mostly Saudis," *Washington Post,* May 15, 2005, A1.

213   *I had a chance during my visit,* conversation with Crown Prince Abdullah, Riyadh, Saudi Arabia, February 22, 2005.

214   *He has allocated $3.3 billion,* Edward S. Walker, "Islam's Battle within Itself," *Baltimore Sun,* October 12, 2005.

215   *"a sort of oily heart,"* Max Rodenbeck, "Unloved in Arabia," *New York Review of Books,* October 21, 2004. (Rodenbeck is characterizing a general perception.)

FIFTEEN: ARAB DEMOCRACY

217   *"the most powerful force,"* Senator John F. Kennedy, cited in Thurston Clarke, *Ask Not: The Inauguration of John F. Kennedy and the Speech That Changed America,* Holt, New York, 2004, 83.

217   *"rash intervention,"* ibid, 83.

218   *"stability cannot be purchased,"* President George W. Bush, address to the National Endowment of Democracy, Washington, D.C., November 6, 2003.

220   *Surveys have found that Arab and Muslim populations,* Pew Global Attitudes Project, "Views of a Changing World," June 2003.

221   *"the election system,"* King Fahd, cited in John L. Esposito, *The Islamic Threat: Myth or Reality?* Oxford University Press, New York, 1999, 242.

222   *"To be a secularist,"* Abdou Filali-Ansary, "Muslims and Democracy," *Journal of Democracy,* July 1999.

223   *"If one were to ask if Muslims,"* Seyyed Hossein Nasr, University Professor of Islamic Studies, George Washington University, cited in Osman bin Bakar, "Pluralism and the 'People of the Book,' " in Seiple, Robert A. and Dennis R. Hoover, eds., *Religion and Security: The New Nexus in International Relations,* Rowman and Littlefield, Lanham, Md., 2004.

224 *"The U.S. and U.K.,"* Prime Minister Ateif Ebeid, cited in David Remnick, "Going Nowhere," *New Yorker,* July 12 and 19, 2004.

226 *"When I was at the Department of State,"* "Interview with James A. Baker III," *Middle East Quarterly,* Vol. 1, No. 3, September 1994, 83.

227 *"Even the most moderate,"* dissent by F. Gregory Gause III to Council on Foreign Relations Independent Task Force Special Report No. 54 (cochaired by Vin Weber and Madeleine K. Albright), "In Support of Democracy: Why and How."

228 *"As for these Islamists,"* Orhan Pamuk, *Snow,* Knopf, New York, 2004, 26.

230 *"Maybe some will...say,"* President George W. Bush, cited in Michael Hirsch and Dan Ephron, "Can Elections Modify the Behavior of Islam's Militant Groups Fighting Occupation?" *Newsweek,* June 20, 2005.

230 *"From the day of our founding,"* President George W. Bush, inaugural address, Washington, D.C., January 20, 2005.

SIXTEEN: ISLAM IN THE WEST

235 *"The countries of Europe,"* Dr. Gerhard Ludwig Müller, cited in Elyse Schneiderman and Caroline Vazquez, "Immigration and Its Discontents," *Yale Globalist,* October 2004, 13.

239 *The bombings in London* [footnote], *Voice of America,* editorial, "Muslim Leaders Confront Terrorism," September 13, 2005.

239 *the Spanish police apprehended,* Elaine Sciolino, "Spain Continues to Uncover Terrorist Plots, Officials Say," *New York Times,* March 13, 2005, 11.

239 *German and French police broke up cells,* Elaine Sciolino, "France Seizes 11 Accused of Plotting Iraq Attacks," *New York Times,* January 27, 2005, A8.

240 *Operatives of Abu Musab al-Zarqawi's terrorist organization,* Craig Whitlock, "In Europe, New Force for Recruiting Radicals," *Washington Post Foreign Service,* February 18, 2005.

240 *British officials estimate,* counterterrorism officials cited anonymously, ibid.

240 *"Part of the Muslim community,"* interview with Prime Minister Tony Blair, London, October 17, 2005.

240 *"In these neighborhoods,"* ibid.

243 *"Staying here carries with it a duty,"* Tony Blair, quoted in Irshad Manji, "Why Tolerate the Hate?" *New York Times,* August 9, 2005. (Op-ed article.)

244 *"I flatly refuse to believe,"* Kemal Atatürk, quoted in Margaret MacMillan, *Paris 1919,* Random House, New York, 2001, 370.

245 *"At a time when people,"* Abdullah Gül, quoted in Amer Tahiri, "Turkey's Bid to Raise Its Islamic Profile and Court Europe May Backfire," *Arab News,* October 6, 2004.

245 *"To modernize an Islamic country,"* Joschka Fischer, quoted in David Masci, "An Uncertain Road: Muslims and the Future of Europe," Pew Forum on Religion and Public Life, Pew Research Center, December 2004.

246 *a per capita income, World Development Indicators,* World Bank, 2003.

246 *Prime Minister Silvio Berlusconi.* The quotations from Berlusconi and Giscard d'Estaing are cited in Masci, op. cit.

246 *"Turkey has always represented,"* Cardinal Joseph Ratzinger, cited in Ian Fisher, "Issue for Cardinals: Islam as Rival or Partner in Talks," *New York Times,* April 12, 2005.

248 *"No doubt very few countries,"* interview with Prime Minister Tony Blair, London, October 17, 2005.

248 *40 percent of whom,* survey cited in Karl Vick, "In Many Turks' Eyes, U.S. Remains the Enemy," *Washington Post,* April 10, 2005.

249 *"a splendid piece,"* Vincent Boland, "Faith, Hope, and Parity," *Financial Times Weekend,* August 27–28, 2005.

SEVENTEEN: AFRICA: A RACE FOR SOULS

251 *"We are heading,"* Andrew Rice, "Evangelicals v. Muslims in Africa," *New Republic,* August 9, 2004.

251 *"There is a race,"* ibid.

263 *in Nigeria's central highlands,* Somini Sengupta, "Where the Land Is a Tinderbox," *New York Times International,* June 16, 2004, A4.

264 *"We didn't see the chaos growing,"* Ben Okri, *Songs of Enchantment,* Cape, London, 1993.

EIGHTEEN: THE WHOLE SHOOTING MATCH

268 *Surveys have found,* Center for Strategic Studies, University of Jordan, "Revisiting the Arab Street: Research from Within," February, 2005, 46. (Study.)

268 *Robertson told an audience* [footnote], Pat Robertson home-page online, www.PatRobertson.com/speeches.

268 *A plurality think Islam,* survey, Pew Forum on Religion and Public Life, Pew Research Center for the People and the Press, July 2005.

270 *according to one joint study,* "An Arab-American Relationship for the Twenty-First Century," Report of the Middle East Institute in Washington, D.C.; and the Al Ahram Center for Political and Strategic Studies in Cairo, with the Support and Participation of the Ford Foundation, March 2005.

270 *A second survey,* Pew Global Attitudes Project, "Unfavorable Image of U.S. Is Largely Unchanged," Pew Research Center for the People and the Press, Washington, D.C., June 2005.

270 *"every agency and department,"* President George W. Bush, U.S. Department of State, September 9, 2005.

271 *Some are actually convinced,* Craig R. Charney and Nicole Yakatan, "A New Beginning: Strategies for a More Fruitful Dialogue with the Muslim World," Council on Foreign Relations, May 2005.

274 *The Saudi embassy in Washington* [footnote], cited in Jessica Stern, *Terror in the Name of God: Why Religious Militants Kill*, HarperCollins, New York, 2003, 49.

275 *"there should be a clear distinction,"* Sayd Mohammed al-Musawi, quoted in Mona Eltahawy, "After London, Tough Questions for Muslims," *Washington Post*, July 24, 2005.

275 *Clausewitz was right*, Carl von Clausewitz, *On War*, 1832, cited in Wikipedia entry for "Fog of War."

277 *"It is OK,"* telephone conversation between the author and Bill Clinton, August 17, 2005.

278 *"For now, I see through a glass darkly,"* I Corinthians 13:12.

278 *"If you accept that you may not know everything,"* interview with Bill Clinton, Chappaqua, New York, September 27, 2005.

278 *"Compete with one another,"* Quran 5:48.

278 *"if Allah did not check,"* Quran 2:251.

281 *"full partners in the development of human civilization,"* message of King Abdullah, Amman, Jordan, November 9, 2004. Viewed at http//:www.kingabdullah.jo/body.php?page_id=464&menu_id=&lang_hmkal=1.

NINETEEN: SUMMONING THE BETTER ANGELS

283 *"Christians and their opponents,"* C. S. Lewis, *The World's Last Night* (ch. 6), cited in Clyde Kilby, ed., *A Mind Awake: An Anthology of C. S. Lewis*, Harcourt, 1968, 226.

284 *"Doubt is not the opposite,"* Tillich's aphorism appears in numerous collections of quotations, including Brainyquote, Tentmaker Quotes, and Use Wisdom online.

286 *"Social conflict,"* Reinhold Niebuhr, *Moral Man and Immoral Society*, Scribner, 1932.

288 *"answer to a calling,"* President George W. Bush, speech to Republican National Convention, New York, September 2, 2004.

288 *"What's wrong with dominance,"* William Kristol, cited in Jim Wallis, *"God's Politics: Why the Right Gets It Wrong and the Left Doesn't Get It,"* Harper San Francisco, 2005, 138.

290 *"most acceptable service,"* Benjamin Franklin, *The Autobiography of Benjamin Franklin*, Washington Square, New York, 1975, 99.

290 *According to the poem by Yeats*, William Butler Yeats, "The Second Coming." *Selected Poems and Two Plays of William Butler Yeats*, Collier Books, New York, 1962, 91.

Acknowledgments

In the spring of 2004, I was invited to address the Yale Divinity School. Clyde Tuggle, a friend and an alumnus of the school, had initiated the idea. Since leaving government, I had spoken to groups of almost every description, and I am not usually at a loss for words, but I was unsure what would interest a hall full of aspiring ministers and theologians. Rule one in any speech is to start off on a light note, so I dredged up the only story I knew featuring both God and a former secretary of state:

> A man dies and goes to heaven. At the pearly gates, he tells Saint Peter how happy he is to be there because he had always wanted to meet Henry Kissinger. Peter replies that Dr. Kissinger is still alive and not expected for some time. Disappointed, the man enters Heaven but soon rushes out very excited. "Saint Peter," he exclaims, "Henry Kissinger *is* in there; I just saw him. He is pacing around with his hands behind his back muttering about the Middle East." Peter shakes his head sadly, "No, I'm afraid you're wrong. That wasn't Kissinger; that was God. He just *thinks* he's Henry Kissinger."

A story, however, takes one only so far. For publicity purposes, Yale wanted to know in advance the title of my remarks. That is when this book, *The Mighty and the Almighty*, was truly born. I prepared the speech and delivered it to a positive reception but realized at the time that I had merely skimmed the surface of a subject of boundless importance and depth.

When I was in college, I had reported for the school newspaper and dreamed about a career in journalism. *The Mighty and the Almighty* gave me a chance to play reporter. I began by interviewing two people uniquely qualified to discuss religion and U.S. foreign policy, former presidents Jimmy Carter and Bill Clinton. Both men have hectic schedules, but both still took time to share with me insights that have immeasurably enriched this book. I especially want to thank President Clinton for doing me the honor of writing such a superb introduction to this book. I am grateful, as well, to Prime Minister Tony Blair, King Abdullah of Saudi Arabia, King Abdullah of Jordan, and former president Václav Havel of the Czech Republic for allowing me to discuss this project with them and for giving me the benefit of their experience and thoughts.

Early in my career, I came to appreciate the truism that a little knowledge is a dangerous thing. In writing this book, I knew that I would be touching on volatile subjects. I worried that I might mischaracterize religious beliefs, get part of the history wrong, offend people unintentionally, or fail to raise obvious issues. In other words, I needed help. For that, I turned to old friends and new. Bob Seiple, former U.S. ambassador for international religious freedom, was the first to review a draft of this text with an expert's eye. I am grateful to him for supporting this project so strongly and for his many helpful suggestions. Ambassador Seiple and I do not see every issue the same way, but we agree fully on the close connection between knowledge of religion and the protection of international security.

I turned next to Imam Abdul Feisal because he is a wise man and could read the draft from a Muslim perspective. He responded to my request for help by clearing his calendar, reading the entire book, commenting in depth on every chapter, correcting my punctuation, and extending a blessing to me and my loved ones—all within four days. He, too, will not agree with everything in these pages, but because of his contributions it is a far better volume (and more grammatical) than it otherwise would have been.

Hard as it was for me to believe, Rabbi David Saperstein, director of the Religious Action Center of Reform Judaism, matched Imam Feisel in the energy and care with which he reviewed the draft. His page-by-page comments on issues large and small were uniformly helpful if not always decipherable. The memo he attached, thankfully typewritten, contained a wealth of superb suggestions. I am deeply in his debt.

During the eighteen months of this book's evolution, I have become a skilled and diligent picker of brains, ruthlessly tapping the best ones I know. Among those who have willingly (or at least politely) succumbed to this treatment are Zbigniew Brzezinski, my former boss at the National Security Council; Reverend Susan Thistlewaite of the Chicago Theological Seminary; the scholar Elaine Pagels of Princeton University; Senator Sam Brownback of Kansas; Walter Isaacson, president of the Aspen Institute; Fareed Zakaria; Vin Weber, chair of the National Endowment for Democracy; Reverend Donald Argue, former president of the National Association of Evangelicals; Father Alexander Karloutsos of the Greek Orthodox Archdiocese of America; Dr. Richard Land of the Southern Baptist Convention; M.K. Rabbi Michael Melchior, Israel's deputy minister for the Israeli Society and World Jewish Community; Dr. Mustafa Cerić, the Grand Mufti of Bosnia; John Podesta, president of the Center for American Progress;

and Douglas Johnston, president of the International Center for Religion and Diplomacy.

Given my other activities, I also needed help with research. As I have walked by his office over the past year, I have watched as the pile of books on Bill Woodward's desk has grown until it became a mountain range whose peaks are labeled with such names as Armstrong, Novak, Neibuhr, Esposito, Benjamin, Weigel, Wallis, Reston, MacKey, Ross, and King James. In the crevices are crumpled think-tank studies, ripped-out news clippings, a letter from a woman in New Jersey explaining about Satan, and—from a man who had done work on my farm—a brochure entitled "Are You Going to Heaven?" Bill, who was my speechwriter while I was in government, did much of the hardest work on this book, helped with the writing, pushed me to think more deeply, and contributed many ideas of his own.

Elaine Shocas, formerly my chief of staff at the State Department, provided invaluable assistance through her repeated careful readings of the manuscript and her thoughtful suggestions and advice. Elaine helps me decide what to say and, even more important, what *not* to say.

In the course of preparing my memoir, *Madam Secretary*, I had my first experience—a humbling one—of working with that subspecies of magician known as a professional editor. It was my luck to get the best in the business and to have him back now for a second go. Richard Cohen, a marvelous author in his own right, is expert at rearranging sentences (and whole chapters), deleting excess verbiage, and finding the right tone. It didn't hurt that he had spent some time in a Benedictine monastery when younger and helped me avoid at least one unintentional act of heresy. I am pleased to be able to count Richard and his talented wife, Kathy Robbins, among my good friends.

Others who deserve thanks for reading and providing perceptive comments on the draft include my brother and sister, John Korbel and Kathy Silva; Ambassador Wendy Sherman, a partner in the Albright Group and my counselor while at the State Department; Evelyn Lieberman, former undersecretary of state for public diplomacy; Ambassador Dennis Ross; Jamie Rubin, former State Department spokesman; Susan Rice, former assistant secretary of state for Africa; Toni Verstandig, former deputy assistant secretary of state for Near East affairs; Suzy George, my present chief-of-staff; Jamie Smith, my director of communications; and Thomas Oliphant, columnist for the *Boston Globe*. I should also single out Dan Consolatare, who, in the initial stages of this project, helped creatively both in research and in the suggestion of themes. My colleagues Carol Browner, Jim O'Brien, Diana Sierra, Margo Morris, Amy McDowell, Laurie Dunden, Drew McCracken, and Anna Cronin-Scott provided the much-needed—and much-appreciated—daily support.

It is no secret that I went to HarperCollins because of one man—Jonathan Burnham. As senior vice president and publisher, Jonathan has advised me, anchored me, and guided me during the writing of this book. In my memoir published in 2003, I described him as "that rarity, a man both elegant and modest." He may not be infallible, but you could not prove it by me; he has yet to steer me in any direction except the right one.

I am grateful to Jane Friedman, president and CEO of HarperCollins; and Michael Morrison, president and group publisher, Harper/Morrow Division, for welcoming me so warmly into the HarperCollins family. They and every member of this legendary publishing house have provided a remarkable level of encouragement, and I thank them all. Tim Duggan, executive editor, has shepherded me through every stage of the editing and production with his good counsel, good company, and patience. I have been fortunate to work again with the creative vice president and associate publisher Kathy Schneider and all the members of the sales force—a talented group whose enthusiasm is contagious. Vice president and art director Roberto de Vicq has produced a wonderful design for the jacket—not an easy task when the Almighty is involved. Tina Andreadis, vice president and director of publicity, has worked very hard to make the book a success. I particularly want to thank Caroline Clayton and Allison Lorentzen of HarperCollins for their assistance no matter what the hour. Timothy Greenfield Sanders is an extraordinary photographer; a session with him is a grand adventure. I thank him for again doing the best he could with the material before his lens.

For over thirty years, Bob Barnett has been a close personal friend, political comrade, and legal counsel. He has advised me well, as they say, in good times and in bad. I thank him and his talented colleague, Deneen Howell of Williams and Connolly, LLP, for guiding me in my newest career as an author and through the fascinating maze of the publishing world.

I cannot conclude these acknowledgements without expressing appreciation to all the members of what has become a large family for their companionship, support, and love. With them in my life, I know I am truly blessed.

Index

Writing
Articles

ABOUT THE WORLD
AROUND YOU

Marcia Yudkin

WRITER'S DIGEST BOOKS
CINCINNATI, OH

Dedication

To reference librarians everywhere

—a freelance writer's best friends

Writing Articles About the World Around You. Copyright © 1998 by Marcia Yudkin. Printed and bound in the United States of America. All rights reserved. No part of this book may be reproduced in any form or by any electronic or mechanical means including information storage and retrieval systems without permission in writing from the publisher, except by a reviewer, who may quote brief passages in a review. Published by Writer's Digest Books, an imprint of F&W Publications, Inc., 1507 Dana Avenue, Cincinnati, Ohio 45207. (800) 289-0963. First edition.

This hardcover edition of *Writing Articles About the World Around You* features a "self-jacket" that eliminates the need for a separate dust jacket. It provides sturdy protection for your book while it saves paper, trees and energy.

Other fine Writer's Digest Books are available from your local bookstore or direct from the publisher.

02 01 00 99 98   5 4 3 2 1

Library of Congress Cataloging-in-Publication Data

Yudkin, Marcia.
    Writing articles about the world around you / by Marcia Yudkin.
        p.   cm.
    Includes bibliographical references and index.
    ISBN 0-89879-814-0 (hardcover : alk. paper)
    1. Journalism—Authorship. 2. Feature writing. I. Title.
PN147.Y83   1998
808'.02—dc21   97-40672
                                                CIP

Edited by Jack Heffron and Roseann S. Biederman
Production edited by Amanda Magoto
Cover designed by Chad Planner

Praise for *Writing Articles About the World Around You*

"Whether you're a newcomer gearing up to dive into the writing pool or an old-timer needing to revive a neglected writing career, *Writing Articles About the World Around You* will point you in the right direction, and, even better, stir up all sorts of new, useable ideas that may be hiding in plain sight."

—*Barbara J. Winter*, author of
Making a Living Without a Job

"The book is professional yet accessible, knowledgeable, authoritative, straightforward and engaging, offering lots of real-life examples and nitty-gritty details on everything from interviews to invoices. She offers plenty of 'reach for the stars' encouragement, but also reminds us to stay full grounded in the realities of the publishing world."

—*Anne Stuart*, managing editor of
CIO and *WebMaster* magazines,
freelance writer and writing instructor

"So how does one break into publishing? From ideas to print, Yudkin answers the question clearly and directly. It's a complete workshop between covers."

—*Kitty Werner*,
Dorothy Canfield Fisher Writers Conference

"*Writing Articles About the World Around You* is filled with practical advice on how real people make real money writing about what they know. The stories from people who've been there done that, and sold their stories demystify the process of making a living as a freelance writer."

—*Teresa Mears*, editor and publisher
of *Freelance Success* newsletter for writers

TABLE OF CONTENTS

PART THREE
Resources

ABOUT THE AUTHOR

Marcia Yudkin is a Boston-based writer, consultant and seminar leader who specializes in helping people communicate creatively. She launched her freelance writing career with an article in the very first Sunday *New York Times* Education section in 1981, and went on to publish articles in hundreds of magazines from *USAir Magazine* and *Psychology Today* to *New Age Journal* and *Cosmopolitan*. Her eight previous books include *Marketing Online, Six Steps to Free Publicity* and *Freelance Writing for Magazines & Newspapers*. She has taught or spoken at more than fifty writers' conferences over the years and, through her Protégé Program, coaches writers one-on-one by e-mail, fax and mail.

Marcia Yudkin
P.O. Box 1310
Boston, MA 02117
(617) 266-1613
marcia@yudkin.com

Ideas From Home

Chapter One

Starting From Home

Perhaps as I once did, you believe that "real writers write novels." Or perhaps you treasure journalism and fantasize about breaking into print with a Watergate-style exposé or an astonishing interview with Madonna. Or you dream of a fan club of millions for your humor or political column. Or being flown all expenses paid to exotic corners of the earth, to report back on penguin-dotted glaciers or a never-before-explored rain forest.

Ambitions are wonderful, but when it comes to getting from being unpublished or barely published to the pinnacles of the profession, you need realistic ways of getting started in freelance writing and amassing a track record. Most successful writers launched their careers by translating what they already knew to a format that met the needs of some specific newspaper or magazine.

And that's the mission of this book—showing you in concrete detail how you can publish articles in local, regional and national publications without venturing beyond the boundaries of your hometown. You don't need to scheme your way behind locked gates in Hollywood or uncover the smoking gun for our next national scandal in order to attract the attention of editors who have the power to publish you. On the contrary, chances are that your best opportunities lie in topics so near to you that you don't yet recognize their potential.

How can I be so sure of this? I've lived largely on my writing income since January 1981, when I sold my first article to *The New York Times'* first educational supplement. (You'll learn the story behind that sale in chapter twelve.) I've discussed article

ideas person to person with dozens of editors, coached scores of writers to publication, traded stories with hundreds of fellow freelancers and taken questions from thousands of aspiring writers at conferences and workshops or in online forums.

THE DELIGHTS OF FREELANCE WRITING

From 1978 through the end of 1980, I worked as a college professor. After the first year, I became bored and dismayed by the prospect of teaching the same subjects year after year. I can't ever remember being bored during the next sixteen years as I sold my work to hundreds upon hundreds of magazines and newspapers, tackling topics ranging from nanny training to capital punishment. Each new assignment offered a fresh challenge and an opportunity to get paid for a real-world education. I found writing for publication incredibly fun. In fact, though, there are as many possible satisfactions in freelance writing as there are freelance writers.

When Kelly Boyer Sagert of Lorain, Ohio, took maternity leave from her job as a loan officer in 1991, she looked around for another career that wouldn't require the long hours she had to put in at the bank. She made her first sale to *Cats Magazine* that year with a piece about a stray cat that had moved into her father's funeral home and endeared itself to mourners. The magazine paid her just $35, but by early 1996 Sagert had two book contracts lined up, about 50 magazine and 250 newspaper articles behind her, a weekly "What's Happening" column, and public relations experience for the County Visitors Bureau.

"I like being able to work at home, being my own boss and meeting interesting people that I'm writing about. For example, I'm doing a book on boomerangs, and the people who compete on the national circuit are crazy, enthusiastic folks who it's a joy to be around," Sagert says.

Veterinarian Brad Swift of Flat Rock, North Carolina, freelanced part time for animal and pet-related magazines for about ten years before he took the leap of quitting his medical career. "People ask me if I miss being a vet, and I always look closely at my situation before replying. So far the answer has always been the same: 'Are you kidding? No!' " Swift reflects.

"I love the opportunity freelance writing gives me to express my creativity—taking the spark of an idea and fanning it into the flames of a finished article. I also feel like I'm contributing to others by thinking carefully about the message I'm about to deliver and then doing that to the best of my ability. And I love the freedom to write about things I'm excited, passionate or curious about."

Not all successful freelancers abandon their previous career, of course. Erik Sherman of Marshfield, Massachusetts, makes most of his livelihood as a marketing and public relations consultant, but writes regularly for *MacWeek,* the business section of *The Boston Globe* and elsewhere. Why?

"Covering a wide variety of topics, including technology, business, food and theater, suits my nature. Call it unfocused if you will, but it fits with freelancing. I also like the fact that I'm not under allegiance to any particular corporation. If I don't like the way they work, I can just pick up my computer and take its output elsewhere." Sherman has established relationships with some high-paying magazines that add considerably to his income. "There are few other tasks that allow me to make $1,500 in under a day," he notes.

Tom Przybylski of St. Louis, Missouri, cites two different rewards of writing articles for magazines in addition to his regular work as a direct-marketing consultant. "Nothing creates authority better than being an author, and the exposure is invaluable. *Marketing Tools* magazine, where I published two articles in 1995, is read both inside and outside the direct-marketing community. Having these couple of articles available to show prospective clients lends credence to what I'm saying and gives me a competitive edge."

Even employed journalists find enjoyment in moonlighting for magazines other than the one that signs their paycheck. "Freelancing allows me to write about subjects I don't ordinarily cover in my day job, reporting on the IRS and Congress for *Tax Notes* magazine," says Ryan Donmoyer of Alexandria, Virginia. "Through freelancing, I can write about the Internet, personal finance, entertainment—anything besides taxes or politics. It keeps me sane."

Anne Stuart, a former reporter for the Associated Press now

employed as a writer/editor for *WebMaster* magazine, agrees about the appeal of variety. "I like to keep my hand in on topics other than doing business on the Internet, and when I write for a general audience, my friends and relatives get the chance to read my work. The extra money is always welcome, too."

WHAT YOU NEED TO SUCCEED

Using my understanding of the writing business and examples and testimony from other writers, I'll explain how to come up with promising article ideas, place a spin on them so they'll appeal to a category of publications likely to take an interest in them and secure an editor's commitment to at least look at your work. I'll also explain how to research, write and polish your articles and end up with bylines to be proud of.

You in turn need only a few qualifications to benefit from the comprehensive instructions in this book:

- *Curiosity*. Freelance writers who succeed ardently want to know about the subjects they cover and enjoy passing on their discoveries and insights to others. If you have any topic you've ever investigated only because you wanted to know more, you pass this test.

- *Respect for the English language*. As melodies and rhythm make up the very substance of music, words are the medium for writing. You don't need a huge vocabulary or all the rules of grammar at your command, but when someone points out that you wrote "lightening" instead of "lightning" for the phenomenon accompanying thunder, you need to feel something akin to "Oh! Imagine that!" rather than "Big deal."

- *Flexibility*. If you believe you already know what people want to read, or how something must be written, then your mind may be too rigid to slip around, over or under the hurdles that stand between you and publication. Successful writers adjust their approach to a topic, their style and their execution of an idea according to input they receive from the publishing world. So long as you're open to learning better ways of communicating ideas, you fit my third and final prerequisite for becoming a successful freelance writer.

MYTHS ABOUT GETTING PUBLISHED

Did you notice that I didn't mention degrees or education in my list of qualifications? Here are a few misconceptions about what it takes to get published that appear to be widespread.

• *To publish articles, you need a college education or a journalism degree.* You don't need any educational credentials at all to get published. In fact, submitting a resume to an editor is a dead giveaway that you don't understand the freelance business. Skill in written communication, which some undereducated people have and many highly educated folks lack, gives you entrée to the publishing world. Your sole relevant proof of that is the way you submit your ideas.

• *You need personal connections with editors.* Wrong again! If you can write a terrific query letter, as described in chapter seven, you can get a go-ahead from an editor who doesn't know your name, your face, or your personal charm or lack of it.

• *You can't get published without a literary agent.* For the world of magazines and newspapers, this claim is a generation or more out of date. Most literary agents no longer handle periodical submissions, even for favored clients, because their commissions from article payments would barely cover postage and telephone expenses.

• *You must take precautions to prevent people from stealing your ideas.* This one comes up at almost every workshop I teach. Contrary to beginners' suspicions, however, ideas are just about never snatched from the mail and given to staff or regular contributors to pursue. If you haven't worked in an editorial office, you have no notion how common it is for people to propose independently virtually the same article. I return to this theme in chapter eleven. Instead of worrying about unlikely rip-offs, spend your energy coming up with original ideas interestingly presented.

• *No one wants to publish beginners.* Logically, this myth couldn't be true. Every now-successful writer once made a first sale. If you've never been published before, you just have to be all the more bewitching and relevant in your article proposals. Follow the guidelines in this book, be persistent and you will get your chance.

• *The odds stand overwhelmingly against you when you try to submit your work.* True, the most visible magazines on the newsstand receive bagfuls of mail from aspiring writers each week. But editors at such magazines have told me that only a small percentage of the ideas they receive are on target, timely and appetizingly presented. Once you master the process of proposing in a well-written letter an article that matches a certain magazine, your chances rise to a reasonable level.

• *You need fancy computer equipment before you can submit your work.* I hear this one often from people who haven't gotten down to the business of approaching editors yet: "After I get my computer . . ." or "Please tell me which software and printer I need." In fact, you don't need any computer of your own at all. Michael Brennan, a writer formerly from the Boston area, broke into print when he was homeless by using a computer at a local university. In many cities and towns you can rent enough time at copy centers like Kinko's to type and print a letter for only a few dollars. And the last I heard, neat typewritten queries were accepted on equal footing with computer-printed ones.

A WEALTH OF OPPORTUNITY

Before we get into coming up with publishable ideas, it's important that you increase your awareness of the enormous quantity and range of existing magazines. Each year when I buy the latest edition of *Writer's Market*, the best market guide for writers, I'm amazed all over again at the thousands of magazines profiled there that I've never heard of. Have you ever run across a copy of *National Dragster*? How about *Norway at Your Service*? *Texas Gardener* or *Southern Lumberman*? Or *Chile Pepper: The Magazine of Spicy Foods*, *Twins*, *Episcopal Life* or *Tropical Fish Hobbyist*? Each has a circulation of 12,000 or more and buys from 10 to 150 articles a year from freelancers.

According to *Ulrich's International Periodicals Directory*, at least 79,000 magazines publish regularly in the United States alone. In addition to *Writer's Market*, several other listings of magazines, such as the *Standard Rate & Data Service* guides or *Bacon's* (see Resources, p. 198), can lead you to unfamiliar periodicals. Once you get serious about writing for magazines, you may also turn up useful markets when you visit friends'

bathrooms, explore the seat pockets of airlines and haunt a variety of newsstands.

Don't forget to start hunting for different newspapers as well. If you've read nothing but the *Hometown News* and *USA Today* for the past several years, you may be overlooking other local opportunities. Peruse the racks at convenience stores and laundromats, look at what arrives free in your mailbox or on your doorstep and check out the holdings in your public library. In the Boston area, besides the ubiquitous *Globe* and *Herald*, you can find the *Boston Business Journal* for sale and *The Tab*, *The Improper Bostonian* and *Editorial Humor* for free in street boxes. At some health clubs in the suburbs you'll see stacks of *128 News*, and in certain neighborhoods, the *South End News*, the *Brookline Citizen*, the *Jewish Advocate, Sojourner* (for women) and *Gay Community News*. Even in the papers you regularly read, look beyond the sections you normally focus on to get a sense of the full range of topics covered.

Beyond magazines and newspapers lie a panoply of newsletters. Practically every organization sends something to its members every month or quarter that includes short articles. As I explain further in chapter twelve, when you start from the bottom and work your way up, your first step is to get your work published somewhere, anywhere. Newsletters generally won't pay you for submissions, but depending on how sophisticated their pages look, they can provide you with an easy route to your all-important first "clips"—copies of your published work, which in turn open doors for assignments for pay.

Except for the most visible and popular magazines, which receive an overabundance of mail from people like you, you'll find that editors have a large, constant appetite for fresh, well-targeted freelance material. Trade magazines, edited for specialists working in an industry or profession, almost never appear on newsstands and are particularly receptive to approaches from knowledgeable writers. Amy Sitze, editor of the 27,000-circulation trade tabloid, *The Inside Line*, told me that she hardly ever receives any query letters, and only once or twice in three years heard from a writer who had good clips as well as knowledge of the electronics industry. "That person would be my dream," she says.

SCOPING OUT A MAGAZINE OR NEWSPAPER

Although you may have read thousands of magazines in your lifetime, you need to learn a new way of looking at these familiar entities if you are to interest them regularly in your written work. The first thing to understand is every magazine has a readership and a focus. Although an editorial statement contained in the magazine or in a market guide for writers provides important clues to the essence of that publication, you can get a much more specific "take" on its target audience by studying the advertisements. For instance, the Saab car ad on the back cover of the premiere issue of *Self-Employed Professional* tells us that its readers are worldly and well-heeled. In *American Woman,* a series of ads for home-study courses on bookkeeping, real-estate appraising and paralegal studies indicates that many of its readers are high-school graduates in need of specific job skills. For a freelance writer, the ads serve as pointers toward the magazine audience's age, geographical distribution, job level, income, family status, technological and cultural sophistication, tastes and so on.

Refine your hypotheses from examining the ads by assessing the range of content you find in a sample issue or two. Often surprises turn up that you would never have predicted from a magazine's title. For instance, if you'd wanted to write an article on Los Angeles a few years back, probably the last magazine to come to mind would have been *New York Woman.* Yet you'd have learned from looking at it that the now-defunct magazine included a regular department called "The Other Coast." Similarly, if you wanted to write about investment strategies and managing personal finances, you'd think of a magazine like *Your Money,* not *RDH: The National Magazine for Dental Hygiene Professionals.* Yet the latter stated in its *Writer's Market* listing that it wanted to see queries on all types of personal growth and lifestyle topics—including finances.

Editors are constantly on the lookout for writers capable of matching their publication's characteristic tone—the attitude and flavor of the writing. You can understand significant differences here by comparing randomly chosen paragraphs from publications that might appear to be similar. Are the articles full of the pronoun "I," do they speak directly to the reader as "you" or are they more impersonal? Do you find slang and informal

diction, like "one day this bozo I knew in high school called me," or a lot of technical terms like "flow-through percentage" and precise numbers like "38.9 percent"? Are the sentences long and convoluted or crisp and snappy? Do snobbish judgments come through in the writing or a "you-can-do-it" spirit? When it's time to choose places to write for, sensitivity to tone helps you avoid publications you don't match well with or to modify your writing appropriately.

In becoming acquainted with particular magazines, keep an eye out for the length of articles, which may vary greatly from publication to publication and within different sections of the same one. Generally department articles or columns—pieces on topics that run under one heading issue after issue—run much shorter than features, the one-shot pieces. But in a magazine like *Inc.*, features might run 4,500 words, while several years back in *Vis-a-Vis*, the United in-flight magazine, the very longest articles consisted of around 800 words. Also, by examining half a year's issues, you can get a sense of whether the same names turn up in bylines again and again or whether abundant new names show that work is spread around among a lot of freelancers.

To size up a newspaper you might want to write for, look at one whole week's worth of issues. Note which topics are covered once a week, and which every day, the percentage of local contributors versus syndicated or nationally generated material along with the other factors discussed above. Pay special attention to the editorial section and coverage of special topics such as travel, computers, education and food.

IDEAS VERSUS ANGLES

Although nonfiction writers talk amongst each other about coming up with ideas, in truth, ideas are never enough for pitching a proposed story to an editor. You need an *angle*, a distinctive spin on an idea that indicates why or what about that idea would interest a specific audience. Editors never hand out assignments for ideas; they contract with freelancers who propose angles.

Here's the difference. Suppose you're thinking you want to write an article about raising twins: that's an idea, a topic. Well, what *about* raising twins? About the effect on older siblings of the birth of twins? About home remodeling that facilitates the

upbringing of twins? About traveling by train with toddler twins? About what bringing up identical twins taught you about everyone's need for individuality? Those are four angles for, perhaps, a parenting magazine, an architecture magazine, the travel section of a newspaper and a psychology magazine, respectively.

In my workshops, I convey the difference between ideas and angles through an exercise that begins with asking for volunteered article topics. Then I take one of the suggested ideas and ask how we could match that idea with each of several categories of magazines from *Writer's Market*.

For instance, if someone had wanted to write an article on corporate downsizing, I might ask, Is there a spin we can put on the topic of corporate downsizing to make it fit an ethnic/ minority magazine, like *African-American Heritage*, *Hispanic* or *Polish American Journal*? Inevitably someone will suggest the angle of whether or not minorities are losing ground in the era of downsizing. How about making it suitable for a regional magazine, like *Pensacola Magazine* or *Detroit Monthly*—something on the ripple effect in the regional economy of big-employer downsizing? How about targeting a pet magazine with an article called "When Your Pet Picks Up Your Depression"? And so on. Each of these angles will fare far better with editors than the generic, murky idea we started out with. Indeed, the more remote the matchup you attempt, the fresher and more publishable the angle you arrive at tends to be.

Let's try this together. Imagine that you've become excited about some research that says that people who listen well (judged by others, not themselves) make more money and express more satisfaction with their lives. Can you list at least a dozen angles for this budding article idea, along with the kinds of periodicals each angle might match well with?

Please do try this exercise before you peek at my list, which of course doesn't exhaust the possibilities. Specific angles and markets include:

1. *Local psychologist discovers that great listeners lead happier and wealthier lives*, for a city or regional magazine that covers the area where the person who conducted the study lives. This article would focus on the researcher, as someone rooted

in the area the magazine covers.

2. *Listening feeds the spirit—as well as the purse*, for a religious magazine. Notice how you would tailor the language you use to the audience—for instance, "spirit" and "spiritual" for the religious market versus "happy" or "fulfilled" for a secular orientation.

3. *Good listeners get ahead in life and have more fun!*, for a teen magazine. Here all the examples need to be geared to what teenagers relate to—having others like you, joining a group, understanding yourself, doing well at a job, acing a college interview, etc. It would have to avoid preachiness to work for this audience.

4. *The golden rewards of listening*, for a general business magazine. For this angle, emphasize the specific dollar amount payoffs discovered by the researcher as characterizing the good listeners rather than the lousy ones. You could also elaborate on ways that this contradicts some business stereotypes.

5. *Good listening not only saves lives—it fattens your wallet*, for a pilots' magazine. This angle connects the research that forms the premise of this exercise with other research showing that many deadly airline accidents stem from poor listening.

6. *For a healthier bottom line, develop this surprising business skill—listening*, for a business magazine focusing on the start-up phase. For this audience, stress how listening can help you choose the right business to launch, act appropriately on advice, hire well, etc.

7. *Great listeners yesterday and today*, for a historical magazine. You'd scour the past for prominent politicians, business figures and entertainers renowned for being either magnificent or atrocious listeners to see whether these cases seem to corroborate or refute the research in question. You could bring it up to today as well with a discussion of a few prominent individuals' listening profile.

8. *Listening to the electorate—too much of a good thing?* for a political magazine. The premise here would be that good listeners tend to get ahead in life, but does that apply to political campaigns, where those running sometimes appear to sacrifice their integrity to sway with the polls?

9. *Listening as a survival skill,* for an outdoor/mountaineering

magazine. As with the aviation angle, you might be able to cite anecdotes on poor listening contributing to some well-known mountaineering disaster, and put these in the context of the new, more general research.

10. *Good listening builds healthier families, ten ways,* for one of the home-oriented women's magazines. You could seek out similar research to draw out its implications for happiness at home.

11. *To build better listeners, appeal to self-interest,* for a management magazine. Explain that research done by so-and-so points to a better way than exhortation to motivate staff members to pay attention: by becoming better listeners, they increase their chances of earning more and enjoying life more, on and off the job.

12. *Listening to your customers and reaping the rewards,* for a grocers' (or printers', realtors', etc.) magazine. For this angle, focus on the benefits not of listening in general but of specifically listening to customers. Tailor your examples to the specific trade served by a magazine.

13. *Good listening earned me a fortune,* for the business section of a newspaper. If you can recount a dramatic experience of yours that illustrates the benefits of close listening, even if it occurred many years ago, this research study would make your personal essay about it appear timely.

Probably you've generated a few angles that don't overlap with mine. Incidentally, I made up this research, so pursue any of the above angles at your peril! Seriously, when you begin generating ideas for freelancing, brainstorm a lot of possible angles for them. Then choose the less predictable ones that excite you the most to start off with. Nothing stands in the way of you pursuing half a dozen or more of the angles, because they'd end up being substantially different articles, with some overlapping content.

In the rest of Part One, I help you understand the process of coming up with promising article ideas you can execute right where you are. Part Two describes the process of selling those ideas to editors, researching and writing a respectable article and building a satisfying freelance career.

Chapter Two

Your Experiences
as a Resource

In 1994, Kathi Geisler of Chelmsford, Massachusetts, had published just a handful of newspaper articles and done work-related writing when she contacted *Ladies' Home Journal.* She was launching a newsletter called *Food Issues* and presented herself as an expert on the topic of eating disorders, having lost one-hundred pounds and having recovered from a newly identified psychological syndrome called binge eating disorder. "My idea was that I'd be interviewed in the magazine as publicity for the newsletter," she recalls. "But an assistant editor called and suggested I write my own story for their column, 'A Woman Today.' This was the last thing I expected. I hung up the phone and went wild."

As Geisler discovered, many magazines value the authenticity of personal stories to an extent that they offer opportunities to inexperienced writers whom they might not otherwise be eager to deal with. The editor who called her explained that they often assigned a writer they knew to interview people like her and assemble the article in an "as told to" format. Geisler pointed out that she had *some* background as a writer and asked if she could put together the article herself. The editor invited her to try, reserving the right to decide on who would be the actual writer after seeing Geisler's initial draft.

After receiving the first version of her piece, the editor responded with a long list of questions and suggestions for revisions, and the final version of the piece appeared with Kathi Geisler's byline in *Ladies' Home Journal* in July 1995. Geisler negotiated a blurb about her newsletter to accompany the article, and not only received $750 from the magazine for the 2,000-

word piece but also more than 1,000 subscriptions from inter-ested readers. "They told me later it was the most popular article they ran that year, and maybe ever," she adds.

NOURISHING PROMISING IDEA SEEDS

Since as long as you are intelligently alive, you are continually having experiences, the notion that you may need guidance and practice in recognizing experiences to write about may strike you as peculiar. Even *with* plenty of practice, though, recognizing experiences worth writing about doesn't happen automatically. Six or seven years into my writing career, I found myself face to face with Rona Cherry, executive editor of *Glamour* magazine. She had invited me to meet with her when I came to New York City, and I had shown up for our appointment clutching a list of article ideas I thought suitable for *Glamour*.

One by one I pitched the topics and angles I had slaved over, and one by one she shot them down. After she said no to the eighth and final idea, I sat frozen, expecting her to stand up and usher me out. Instead she sat back, touched her fingers together in the shape of a steeple and said, "So, tell me about yourself."

Cherry didn't really do that out of a friendly impulse, I soon realized, because every once in a while as I mentioned something about my interests, background or circumstances, she would say, "Maybe there's an article there." I told Cherry that I was married to a Chinese man I'd met in China, and that the relation-ship presented quite a lot of challenges. "Maybe there's an article there," she said, and it hit me for the first time that although I'd published a piece about our courtship (in *Ms.* magazine), I hadn't written anything about what had happened since Chen arrived in the United States to live with me. Somehow I'd overlooked the most obvious writing fodder, right next to me in bed every night and padding around my writing desk day after day.

At the end of our meeting, we decided that I would prepare a proposal for an article on living with someone from another culture. *Glamour* ended up not assigning the article, but now that I'd awakened to the topic, I reworked it for an assignment from and publication in *TWA Ambassador*.

Like me, you may be overlooking life experiences that you take for granted but could interest people who do not know

you. You can duplicate my interview with Rona Cherry by writing down every fact about yourself that you might mention if someone prodded you to talk about yourself. Your list might include things like this:

- My fifth career, as flight attendant.
- Used to be an EMT, found it too stressful.
- Married high-school sweetheart.
- Have identical twins that I sometimes can't tell apart.
- Can't stand my father-in-law.
- Spouse almost went bankrupt last year.
- Live in Victorian house we restored.
- Worried about quality of water in our town.
- Am a sucker for charity appeals.
- Enjoy flirting, which bothers some others besides spouse.
- Collect Afro-American dolls.
- Last summer, had nothing but "bad hair days."

You could wrap an article around each of the above facts, if you had enough enthusiasm to try it. After you run out of items to add to your list, place a star next to those you feel ready and able to write about now.

For Susan Tiberghien, an American based in Geneva, Switzerland, who has devoted herself full-time to writing since her fiftieth birthday in 1985, personal experiences begin their journey toward published articles in a journal she keeps. About twice a week she'll record reflections, perceptions, reminiscences, observations and incidents—what she calls "gleanings" from her life, rather than a rigorous day-to-day memorializing of what she is doing. Experiences on which she's published pieces range from picking up her to-be-adopted Vietnamese son at the airport to watching trees being cleared near her home for a new housing development. You could keep such a journal in an attractive notebook, if that motivates you, on scraps of paper collected in a file, on your computer or even on a tape recorder into which you speak while you're driving to and from your job.

Besides the solitary exercise of keeping a journal, you can discover topics worth writing about by noticing what interests others in your daily conversations. If acquaintances lean forward or nudge the person next to them to listen in when you are telling

a story, you may have compelling material for print. If people laugh and cry when you talk about something that happened to you, try translating your perspective to the page.

Barbara Beckwith of Cambridge, Massachusetts, says she recognizes a marketable experience when she tells a story and listeners exclaim "Wow!" She noticed that whenever she told friends she and her husband were setting off for a "reading weekend," people would ask, "What's that?", intrigued. Five newspapers rejected her essay describing how she and her husband would hole up in a picturesque inn and read their way through the books that had piled up to a teetering, neglected stack at home. After she recast her focus from the inns to the works the two of them read, a *New York Times* book review editor liked her piece well enough to pass it along to her colleague in the travel section, who published it in December 1993 as "The Bookworm's Weekend Retreat."

In the writing class Mopsy Strange Kennedy has taught at the Cambridge Center for Adult Education throughout the 1980s and 1990s, participants receive a handful of new suggested personal experience topics at every session. These prompts include "the first (or last) time I saw him (or her)"; "an experience of love and loss in which you gained something of enduring value"; "an inanimate object and its meaning to you"; and "two very different friends who have each influenced you."

Colleen Kilcoyne, who attended Kennedy's class for a year and a half, says that she's kept all the assignment lists, which have spanned the gamut from the mundane to the bizarre. "The topics were a running joke for some of us in the class, and you didn't have to use them, but a lot of class members found them helpful." Kilcoyne's first published piece, "I Killed June Cleaver," which appeared in the *Lexington Minuteman* as well as in *Hysteria* and a collection of parental humor, originated in a conversation with her brother. But she says that the weekly assignments left her hopeful that almost anything with the slightest twist could serve as decent material for a piece.

To spark article ideas based on your experiences, you can take a trip to the library and scan magazines and newspapers for personal-experience articles until you explode with a thought like "Geez, if this person can get paid to write about _____, I

could write about _____." You'll find that people have profitably written about life-changing events like the death of a parent as well as lighter moments and commonplace incidents, like cheering kids on at Little League or sharing a recipe with a friend.

Miami-based Teresa Mears's first published piece, as a college student, played on the pun "Spring Break" in an account of breaking her finger in her apartment when she stayed home during spring vacation. She went on to publish columns on such minor events as her family not liking traditional Thanksgiving food and having a mouse in her car. Similarly, Marilyn Pribus of Fair Oaks, California, wonders what can be more ordinary than selling your old car when you buy a new one. Yet, both the *Sacramento Bee* and the *Los Angeles Herald-Examiner* published her piece on selling her beloved old Valiant. Titled "Emotional Mileage" and then "A Car Called Blueberry" when it was later reprinted in *Reader's Digest*, the article still makes Pribus cry when she reads it, and it struck a chord with readers who called long-distance or wrote to talk about their old cars.

If you're still floundering around for experiences to turn into articles, you can always specifically sign yourself up for out-of-the-ordinary adventures. As a kid reporter for the *Times Herald Record* in Middletown, New York, Fern Reiss wrote a "Let's Go" column that gave her the excuse to try pastimes like hot-air ballooning and flying in a two-seater plane that would otherwise be off-limits for her as too expensive and dangerous. "Motorcycling was the most terrifying," she recalls. "I intended to write about it in the third person, but a guy I interviewed wouldn't answer my questions unless I rode with him. He gave me a wild ride with a lot of fancy turns. It felt a little safer doing it as a journalist, but I was still pretty scared. The whole idea of the column was to include the excitement of doing something for the first time, though, so I guess that was appropriate."

HARVESTING YOUR EXPERIENCES FOR ARTICLES

Don't exclude topics from your list because you can't abide the thought of exposing your personal situation or feelings about it to strangers. I called this chapter "Your Experiences as a Resource" rather than "Writing About Your Experiences" because

you don't have to undress yourself in public in order to use the assets concealed in your past and present. Actually, three possibilities exist:

1. Write directly about your own experiences.
2. Use your experiences to uncover topics to write about journalistically and impersonally—leaving yourself out.
3. Incorporate your experiences into an article that otherwise mostly treats the topic dispassionately.

Option number two embodies an important means to get a fast, powerful start in freelancing, because it guarantees that you've chosen a topic about which you have strong feelings. Spirited motivation makes dedicated research, pungent writing and committed follow-through more likely. Option number three represents a hybrid of the personal and the impersonal, where your experience provides the spice of authenticity. You'll have research, background and perspective from experts along with your own story as a jumping-off place or as one example among many.

In all three cases, it's crucial to think through the issue of marketability before you pour too much effort into a piece. Everyone's suffered through droning blow-by-blow spoken accounts of others' operations, vacations, lawsuits and marathons, and these rarely become any more interesting when written down. You'll get a better handle on how to slant a piece or on formulating an angle, as I called it in the previous chapter, if you ask yourself, "Who might care about this sort of experience and why?" Even if you decide on option number one, to work on an account focused on yourself from beginning to end, you'll choose the content, set your experience in context and describe it more effectively when you understand that you have to earn readers' attention and ensure that your experiences have relevance for them.

Let's take, for instance, the fact that you married your high-school sweetheart as the experience you're considering as the basis for an article. Who else might care about this and why? Well, lots of people past the age of twenty-five who've been married or want to get married wonder how to keep a relationship alive when those in it undergo significant changes. With a

pair of high-school sweethearts it seems inevitable that one or both of those involved would become a different person. How has your relationship weathered such changes—or not? That's one possible angle. Similarly, people who fell in love intensely in their teens often look back decades later and wonder what it would have been like to sustain or reawaken that first intense relationship. You don't need to wonder—you know. Answering that question constitutes another angle.

If you choose the journalistic approach to these topics, the angles turn into "Can high-school sweethearts make it to a truly golden anniversary?" or "What if you had never broken up with Bobby Rae?" By considering the issue of relevance, you come up with a sharper focus. You recognize that merely surveying your spouse's strengths and weaknesses or recounting a series of incidents without a larger point in mind probably won't engage someone who doesn't already know you.

Or suppose, as the basis for an article, you seize on the fact that you're a sucker for charity appeals. Who else would care about this and why? Well, many people would become concerned that those who can least afford to give away what they have are vulnerable to slick, professional fundraisers. In a hybrid article following option number three above, you might relate your vulnerability and argue that there should be more safeguards in fundraising. Or you might note that some national politicians are advocating less government assistance to the downtrodden. In an opinion piece you could argue that, while you give a lot of money to causes, you're unusual in your circle of acquaintances and that therefore shifting the burden to private charity bodes disaster. Or, others besides yourself might wonder whether fundraisers are relying on sophisticated, tested tactics designed to part rich people from their wealth. An impersonal journalistic investigation of this issue might enlighten the concerned public.

SOME REASONS PEOPLE CARE

If the "Who might care and why?" question has stumped you, here are some reasons people appreciate reading about other people's experiences:

Timeliness

Poet Philip Levine's reminiscences about his romantic poetry class with Professor A.D. Wooly became timely—to the tune of publication in *The New York Times* and the *International Herald Tribune*—on the occasion of the 200th anniversary of John Keats's birth. In 1978, Tom Yates's first published piece, about collecting bottles for two cents each when he was young, appealed to the *Detroit News* because Michigan had just passed a bottle deposit law. Anniversaries, holidays and related events dominating the news all affect what people find fascinating. On an ordinary day people might not take an interest in your meditations about having narrowly escaped death in the Northridge earthquake. But if the ground has just shifted again and rattled Californians, your account becomes highly marketable.

"I Can Relate to That"

Certain recounted experiences evoke enjoyment because people recognize themselves in the stories. Sophia Dembling remembers receiving a lot of fan mail for personal-experience columns she wrote early in her career for the *Dallas Morning News*, on being clumsy, shopping for Christmas gifts, being not such a good sport, double-edged compliments, the *Sports Illustrated* swimsuit issue, and many other topics. "My assumption is that I may be writing about a personal episode but I am not all that different from jillions of other people," she says. "If I feel and experience something, chances are good that lots of other people in the world do too. You just have to make sure you're not digressing into elements so personal as to leave the readers outside."

The Curiosity Factor

We can't say that experiences have to be universal to merit retelling in writing, though, because readers who've never done any such thing can delight in the story of your telling off a policeman or wrestling with an alligator. After I heard that the editor of the "Hers" column of the Sunday *New York Times Magazine* said they were having trouble finding fresh topics, I approached her with a piece about meeting my Chinese mother-in-law for the first time, seven years into my marriage. "I don't imagine

you've gotten many submissions along those lines," I remarked after the essay was accepted. "No, yours was the only one," she admitted dryly. I know that my uncommon experience had an impact on people, though, because four years after I published it, I mentioned to a table full of writers that I had authored that piece, and several people who didn't know me exclaimed in unison, "I read that!"

The Compassion Factor

Readers don't expose themselves to essays about events like rape, illness, the untimely death of a loved one or a fire that destroys everything one owns because of curiosity or any ordinary form of enjoyment, but rather for three closely related reasons, I think. First, many feel "that could just as well have happened to me"; second, they feel sympathy for those who did suffer the calamity; and third, a well-constructed story about adversity often evokes a catharsis, or emotional climax and release. Because of that third element, you'll find it easier to peddle a piece on a devastating experience that hints at some redemption than an unrelievedly dark, grim essay.

Insight

Some writers take something that happened to them and wring instructive lessons from it. Evan Hunter, who publishes novels under that name and mysteries as Ed McBain, got irritated when his publisher tagged what Hunter calls his "straight fiction" novel *Privileged Conversation* as "an explosive classic of suspense." He transformed that irritation into an illuminating article in *Writer's Digest* magazine that explained the difference between "straight fiction" and mystery or crime fiction.

Entertainment

I read Dave Barry's humor column every Sunday not because it's timely, or because I relate to his outlandish tales or because I admire his insights, but because he makes me laugh. Humor that works on the printed page is difficult for editors to find, so if you have the gift of making your experiences hilarious, get busy polishing your schtick for submission.

CRAFTING A PERSONAL ESSAY

Besides the tips on article structure that you'll find in chapter nine, I'd like to comment on some factors that distinguish writing about yourself from other kinds of writing which do not involve you as a participant. Editors and readers of personal essays expect that you'll have digested what happened to you enough to present your experience as having a particular meaning. They also usually demand more artful shaping and telling of your own story than if, say, you were reporting on the latest school board decisions or describing how to grill vegetables. Thus, although personal essays don't require research, they need an especially careful process of development, and may demand as much rewriting and literary care as the best fiction.

Susan Tiberghien's personal essays always originate in her notebook of "gleanings." When a theme gathers enough momentum, she'll write a draft of the story in one sitting. She'll try to set that draft aside until she can look at it with workmanlike detachment:

- Has she depicted the setting and characters with significant details?
- Is there tension in the form of a conflict portrayed in action and dialogue, and a plot, leading to a climax?
- Does the story conclude with a resolution, a discovery on the part of the narrator?

With such thoughts in mind, she'll rework the story into a second draft. Sometimes at this point she'll realize that she still doesn't have a sufficient handle on the meaning of her experience, making more waiting and rewriting necessary. An essay called "The Train Whistle," for instance, described how her two-year-old grandson arrived at a French train station upset because he'd missed the arrival of the train. To cheer him up, Tiberghien pretended she was the train whistle. "As I wrote and rewrote this piece, I realized I was whistling for myself, not for him," she reflects. "Train whistles don't sound like that in Europe, only in America. I was whistling for myself, as the lonely American among four French people." Once she feels satisfied that she's expressed the meaning, Tiberghien clears out unnecessary words, expands her use of imagery and refines the rhythm

and sounds of her writing.

As Tiberghien's realization about the train whistle shows, often when we undertake a piece about something that happened to us, we don't fully grasp the impact the experience had. Writing takes us farther along toward understanding. When I wrote my article, "Falling in Love in China," I had trouble dramatizing in just a few paragraphs my transformation from yearning for love affairs to welcoming a deep, committed connection with my Chinese boyfriend. After many, many versions I conveyed the change in a crucial sentence, after being told that sex was only ten percent, twenty percent at most, of a relationship: "As I stood taking this in, it dawned on me that the Chinese way, where 80 or 90 percent was loyalty, affection and mutual respect, was what I had always wanted." Having to articulate what I learned felt as illuminating and revealing to me as it would to readers.

In a personal essay intended to have depth and power, the compression of your story requires that you shed a distracting fidelity to every last detail of what happened in favor of overall truthfulness. When she writes about her husband, Susan Tiberghien refers to him as "Pierre" rather than "Pierre-Yves," because the more cumbersome actual name doesn't bear on either the drama or the meaning of the events she's recounting. Similarly, I feel free to change the order of events if a rearrangement helps me drive my point home more clearly, to mention only the momentous steps in a series of events and to combine things that may have happened separately so that I can complete the essence of my story in a given number of words.

This doesn't mean that you should feel free to fantasize an experience and present your vivid imagining of it as truth. Lois Duncan, author of *How to Write and Sell Your Personal Experiences* and dozens of other books, rued her decision to sell a first-person tale about being widowed with three small children to a magazine called *Guideposts*, which she'd read was seeking "first person, inspirational stories about people who face and overcome problems."

Too late she realized that this publication, of which she'd never heard, had millions of readers, including strangers who recognized her on the street from the photo that accompanied

her concoction. Duncan, who was actually married and eight-and-a-half months pregnant when the article appeared, endured scathing condemnation of her "fraud" from readers and editors. Years later a student of hers who had had an article accepted at *Guideposts* mentioned that she was asked to provide her written assurance that the article was factual, "as there had been an embarrassing incident once when an unscrupulous contributor had sold them a fictionalized story disguised as fact." Duncan certainly learned her lesson, having lived in fear for months that the magazine would sue her.

PITFALLS OF "I" WORK

Having looked at scores of personal essays in progress, I've noticed several traps that ensnare many writers when they begin to write about themselves for publication. First, although writing about intense episodes from your life may feel therapeutic, telling true stories on paper necessitates framing them, rather than just spilling them out as you might to your journal, your best friend or a therapist.

"Personal writing demands that you get inside an experience with all its imagery, symbolism, meaning and present-tense vividness while also getting sufficiently outside that experience to see its larger shape," reflects Mopsy Kennedy, who works as a psychotherapist in addition to writing and teaching writing. "It's a broad, aesthetic way of looking at your life and suffering, a wonderful combination of immersion and perspective."

Instead of piled-up emotion, a personal-experience piece needs to concentrate on making your story come alive for a reader whose sympathy you cannot take for granted. The motto of creative-writing teachers everywhere, "Show, don't tell," should become your watchword as well. "Telling" means merely summarizing an event and its impact, while "showing" means bringing the readers to feel the impact for themselves by recreating the experience step by step on the page with specific scenes and vivid details. I'd be "telling" if I wrote, "When I moved to a new community, the sheriff irritated me by trying to serve papers on me repeatedly for the previous occupant." To "show" this event, I'd have to write more along the lines of this:

> *Almost always the doorbell meant a package from the UPS man. This time the man in brown was dumpy and middleaged, without any logo on his pocket.*
>
> *"Jeanne Thomas?" he asked, holding out an envelope and smiling to show several cracked teeth.*
>
> *"No, she doesn't live here any more. Sir, this is the third time you've come here trying to serve papers on her," I said. "Could you please not bother me again?' "*

Notice that in the second version I don't need to say I found this irritating; it comes across on its own through the dialogue.

Beginning writers often neglect to fill in enough context and background for their story to make sense to people who don't know them. Depending on your tale, facts like your age, your ethnicity, the history and size of your town, your level of wealth or poverty may need spelling out to prevent confusion on the part of readers. For this and other reasons, feedback from people who will be constructively candid on your personal pieces can prove tremendously valuable to you.

"The other people in Mopsy Kennedy's class would tell us what they liked about our piece and where they got confused. Did they laugh, did they relate to it? We had an audience to get a reaction from," recalls Colleen Kilcoyne. Chapter eleven includes pointers for eliciting helpful feedback from friends, relatives or other writers. Feedback clues you in on whether you've spilled your guts revoltingly onto the page or created a moving narrative to which strangers can respond.

Since some motives for writing interfere with the ability to engage readers, reflect on whether or not you're detached enough to rivet your efforts on your story rather than the desire to vent anger or wreak revenge. Write it all down just to get it off your chest if you're hell-bent on humiliating your former boss in print or driving a company that you felt cheated you into bankruptcy. Then either get to work on a more even-tempered version or file your ravings away for a sunnier day. "There has to be some creation of warmth and intimacy between the writer and the audience, a bonhomie," says Mopsy Kennedy. "Rarely does a cranky voice seem to get published unless the vinegar is warmed up with humor or something. I know that after six years

I still don't have the transcendence to make my hatred of Andie, an editor I dealt with, sell."

A final pitfall, which I can't completely warn you away from, is the fear that exposing your deep feelings publicly will make you vulnerable to criticism or might infuriate those you've written about. If you bare your soul about mistakes you made, readers could indeed write in scoffing at you for having been naive. I can't decide whether or not Ralph Keyes has done writers a service in his book, *The Courage to Write,* collecting cases where displaying personal linen in print caused longlasting rifts with family members.

For instance, Paul Hemphill's mother and sister did their best to buy up all locally available copies of *The New York Times* and feed them to a bonfire the Sunday it published his portrait of his hard-drinking father. In my view, Keyes doesn't quite balance such anecdotes with the other side of the coin, like the fact, revealed later in his book, that years afterwards, Hemphill discovered in his deceased father's papers a copy of that essay with "All true. All true" scribbled across the top. I've brooded about this danger occasionally myself, but so far nothing I've written has lost me a friend or earned me a family tongue-lashing.

New York City freelancer Mary Beth Coudal faced a slightly different dilemma when she told editors at *Self* that she was undergoing in vitro fertilization. In preparation for a possible article, the editors asked her and her husband to keep a journal of their experiences and feelings, which they did. Along with the medical procedures, they were participating in a therapist-led support group with other couples in their situation. And around the time that Coudal learned she was pregnant, she also realized that the therapist and others in the support group didn't like the idea that she might publish something revealing from their confidential group sessions.

After discussing the ethical dimensions of privacy with the therapist and other writers, Coudal decided that it wouldn't be right for her to say anything more about her support group than that she attended it. "Couples involved in infertility procedures have a lot of problems with trust, and I didn't want anyone to feel hurt because of something I wrote," she says. "The therapist told me that the doctor of some clients of hers was writing up

their case for a medical journal, and they felt invaded even though he was going to disguise them so that no one would know it was them. I can see that and respect that."

JOURNALISTIC PIECES GROUNDED IN EXPERIENCE

As I said earlier, a sure way to avoid alienating friends, associates and relatives is to use your experience as a springboard to a third-person treatment of an issue you care deeply about. Once you leave yourself out of the picture, return to the question, "Who would care about this topic and why?" to point toward audiences and angles for an impersonal piece. For example, that worry about your spouse's income that you don't want to confess in print might suggest a piece for a business magazine on how to come back from the brink of bankruptcy, or an article for a city magazine profiling a therapist who helps people suffering money problems. Having restored a Victorian house might lead to work on an article for a home-and-garden magazine on authentic Victorian detailing or for the real estate section of the newspaper on how to accurately estimate your renovation costs in time and hassle as well as money.

Because such a piece emerges from things you've experienced, you'll often have a head start on people to interview, questions to pursue and points to make in the article. Once you have an angle and audience firmed up, find specific appropriate markets to query, as explained in chapter seven. Writing a journalistic piece without an explicit go-ahead from a magazine or newspaper represents a foolhardy risk. With that go-ahead in hand, however, your next step would be to track down people to interview and to arrange in-person or telephone appointments to draw the information you need out of them. I describe that process in chapter eight. With the interviews completed, you move on to outlining and drafting your article, as discussed in chapter nine. You'll write and rewrite it—as chapter ten and eleven set out—and if all goes well, you'll end up with a respectable publication that's not about you, and a check for it.

Cynthia Myers of Wimberly, Texas, used this strategy to sell two articles to *Modern Bride* early in her career. Having married someone whose job kept him on the road about two-thirds of the year, she proposed an article on coping with separations.

Among those she interviewed for "Long Distance Love" were her mother-in-law, whose husband worked for the same company as her own husband, and a marriage counselor. She also drew on her experience in getting married as a sophomore in college to propose and sell an article on combining marriage and school, interviewing other married students and a college counselor. "I didn't have to do a lot of preliminary research prior to the interviews, and I knew which questions to ask those I interviewed," Myers says. "I also think I could readily identify with my readers and that helped me organize the articles. And having lived my topics, I was an automatic expert when I approached *Modern Bride*, even though I didn't have a lot of writing experience at the time."

Similarly, when my husband was having trouble finding work, I got to know several other women with low-earning husbands, prompting the query to *Ladies' Home Journal* that I've reprinted in chapter seven. Just through living I'd already found all the interviewees I needed for the article except for the psychologists. I never mentioned to the magazine why I had become interested in women who made more money than their husbands, and it didn't matter because the editors agreed it was a valuable topic for their readers.

When you decide on a neutral treatment of an issue you're involved in, your most important task is to set the phenomenon in context by providing hard facts, subjective testimony and perspective. The venerable "Who, What, When, Where and Why or How" of Journalism 101 provides a reliable guideline for collecting and structuring your material. For instance, for an impersonal article along the lines of "Is Your Drinking Water Safe?" those questions would suggest finding out at least the following:

- *Who:* Who needs to worry about unsafe drinking water? Who are the other parties or entities involved in the issue besides residents?
- *What:* What substances rank as water contaminants, and what harm can each of them do?
- *When:* When did drinking water begin to pose health risks? Are the risks immediate or long-term?

- *Where:* Where geographically are the biggest problems? How do the risks compare in rural areas versus big cities, with wells versus town water, in the desert versus in rainy, mountainous regions?
- *Why or How:* Why does water pollution persist? How can it be remedied? How can consumers know their level of risk and protect themselves? How can we improve the situation through political action?

You'll want to find out whether the publication you're writing for prefers you to present both sides of such an issue in a balanced fashion, to include both sides while coming down clearly on one of them, or to argue your case passionately without much more than a nod or a scowl at those who disagree.

In all three cases, you must make clear to readers not only what the situation is, but who says it is that way. That is, you wouldn't normally write just, "Even before the twentieth century, health-conscious observers called attention to the harm of manmade pollutants from mining, manufacturing and the dumping of household garbage in rivers and streams," without an attribution like, "According to Helen Griceny, professor of water resources at the University of Southern Oklahoma. . . ." You maintain your credibility with readers by showing where your information came from. See chapter eight for tips on research techniques.

HYBRID PIECES

Between the intimacy of an article based only on your experience and the authoritative approach of a journalistic piece lies a middle option, where you combine your personal story with facts, figures, expert commentary and sometimes testimony from others like yourself. To propose what I'm calling here a hybrid piece, you'd normally explain the article first in terms of the impersonal information you plan to include, and then mention that you'll also insert your own experiences and perspectives. Editors who would never accept a personal essay may welcome this combination.

Stephanie Howard of Santa Clarita, California, had often thought that she should write an article about infants and

toddlers wearing contact lenses. "My son has worn a lens since he was 14 months old, and people are always amazed that we've done this," she says. She queried *Parenting* on the topic and got an assignment to write a 200-word piece to accompany a larger story by someone else on children and vision. Howard interviewed her son's doctors first and got their recommendations of other specialists who would have useful information. "I used my own observations as a parent to flesh out the piece," she says.

In the article on cross-cultural relationships that I wrote for *TWA Ambassador*, I used the experience of meeting my husband in China to begin and end the piece. Everything else derived from interviews I did with experts on relationships or with others who had fallen in love across cultural boundaries. Thus only the first and last paragraphs included an "I," with the rest written in third person. Other patterns, such as starting off in third person and including a first-person anecdote within the piece, may work but are more difficult technically to pull off.

Chapter Three

Using What You Know

A nybody who has survived his childhood," Flannery O'Connor once advised other writers, "has enough information about life to last him the rest of his days." Although O'Connor, master of the short story, probably had fiction in mind, her precept applies to article writing as well. If you're old enough to read this book, you undoubtedly know a multitude of things that could serve as a foundation for nonfiction articles. They could be as esoteric as the physics of a speeding baseball, or as mundane as twenty-one ways to cook rhubarb. You just need more consciousness about how what you know might be of value to others, and awareness of more ways to cash in on your treasury of expertise.

CASHING IN ON YOUR HOBBIES

Two writers told me that they published articles derived from their boyhood hobbies while still in their teens. British science writer Phil Bagnall developed a fascination with meteors as a small child and read everything he could find on the subject. At the age of fourteen he broke into print with an article in a specialty astronomy journal called *Meteoros* and continued writing in that field. In 1987 he interested the American magazine *Astronomy* in a piece on a meteor shower that had produced unusually brilliant shooting stars but was largely ignored because it occurred around the New Year's holiday. "I've been their 'meteor man' ever since," he says. High-tech public relations specialist Marty Winston of Novelty, Ohio, became obsessed with electronics from the age of eight or nine on, so much so that he published several technical articles and photos in ham

radio magazines a few years before he earned his own license. During the next decade he completed thousands of instructional pieces on construction projects for electronics magazines.

In her early twenties, Nancy Mingus ended up with her first published article because an editor for a regional newspaper who participated in a writers' group with her knew of her interest in watching hot-air balloon rallies. "There were about fifteen writers in that group, and I think I was the only one she ever bought material from," Mingus recalls. "During the coffee hour before the meeting I asked her if she'd like an article about the upcoming local balloon rally, which I'd attended in previous years. She knew my enthusiasm for the topic and believed that I'd be able to express that in an article. It took about two seconds to convince her. I had never tried any nonfiction, but I learned to be open to an opportunity if it looks like it wants to knock."

Doug Finch of Old Greenwich, Connecticut, attributes his first sale to the fact that his hobby enabled him to come up with an unusual angle that would never have occurred to a non-hobbyist. "Twenty years back, not many journalists knew much about rugby, but I'd played it during college," he says, "and I learned that although it had a roughneck reputation, a number of sports medicine experts ranked it well below American football for likelihood of serious injury. My rugby club regularly played against several medical school teams, so I figured that if the sport was popular among would-be doctors, there was a story there. I scoured a newly purchased copy of *Writer's Market* and sure enough, I found a physicians' leisure magazine that agreed this would make a good feature." Finch earned $300 for "Rugby: Sport or Religion?"

Cori Kenicer's specialization in golf-related travel articles evolved as a combination of two hobbies. Soon after she left the real estate field to try her hand at writing about travel, an old love, she snagged an invitation to tour health spas in the Basque country of France. "I realized I needed a different angle from the much more experienced writers on the trip, and walking down the street, I spotted a copy of *Golf for Women* magazine on a newsstand. I'd grown up with the game of golf and knew there were a lot of golf courses in that part of the world. I contacted the *Golf for Women* editor by fax, because I was leaving

in less than a week, and he called to say he loved my idea."

Now a member of both the Golf Writers Association of America and the California Golf Writers, Kenicer has flown to Morocco four times as one of only twelve American media guests of the Royal Moroccan Golf Federation to cover its annual King Hassan II Pro-Am tournament. She evaluates the courses she visits as well as instructional opportunities and tee-time availability in ways that I, totally ignorant about golf, certainly couldn't.

You run one considerable danger, though, in making money from pastimes you love. When an avocation turns into a vocation, the pleasure sometimes slides away. In 1979 avid gardener Barbara Pleasant sold a piece to *Organic Gardening* on growing spinach in winter in a climate like hers in Huntsville, Alabama. In 1988 her relationship with the magazine became formalized when it made her a contributing editor under contract to them for eleven features a year. When I spoke with her, she had just passed in the manuscript for her sixth gardening book.

"The good side of making a livelihood from your hobby is that you know the significant revelations about the subject matter and how communication with the reader should proceed," Pleasant reflects. "The bad side is that successful garden writers get so busy they don't have time to garden any more. It almost happened to me, and I cut back on my travel schedule as a result."

LEVERAGING YOUR EDUCATION OR WORK EXPERIENCE

Whatever you've studied or accomplished in the work world can give you a huge advantage over other writers in launching yourself as a freelancer. John McCormick, who now writes about computers from his homestead in central Pennsylvania, learned this lesson years ago when he was living on his boat in Boston harbor and earning money by fixing cars and boats. The guy on the boat docked next to him happened to be working for the magazine *Cruise World* and asked him to write a piece on emergency engine repair for sailors.

"The editor liked it so well he ordered a series of articles," McCormick says. "This gave me the courage to strike up a con-

versation with an important-acting 'author' on yet another boat nearby. I asked him where he was published and he became rather nasty. I found out later that he had nothing but a large collection of rejection slips. He lived on a boat which never left the dock, knew nothing about the ocean, navigation, seamanship or any such thing, and yet was writing mystery stories involving boats. I was working part time at a detective agency and ran a charter boat so I had an inkling why this writer with absolutely no background in what he was writing wasn't having anything like the sales success I experienced right from the beginning."

As McCormick discovered, having substantive knowledge can put you in the position of having what editors want, if you make contact with the publications eager for your expertise and deliver publishable work. Perhaps a mystery novel with your byline represents your ultimate dream, but in the meanwhile, why not establish a track record and make some money using what you know well, whatever that is?

Elayne Robertson Demby, based in Weston, Connecticut, lost her job as a corporate attorney and gave writing a whirl by approaching a friend of a friend who edited a leading trade journal on pension plans, which had been one of her areas of specialization. She now writes two to six articles a month for *Planned Sponsor* while progressing slowly toward her goal of writing for *Bon Appetit* and *Gourmet* and publishing a cookbook. "First I wrote for some gardening magazines, then I did gardening with recipes, and then I was writing for food magazines, including *Fine Cooking*, although it's still not up to par with what I make writing about benefits."

Green Beret Mike O'Rourke, while still on active duty, likewise used what he knew to ace his first sale. "In the U.S. Army Special Forces, I was working as a sniper instructor," he says. "Since I work with weapons every day, I enjoy reading gun magazines, and thought our technique for zeroing (sighting in) our sniper rifles would make a good article if slanted for hunters and their rifles. With what I now know was a sorry excuse for a query letter, I hit pay dirt with *Guns*, a prestigious magazine in the field, which paid me $400. I'm still new at this, but success is a great learning tool." Note that O'Rourke did an excellent

job of thinking through the question I introduced to you in the previous chapter: "Who might care about this and why?" He brought a technique developed in one arena to a second, more sizable market that hadn't yet learned about it.

Gary Dawson, a goldsmith in Eugene, Oregon, used much the same strategy in writing up something he'd discovered in his professional life for another audience. Over a period of years, he'd worked hard at developing a technique for photographing the jewelry he creates. "Photographing jewelry is really a specialized niche in the photo business," he says, "and as I began to realize some success in my efforts, I felt I had become qualified to address some of the questions that seemed to come up again and again." Dawson queried *Shutterbug Magazine*, for skilled amateur and professional photographers, about an article on what he'd learned and got a rapid go-ahead. The magazine soon bought his article and accompanying photos, and within two years writing had become an important secondary income stream for Dawson.

Sometimes a market is so eager for knowledgeable writers that you can quickly build a thriving career as a specialty writer. Bruce Goldfarb parleyed his background as a paramedic and firefighter into a new line of work when he noticed that a columnist for a magazine he regularly read, the *Journal of Emergency Medical Services*, appeared to be slacking off. "I called up the editor and said I could do a better job," Goldfarb says. "The editor gave me a three-month trial period." Not only did Goldfarb branch out from that column, called "Current Research," to features, news stories and editorials for that magazine, he learned how to multiply his earnings by retargeting the research he was turning up for the column for noncompeting markets like *Medical Tribune, American Medical News, USA Today, American Health* and others. "I've been very, very lucky. I developed a following, got invited to conferences and even ended up marrying my editor at JEMS."

Pilot and flight instructor Mal Gormley also became a full-time writer because of great demand for his combination of technical knowledge and wordsmithing skills. *Business & Commercial Aviation* magazine hired him as a copy editor, after a string of copy editors with a good knowledge of English but

no background in aviation hurt their image. (A copy editor, as I'll discuss at greater length in chapter eleven, functions as the last line of defense in making sure prose is accurate, concise, clear and consistent in style.) "Then I mentioned to an editor that I'd once worked for *Reader's Digest's* computer department, and bang, I found myself saddled with responsibility for an area no one else was covering—aviation computing." In addition to selling articles regularly to *Business & Commercial Aviation*, *Aviation Week* and similar trade magazines, he's sold a book on aviation computing to McGraw-Hill. Gormley finds writing less strenuous and demanding than flying, and freelancing less stressful than working on staff. Now that he's moved to the coast of Maine, "It doesn't get any better than this. I have a life now, more control over what and when I write, and make the same as I did before."

If you're protesting after all these examples that you don't have any specialized or advanced knowledge, keep in mind that the expertise you feature doesn't even have to be yours. Lance Zedric told me that in addition to writing, he works at his family's scrap metal business. One day he asked his father and cousin how they know if they would be getting ripped off when they are looking at a used car to buy. They did indeed have numerous interesting tips for him, such as putting a tissue over the tailpipe to see if a problematic motor causes it to be sucked in, enabling him to sell an article called "Buying a Used Car" to *Heartland USA*. So in addition to surveying your own vocational knowledge, think about whether anyone you know well has pointers that would benefit readers, if you presented them in writing.

HOW-TO ARTICLES

Much of the time articles grounded in your hobbies or your profession fall into the "how-to" genre—they advise or instruct. Once you have the information and have chosen an appropriate target audience, these are among the least demanding kinds of articles to write. Readers and editors will be expecting just clear, interesting content, not paragons of style or profundity. A formulaic structure, as encapsulated in titles like "Six Steps to a Worry-Free Early Retirement," "Ten Tactics for Yawn-Free Home Videos," or "The Secrets of Refinishing Heirloom

Furniture," often works quite well. I've written scores of these over the years, and find that they don't take anywhere near the time or brain strain that personal essays require. And although you may have to do some research, that would represent a molehill next to the mound necessary for a solid journalistic piece.

Let's say you've inventoried what you know and who might find that valuable, and arrived at an angle suitable for a particular audience. Following the instructions in chapter seven, you craft a query letter proposing your article idea, and you receive a go-ahead. The next step involves cataloging what you already know and finding the gaps you need to fill to round out an article.

Suppose I wanted to branch into food writing, a completely new arena for me, for instance, and I'd gotten an assignment for one of the few food-related articles I could write partly out of my head—"Improvisatory Chinese Cooking." To get started I'd brainstorm a list of the main points I wanted to make:

- Cookbooks and recipes largely absent in China
- Home cooking not named dishes with specified ingredients, but concoctions from what's available in refrigerator, at the market
- Measuring never necessary
- Dry, unrefrigerated ingredients to have on hand
- Basic stir-fry and rice-cooking techniques
- Trial and error lessons about specific ingredients

Very quickly I'd realize that my knowledge for this article was thinner and less remarkable than I'd claimed in my query, and I'd have to plump it up with anecdotes about how I learned all the above from my Chinese husband and in-laws. So I'd make a list of stories illustrating my points, such as myself teaching an American cousin how to make boiled rice without measuring, and my husband teaching me the proper flavors through taste tests. Looking one more time at the original list, I'd make another enumeration of things to find out from others, particularly my brother-in-law, who once worked as a sub-chef in a Chinese restaurant and has a much larger repertoire of cooking techniques than my husband or I.

As a financial planner or accountant working on the early

retirement piece, you would similarly assemble a roster of your major points and then itemize the missing pieces, such as numbers demonstrating the trend toward early retirement, and the correct names and details of relevant regulations. Nothing dampens your progress as a writer more than presenting inaccurate information, and even if your memory gets you by in day-to-day transactions, for advice enshrined in print a lot more caution makes sense. For the home-video article, you might inventory your tips and then realize that asking your friends for samples of their home videos to watch would probably yield more examples to weave around your advice. Or for the furniture-refinishing piece you might decide to interview an antiques dealer you know, to include her comments on varnishing do's and don'ts, a step you know you're no expert on.

Before you write a word of the article, fix in your mind who you're writing to, since the particular audience must influence the content, terminology and level of explanation you use. For unsophisticated home-office computer users you couldn't write about "second-generation client-server interfaces" and expect understanding, or spend five paragraphs on defending against sabotage-bent hackers when this represents a danger only for large companies whose computers interact regularly with other computers outside the company premises. Years ago, when home computers first became popular, a woman who wrote for computer novices with her husband told me that they passed everything by her grandmother before sending it in to the editor, figuring that if their guidelines passed the "grandmother" test, they'd expressed themselves clearly enough.

Since I too write more for novices than for specialists, I try to avoid jargon as much as possible, and build in redundancy for any terms some readers may not find familiar. For example, a few sentences back it occurred to me that some readers may not understand what a "hacker" really does; by adding the adjective "sabotage-bent" I made it possible for those who couldn't give a definition of the term to understand it in context. I've found that sophisticated readers don't mind such subtle clarifiers, while readers newer to the subject appreciate them.

Your final concern in preparing a publishable how-to piece is ensuring that your writing has some personality and doesn't just

serve up the reader dry nuggets of advice. You can engage the reader by texturizing the "how-to" with a chatty personal overlay, as I outlined above for the "Improvisatory Chinese Cooking" article. Or you can keep yourself out of the article and inject some pizzazz with historical or contemporary anecdotes, dramatically or humorously told. See chapter ten for some comments on developing a distinctive voice that enlivens your prose.

DISHING UP YOUR TASTES

Perhaps when you survey what you know, being a discriminating consumer in some specialized realm of life comes to mind. If you love to discuss films till the cows come home, why not try film reviews? If exotic cuisines send you into raptures, why not take a stab at restaurant reviews? Reviewing books, music, dance, cars, computer systems and programs, aerobics classes, fishing spots, ski equipment or shop windows are some other options. Since I've only done one piece ever of this genre of writing, I went in search of writers with more experience and tips to share with you.

Erik Sherman, who has published numerous restaurant reviews, stresses the importance of venturing into reviewing only when you have a more solid foundation than strong opinions. "For restaurant reviewing, you should know a lot about food. I've been cooking more and more seriously since I was seven years old," he says. "The point of your piece isn't, did you like the food or not, but assessing how close the restaurant came to achieving what they're trying to do. For instance, you have to know what French food is supposed to taste like, because it's very structured. You need to know to ask, when your plate arrives, do things look harmonious? For Chinese food, are the sauces crisp, with clearly defined flavors?" Sherman also considers himself qualified to review plays, and has. "My parents were in theater, and I've acted, directed and studied theater. I can tell if the lead is very stiff, or creating a caricature out of the role," he says. Because he knows little about architecture or popular music, however, he'd stay away from reviewing in those areas.

Robin Brooker, who reviews computer software and hardware from his home in a small town north of Manchester, England, says he tries to keep as his paramount concern the

reader's questions, "Is this item worth buying *for me*? How will it help me?" Rather than aiming to impress strangers with his knowledge, which he knows would turn editors off, he imagines the reader as a friend sitting across the desk from him. "I try to convey what it feels like to operate the computer system I am using, not just the technical specifications," he says. "If I'm writing about CD-ROMs for children, I enlist the aid of my five-year-old granddaughter." Brooker does his best to mention both positive and negative points about the item he's reviewing, "and unless the thing is complete rubbish, I always try to end on a positive note."

The quest for balance came up in every exchange I had with writers about reviewing. Erik Sherman told me he would avoid an assignment if his experience at a restaurant was completely dreadful. "If the place was so bad I'd never eat there again, I wouldn't do the review. It would be too unpleasant for me," he said. Holly Moore, who reviewed food and restaurants for *The Philadelphia City Paper* for fourteen years, said much the same: "Many new restaurant reviewers try to make a name for themselves by attacking established restaurants and by being more interested in packing their reviews with cute cheap shots than in writing about the substance of the restaurant. My view was that most people dine out for a good time, not to achieve gastronomical nirvana, so I made it a policy not to write bad reviews. Instead I defined the mission of my column as discovering enjoyable or fun dining experiences. Not many newspapers will let you get away with this, though. Most review readers are vicarious 'armchair' diners, like the drivers who slow down to gape at a car wreck. They're not happy unless blood is spilled."

Moore was happiest with the reviews she wrote that took in not only the meal she'd eaten, but also a conversation the following day with the owner and/or the chef. "You can capture the restaurant's essence much more surely if you spend some time with the people who run the place rather than writing solely as an observer."

Beware of overly formulaic material when you write your review. For book reviews, one danger is sticking too close to relating the plot, as in the kind of reports we had to do for school to prove we'd read the book. According to Kathryn Lively, editor

of the literary magazine *Athena*, book reviews may need to summarize the story for the reader, but also need to include detailed criticism. Are the characters believable? Does the story line generate enough interest to keep a reader alert for 300-plus pages? Is the book worth the $25 price tag?

With food reviews, too many writers follow this recipe, claims Holly Moore: "Two paragraphs on the restaurant in general, one paragraph each on service and ambience. A bunch of bite-by-bite paragraphs on 'I ate this, my table mate ate that and then I ate this,' wrapped up by a final paragraph about returning/never returning. Try to break away from this formula. I'm of the opinion that most readers don't really like reading about what a reviewer ate, and limit their reading to the review's opening and closing paragraphs."

So long as you understand that reviewing presents a service for the reader rather than a venue for an ego trip, you're ready to begin your search for a periodical that might benefit from your insights. Rarely will an editor bump a reliable reviewer to make room for an untried, fresh voice, but it doesn't hurt to send an inquiry with the message, "If you ever need someone new. . . ." The regular columnist may have just requested to be released from his or her responsibilities, or the editor may have been looking for someone younger, or more knowledgeable, or with a livelier style.

Almost always an editor will want to see a few sample reviews before making any commitment to you. If you prove to have writing skills and educated tastes, you may even find editors pursuing you after your reviews appear here and there. Susan Peña, a freelance music critic in Reading, Pennsylvania, has gotten calls from editors at *Chamber Music* and *Sojourners* magazines who had read other work of hers and recognized that she had a head start over many other writers on classical music. Along the way, she's interviewed many major figures in the music world, like Riccardo Muti, Andre Watts and James Galway, a privilege never available to mere fans or aficionados.

PEDDLING YOUR PASSIONS
Besides using what you know and your capacity to evaluate subjective phenomena such as food and the arts, you can find prom-

ising article material in things you believe—the more passion-ately, the better. Around New Year's 1994, Quebec writer Carol Krenz got so fed up with the fact that no country would lift a finger to help Bosnia that she wrote an opinion piece and called the editor of the *Montreal Gazette* to warn him that it was on the way.

Upon receiving it, the editor called her to ask for a tighter focus and then published the revised piece the day after the Sara-jevo marketplace was bombed. Through the wire services, the story appeared in the *Calgary Herald* as well as in Montreal, prompting more than 1,000 people to write Krenz letters in re-sponse. "It succeeded in moving so many people, stirred up a lot of political activism and made me feel better for having done something to coax everyone out of their stupor and pay atten-tion," she says.

I don't want to give the impression that world events serve as the preponderant theme for opinion pieces, though, because you can equally build these pieces around everyday issues, such as colleagues at a dinner of four who order more drinks than any-one else and then suggest splitting the check four ways.

Californian Marie Faust Evitt had published just three essays with the *San Jose Mercury News* when she sold a piece to *Newsweek*'s prestigious "My Turn" column about adults glori-fying summer vacation and implying to kids that school was best when it was finished for the year. "You might not think this is an issue one could feel passionately about, but each June virtu-ally all my relatives, neighbors and store clerks ask my kids if they are glad school is out for the summer," Evitt says. "That year, the first time someone asked my first grader if he were looking forward to summer I got so steamed that I sent this piece right out to *Newsweek*. They published it a few weeks later."

Different as their topics were, both Krenz and Evitt had one factor working in their favor: timeliness. The Bosnia editorial related to events in the news, while Evitt's piece reached *Newsweek* just before that year's national summer vacation. If your message isn't intrinsically well timed, you can increase its appeal for editors by using a so-called news hook or news peg—that is, tying it in to something people are currently thinking and talking about.

Judith Schlesinger, a clinical psychologist in Dobbs Ferry, New York, felt moved to sound off when she heard both President Clinton and the governor of Oklahoma refer to the Oklahoma City bombers as "evil." Her piece used that as the lead for her reflections on what it meant that her field of psychology never used such moralistic language. Instead, whether it's Charles Manson, Jeffrey Dahmer or Susan Smith in question, psychologists seemed to examine criminals' motives so minutely that they wound up obscuring the misdeed itself. Schlesinger mentioned recent signs that psychology was beginning to narrow its gap with respect to religious perspectives—another timely element. Her editorial ran in nine editions of the Gannett newspaper chain in Westchester and Putnam counties.

To capitalize on the timeliness factor, you have several options. One is to seize the inspiration of the moment and finish and submit your essay that very day or the next. Since newspaper editorials usually run from 600 to 800 words, this shouldn't present insuperable problems for many of you. Call your target newspaper's editorial department to find out if they prefer to receive your timely editorial by mail or by fax. Another is to have much of an editorial written and to wait until current events provide a suitable hook, and then to incorporate what just occurred into your piece's lead and change other sections of it where necessary to fit.

For monthly magazines which include an opinion column, keep in mind in using a timely hook that readers would be encountering your piece roughly four months after you wrote it. Because memories of the details of transitory news events would by then already have faded, make sure any news hook concerns larger, less forgettable events—a terrorist bombing, say, rather than a politician's slip of the tongue. Although you'll see in chapter seven that I recommend on the whole sending editors query letters rather than completed articles, short editorials constitute a major exception. Send in the whole piece, ready to be slipped right in to the publication.

In discussions with newspaper editors and other writers, you might hear the expression "op-ed piece." Short for "opposite the editorial page," this term derives from a pioneering innovation of *The New York Times* in the early seventies. Until then, editori-

als usually shared one page with letters to the editor, leaving little space for outside contributors. With the addition of a whole extra page for commentary, an idea which soon spread to newspapers all over the country, unknown freelance writers and recognized authorities began to have their say along with syndicated columnists. Because you'll be among distinguished company, your editorial contribution must have much more substance than the sort of monologue you'd deliver to people hearing you sputter over something in the newspaper.

R.G. Schmidt, who has published more than 750 op-ed pieces, mostly for Florida newspapers, warns that the word "opinion" may mislead writers into misconstruing what editors expect in an editorial. "The purpose is not to persuade readers to think your way so much as to make the readers think about an issue in a way they might not have before. You encourage the reader to look at the matter further," he says.

For instance, in 1996 when people were accusing former President George Bush of not having gone far enough in the Gulf War to get rid of Saddam Hussein, Schmidt pointed out in reply that the United States was never formally at war with Iraq. "Congress gave the President authorization to reinforce two United Nations resolutions which said, 'Get Iraq out of Kuwait,' " he says. "George Bush had no authority to go across the border of Iraq. I told readers, this was the resolution number, check it out and then decide for yourself whether Clinton is finishing up something George Bush couldn't handle, or whether George Bush did everything he was legally empowered to do. You can't ever go off half-cocked in an op-ed. You need to back up your view with facts." In order to get his hands on those backup facts, Schmidt engages in an average of fifteen hours of research for a column that may take an hour and a half to two hours to write.

Besides short editorials, your convictions can furnish the grist for feature-length articles that argue for a point of view. I wrote one such piece early in my career when I learned that Massachusetts had a question on the upcoming Election Day ballots asking voters whether or not the state should bring back the death penalty. The topic seemed perfect for the *Valley Advocate*, my local alternative weekly paper, and when I proposed it to the editor,

for whom I'd already done several assignments, I got a quick go-ahead. I spent about a week collecting information from activists on both sides of the issue, and made numerous calls to find out the exact location of the state's long-unused electric chair, and how it worked. My idea was to shock readers into realizing that their vote could lead to the state killing a person, and then to counter each of the most popular arguments in favor of capital punishment with hard data.

Although my article didn't turn the tide in the referendum, a call from a criminal lawyer telling me it was the best thing he'd ever read on the topic made me hopeful that I'd softened a few harsh attitudes in the paper's circulation area. These longer argumentative pieces usually do best with publications aligned with your own views, although some magazine editors use whether or not the article will spark controversy as their decisive criterion.

Philadelphia attorney Bill Smith says that although he knows that magazines and newspapers no longer serve as the prime source of information for most people, he still enjoys the chance to startle people into looking at issues in a different way. Besides several features on the death penalty, Smith wrote a piece for the *ABA Journal* of the American Bar Association on constitutional law according to the militia movement, based on documents he stumbled across on the Internet, as well as an open letter to the militia movement explaining that if they believed the federal government represented a monolithic conspiracy, they'd obviously never worked for the government. The latter appeared in the *Columbus Guardian* in Ohio and Smith's local bar association magazine. "Sometimes readers write to you," says Smith, "and it's a real kick to realize that you've written something that revved someone up enough to stop what they're doing and get something off their chest."

Chapter Four

The People Around You

How would you rate the odds that, once you thought about it, you would be able to name someone you personally know who could serve as a worthy focus of an article? Even though you probably don't know any celebrities, notorious criminals or prominent geniuses, I'd put the chances at more than 90 percent. If we add in those whom you may not know but whom someone you know knows, the probability shoots up to 100 percent. So your question becomes not "Do you know anyone who merits an article?" but "Who is a good subject to start with?" Let's address that first, then turn to several different kinds of people articles.

WHAT MAKES A PERSON INTERESTING?

If you're still coming up empty, it might help to mull over the factors that influence editors to nod their heads and agree that a piece about so-and-so might appeal to a particular group of readers. Stories about people with the following qualifications represent the most common choices.

A Person Who Is Prominent or Already Well-Known

The public has an abiding curiosity about illustrious individuals, such as software mogul Bill Gates, ex-Texas governor Ann Richards, cellist Yo-Yo Ma or champion skater Kristi Yamaguchi. Your challenge here will be coming up with a fresh angle on someone readers probably have already heard about, and explaining to editors what makes that person particularly relevant to their readers.

For instance, a parenting magazine might welcome a profile of Gates as a father, highlighting how he carves out quality family time despite his business responsibilities. (*If* he does—I'm merely brainstorming here.) If Ann Richards, often pictured during her campaigns on a motorcycle, is spending her retirement riding around, she could provide a charming change of pace for a motorcycle owners' magazine. Or suppose your daughter has worshipped Yo-Yo Ma and practiced harder on her violin since he made an appearance at her elementary school—this suggests the angle of Ma's commitment to his child fans. And the question of whether or not Yamaguchi has done well with endorsements and post-Olympic promotions might grab an ethnic magazine like *Rice* or *Asiam*. Even if you happen to have easy access to someone of their prominence, however, you can't expect a go-ahead for an article about them without a compelling angle.

Other High Achievers

Numerous people in your community have accomplished something that makes them stand out without becoming household names. Keep your nose to the ground about this, and you might learn that two doors down lives a flower lover who breeds orchids and had a new strain named after her. When Kelly Sagert was asked to write profiles for her local newspaper, she wanted someone splashy to start off her series. She serves as recreation director of her church and bible school, and one night while she and the minister's wife were slinging the ball around among screaming kids, Kelly asked her if she knew anyone she could interview. The minister's wife said there was a guy in the county who was one of the top-ranked boomerang players in the world—and the newspaper was thrilled to get the story.

A Person With a Passion

Whether or not their fervor has produced results, the fact that someone cares enough about some wrong to try to do something about it can attract admiration. The home-based image consultant in your town crusading to change the zoning laws might interest a national magazine on entrepreneurship. A gun store owner who takes a public stand against inhumane animal traps may deserve coverage in a publication like *Wildlife Conservation*

Magazine. The fourteen-year-old who showed up at a school board meeting to denounce tracking into ability levels in school as discriminatory could serve as the focus for a serious exploration of the issue in a magazine for educators.

The Originator of a New Idea

As with evangelists for a cause, we like to read about people trying something new, regardless of their degree of success. Someone who's invented an electromagnetic anti-smoking treatment would make for a fascinating article. Likewise, get those freelancer's wheels turning when you learn about someone opening up a dating service in a health club, or an attorney who offers free legal advice the first Friday of every month.

The Last of an Era

While we're drawn to "firsts," we also appreciate "lasts." The last village blacksmith in New England, the last typewriter repairer in your town, the last survivor of the 1906 San Francisco earthquake, the last descendant of the city founder—all represent promising article topics.

Someone who Overcame Tragedy

Think about people whose recovery from misfortune you've found inspirational. Perhaps someone you know who has a family history of suicide and resisted the impulse himself when his life spiralled downward. Or a single mother who copes admirably with a multiple-handicapped daughter. Or a former drug addict who runs a charity for foreign war orphans. If you enjoy the kind of stories that pull at readers' heartstrings, why not set out to write some? These can interest community newspapers, city or regional magazines and inspirational magazines, especially those serving the same religious denomination as your subject. Your biggest challenge may be persuading your subjects to allow you to place them in the limelight.

Someone Felled by Tragedy

Some compelling people stories concern those who have failed to overcome tough circumstances, such as teen parents trying without enough resources to raise their child responsibly. Or a

compulsive gambler who caused a family bankruptcy, cast a shadow over his children and prompted his wife to resume problem drinking. Or the mayor who lost reelection by five votes and has never been able to get beyond his setback. These true-life tales work best when they yield an implicit moral lesson for the reader.

A Person With a Bizarre but True Story

Sometimes you run across people with amazing stories like spending years searching the world for a birth mother only to discover that she lived two miles away. Such believe-it-or-not sagas can earn space in small local periodicals or mass-readership markets like *People*, the *National Enquirer* or *Parade*.

They Do What?

Your mental survey of people you know may land on someone who pursues a strange or rare hobby or profession. Your eighty-year-old Uncle Osbert's antique doll collection might make him the laughingstock of his neighborhood, but it qualifies him for a profile in *Doll World*, *Antique Review*, or perhaps an inflight magazine for an airline that services your area. Similarly, meeting someone who studies bereavement among pets should send you to the computer keyboard to propose a piece for *Pet Focus* or *I Love Cats*.

Someone Who Has Made an Unusual Life Choice

I'd sure enjoy reading about someone who won the state lottery and gave every last cent of the million dollars to leukemia research. Or an adoptee who decided not to search for his birth parents. Remember that people can stand out from the crowd for many, many reasons, some of which wouldn't be known to their casual acquaintances. Until you asked a lot of questions about the man who was always taking notes on the beach, you wouldn't know that he was the former CEO of a multinational corporation now chronicling the habits of the wild birds that make their home on your remote island.

THE CHALLENGES OF PROFILE ARTICLES

Early in my career I profiled a woman who had been dead for more than seventy years. I'd read references to Ellen Swallow Richards as the founder of the science of ecology, and I dug around in the library to uncover information about her research on air and water quality and the way she spread environmental awareness early in the twentieth century. In that case, my challenge was to provide a vivid portrait relevant to today's readers from historic sources. Usually, though, you'll construct a profile after background research, live person-to-person contact and, often, interviewing of colleagues, family members or other associates of your subject.

Profile articles tend to have a wide-angle focus on a person, offering both a close-up look at what he or she is like and a broad perspective on his or her personality, life journey and impact. With a living subject, you'll have a hard time selling a profile without having interviewed the individual in person. Readers expect description and insights from you that they couldn't formulate themselves from reading news accounts, gazing at a still photograph of the person or watching a TV interview. This means that for a profile you confront double the challenge of doing an interview where your goal is simply obtaining informational content. (Chapter eight offers advice on interviewing.) Besides having to ask great questions and perform the follow-up necessary for punchy quotes, you must also be making observations that will enable you to provide that "inside look."

For the broad perspective, you often need sources for information beyond what you can turn up during your one-on-one time with the subject. If the person has been featured in the media before, you should look up previous profiles and news stories at the library so that you can spend less of your time together going over basic facts. You can also get clippings—at least the favorable ones—with a call to the public relations department of the organization the person belongs to, or directly from your subject. But you might need more big-picture preliminary research, too. For the profile of someone opening up a dating service in a health club, for example, a search for data on how dating-services and health clubs are currently faring in the

marketplace would make your interview and your article better informed. Similarly, you won't start off on the best foot with your subject if you have to walk in and ask a question as basic as, "Now I know you're the first English horn player to make a solo recording, but what's an English horn?"

While your interview with the subject will prove pivotal, conversations with the person's associates help you round out a picture beyond information provided by the subject that might be self-serving, one-dimensional, overly modest or just limited in amount. Interview the main quarry last whenever you can. B.J. Roche, a freelancer in Rowe, Massachusetts, hadn't done many profiles when she received the assignment to interview Ruth Simmons, president of Smith College. After the interview Roche spoke with about thirty people who knew Simmons, including Smith professors and students, members of the presidential search committee and Simmons's brothers and sisters. Then she realized, too late, that she might have had an easier time during the interview had she done all that before rather than after her appointed time with Simmons herself.

"Talking to her last would probably have given me a deeper understanding of who she really was," Roche reflects. "Since her story, that of a great-granddaughter of slaves becoming the head of a top, elite college, was a compelling and personal one, I wanted to get that from her, but she was a little unwilling to give it to me. If I had gone in there armed with the anecdotes that I later got, I could have said, 'Tell me about the time you . . .' and opened her up a little more. As it was, I did do some follow-up over the phone, but we didn't get the kind of give-and-take you get by sitting over a cup of coffee."

If you jump to the assumption that you'll need an entire day or even a week of following your subject around in order to write an acceptable profile, scale back your expectations. Not only does that kind of access tend to be unobtainable, it's overkill. You'd end up with mounds more information than you could use in a 2,000-word profile and much irrelevant material, and perhaps even come up short on good, pertinent quotes.

Leonard Felson, a former *Hartford Courant* staff reporter now freelancing, can cite a few times though where riding around with a person helped round out a profile. Felson became

interested in a Glastonbury, Connecticut, lawyer and city councillor who always voted his conscience and was hated by his fellow Democrats. Joining him on errands around town for a few hours over several separate days, Felson picked up revealing details such as the man always leaving his keys in the car when he went to get coffee and asking Felson not to let people in the restaurant figure out that he was a reporter. In many cases, however, by doing your homework and deciding on a focus beforehand, you can gather enough material for a substantive profile in just one or two hours of talking with the person.

Freelance writer Judith Montminy, who has published more than five hundred arts-related profiles in the "South Weekly" section of the Sunday *Boston Globe,* says she manages to keep turning in one or two profiles a week by knowing her angle before she sits down to interview her subject. Montminy points out that she gets a go-ahead from her editor only after she's answered the question, "Why feature this person now?" This furnishes the focus for her session with the interviewee. For instance, when she profiled pediatrician Mark Vonnegut, she presented the angle to her editor of his growing involvement with painting, culminating in his upcoming first one-person show. That, more than his having grown up with a famous father, novelist Kurt Vonnegut, drove both her conversation with Mark Vonnegut and the resulting article.

Similarly, when her editor "bit" at a story about a local poet coming out with a personally revealing book, Montminy zeroed in on the difficulties and benefits of using personal life as your material, not every aspect of the poet's career, when they spoke. Keeping her finger on the pulse of the arts in her area amounts to practically a full-time job, but it enables her to select the timely stories likely to get a go-ahead from her editor and make the best use of her time with her interview subjects.

Having an angle in mind in advance doesn't mean Montminy stays with it rigidly. "I have a religious conviction that I have to be true to what comes up in the interview," she says. Once she was expecting to portray the new director of an organization as preparing to make big changes, but instead of having a long list of things he wanted to accomplish, the new director turned out to be quite cautious. In a case like this, you should of course not

only adjust your approach for the article, but also explain to the editor who made the assignment why you'll be passing in an article with an angle different from the one you earlier pitched.

Writing up a profile doesn't involve a different process than crafting any other kind of article. As explained in chapter nine, you'll need to find a lead, a stated focus, a flow for the body of the piece and a satisfying wrap-up. Throughout you'll marshall descriptions, incidents and quotes to keep the profile from coming across like a dry recital of biographical details.

MASTERING THE "Q&A" FORMAT

If profiles sound challenging, you may decide to start writing about people in a Q&A format, where an initial paragraph or two introduces your subject and the rest of the article takes the form of questions from you and longer answers from your interviewee. Chicago-based freelancer Gene Koprowski, whose more than one-hundred published Q&A interviews include many with luminaries such as Vice President Al Gore and America OnLine CEO Steve Case, provided insights into why some publications prefer the rather limited, stark format of questions and answers to a profile. "The Q&A format works well for controversial people, such as business leaders, who have been covered a lot in regular articles, where it's hard for readers to discern what's the person's own 'spin' and what's the writer's interpretation," he says. "A Q&A is almost like a lengthy TV interview. It gives you a way to let these leaders hang themselves with their own rope."

With Steve Case, for instance, Koprowski asked about his company's big computer crash during the summer of 1996, when millions of America OnLine users couldn't gain access to the system. "Usually Case gives the same pat answers to everyone," Koprowski says. "But when he just says something like 'Oh well, we learned a lot from the blackout' in a Q&A, it shows that the writer's not lazy. It really is that Case is trying to put a good face on things. Other times, if the subject knows it's going to be Q&A, they know whatever they say can show up and they have a powerful incentive to be truthful."

Yet several experienced writers who have published both profiles and Q&A pieces told me that, contrary to appearances,

they found the latter more demanding. Whereas in profiles you need to punch up the color so that your portrait is vivid and dramatic, the Q&A format gives you little scope to add your observations and perspective. Beyond your introduction, the reader gets only what came up in conversation. "I don't like Q&A because it feels dry and stilted and formal," says Jerry Vovcsko, who writes regularly for the trade magazine *National Fisherman*. "There's little if any chance to color in the background and context of the individual and events you're writing about."

"With a profile you have more room for creativity," agrees Robin DeMattia, who did a Q&A article about the state archaeologist of Connecticut for the Connecticut Weekly section of *The New York Times*. "I found Q&A a very difficult process." Before querying the *Times*, DeMattia knew that the archaeologist was very quotable—an absolute requirement for Q&A, since your subject's actual sentences constitute the content. A local museum had referred her to him while she was researching a previous article on scuba diving in Connecticut and needed to find out people's rights to take things from the ocean floor.

DeMattia cited the frustrations of having to keep a sharp eye on her tape recorder during the interview to see when the tape was running out, and needing to transcribe her whole hour and a half interview and then cut, cut, cut. She also had to keep her ears open throughout the interview for segments that wouldn't read well as spoken. "People cut off in the middle of a sentence a lot. You have to listen for that and get them to restate things during the interview," she says. Staying on topic during the interview is essential too. DeMattia kept the archaeologist talking about the richness of Connecticut's historic resources, sites that might be in people's own backyards and how we can preserve archaeological sites and learn from them.

You absolutely need reliable technology to generate a word-for-word text for a Q&A article. Gene Koprowski sometimes has two tape recorders going at once as insurance for this. He also recommends that you try to secure two hours with your target so that you'll have enough material from which to select the sparkling parts and shape them into a piece that has a nice flow. "Often you have to push several times to get a unique

answer. Don't be afraid to repeat yourself, since your job is to get revelations, or at least not what everyone gets. Ask the same question different ways." With prominent people who have a lot to lose if they misspeak, Koprowski suggests using a broadcast-quality tape recorder, which would provide better proof that they really did say what they said. "Bob Palmer, CEO of Digital, the computer company, said to me that when he first came to Digital in the early eighties it was 'Greed Land.' Digital's PR person claimed Palmer had said 'Dream Land.' But it was very clear on the tape."

Q&A's are less charged and confrontational, of course, when you're not aiming to pin someone to the wall so much as trying to elicit her knowledge, experience and views. Chess champions unknown to the general public, fourth-generation Nebraska farmers, campaign workers for a fringe candidate might all serve as interesting Q&A subjects—so long as they express themselves well verbally. Robin DeMattia warns against committing yourself to a Q&A until you screen the person. "You might be in for a rude awakening if you sat down with someone who used terminology your readers wouldn't understand, or couldn't give examples, or just wasn't articulate."

OTHER KINDS OF PEOPLE ARTICLES

Besides profiles and Q&A columns, the interesting people you know and discover can inspire other types of articles. Sometimes you'll want to profile not one person but a group of individuals. The group might comprise a rock band, a team of inventors, a prominent family, a nonprofit organization or a business firm. In those cases you'd portray the group identity and history, punctuating it with appearances of the individuals who serve as a part of the group. In other cases, your group might include people who don't work together in any sense and may not even know each other—such as the Wharton Class of 1973, third basemen, or women who got off and stayed off welfare. That kind of group profile requires that each person you depict comes across both as a distinct individual and as an instance of the points you are trying to make about the group. Not easy!

The group counterpart to Q&A articles would be roundups, where you pose one question and show how different people

responded to it. These appear in periodicals as diverse as *The New York Times Book Review* ("What's the best book you read this year?" "Which book do you most wish you had written?"), *Cosmopolitan* ("Tell us about your first date/first kiss/first heartbreak") and daily newspapers ("What do you think the government should do about Social Security?"). Those highlighted in the roundup might be celebrities, whose answers give us a look into their inner lives, or ordinary persons in the street, whose responses reveal a range of opinions. You'd definitely want to get an editor's commitment on this type of article before going to all the trouble of soliciting the replies.

The opportunity for another type of people article might come up when you meet someone who has a dramatic story that they can't write themselves. In an "as-told-to" piece, after extensive interviewing for anecdotes, details and emotions, you create a reconstruction of the story in the first person—in the subject's voice, not yours. I've seen this sort of piece both in women's magazines, where the writer appears to have a good deal of literary license, and in daily newspapers, where the reconstruction has more fidelity to the subject's actual words.

Yet another kind of people article resembles a personal essay, but the focus is on another person rather than oneself. These other-oriented essays often contain nostalgia about, say, a former teacher or a dead relative. They need a finely tuned emotional tone, so that they affect readers who didn't know the person in question, without sinking into raw sorrow, anger or remorse. Profiles wouldn't normally contain the current of emotion of this type of essay, so it would be important to present such a nostalgic piece to editors as a personal essay rather than a profile.

GOING BEYOND PERSONALITIES

Probably the most common remaining kind of people article is a journalistic piece that results from your having encountered a fascinating person who ends up not becoming the focus of the resulting article. Leonard Felson told me about a couple of instances where he initially pursued a person but later realized the real story lay in a general issue or trend that the person exemplified. Once at a dinner party, he heard about a man

named Carlos Cardoso, a vice-president at Colt who had helped to turn around the famous old gun manufacturer from bankruptcy. As he looked into the situation, he recognized that a story about how the company found a way to remain operating in New England made more sense than a profile of Cardoso. "I pitched it as a business story with lessons for other manufacturers," he says, "since a prevailing view is that companies can no longer compete being based in New England." This story sold to *Connecticut* magazine.

Another time Felson learned about a group of neighbors who had become involved in the issue of technology and education, establishing a program that connected the city and the suburbs through computers, enabling kids separated by social class and geography to work on school projects together. "I thought at first the story was about two parents who put together a conference, but decided instead to focus on the issue of bringing computers into schools." His article about efforts throughout the state, including contributions from the business sector, to wire school systems for computer use ran in *The New York Times*'s Connecticut section. "Often the people you meet are the trees in the forest and not the best people to focus on. Ask them if others are doing what they're doing. Ask about someone who's above the fray who can give an overview of the phenomenon they're involved with. That person might be a professor or a president of a trade association. Then the person you first met becomes one of several people you interview."

Conversely, Felson recalled a case where he thought at first about an issue-oriented piece and then channeled his research into a profile. With the backdrop of many people in the Hartford suburbs being afraid to venture into the city, day or night, an urban minister had created a program where suburbanites slept at his church and toured inner-city neighborhoods for three weekends. As Felson looked into the program, he decided that a profile of the minister rather than a wider piece on suburban fear of the city was most appropriate. "The minister's personality and philosophy drove the program, which was unique in the region and one of only a few in the country," he explains. "Uniqueness is a good reason for a profile."

EXTRA MILEAGE FROM THE PEOPLE YOU MEET

Once you've spent the energy to collect and digest information about people you've interviewed, don't put it away in your files after just one article. Ponder whether or not you can recycle some of your research by concocting a new angle for a different audience. Often a point that didn't get much prominence in your first article hints at another possibility. For instance, I profiled Ellen Swallow Richards for *Vassar Quarterly* because she graduated from that college, but she taught for years at MIT, for whose alumni magazine I could portray her as a pioneering woman professor. Likewise, when the twenty-fifth anniversary of the Clean Water Act was approaching, I could propose an article on her for *Sierra* or another environmental magazine depicting her as one of the nation's first clean-water activists.

Besides browsing back through your notes, you can generate angles for reselling your research by sitting back and analyzing facts about the person you interviewed. Often these categories help you arrive at a promising new angle:

- *Geography.* The place where someone was born ("Cleveland native . . ."), spent formative years ("former Plainviller . . .") or lives now ("Miamian . . .") may furnish an additional slant. Look for correspondingly geographical publications to query, such as daily newspapers, special regional sections of Sunday newspapers, Sunday magazines, regional magazines and in-flight magazines of airlines that fly to that area.
- *Gender.* Does your subject stand out as being especially notable as a man, say as having doubled as a stay-at-home dad during the time he wrote his hit play? Or as a woman, say as heading the largest woman-owned public-works contracting business in the state? Given that more magazines exist that target women than men and that high-achieving women tend not to receive their fair share of publicity in general media, the gender angle works out more for women subjects than for men.
- *Race, nationality, religion or ethnicity.* I know an Armenian-American man who is trying to market the inventions of Armenian pharmaceutical scientists in the former Soviet Union to the American health food industry. When he's farther along in his project, he might merit coverage in *Ararat* (for Americans

of Armenian descent) as well as in health food magazines. Other periodicals serve the African-American, Hispanic, Italian-American, Catholic, Episcopal and Jewish communities.

• *Age.* Can you find an additional focus in the age of the person you interviewed? Dorah Blume of Cambridge, Massachusetts, became interested in emu farming, and visited with a retired couple in Vermont who were raising the ostrich-like birds for food. While she was waiting for a reply from *Natural Health* on a query about the healthfulness of emu meat, she received a positive response from *Modern Maturity* to a separate query portraying emu farming as a comfortable and profitable profession ideal for older men and women.

• *Lifestyle.* If you established a terrific rapport with Martina Navratilova when you interviewed her for *Racquet* magazine, you might have the beginnings of another story on her for *Girlfriends* or *Curve* magazines, with the angle of how the tennis world views her as someone who has "come out." Or perhaps you learn that an executive whose business triumphs you covered lives in a recreational vehicle year-round. *MotorHome* and *RV Times Magazine* sure seem like logical prospects for the RV angle.

• *Hobbies.* When the crusader for zoning rights turns out to spend summers scuba diving for buried treasure, when the photographer mounting a pathbreaking exhibition moonlights as a square dance caller, when the history professor has a collection of rare turn-of-the-century postcards, you have profitable extra angles staring you in the face.

• *Tie-ins with current events.* Do today's front-page stories provide good reason to reevaluate someone's crime, exploit or achievements? For instance, with the media in a hubbub about rocks that reveal that life once existed on Mars, you might profitably re-spin the interview you did with a computer scientist who helped create the imaging system on the Viking spaceship.

• *Profession.* Keep in mind that if you profile an innovative bookseller, grocer or lawyer for your local paper, you may be able to reslant your material and sell it to *Publishers Weekly*, *The Gourmet Retailer* or *Barrister*, respectively.

• *Political views.* Similarly, a politician, business leader or community activist whom you portray in a local context may

merit national coverage in a magazine sympathetic to his or her convictions, such as the leftist periodical *The Progressive* or the right-wing *National Review*. Here, as above, you may need to shift your focus to a more issue-oriented than a person-oriented approach.

Many times the recycling comes about when you shift from spotlighting an individual to depicting that person as one instance among others of a trend. The retired executive you discovered chronicling the wildlife on your island might spur not only a profile but also a wider piece on "refugee CEOs." The newly elected Republican politician whom you discovered has a staunchly Democratic twin sister might spark a piece on "opposite twins" for the lifestyle section of a newspaper or for *Twins* magazine. The top-ranked boomerang player discovered by Kelly Sagert might serve as one part of an article on champions of arcane outdoor sports for *Outside* magazine.

Chapter Five

Places Near Home

Once or twice a week my husband invites me to accompany him to the supermarket, the electronics store or a nearby beach. Sometimes I'll grumble, since it's an interruption, but often I'll go along for the ride. We'll warm up the car, which he'll verbally praise, as if it's a well-fed steed, and then ease it out of the driveway. Although we're journeying less than ten miles, one of us will then put smiles on both our faces with the delighted phrase, "Small trip!" The ritual never fails to refresh us, providing a mini-vacation at virtually no expense.

Finding adventure in the familiar is the spirit in which you can get started in travel writing without hopping aboard a plane, shelling out big bucks on a trip or driving beyond your everyday circuit. "Remember, no matter where you live, it's a travel destination for someone. Someone, somewhere thinks it's remote and exotic and wants to read about it," says Jules Older, who along with his wife Effin Older teaches travel writing workshops in the so-called Northeast Kingdom, a rural but not always picturesque corner of Vermont. The Olders once dramatized this claim for New England writers at a conference with reference to Worcester, Massachusetts, a city that throughout my childhood was known as "the armpit of the East." Their patter ran something like this:

> *No matter where you live, someone, somewhere wants to read about it.*
> *Except Worcester. No one wants to read about Worcester.*

> *You mean Worcester, the city where Freud gave his fa-*
> *mous American lectures? Worcester, the home of the Amer-*
> *ican Antiquarian Society? Worcester, which houses the*
> *largest collection of armor in the Western hemisphere?*
> *Worcester, home of the New England Science Center?*
> *Worcester, the birthplace of Clara Barton—you mean that*
> *Worcester?*
> *Yeah, I knew that.*

At their workshops, the Olders ask participants to come up with at least three story ideas about places within a ten-mile radius of home. Once one fellow flatly contended that there weren't any noteworthy places in his area. Effin stunned him by reeling off five for him off the top of her head, including the state fair. Why would anyone be interested in the state fair? he asked. Not everyone has one, the Olders reminded him. Once his eyes were opened, the man who had claimed his area had no travel appeal came up with ten more story ideas before lunch.

Right now, see if you can complete this exercise by coming up with at least three ideas for articles about your home turf.

How did you do? If you came up dry, the rest of this chapter should prime your mental pump so that it flows with promising possibilities. If you came up with three, you'll learn that the options are virtually endless. Once you've listed seven or more, you're ready to start building the kind of track record that enables you to get sent all-expenses-paid to Hawaii, Budapest or the Galapagos Islands—if that's your dream.

AN IMPROMPTU TOUR OF TRAVEL WRITING POSSIBILITIES

To demonstrate to you that the options for writing travel pieces without leaving home range far beyond straightforward destination pieces, I went browsing in the periodical section of my public library. Within fifteen minutes I'd collected half a dozen interesting examples of travel-related articles in nontravel magazines. Each could have been written by someone who hadn't budged from home to research it. Following the name of the magazine and the title of the article are some comments and a lesson or two for freelancers from the example. Do this exercise yourself

and you'll undoubtedly discover many more kinds of opportunities than those I ran into.

Early American Life

"Newport Christmas," accompanied by a shorter piece called "Bed and Breakfast in Newport." The angle for the main piece isn't just historic Newport, Rhode Island, but how Newport celebrates its annual yuletime festival. It's a perfect match for the December issue of this magazine devoted to architecture, decorating and lifestyles in the seventeenth and eighteenth centuries. The accompanying article profiles a few colonial-era homes in Newport that have opened their doors to guests, and ends with addresses and telephone numbers for eight of them. The moral: think about time tie-ins as well as topical tie-ins for locales: "Cheyenne at Rodeo Time," "San Francisco in Fog Season," "A Philadelphia Fourth of July." For a monthly magazine, you'll have to contact the editor at least six months ahead of time, at least six weeks ahead for a weekly newspaper section.

Eating Well

"Wetting Your Appetite." A tour of a famous fish market in Seattle, along with tips on buying fish wherever you live. There's also a sidebar called "Fish Facts" and four fish recipes. What foods are special to your area, and what places could you feature to highlight them? Think about planning a unique culinary experience for a visitor to your area: a clambake, a teahouse tour, "Cambridge's Cybercafes," "Milwaukee's Mini-breweries."

Health

"Learn to Play Again." How to truly leave stress behind when you go on vacation; the sidebar is headed, "Surviving a Family Vacation." Here we're reminded that traveling itself can be your focus, rather than a place. And you're as eligible to write this sort of piece as someone who flies to a different exotic hideaway every month. For instance, I could probably expand the idea of the "small trip" at the beginning of this chapter into an entire article for a health-related magazine.

Parents

"Ten Great Getaways: Top-Rated Resorts With Families in Mind." A roundup of highlights, prices and pros and cons vis-à-vis kids of ten U.S., Caribbean and Mexican resorts. Ten is a common number for this sort of collective portrait. Your information must be up-to-the-minute accurate, and it will help if you're basing recommendations on more than personal opinion. But you wouldn't necessarily have to leave home to research a roundup, say, of ten overlooked national parks, ten ways to see Minneapolis (by car, bus, bike, plane, skates, kayak, foot, wheelchair, scooter, horse), ten places to worship the sunset or ten great public libraries.

Runner's World

"The Road: Orlando, Florida." You wouldn't have to be a serious runner to write this sort of very targeted guide to a city, only be able to think like one. This article characterizes Orlando in general terms, then zeroes in on what a visiting runner would want to know: where to and not to run, where to get equipped, where to find local runners, where to sleep and eat, and the 5K through marathon races held in the area. The possibilities opened up here are as limitless as the specialty areas for magazines. "A Biker's/Fisherman's/Hangglider's/Doll Collector's/Theater-goer's/Birdwatcher's Guide to the Hudson Valley."

Yankee

"Perfectly Grand in Prouts Neck." One hundred years ago, painter Winslow Homer wintered on a rocky stretch of land called Prouts Neck and rendered it on canvas. This piece is breathtakingly illustrated with reproductions of Homer paintings, contemporary color panoramas and historic black-and-white photographs. Think about retracing the steps of someone famous who once lived in your area, as in "Jack Kerouac's Lowell, Massachusetts"; "The Suffragettes' Seneca Falls"; "Ross Perot's Texarkana."

HOME, STRANGE, HOME

When I went around looking for people who had succeeded in writing about places close to home as tourist destinations, I

found that many of their stories held lessons for those who need extra help to locate the article gold in familiar areas. The old advice from writing teachers, "Write about what you know," emerges as a productive tip for getting started from Karen Gibson's experience. Gibson, based in Norman, Oklahoma, says that when she started brainstorming for article ideas, she quickly realized that her home state was virtually ignored by the travel industry. After making a list of Oklahoma places of interest that she already knew about, she queried *Backpacker* for a piece on trails in Oklahoma. They published it as "Oklahoma's Lush Side" in September 1993.

An avid hiker, Gibson realized that she hadn't exhausted this angle, and sold a second piece to *Backpacker* a few years later on Oklahoma's only national park, Chickasaw National Recreation Area, which boasts not only mineral springs and a freshwater lake but also a colorful history as a gift from the Chickasaw tribe to the federal government. She has also taken advantage of the fact that few Americans realize that Oklahoma has the largest Native American population in the United States.

Just as Karen Gibson was able to surprise me, and presumably non-Oklahoman editors, with a fresh angle on her state, Coloradan Howard Rothman sold an article to *Guest Informant*, an annual magazine distributed in hotel rooms, on Colorado as the state where more beer is brewed than anywhere else. In "Colorado Breweries," he produced a tourist-oriented wrap-up of breweries in the state where visitors can see beer being made. "I found out about Colorado ranking first from one of the innumerable press releases I receive, announcing the opening of a regional Anheuser-Busch brewery in Fort Collins," he recalls. "Since I didn't know Colorado was tops in beer production, I figured it would be news to visitors, too. But I shaped a story by looking beyond the press release for a way that this news could prove of practical use to someone visiting the area."

For a quick overview of your home state's possibly overlooked economic and demographic strengths, look it up in a recent encyclopedia, or request a handbook from the state tourist board. Once you become active in travel writing you'll probably find yourself on lists to receive the kind of press releases Rothman does.

Another idea-producing item obtainable from a state or regional tourist board or local chamber of commerce would be a calendar of upcoming special events. As I mentioned earlier in this chapter, a time-related angle often makes your article more attractive to editors than pieces that could run any old week or month.

Colleen Foye Bollen sold her first travel article when she realized that the upcoming tenth anniversary of the eruption of Mount Saint Helens, which she had originally witnessed from her home in nearby Seattle, would serve as a dramatic hook. Way before the predictable anniversary stories began to surface in the local media, she queried *Seattle's Child* for a piece on the now-quiescent volcano as a destination for families.

"Not many kids have an active volcano in their backyard, especially one that is safe to visit and that showcases the awesome power of Mother Nature. This was a great article for a beginner to write, because the story was so dramatic," she says. "All I had to do was remind readers about the eruption, tell them about the rejuvenation of plant and animal life in the ensuing years, and describe what they would be able to see when they visited." Bollen resold versions of the article to *RV West* and *Northwest Baby & Child*, a publication issued by a diaper company, which paid her with a free month of diapers.

Note that you can often interest nearby publications in articles featuring local places. Lee Daley of Corte Madera, California, named four attractions within one-hundred miles of her home that she had written about for Northern California newspapers—whose readers also lived just a couple of hours away or less from the destinations. One article concerned bed-and-breakfast inns on Point Reyes, a scenic area across the Golden Gate Bridge from San Francisco, and another highlighted one bed-and-breakfast place at Stinson Beach, even closer to San Francisco. "When you're writing about nearby places for local readers, you need a narrower focus than otherwise," Daley suggests. "People already have a general idea of the area, and they're looking for something unique or new, and for insider information. For example, at Stinson Beach I knew the history of the gardens at the bed and breakfast and a particular inlet where sea otters play." Her local readers wouldn't need the kind of

orientation to comparatively rural Marin County necessary for and of interest to readers in, say, Baltimore or Milwaukee.

Keep relatively local publications in mind, then, as you keep adding to your list of article topics you can write about places close to home. One writer who returned from a travel writing seminar at the National Press Club in Washington, DC, reported that the travel section assistant editor said *The Washington Post* had submissions coming out its ears on exotic locations, but needed more about places to visit in Delaware, Pennsylvania, Maryland and Virginia. A comparable need probably exists at regional newspapers and magazines near you.

MASTERING THE DESTINATION PIECE

As with profiles, where your ability to craft a captivating portrait depends on having gathered outstanding quotes and cogent observations during your interview, any first-rate destination piece begins with careful on-site research. Grab up current printed brochures and fact sheets, make notes of what you see, hear, smell and experience, and seek out people who can provide dependable information that can't be picked up merely by observation. When visiting a site like a museum for an article, travel columnist Doris Larson of Kent, Ohio, often calls ahead to make an appointment with the curator to facilitate her information gathering.

Two important responsibilities should guide your questioning and note taking: you'll need perspective that only an ideally observant visitor could provide, and you'll need accurate facts, details and anecdotes that most visitors wouldn't bother to collect. Your duty of accuracy means that you must do your best to personally confirm important items like prices, hours of operation, telephone numbers and so on. Never use information from printed guidebooks that you haven't checked on your own. And even if you don't intend to sell photos of the place, pictures can help you round out the notes you took at the time by reminding you of the atmosphere and setting.

The range of information you collect should relate to the interests and needs of the audience for whom you'll be writing about this destination. To a certain extent this means obvious moves like, if you're aiming at *Sober Times*, make a special effort to

find nonalcoholic venues and don't bother with breweries and bars, while if you'll be writing up Memphis for a student publication, find out the local drinking age and seek out budget restaurants that have an appealing attitude. The more you think through what your audience might want and need to know about a destination, the more you'll include special touches like restaurant and inn family rates for parenting magazines, corporate discounts for business travelers or mentions of local synagogues and kosher restaurants for a Jewish publication. Given an extra day on the town, would your particular group of readers rather head out to the golf course, shop for bargains or eagerly stay out past midnight to hit the jazz clubs? The ads and articles in previous issues of your target publication will provide valuable clues.

When you sit down to plan out your travel piece, the most important decision to make concerns your point of view. If you didn't already formulate an argument when you pitched your article in advance, come up with a sentence or headline statement now that encapsulates your perspective on this place, such as: "In August, New York City is as cool as ever." "Even without sightings, a Newfoundland whale-watching trip offers delights." "Boston beaches eighty-five cents away from downtown." "A sunset lover's guide to Utah." When you're stuck, make a list of stereotypes about the locale in question and see which ring true when turned upside down. Or look through your notes for one feature of the place that could typify its appeal for your audience.

Beneath the umbrella of that point of view belong descriptions of your destination. These must have a fresh, original flavor so that they entertain and enlighten as well as inform readers. Shun predictable or general statements like "New England weather is famous for being changeable" in favor of more precise, unexpected characterizations like "April temperatures have been known to range from a blizzardy 30° to balmy T-shirt weather—within 36 hours." Liberally toss in anecdotes and details that you uncovered during your research, such as the lawsuits that plagued the construction of the building and the number of steps in the fire tower. And don't mechanically catalog what visitors can see and do there. Readers expect you to sort through the possibilities and offer well-informed, reliable recommendations—

the must-sees, the little-known treasures, the overrated has-beens.

Most destination pieces include one or more practical "If you go . . ." sidebars. These put together in handy list fashion the top travel, accommodation and eating establishments along with telephone numbers, prices and addresses. Generally an "If you go . . ." sidebar should contain details for transportation options—by plane, train, ship, car, taxi, subway, bus, foot or camel depending on the destination; places to stay and to eat, each with a thumbnail depiction and price range; and the hours, locations, fees and phone numbers for major attractions at the destination. Don't leave important information out here because it's mentioned in your main narrative, since some readers may make a beeline for the "If you go . . ." section without reading the rest of the article. Wherever possible, end with a resource such as a tourist board or chamber of commerce that a reader can contact with general needs or unanswered questions.

IN A MORE LITERARY VEIN

Although most magazines that buy travel articles seek service-oriented pieces, some welcome travel literature, or travelogues. As compared with the practical, here's-what-you'll-find emphasis of destination pieces, travel literature tells a story about a journey in the first person using a thoughtful, literary tone and an essayistic structure. Such a piece needn't stress the attractiveness of a place, and it doesn't usually presume that the reader would want to follow in the writer's footsteps. A lesson or at least a significant theme serves as the backbone of the piece, and it may include dialogue, suspense, symbolism and other elements imported from fiction woven along with description.

Travel literature can have a leisurely pace, but rarely will anyone welcome your day-by-day touring log, however nicely written. Instead, select the aspects of your journey to reveal dramatic action, with something vital at stake that others might relate to as well. "Establish a ground situation early in the essay," advises Lucy McCauley, a writer and editor of travel literature based in Cambridge, Massachusetts. "Then complicate the situation. Then provide a climax and resolution, wherein the reader learns something along with the writer." The driving force might be some sort of personal quest, such as for healing or for discovery

of one's roots, or an unwilling confrontation with some travel obstacle, like bureaucracy or incompatible companions, or discoveries by an uninvolved but caring observer, as of recovery of an area from war or famine.

In the last category was a piece McCauley published in the "Letters from . . ." column of *Harvard Review* about visiting Budapest with Holocaust survivors, trying to see it through their eyes. In the traveler's obstacle category, she published a personal story about dealing with the attentions of a married man in Bolivia, in an anthology of travel tales by women. And in the personal quest category, a story about connecting with her mother during a trip they took together to Guatemala, appeared in *International Quarterly*, a literary magazine. The drama of that tale had to do with the ranch where McCauley's mother grew up and her grandfather was murdered, as well as with McCauley's difficulty in telling her mother she was getting divorced. Nothing in these categories necessitates going far away from home, she notes, and in fact she is currently writing something about Walden Pond, made famous by Henry David Thoreau and just eleven miles west of her Cambridge home.

McCauley had occasion to review some three hundred literary travel submissions and previously published pieces when she compiled an anthology called *Traveler's Tales: Spain*. She rejected a good number of pieces that read like travel diaries, closely following someone's whole itinerary, and quite a few others filled with stereotypes, flat writing and clichéd descriptions. "The more a subject's been written about, like bullfighting, the more terrific the writing has to be, and the more you need a unique approach," she says. She also shied away from pieces with no conflict or tension, just straight description— "even if it was nice description." Pieces that she selected included ones where the writer learned something abroad, like flamenco guitar, or where some event coming at a critical time in life truly changed the writer.

It'll take a sharp eye and a lot of digging to uncover markets for magazine-length travel literature, since destination coverage dominates the field. Look beyond the self-evident travel-related magazines to markets concerned with the theme you're writing about, such as mother-daughter relationships, thriving with a

disability or finding your particular ethnic roots. In addition to periodicals that you can track down at the library, on newsstands and in market guides, people collecting stories for anthologies often put out calls for contributions through the newsletters of writers' organizations such as Poets & Writers or the International Women's Writing Guild.

WHAT ABOUT PHOTOS?

If you enjoy the process of photographing places you visit, you have the potential to multiply your income from writing travel pieces. From my study of *Writers' Market*, it seems that selling photos and articles would typically double your fee, as compared with selling only words. Dan Owen, a writer/photographer based in Phoenix, Arizona, says he's done much better than double with some photo-heavy articles. A magazine piece on a vintage speedboat cruise earned him $800 for the article and $1,800 for the photos. Like other professional photographers, Owen also makes extra money from his photos by selling just one-time or first rights (see chapter seven) initially and then reselling the shots to other magazines or to stock photography houses. The latter are companies to which art directors turn when they need a shot of an erupting volcano, a crowded fish market or Victorian row houses in San Francisco.

Owen spends about 80 percent of his on-location time nailing down the photographs he needs and 20 percent on observation and collection of resources and contacts that he can mine for the article copy once he returns home. "If I'm doing a piece on the historic courthouse in Bellefontaine, Ohio, I'll always line up a local person whom I can call for more information later. I'd say, 'Look, I need to concentrate here on the pictures, but when I get back home to Phoenix, may I call you for more background about the courthouse?' People always say, 'Sure, call me any time.' "

Richard Kreitman, who's sold numerous article-plus-photos packages to the travel sections of newspapers, juggles his dual responsibilities on site by dictating all his observations and recording his interviews—as well as keeping a running log identifying his photo subjects—on a mini-cassette recorder. Sometimes he'll switch roles only once, by doing all the information gather-

ing first, then spending the whole next day photographing. Of course, if you're already close to home, limited time at the destination doesn't pose as much of a problem. If you can't stay long enough to switch tracks from writing to photography or vice versa, you can make two trips to the site, one to round up substance and one to take photos.

You'll need a little more than the standard tourist camera for salable photos. A 35mm camera with extra wide-angle and zoom lenses is *de rigueur*, as is non-expired brand-name film (Kodak or Fuji, for example) that you keep away from sunlight, extreme heat and airport X-ray machines. "Always take an extra camera or camera body along in case the other breaks," advises Dan Owen. Most writer/photographers don't bother with so-called medium- and large-format cameras, which produce sharper, larger negatives of buildings and landscapes but cost much more and require much more technical prowess.

And what about color versus black and white, slides versus prints? You might as well shoot in color as a rule, my sources agreed, since color slides or prints can easily be converted to black-and-white prints. But on the slides-or-prints questions, there was less consensus. Dan Owen said flatly, "High-quality magazines always want slides. Any publication working from prints is low-end." Newspapers apparently can handle either color slides—also called "transparencies" in the trade, by the way—or prints, and some tabloids and magazines produced through desktop publishing technology prefer prints, which they run through a scanner.

If you have a pre-trip assignment, find out the publication's preference, which might be quite idiosyncratic. Gardening writer Barbara Pleasant, for instance, says that the gardening magazines are standardized on Fujichrome 50 or 100 so that green and blue hues throughout the magazine match. If you're winging it, hoping to sell an article and pictures later, color slides seem the safest bet. They duplicate easily, and can also be converted to prints.

TAKING AND SUBMITTING SALABLE SHOTS

Everyone who sells photos recommends taking many, many more than you'll need. Sophia Dembling says that she shoots

ten to fifteen rolls of exposures on a weeklong trip, adding, "A professional photographer once told me that if you get one usable photo from each roll, you're doing fine." Besides proper exposure and sharp focus, composition makes the difference between so-so or downright bad photos and salable ones. Richard Kreitman tries to get as much bright color as possible into his photos, indicators of action such as waving flags and either street signs or ads that reveal at a glance the location of that particular sunset or stadium. Also, photos taken either early or late in the day yield the best colors, he notes. The husband-and-wife travel-writing team of Marilyn and Glenn Pribus meet the mandate for bright colors by always wearing something red and appearing in each other's photos. They also make sure they take both vertical and horizontal shots, the difference coming about from the position of the camera.

Dembling says her main rule of thumb with respect to composition is "If it doesn't look good in the viewfinder, I don't press the shutter." Pitfalls like too-busy backgrounds, a kid picking his nose next to the person you were aiming the camera at or a flagpole seeming to grow out of the subject's head require constant vigilance, she says. "Shots with no discernible focal point— milling crowds, wishy-washy scenes, meaningless interiors—are very unappealing to editors." She tries to take both wide scene-setting shots and close-up details, which give editors and art directors interesting options for contrast. London writer and editor Victoria Stagg Elliott adds, "Unpublishable snapshots have a friend standing in front of one of the seven wonders of the world, while publishable photos have been thought through in terms of lighting, position and framing."

"Whenever you submit photos, publications judge them against those produced by professionals who do nothing else," warns Dan Owen. Snapshot quality just won't cut it. But achieving acceptable quality in photography is not as difficult as, say, playing violin in an orchestra or completing a marathon. Owen suggests practicing by shooting often-photographed scenic sights in your area and comparing your results with what you see in newspapers, guidebooks and magazines. Similarly, Kreitman recommends creative borrowing while you're learning—looking over how published professionals have photographed the sites

you're planning to visit and trying to replicate those angles and compositions.

Most writer/photographers I spoke with do not submit photos in any form except when an assigning editor has requested them. Slides are best presented in 8½″ × 11″ acetate sleeves, purchasable at any good camera store. Make sure you stamp or write your name and telephone number on each slide, along with a number keyed to a legend on a caption sheet. When submitting prints, likewise label each one on the back with your contact information and either the caption or a number keyed to your caption sheet.

Richard Kreitman successfully used a different approach in his submissions to newspaper travel editors—a montage sampler of photos and captions on an 11″ × 17″ page that he'd duplicate for about $2.50 each on a color copier. Compose captions carefully as a dynamic part of your storytelling, rather than as dry identifiers of the contents of the image. For instance, notice how much interesting information not visible in the picture this caption from a piece by Kreitman on whale-watching offers: "Passengers aboard Oceanic Society boat to Farallon Islands scan the granite outposts for the plentiful wildlife living there. This includes several species of whales, plus porpoises, dolphins, seals, sea lions, elephant seals, birds and sharks."

Although my sources agreed that formal signed releases from the people in your pictures aren't usually required for editorial (as opposed to commercial) photography, Dan Owen pointed out that if you plan to resell your photos to stock houses, they always require releases, so that it's safest to get signed permission from identifiable subjects and from the owners of cars, boats, planes and houses that figure prominently in your shots.

If all this seems overwhelming, keep in mind alternative ways of meeting editors' needs for photography. Cori Kenicer, who specializes in golf-related travel pieces, says that she finds writing and photographing incompatible. "If I have one day to look at a golf resort, I want to talk to people, get a feel for the place, see how the energy is, how the service is. How can I do all that when I'm looking around for the right lighting, or trying to line up the perfect shot?"

Instead of taking photos herself, she either submits photos

taken by her husband when he's accompanied her on a trip, tells the editor about sources of free photos from golf properties she's reviewed or regional tourist bureaus, or calls around her network of writer/photographers for someone who might have just the shots to illustrate her stories. "It's never been a problem that I don't supply photos of my own," she says. So if you just can't hold a camera still or master the technicalities, you're not necessarily sabotaging your travel writing opportunities. Team up with someone else or bone up on specific sources for the photographs that round out your stories.

VENTURING BEYOND HOME

Launching a travel writing career with portraits of places close to home requires minimal outlay in expenses and pays off handsomely in credentials and experience. If writing about far-away places represents an ultimate ambition, these easy-to-start-with clips can help you reach that goal. You can also earn opportunities to write travel pieces for prestigious magazines once you pay your dues with articles about trips you were planning to take in any case. Richard Kreitman generated a major article sale about his honeymoon destination, Costa Rica. Your previously published work, of whatever sort, qualifies you for subsidized travel, both in the form of transportation, food and lodging paid for by parties at your destination, and invitation-only press tours, where writers are taken to an area all expenses paid.

Says Cori Kenicer, who estimates that she's taken advantage of subsidized travel about twenty times, "It gives you access to places, properties and attractions that most publications wouldn't finance and that you might not be able to afford yourself as a writer. It's also convenient because you're hosted by people who smooth the way for you instead of having to drive around on your own getting lost." Just as valuable, press trips provide opportunities to network with other writers. "That's given me the chance to learn about organizations, events and publications that helped my career, and I've even gotten a crack at assignments that someone else on the trip couldn't handle."

Individualized subsidized travel involves first getting an article assignment and then asking hotels, airlines and tourist organizations to defray your expenses for researching that destination.

For instance, if Kenicer receives an assignment to write about golfing in the Canadian Rockies, she'll begin calling the public relations people at the resorts she'd be covering. She'd also look into whether a regional association exists that might take care of her expenses.

"There is some implicit quid pro quo," she admits, "in that they might expect you to say only good things, or give their place more space if you stayed there, but I like to think of it in terms of them showing you their place at its best, hoping that you'll like it. My responsibility, though, is to the reader rather than the people who subsidized the trip." Only once can she recall a host complaining—when she gave the lead of an article to a place where she hadn't stayed. She placated that public relations person by reminding him that her assignment focused on "What's New in Arizona," so that top billing properly belonged to the state's newest golf course, not the one he represented. In one way or another, Kenicer usually goes all expenses paid—travel expenses she can't find someone at the destination to take care of she'll negotiate with the magazine to pay.

Press trips, which I've often heard described as "grueling," involve a nonstop schedule for a group of writers to experience as much as possible of a destination together, all expenses paid. Writers usually get invited based on being listed with their credentials in the membership directory of a travel writers' organization, or because the trip organizer saw someone's published work. Sponsors expect that invited writers will do their best to line up assignments before going on the trip, and to generate published pieces promoting the area. Cori Kenicer encourages anyone going on a press trip to tell the sponsors about special research needs and interests. "They're usually very accommodating because their ultimate goal is for you to get what you need to write a positive story." On the downside, she finds that press tour organizers often like to showcase the culinary skills of the sponsors, which means dinners can be overly heavy, time-consuming and tiring from the perspective of writers focusing on special arenas besides food.

Because of the usually unstated expectations of the establishments and organizations paying for the writers' trips, sponsored travel has a controversial status within the journalism

profession. Many newspapers ask freelance contributors of travel pieces to certify that they have not received any unpaid transportation, lodging or food. Writers who do accept subsidies point out the absurdity of this ethical position, since the policy that writers must pay for their own trips makes it difficult to break even on the work, much less earn decent pay after expenses. Sophia Dembling, who has taken press trips as a writer and detected telltale signs of sponsorship in work submitted to her as an editor, says that it's possible for writers to avoid the pitfalls of the practice. "The risk, of course, is that freelancers will be so afraid of alienating their sponsors and losing invitations that they won't write anything negative. Well, honest writers write honest stories. I have written negative stories off sponsored trips."

As an editor, Dembling recalls being able to spot payback stories because they tended to be jam-packed with superlatives and mentioned properties with no relevance to the story. Her own guidelines include accepting government-sponsored trips, which focus on a country or region, and not hotel-sponsored trips, to avoid any pressure from publicists to fit a particular property into a story where it doesn't belong.

Some organizers of press trips try to accommodate editorial sensitivities by offering a discounted daily rate for writers aiming at publications that disallow subsidies. Kenicer can't recall ever meeting anyone on a press tour participating on that basis, however.

Chapter Six

Local News Worth Spreading

After I had been writing articles for about six years, I had enough clips and enough nerve to make appointments for personal story conferences with editors at some of the largest women's magazines. I'll tell you more about this strategy in chapter twelve, but here I'd like to share one of my biggest surprises at these conferences. For me the distance from Boston to New York City was only a leisurely train ride or a short hop by plane, something I'd done countless times in my life. Yet almost every time, when I walked into an editor's office, the opening question was, "How was your trip?," as if I'd stepped off the Concorde.

Gradually I realized that for these New York editors, Boston felt much farther away than New York felt to me. On their mental map, anything east of Greenwich, Connecticut, was off in the wilds. My students in Providence told me confirming stories of meeting New Yorkers who had only a foggy notion where the state of Rhode Island was. Even Brooklyn, the Bronx and Staten Island—officially portions of New York City—feel foreign to some confirmed Manhattanites.

The insularity of Manhattan, where perhaps close to half of national magazine headquarters are rooted, represents tremendous opportunity for an enterprising freelancer. Magazines with a national readership need stories set outside of their home base, wherever that is. As someone based elsewhere, you're in an ideal position to inform them about, and get assignments for covering, newsworthy events and significant developments in your neck of the woods. Often the stories filling the front pages of your hometown newspapers and leading area newscasts never make

it beyond your locale, and some of those deserve to. Once you understand how to tailor a local story for a national publication, every local newspaper you read or newscast that you listen to—and even gossip at the local bar—offers a rich mine for potential articles.

THE INVISIBILITY OF THE FAMILIAR

In order to make hay of occurrences close to you, you have to overcome the barrier of not seeing the newsworthiness of events that may appear as ordinary and unremarkable to you as the bushes growing around your house. I learned this in the early 1980s after I got the bright idea that I could get a press pass to a local conference on the psychology of the nuclear threat if I could find a magazine that wanted an article about it. I approached an editor at *Psychology Today* whom I'd met, thinking they might want a short news item about the conference. "We don't cover conferences—why don't you get the program and see if there's something in particular to focus on," suggested the editor. To my amazement, I got an assignment to write a full-length feature story on the psychological impact of the nuclear arms race on children. At that time, I was deeply involved in the anti-nuclear movement, and since everyone I knew knew that kids were scared of nuclear bombs, I presumed everyone else knew it too. When my article not only became *Psychology Today's* cover story but was mentioned by Tom Brokaw on the NBC Nightly News, I realized with a start how wrong my assumption had been.

As this anecdote shows, the local story you may be sitting on may relate to events known within some political, social or occupational group, not only a geographical locale. It's equally important to understand that the category of "news" includes much more than front-page stuff like plane crashes, bombings, elections, mass layoffs and peace talks. Here are some additional categories of news stories you should have in mind.

• *Controversies.* Native Americans decide to build a toxic waste dump on their reservation, whose streams feed into the municipal water system. Or, consumer advocates are criticizing health maintenance organizations that reward doctors for refer-

ring fewer patients to specialists. Or, First-Amendment champions are clashing with parent groups that want the power of overseeing school library acquisitions. Such conflicts raise such important issues that articles presenting each point of view could hold appeal for magazine and Sunday supplement editors locally, regionally and nationally.

• *Legal cases.* If an entrepreneur in your town has been prosecuted for scamming buyers or violating zoning laws with a home office, small-business magazines might be interested in the story. If members of a prominent family are suing one another, or taking different sides in a child custody dispute, this could serve as the basis of a gripping human interest drama. When a peculiar, pathbreaking or high-stakes case comes to your attention, think "Who would care about this and why?" to identify kinds of publications that might welcome the story.

• *Crimes.* The man serving your town as superintendent of schools gets stopped by police for drunk driving while he is wearing women's clothes. An article on how parents explained this to their kids might interest parenting or religious magazines. One year after a Harvard University junior stabbed her roommate forty-five times and hung herself, an instructor who had rejected the murderer for an autobiographical writing seminar published a probing article on the tragedy in *The New Yorker*. Even without any personal involvement, you could revisit your community's most notorious unsolved robberies, murders or kidnappings five, twenty-five or fifty years later.

• *Community success stories.* Is some program that solves a problem on a lot of people's minds working fabulously in your community? Whether that's cutting down prom-weekend accidents, air pollution or the isolation of senior citizens, publications elsewhere might appreciate such news.

• *Exposés.* Because the research can require tremendous amounts of time, energy and resources, staff reporters, not freelancers, perform most of the nation's muckraking. But if you can demonstrate that the government, an organization or a prominent individual has been doing something wrong, you may have an explosive and publishable article on your hands.

• *Offbeat gatherings.* In a calendar of upcoming local events you learn that the Guild of Vedic Astrologers, the National

Committee to Preserve the Manatee and the statewide Karate for Kids championship matches will be meeting in your city. Each event offers promising material for articles. Snag an assignment and you should be able to go to the events for free.

• *Social/family/educational difficulties.* Private struggles become news when they repeat in many households. You may have a good article topic in hand when you hear about families having trouble combining siblings, step-siblings and half-siblings; about parent-child drug habits; about a tidal wave of neighborly feuds; or an epidemic of exotic learning disabilities.

• *Trends.* Editors perk up when phenomena of all sorts increase or decrease in popularity, experience a revival or keel over and vanish. Almost any sizable change, innovation or eclipse has relevance for someone, sometimes for many different identifiable groups. Notice that religious wedding ceremonies are rising, and you could sell articles on the new tendency to bridal, religious, ethnic, advertising and church administration magazines.

• *Exceptions to a trend.* There's a story there when you learn of someone or something bucking a trend. Aaron Feuerstein, the elderly mill owner in Lawrence, Massachusetts, who kept idled workers on his payroll after a fire destroyed their workplace, won national acclaim because people viewed him as combatting the bottom-line-rules mentality. Similarly, the extinction-threatened spotted owls nesting in your woods offer you more possibilities than the robins and squirrels around them.

• *Harbinger stories.* Sometimes you can answer the question "What's ahead?" with predictions that are more grounded than images in a crystal ball. This might involve upcoming demographics, like a baby boomlet, what-if scenarios based on a current scare, or once-in-a-lifetime glitches like the havoc forecast for computers unprogrammed for the year 2000—all fertile article topics.

• *Anniversaries, updates and milestones.* Suppose the tenth anniversary of a deadly tornado that ripped through your town is coming up: Has everyone touched by the destruction recovered? Or no one has seemed to wonder how new environmental regulations put into effect a few years back are working: Why not you? Or the ten-millionth nurse's uniform has rolled off the assembly line at the factory down the street: Does this fly in the

face of experts who said uniforms for nurses would go out of style?

- *Release of new products, services.* Stay on the lookout for cute, clever, outrageous or surprising business innovations. Run to your computer to query when someone near you offers 24-hour legal advice, 240-day guarantees for floor cleaning or 2,400 varieties of coffee.

- *Surveys and research.* Every day of the year, professors and privately employed researchers in your area collect data that can illuminate what's happening in society, among particular groups of people and in nature. You can be among the first to know this news by calling local colleges, nonprofit organizations and fact-finding organizations and asking to be put on their public relations mailing list.

SNIFFING OUT TRENDS

"Keep your eyes and ears open," advises Leslie Petrovski, who sells about one article a month to the Living section of her home-town paper, the *Denver Post.* One piece of hers on women over sixty who had started new careers originated in just listening to her mother talk about what was new with her friends. One on the contemplative prayer movement, which she considers to be "meditation repackaged for Christians," came about from listening to her own contemporaries. Another on the resurgence of yoga among baby boomers came about after she enrolled in a yoga class herself and chatted with the teacher.

Petrovski says that after grabbing onto a few examples, the next step for a trend story usually involves seeking confirmation that these cases do actually represent a trend. For the older women starting new careers, she called senior organizations to find out if they had noticed this. They had, and arranged conversations with experts in the field. When someone has gathered statistics, that goes into the story, of course, but often anecdotal evidence and testimony from specialists can substitute for hard data. Petrovski also keeps trend books like Faith Popcorn's *Clicking* and John Naisbitt's *Megatrends* on her bookshelf for their broad interpretations of where Americans and others are heading.

Keep in mind that trend stories travel well both locally to

nationally and nationally to locally. That is, you can interest national publications in something new happening in your area if you live in a place where the next cool things tend to spawn. You can also watch the national media for accounts of spreading fads and report for your local media on the telltale signs of them beginning to catch on in your area. For instance, Petrovski had read about tea salons opening in New York City and Los Angeles, and found out that although none had arrived yet in Denver, coffeehouses were offering more teas. When she proposed the story to her editor at the *Denver Post*, she learned that her instinct was right on target, since the paper had already run a similar story she hadn't remembered.

The same principle applies to highlighting the relevance of general trends to particular ethnic, occupational or lifestyle groups. In London, Victoria Stagg Elliott writes a lot for Jewish publications, and sells numerous articles on what trends in the larger society might mean for Jews. "About half a dozen books about angels hit the shelves in one month, and I knew that a couple of angel-related documentaries were in the works," she says. "I turned that into an article about what angels mean and what they are within the context of Judaism." Another time, when "mad cow disease" was slaughtering the beef business in Britain, Elliott investigated whether kosher beef, considered more healthful than ordinary beef, was seeing increased sales from nonobservant Jews or gentiles. No, she learned, people were buying more poultry and fish, but the question and the answer still held interest for Jewish readers.

Yet another method of formulating trends consists of noticing a particular event or two and devising a generalization for which it serves as an illustration. Sophia Dembling loves this sort of exercise and publishes them often in her local paper, the *Dallas Morning News*. After glazing over and going into overload at Blockbuster Video, she wrote an article on the glut of options available to people nowadays, in everything from videos to the number of books designed to help you select videos. Another piece, called "The Rise and Fall of American Icons," hatched when Nelson Mandela burst the bubble of international adoration after he was released from jail by speaking up in favor of violence. "We're Having Some Serious Fun" portrayed the grim

pursuit of leisure sports she'd noticed in local parks and in the prickly attitude of salespeople at a bicycle shop when she tried to buy accessories for her $100 bike. "If I'm feeling something in particular about society, I figure a lot of other people are too," she says, and obviously her editor at the *Morning News* agrees.

Besides these accomplished trendwatchers' tips, you can make it a habit to ask friends, business acquaintances, even strangers you meet waiting to pay for your parking tickets, "What's new?" or "What's the latest headache in your life?" Even ordinary items in your mail can become seeds for articles when you adopt an ever-watchful mindset. For instance, I recognized a trend when I received a notice from my bank saying that they had to expand the number of telephone lines for their online banking service because the response was many times higher than they'd anticipated. If I weren't too busy with other projects, I could have investigated and then queried business magazines for a piece on the extent to which computerized banking was catching on. The trials and tribulations of friends may provide trend ideas, too.

REPACKAGING LOCAL NEWS

To illustrate the process of creatively recycling news items in your local paper, in January 1997 I pondered *The Boston Globe's* selection of the top ten local news stories of 1996 and was able, without too much painful brain work, to come up with fresh angles worthy of regional or national magazines for half of them:

1. John Salvi, who murdered two reproductive health clinic workers, received a sentence of life in prison and killed himself in his cell. *Ms., Glamour* or *McCall's* might be interested in an article about how patrons and staff of Boston-area clinics now cope with the threat of that violence.

2. Boston reported its lowest murder rate in thirty years. Given that fact, have ordinary residents changed their behavior? For *Boston Magazine* you could propose an article on how those living on one city street now feel and act with respect to crime.

3. Thanks to several brutal blizzards, cumulative snowfall for the winter of 1996 smashed all Boston records. In the early winter of 1997, you could investigate how memories of the previous

year's wallop were affecting snow removal contractors, insurance companies, travel agencies and hardware stores and sell articles about your findings to relevant trade magazines.

4. Dr. Jack Kevorkian helped a local woman suffering from fibromyalgia and chronic fatigue syndrome kill herself. *American Health* or *Redbook* might be interested in your proposed peek into the homes of three area women bedridden with these maladies. Are their conditions also that desperate and the prospects of relief that remote?

5. South Boston activists had so far managed to stave off the $4 million efforts of New England Patriots owner Robert Kraft to build a football stadium in their neighborhood. An in-depth analysis of the community activists' strategies and strengths might interest a political magazine like *Mother Jones* or the *New Republic*. A portrait of the controversy from the owner's point of view might appeal to one of the in-flight magazines connected to an airline that lands in Boston.

Note that I could have been visiting Boston from Albany, Hartford, Pittsburgh or Chicago and have translated several of these top news stories into angles for articles I would propose about my own area. Since all these stories reverberated throughout a major metropolitan area, though, I repeated this exercise with a look at my weekly hometown newspaper, a publication serving 7,000 or so residents. Amidst many fewer pages than *The Boston Globe* I did discover one article possibility: a controversy over a corporation's proposal to construct a cranberry bog in my town, which has more than five-hundred acres of salt marsh set aside as conservation land. I hadn't been following this debate, but I do know that cranberries don't grow well in many places, so that this dispute might upon further inquiry yield a sufficiently distinctive query for environmental magazines.

Many small-town papers publish a police report which can hide, amidst a numbing litany of who was arrested for assaulting or robbing whom, incredible stories of bungled crimes that could be retold and sold as humor or as revealing windows on a particular city or region. When I lived in Boston's South End, I looked forward to my weekly laundry run because I would read the police report in the neighborhood paper at the laundromat.

To demonstrate opportunities for repackaging local news I also investigated at the other end of the process by searching at the library for published articles that could have originated in a writer snatching a story out of a local paper or newscast. I narrowed my findings to half a dozen articles that suggested important lessons to me. They included some formats I might not have thought of without this look.

In *E: The Environmental Magazine,* I discovered a charming short piece taking off from the story of an 82-year-old Tulsa, Oklahoma, natural gardener who received a citation for violating the city's weed ordinance the same day she hosted more than 800 admirers of the waist-high colorful wildflowers comprising her front lawn. The 12-paragraph article about her featured three other people as well—an Indiana professor facing a $1 million fine for refusing to mow her prairie grass and wildflowers, a similarly cited Maryland couple and a Chicago lawyer who, so the article says, specializes in fighting weed laws. This example reminded me to remind you to think about whether the readers of the outlets you plan to pitch the story to would find the story you initially heard or read enough, or if they'd need additional examples and perspective.

An article in *Redbook* similarly put together several newsworthy cases of one phenomenon, but in quite a different format. The *E* piece flowed with conventional transitions straight through from beginning to end. The *Redbook* piece, called "I Met the Man Who Got My Son's Heart," began with five paragraphs on the growing numbers of friendships between families where a member who unexpectedly died donated an organ and families with a recipient of that organ whose life was saved. Following the introduction were four separate stories, told in the voices of three women whose son or brother had died, and of one woman who had received a heart. Meetings between the two families had taken place in three out of the four cases, which side by side revealed more dimensions of this complicated new kind of human relationship than would have emerged from just one story. Editors often call this article structure a roundup format, and here it also included a sidebar on the emotional dynamics of this relationship, quoting two transplant experts. Since the four women in this roundup live in different parts of

the country, and none of the deaths, transplants or meetings just took place, this piece illustrates an approach much more likely to work in a magazine than in a newspaper, which would usually cover only the case within its territory when a dramatic step in the saga had taken place.

In another issue of *Redbook* I became interested in a tale that also involved several women, but read like a frightening detective story without any heartwarming overtones or emotional closure. Set in Pitman, New Jersey, a small town where at least some elements of this story undoubtedly appeared in the local paper, the article traced the troubles of three young women who suffered from a tumor, cysts and infertility, and who had all years before attended a Girl Scout camp situated beside the number one toxic waste dump in the United States. With frequent shifts in focus signalled by the subheads "The Town," "The Camp" and "The Women," the story took the reader through the mounting evidence and the government and townspeople's denials of the problem. A sidebar headlined "Could You Be At Risk?" offered tips for readers concerned about the effects of toxic wastes in their neighborhood.

I found this a heart-pounding story, and I suspect that it took Mubarak Dahir, the writer, some digging around to have found the three affected women whose testimony and determination to find answers give the story power. From this and the preceding example, a lesson would be for you to ponder exactly where the greatest emotional impact of your story lies. Here the tribulations of desperate, innocent victims with one apparent culprit make for much more drama than would a more scattered depiction of the problem without any central characters.

Whereas the *Redbook* piece leaves little room for doubt about whether or not toxic waste created those women's troubles, a comparably dramatic article that I found in *Boston* magazine seesawed back and forth on the "Was it or was it not?" dilemma. Again, the article focused on a case that certainly made a big splash locally: a Worcester prep school student accused a teacher at her school of rape. The girl had no evidence to offer beyond her own word, however, and many at the school claimed she habitually made up stories. A grand jury refused to indict the teacher, and there the matter still inconclusively rests. In this

piece the writer did an excellent job, I thought, of narrating both sides of the case without giving more credence to either of the antagonists. I would guess that much of this story's appeal for the editors—and the readers—had to do with the prevalence of "he said/she said" situations and the opportunity for a magazine piece to put all the pieces of such a story together in one place and to explore its ramifications in the lives of all involved.

Another narration of a local event, in *Yankee* magazine, didn't raise the question of who was right and wrong because the drama concerned residents of Alton, New Hampshire, fighting raging flood waters on March 13, 1996. After introducing the setting and several key characters, this story took a chronological path to describe the flash flood, from 6:30 in the evening through 6:35, 6:46, 6:55, 7:10 and beyond, with just a few backtrackings and forward leaps that were easy to follow because of the time markers. One woman died, and $5 million in damage occurred in the town. Generally speaking, survival narratives are easier to write than stories of human-versus-human conflict, and the raw ingredients show up in news reports all the time. Can you imagine the possibilities inherent in a drama like two twelve-year-olds lost in the woods overnight who survived because of what they remembered from Boy Scout training? Off the top of my head I can think of three decent angles: how Boy Scout training saved their lives; how the parents coped with their harrowing experience; and how townspeople worked together, with life-or-death stakes, to find the boys. A case like this heard on the news can furnish the foundation for an article every bit as gripping as those about the fatal 1996 Mt. Everest expeditions.

The last of the articles I selected, from *Redbook* again, concerned a program in Kingston, New York, that sends rape victims not to the usual Emergency Room but to a private room with a specially trained nurse who collects evidence and comforts the traumatized woman. The author, Christina Frank, explained the rationale and benefits of the program mainly through the perceptions, experiences and duties of one sexual assault nurse examiner. Because the reader has a name, a face and a personal situation to identify with—and besides the nurse, a rape victim given voice with a pseudonym—potentially dry details of the evidence collection process go over easy with the reader. If you

plan to pitch a local program to national periodicals, make sure you use people to humanize the benefits and scale of success.

A final thought: all of these half-dozen local stories gone national involved conflict or loss. I'll let you ruminate on the implications of that observation on your own.

COVERING LOCAL NEWS AS A "STRINGER"

Another option for making the most of where you live is working as a so-called stringer—covering events in your area for national newspapers, the newswires, and specialized magazines that may not have their own reporters close enough to the action. Knowing that few national news organizations kept a staff reporter anywhere in her state, Marialisa Calta of Calais, Vermont, queried *The New York Times'* national desk every week for months with Vermont news ideas. None of her suggestions ignited interest, but one day she received a call from a *Times* editor telling her that Geraldine Ferraro's son had been arrested for cocaine use in Middlebury, about one and a half hours away. Her job was to drive down there immediately, compile a list of sources and telephone numbers for the story, and then pick up the *Times'* staff reporter when he arrived at the airport from his post in Boston. "I didn't write that story for them, but after that they started taking my suggestions—for stories that were timely but not breaking news, such as the resurgence of coyotes in Vermont," she recalls. "I'd proven myself under fire, I guess."

Other instances in which Calta was called upon for "jump and run" journalism either for the *Times* or for the Reuters news organization included the death of Maria von Trapp (the real-life model for Maria in "The Sound of Music") and the discovery that the deed of a Vermont house owned by Supreme Court Justice William Rehnquist had a clause prohibiting sale to Jews. Typically she'd have to file the story, either by modem or by dictating it over the telephone, by the end of the day. "Sometimes you can research these stories right from your home," Calta notes. "They call you because you know the community and can presumably find people faster than their own reporter." With small children, she finds it hard to drop everything and run around the state to cover breaking news, but her dependability gave her an important "in" at the prestigious paper. She's now

written for just about every section of the *Times* except the Book Review and the Week in Review.

Although Marialisa Calta had considerable reporting experience from previously working for the Associated Press and the *Providence Journal,* similar opportunities await aggressive freelancers who have reported for a small-town paper or just have the requisite energy and enthusiasm. Many now-established writers can look back on a stint as a stringer at the start of their career. Years ago Lisa Collier Cool, author of *How to Write Irresistible Query Letters,* besieged an editor for the North American Newspaper Alliance with ideas for short feature articles. She got her break the day before Election Day with a report on a group of Libertarians who started an anti-election campaign on the theme, "Vote for Nobody." Later she covered numerous other events taking place in her home base of Manhattan for the syndicate, such as a science fiction convention, a publishing industry convention and a boy who had collected more than $60,000 worth of comic books. "I liked having press credentials, and knew I was gaining valuable writing experience, but one day it dawned on me that maybe, just maybe, there was somebody out there who paid more than $35 a story." Cool started writing the same length stories for *The Star*, a national tabloid, which paid at that time $350 apiece.

If you have specialized knowledge, you might find opportunities to cover local events for trade journals or special-interest publications. In September 1996, Executive Editor Bill Mahoney of *Multichannel News* in London advertised on CompuServe, the international online service, for stringers in the Nordic region to write spot news articles and features on developments in the television industry. He said he had a network of more than forty stringers worldwide, a dozen of them hired from CompuServe's journalism forum. Ontario equestrienne Karen Briggs covers horse shows in her area for magazines like *Dressage Today,* *Eventing* and *Spur.* She used to provide just text, with a friend who was a professional equine photographer and usually attended the same events supplying photos, but her friend moved to Cuba. "Most of the events I cover don't have professional photographers assigned, or if they do, they're often too slow to meet my deadlines," she says. "As a result, my antiquated Canon

and I have been struggling to remember what we could from undergrad Photography 101."

How can you find stringing opportunities? Calta suggests her strategy of sending clips and then being extremely persistent. Another route is making sure your network of contacts knows of your special interests and experience. Susan Nicol started a long stint as a hockey stringer when she was writing ads for radio station CKRC in Winnipeg, Manitoba, where she still lives. "The news director knew I was freelancing on the side and had written player profiles on the Winnipeg Jets when they were in the World Hockey Association. One day she walked into the station, saw me and stopped dead in her tracks. The local United Press Canada bureau chief had asked her the day before if her sports director could double as a hockey stringer. Since the station didn't have a sports director, she had said no. She told me about the request and gave me the bureau chief's number. I was covering the Jets for UPC by the weekend and did that for five years."

I came across only one person who said he'd been well paid as a stringer, when he covered the trial of accused Nazi war criminal John Demjanjuk in his home state of Ohio for the Toronto *Globe and Mail* on a daily basis. Everyone else told me the money they got was piddling, and almost not worth it except for other compensations. Susan Nicol received season tickets for Jets games. She also noted that her stringer position led to many other opportunities, such as becoming a backup sports reporter for CKRC, a host for an on-air interview program and a copywriter for a national ad agency based in Winnipeg—all at least partly because she had proven her journalistic mettle as a stringer. Lee Hickling of Cobb Island, Maryland, looking back on having worked as a stringer for United Press International, says decades later, "There are only three reasons for a freelance to be a stringer, as I see it, and none of them is money: for the love of it, for the thrill of seeing one's stuff in print, and in order to accumulate clippings."

As for the "love" motivation, Marialisa Calta says, "If you like to know what's going on in your community, stringing gives you an excuse to find out. It puts you in the center of your community so that you hear tons of stories. I love news reporting, and find it exhilarating, a huge amount of fun."

From Idea to Article

Chapter Seven

Query Letters, Assignments and Completed Articles

U p to now we've been focusing on ways of coming up with ideas. Now we get down to nitty-gritty methods of researching, writing, rewriting and getting your work into print. Many beginners assume that writing for publication involves composing a work in the heat of inspiration and then shopping the completed manuscript until someone buys it. But without some preliminary thinking about your audience, the optimal length for a specific publication and the approach you're taking to your subject, you run the risk of writing a piece for which no market, anywhere, exists. Writing first and looking around for a market later thus poses the danger of wasting a lot of your time. You're much more likely to succeed by mastering the art of writing a polished query letter—the tool seasoned writers use to interest publications in their work.

Still, as with any rule of thumb, contrary successes exist. Of the dozens of freelance writers I spoke with for this book, some got started through a lucky accident. Gary Hoff, an osteopathic physician in Des Moines, Iowa, regaled a reporter for a local paper who was interviewing him on some medical topic with examples of malapropisms he'd run across in his practice, such as a woman who complained of "weasels" (wheezes) in her chest or another who said she had "Cadillacs" in her eyes. The reporter shared the examples with her editor, who called Hoff and invited him to write 1,200 words on the topic, instigating a sideline business for Hoff as a medical writer for pay.

Lisa Iannucci of Wappingers Falls, New York, enjoyed a similar serendipity when she followed a tip from *Writer's Market* and began sending away for sample issues of magazines. Some-

one from *Spotlight Magazine* called her and said they didn't send out samples but asked writers to complete a paid test assignment. Would she be willing to try out with a profile of a local cardiologist? Susan Peña received her break when she wrote a letter to the editor of her newspaper in Reading, Pennsylvania, complaining about a condescending and ignorant review of a concert presented by a well-known harpist and flutist. The editor called to ask if she knew anyone who could write arts reviews. "I said, 'Well, I think I could,' and, unbelievably, he asked me to come in and meet with him to discuss it," Peña recalls. Ten years later, she's written more than a thousand reviews and freelance features for that paper, along with articles on the arts for national publications.

By definition, such opportunities fall into your lap, and it wouldn't do you or me much good to turn these stories into a get-started method. I've also run across two or three writers whose first bylines came about after inspiration seized them and they penned an entire article without the least inkling of a magazine or newspaper they might send it to. Colleen Kilcoyne spent a year and a half writing personal essays for an ongoing workshop before she felt confident enough to look around for places to send her favorite pieces. "I Killed June Cleaver," on Kilcoyne's unconventional views on mothering, appeared in her hometown paper in Massachusetts, the *Lexington Minuteman*, and was later republished in *Hysteria,* a feminist humor magazine, as well as in an anthology of parental humor, *Pandemonium.* Elise Griffith of Columbus, Ohio, took a humorous book manuscript that she hadn't been able to publish, chopped it up into short pieces and began sending them out cold to magazines.

"Was my face red when I attended a conference on magazine writing and realized what an impression I must have made on no less than three dozen editors!" says Griffith now. "I even admitted I was 'green' in the cover letter." Even so, a senior editor at *New Covenant Magazine* asked her to rewrite what she'd sent so that it was more suited to his audience. Given what she knows now about the writing business, Griffith calls that opportunity "miraculous." Instead of depending on rare strokes of luck, you should learn the more reliable route to getting your articles into print.

THE LOWDOWN ON QUERIES

You've probably already figured out what a query letter is: a proposal in letter form to an editor offering to write a specific article. Because veteran writers use queries to get assignments for articles, you put yourself in the ranks of the pros when you do likewise. More importantly, you create the opportunity for you and the editor to collaborate so that you deliver an article exactly attuned to the editor's needs. To illustrate that, here's what happened a few years back when an editor at *TWA Ambassador* received a query from me.

I wanted to write an article on cross-cultural marriages, relationships between people from different national or ethnic backgrounds. Since TWA flew a good number of international routes, I figured it would be a good topic for the airline's in-flight magazine. The editor called after receiving my query and clippings of previous work to say that she liked the topic but wanted to assign a slightly different angle. "Instead of cross-cultural marriage, I'd like you to focus on international romance," she said, pausing a moment for the distinction to sink in. "Imagine that you're writing the article for someone getting on the plane and flying off to Paris or Stockholm thinking, 'Maybe I'll meet a nice Frenchman, or a nice Swedish woman. Maybe we'll have a fling—and do these things ever work out, anyway?' " The editor also volunteered a source for my article, a colleague who only dated foreign men, she said. She told me how long the article should be—just 1,200 words, which was much shorter than I'd envisioned. Best of all, she answered a crucial question I had about the article without my having to ask. "I'll be sending you a few copies of the magazine, and pay special attention to the route map at the back that shows where TWA flies. You mentioned at the end of your letter that you're married to a man you met in China. You can include your own story in the article even though TWA doesn't fly to China so long as that's your only anecdote about a country that TWA doesn't fly to."

Consider what she'd revealed in this conversation: the exact angle she wanted, the length, one source and whether or not I should include my personal experience, along with, of course, the deadline, my fee and a few other details. This all helped me tune my efforts to her needs so well that after I passed in the

article, she immediately said "yes" to another article proposal from me.

As the document that initiates this sort of dialogue, a query letter must fulfill several purposes. It must:

1. clearly explain the topic and angle you have in mind
2. establish why the article meets the needs of the publication's target audience if that's not transparently obvious
3. demonstrate your sparkle as a writer within the letter itself
4. present your other credentials for winning the assignment

And all that in, optimally, just one page! I referred above to the "art" of writing a query letter, and it does take practice to do all of that concisely and convincingly. Although a query takes up only a page or so, you shouldn't whip it off and mail it right out. If possible, have another writer look it over to see if you've gotten your message across effectively. Or set it aside for a cold, harsh reexamination in the light of those four purposes. Since the query functions as a door-opener, you should treat each one as seriously as you would a job interview.

Having seen hundreds of query letters from writers of all degrees of experience, I've come to the conclusion that there are two main formats for this key document. The sample from my files on the following page is in the format that I use most of the time. Keep in mind when you read it that in 1992 layoffs were epidemic and unemployment was high.

I call this the indirect format for query letters, because it dispenses with the usual preliminary chitchat of business letters, and instead plunges right into the topic with an opening paragraph or two (or three, as here) that could double as the lead-in to an article. Chapter nine surveys the most popular varieties of lead paragraphs, and any of them could serve as an opener for an indirect-format query letter. I like starting off this way because it gives me a chance to strut my best stuff—anecdotes that I've already collected, arranged as effectively as they might be in the magazine. Editors like this kind of letter because, when done well, it hooks them. They want to keep on reading, and they presume that their readers would feel the same way if an article with that lead were to appear in their publication.

After the lead, the indirect format presents the focus of the

SAMPLE QUERY #1

Marcia Yudkin
P.O. Box 1310
Boston, MA 02117
(617)266-1613

June 22, 1992

Pamela Guthrie O'Brien, Editor
Ladies' Home Journal
100 Park Ave.
New York, NY 10017

Dear Ms. O'Brien:

Three years ago Maureen would come home from her job as a corporate outplacement counselor and find herself face to face with a jobless person she couldn't help: her husband. He had quit a job he didn't like and though he claimed to be looking, in her view he was making only ineffectual moves toward landing new work. As his unemployment stretched out to the one-year mark, her rage and hopelessness threatened the marriage, she says.

Barbara, a graphic artist, confessed to me that she keeps the fact that she supports her husband secret from both of their families and most of her friends. She recently took on a mortgage guaranteed by her income and would like to work out a way to have children, even if her husband's career as a consultant/entrepreneur remains bogged down.

On the other hand, Tamar made her peace with the fact that her husband, who had lost a lucrative sales job at age 45 and was very slowly building up a business, might never recover his former earning power and be able to relieve her of the job as a legal secretary which she holds to fill the gap.

What happens when a woman ends up providing more financial support for their family than her husband? What are the unique strains caused by the fact that we live in a society that still says this is not supposed to happen? I'd like to explore this issue in an article titled, "When You're Carrying the Load." I'd speak to psychologists, ministers and career counselors who witness the pain and need for strength among women whose husbands have become casualties of the recession as well as to women like Maureen, Barbara and Tamar who have stories that would be illuminating for other women.

My credentials include four nonfiction books and articles in magazines ranging from *The New York Times Magazine* and *Cosmopolitan* to *Ms.* and *New Age Journal.* My book *Smart Speaking* was excerpted in *Ladies' Home Journal* last year. Enclosed are two recent clips.

I look forward to your reply.

Sincerely,

Marcia Yudkin

proposed article and explains how you plan to handle the topic. Note that I used three techniques to describe my focus to the *Ladies' Home Journal*: I indicated the questions I'd be trying to answer, provided a title and revealed my intended sources of information for the article. By the end of this section of the query letter, your reader—the editor—should have a clear understanding of your topic, your angle on the topic and how you plan to develop the angle, whether journalistically, reflectively, confessionally, humorously or in some other fashion.

Next you summarize your credentials. If you have writing credits to list, choose the ones that put you in a favorable light for this particular proposed article. This part gives a lot of my writing students headaches. "I've never been published before, so what can I say here?" they wail. Well, don't apologize by disclosing that fact. Instead list other relevant qualifications, like your personal experience, any professional or educational background relating to your topic or even how you came to be interested in writing about it.

For instance, if you're querying for a profile of a local cartoonist, you might say, "I've been interested in cartooning since I learned in grade school that someone actually drew those funny strips I loved to read. In the last few years, I've started to collect original drawings by cartoonists." You might not view this as a credential, but it indicates to the editor a long-standing enthusiasm for the subject, which would presumably inform your reporting. If you have some writing experience but not bylines to brag about, feel free to use the kind of inflationary repackaging beloved by resume writers. A student of mine who wrote software manuals at her job stated in a query letter that her writing "mostly focused on the computer industry." (True, right?)

Close the letter by adding anything else the editor may need to know to evaluate your query. For instance, are you offering photos to accompany the piece? If so, say how many, and whether they'd be black and white or in color. Is there a time tie-in for the topic that isn't obvious? For instance, I mentioned in a query to *Ms.* magazine that the article I was proposing might fit into its annual October back-to-school issue. Do you have unusual access to your subject? If so, explain that here. Just close politely, as I did, if you have nothing else to add.

By the way, the *Ladies' Home Journal* query won me an assignment for a 1,000-word article, for which I was promptly paid. As far as I know, however, the article never appeared in print. Since I had plenty of documented successes by the time I wrote that piece, not seeing it in print wasn't a crippling blow to my pride and didn't hold up my progress as a writer, as it might have had that happened earlier in my career. I knew that it didn't mean there was anything wrong with my article, only that it had been held until an appropriate space in the magazine opened up, and then a few years later perhaps appeared out of sync with the improvement in the U.S. economy. These things happen, and you learn to take them in stride.

The query on the following page is in what I call the direct format. It fulfills the four purposes listed above while following the usual business-letter etiquette. For instance, it begins with a statement of the letter's purpose. Observe, too, how I selected items from my biographical qualifications to suit the business focus of *Inc.* Were I to re-query *Ladies' Home Journal* today, I would not use the same credentials paragraph I used for *Inc.*

I don't like my Sample #2 and wouldn't send it, though, because I feel the flat, straightforward opening handicaps my ability to dance engagingly into my topic. Objectively speaking, however, there's nothing wrong with the letter, and the direct approach may work well for publications that favor a drier, less imaginative writing style.

ALL ABOUT CLIPS

So far I haven't said anything about the "clips" I mentioned in my query letter to the *Ladies' Home Journal*. Because this represents one of the most asked-about topics at my freelancing workshops, I've been able to compile a Q&A that will probably answer every question you can think up on this issue.

Q. What's a "clip"?

A. A photocopy of one of your published articles. One or two clips accompanying a query demonstrate to an editor your writing style and ability.

Q. What do I do when a newspaper article I published is too big to photocopy?

SAMPLE QUERY #2

Marcia Yudkin
P.O. Box 1310
Boston, MA 02117
(617)266-1613

December 22, 1996

George Gendron, Editor
Inc. Magazine
38 Commercial Wharf
Boston, MA 02110

Dear Mr. Gendron:
   I'm writing to propose an essay for your first-person column on why public discussion about the apparent upcoming Social Security crisis misses the mark where entrepreneurs are concerned.
   Practically all the voices in the debate agree on the assumption that work is an unpleasant necessity that everyone wants to and deserves to quit after reaching some advanced age. This doesn't fit the experience and expectations of company founders and self-employed professionals whom I know. "The prospect of playing golf every day and ticking obscure world capitals off my life list doesn't appeal to me one bit," says Rhonda, owner of a 12-person computer consulting firm. "I get more excitement out of going on a sales call."
   The controversy also takes for granted a rigid sequence of life stages, in which we choose a career, work at it until 60, 65 or 70 and then quit active moneymaking for the rest of our lives. I'll remind *Inc.* readers that they have many more options, including taking a mid-life retirement and then starting another company, switching gears from hands-on management to an advisory role or just remaining at the helm of the firm until one's health gives out.
   I'll work into the essay my own feeling of enjoying my vocation of author and consultant too much to envision quitting, and cite people who serve as role models for me, like Herman Holtz, who remembers fighting in World War Two and yet keeps turning out business books of contemporary relevance.
   My eight published nonfiction books include *Marketing Online*, *Persuading on Paper* and *Six Steps to Free Publicity*, all from Plume/Penguin Books, and my articles have appeared in publications ranging from *The New York Times Magazine* to *Mail Order Messenger*. In addition to writing, I advise business owners on publicity and marketing.
   I look forward to your reply.

Sincerely,

Marcia Yudkin

A. A good copy shop can show you how to reduce a large-format clip to $8\frac{1}{2}'' \times 11''$ so that it's still readable. Also, feel free to paste the piece up differently than the way it actually appeared in the newspaper. The contents matter more in a clip than the layout.

Q. How many should I send with a query?

A. You can include up to three. Choose the ones that showcase your best writing of the same sort you are querying to write.

Q. Is there a way to make clips available without actually sending them with the query?

A. Yes. Instead of enclosing clips, I have often substituted this line in my query: "I'd be happy to send along clips if you would like to see them." Editors did call to request them.

Q. What if I didn't get paid for an article, or it's from a magazine no one ever heard of?

A. Any well-written article can make a good clip. Editors want to see them mainly to judge the caliber of your writing and how well your style fits theirs.

Q. My best clip has a horrible typo, or a factual mistake that the editor put in there without consulting me. What can I do?

A. Either ink in the correction onto the photocopy, or add an asterisk in the text with your correction in the margin. Any editor looking at the clip will instantly understand that the error was not yours.

Q. The editor totally rewrote my article and ruined it. Can I submit the pre-edited manuscript instead of the clip, with an explanation?

A. Not a good idea. This makes you look like an overly sensitive scrivener who routinely complains about editing rather than taking it for granted as part of this line of work. Either send the clip without an apology or send nothing.

Q. I've been a news reporter for fifteen years. Can I send those clips to magazines?

A. If they're feature stories in magazine style, yes, but hard reporting, no. The format is too different.

Q. My only publications are a letter to the editor in *The New York Times*, an academic journal article, and an article in our hospital newsletter with no byline.

A. None of these makes a usable clip. Letters to the editor don't "count" as a published article, academic papers are virtually guaranteed to elicit a "No" from a popular magazine, and the unbylined article might just as well have been written by anybody. Sorry!

ADDITIONAL TIPS FOR QUERY WRITING

Since conciseness matters greatly in magazines, there's a tremendous premium if you can fit your query comfortably onto one page. Most of the latest versions of today's software offer the capability of changing the size of the letters and the spacing between the lines. In addition, certain fonts, like Times Roman, use up less space than others. Don't justify the right-hand margin of a query letter, though, by making the right side line up evenly; usually this makes the contents more difficult to read. Dot-matrix printers never were well-liked in the publishing industry, and get an even cooler reception now that the sharp output of laser printers has become commonplace. I'm not aware of any prejudice against typewriters, however, so long as the output is crisp and neat.

Unlike manuscripts, queries should be single-spaced, and most publications expect you to enclose a self-addressed stamped envelope for the editor's reply. Over and over again at writers' conferences I've heard editors complain about distracting or self-important letterheads, so keep the heading with your name, address and phone number simple, and use white or off-white paper.

When you send a query that's clearly focused, well written, relevant and timely, it stands out without any attention-getting gimmicks. A form of effort that seemed to pay off was including just enough preliminary research to convince the editor that I already knew a ton about my topic. One or two key statistics, facts or named sources, woven skillfully into your pitch, can accomplish this. See chapter eight on research shortcuts. Make sure you proofread your letter rigorously. Even one typo, usage glitch or spelling mistake can torpedo your credibility. Several

writers I know kick themselves for having generated a new query to Magazine B on their computer without changing a reference to Magazine A deep within the letter.

Some beginning writers think they can save time by phoning queries in. At worst, you'll annoy editors by interrupting what they are doing, and at best you'll hear, "Send me a query." Similarly, some cyberconnected writers think they can sneak in through a secret express channel by hunting down an editor's unpublished e-mail address. Except when the editor works at a high-tech magazine, this tactic backfires more often than it yields a positive response. And unless your story will be unequivocally out of date tomorrow, stay away from the fax machine for queries as well. Rely on the trusty old postal service to get your letter into the editor's in-box. Once an editor knows you, the telephone, fax and e-mail become acceptable means of communication, but not before.

Multiple queries save you time and rarely land you in trouble. To avoid getting into a situation where you accept a go-ahead from a magazine paying $50 per article and get a "yes" two weeks later from another one offering $2,000 if you'd write it for them, group your queries so that you test the waters with the highest-paying prospects first, then the "B" tier and finally the cheapskates. Although I sometimes sent essentially the same query to four magazines at the same time, I never landed in a situation where two of them wanted the proposed piece. Still, I had prepared what I would say in that instance to the second interested party: "Gee, I was talking to another editor the other day who said she wanted that piece. Is there something else I could do for you?" It's bad form to try to instigate a bidding war by getting offered an assignment and telling other editors they can get the article by offering more than the first party.

WHEN THE EDITOR CALLS

Resist the temptation to yell "Whoopee!" and dance around the room when you receive a go-ahead phone call in response to your query. Have the following checklist handy so that all the essential questions about the assignment get settled and recorded in your notes.

- *The topic and angle.* Make sure you're on the same wavelength about the idea you proposed. If the editor describes your article in terms you don't recognize, now's the time to talk it through, to prevent a misunderstanding.
- *Deadline.* Four to six weeks is usual. You absolutely must meet the due date you agree to during this conversation, so think about your other commitments before you give the editor your word on the deadline. I've been given as little as ten days, and would never agree to that again. It's hard to track down sources, digest new information and create an interesting and valid framework for the article in a colossal rush.
- *Length.* How many words would the editor like? The number named here is the length you'll pass in, plus or minus ten percent. Would the editor like an accompanying sidebar? If you offered photos in your query, discuss now how many you should submit of what kind.
- *Fee.* If the editor doesn't volunteer a payment figure, ask, "For how much?" You needn't automatically accept the amount suggested by the editor. Try to provide a legitimate reason for a higher fee, as in, "I'll have to track down at least a dozen scientists to get the most current data for you. Could we make that $1,500 instead of $1,200?"
- *Pay on acceptance?* The more prestigious markets pay when your article is accepted—which may in practice translate to thirty or sixty days after the editor approves the finished piece. But that's much better than having to wait until the month of publication to get paid, known as pay on publication. Here too there's often room for negotiation. Once an editor assured me that my article was coming out in the January issue, and if he tried to put through payment on acceptance, I wouldn't get it any sooner. To protect myself from the possibility of the article getting bumped from the January issue, I asked, "Can we make it that I'll get paid on publication or in January, whichever is sooner?" He agreed.
- *Kill fee.* When you're writing on assignment, editors customarily offer a guaranteed payment in case you complete the article and it doesn't pass muster. This so-called kill fee gets stated as a percentage of the agreed-upon fee for the article. It usually ranges from one-third to one-half and up. That is, if

you'd be paid $1,000 for the article and the kill fee is 50 percent, you'll get $500 if you submit the article and they reject it for any reason. When an article is "killed," you're then free to sell it elsewhere.

• *Rights.* When you sell your work, you don't sell the actual manuscript on which you've typed or printed the article but the right to publish it under certain circumstances. The term "rights" specifies those circumstances, from among the six most common options:

1. First serial rights. Sometimes called "first North American serial rights," this means you're selling the right to publish your piece for the first time in a periodical. Once the magazine or newspaper publishes the piece, you then own all the other rights, such as the film rights, the book rights, the CD-ROM rights, etc. For many years, this has been the standard deal with the best magazines, as it's fair to both the writer and the publication.

2. Second serial rights, or reprint rights. Once you sell first serial rights and the piece is published, you can't sell first serial rights again. If someone wants to republish it, you'd be selling second serial or reprint rights, which means the right to publish something that has already appeared elsewhere. *Writer's Market* tells you which outlets buy previously published work. For some reason the counting stops at second, so that if something's been published thirteen times before, you're still selling second serial rights.

3. One-time rights. This means the publication wants to publish your piece once, without caring about being first. Often this comes up with respect to newspapers, since almost no one reads both the *Miami Herald* and the *Denver Post*. You could simultaneously sell both one-time rights and forget about worrying where the article appeared first. Newspapers may ask for "one-time rights exclusive to our circulation area," which means you couldn't sell the piece to both the *Miami Herald* and the nearby *Fort Lauderdale Sun-Sentinel*, but one of those and the *Denver Post* would still be fine.

4. All rights. A rotten deal for writers! Whenever possible, avoid selling all rights, which means first, second and two

hundredth rights, movie rights, database rights, etc., forever and ever. One student of mine sold a personal essay to a major women's magazine and got several inquiries from film producers about her story. But since she'd sold "all rights," she would never see a penny if a film were made. She also wouldn't have any input whatsoever with respect to her own story on the big screen.

5. Work for hire. This phrase derives from an exception in the copyright law intended for writing produced in the course of one's regular employment, so that the work belongs to the employer rather than the one who produced it. That's fair, I believe, but it's an entirely different kettle of soup when a corporation asks you to agree that your freelance product is "work for hire" without paying you salary, benefits or unemployment compensation afterwards. With work for hire, you hand over all rights *plus* your copyright and have no legal claim to the original content you pass in.

6. Electronic rights have become a significant battleground between writers and the media in the 1990s, with many publications trying to secure the right to post their complete contents online without paying writers extra. Once you become seriously involved in freelancing, you should join the Authors Guild, the American Society of Journalists and Authors or the National Writers Union, all of which closely monitor the latest developments regarding rights on the magazine and newspaper scene and have systems for aiding freelancers negotiating this important matter. Keep in mind that according to the U.S. Supreme Court, rights you don't specifically sign away in writing still belong to you.

• *Expenses*. Many magazines pay the long-distance telephone charges you rack up while researching an article for them, if that's agreed upon in the initial conversation. Ask. When I received my first assignment from *TWA Ambassador*, I asked if they'd cover my long-distance calls for the article. "No," came the answer, "we don't pay any expenses of any kind." I didn't say anything, and a long silence stretched on the line. That was a smart negotiation tactic on my part, since the editor broke the silence with, "Well, how about if we threw in an extra fifty

dollars to cover your phone calls?" Fine, I told her. A few magazines pay your expenses to travel to the folks you interview in person, and to take them out to lunch, but this must all be settled in advance.

• *Suggestions.* Does the editor have any advice for you about preparing the article? Here the editor may pass on useful information about the target audience or put you on alert about a few pet peeves.

• *Contract.* Inquire whether the publication will be sending you a contract. If not, prepare a letter that recounts what you agreed to in this phone conversation and end with, "If this accurately represents what we agreed to in our phone conversation of November 9, please sign one copy of this letter and keep the other copy for your files." Legally this functions exactly like some more formal document that visually resembles a contract. The contract or its substitute in letter format seals the assignment and protects both you and the place you're writing for against misunderstandings. The National Writers Union has its own standard contract for members who are freelance journalists to use in negotiating with publications. For details, use their contact information in the Resources section, p. 205.

Your conversation with the editor who calls may go off in a somewhat different direction when you hear that it's not a formal assignment and the editor would like you to write the piece on speculation. That means no kill fee, no contract and generally no expenses, but you may still have a deadline they're expecting you to meet. Try to get a sense of whether they have a general policy of having first-timers write "on spec" or if they're not sure about the topic fitting their lineup of contents. In the latter case you run a considerably higher risk when going ahead than in the former case. When you're just getting started, an invitation to write on spec might still represent cause to whoop it up—after you put down the phone—because it means someone is giving you the chance to demonstrate what you can do.

EXCEPTIONS TO THE QUERY STRATEGY

In just a few cases, it makes sense to submit a completed article rather than a query. When sending an editor a finished manu-

script, include your name, address, telephone and fax numbers, the word count, your Social Security number and rights you're offering on the manuscript. An accompanying cover letter needs only to say what it is you're enclosing and who you are.

1. *Humor. Writers' Digest* once published a successful query letter offering to write a funny article about visiting the dentist. What made that query noteworthy, though, was that its success was so rare. Usually editors stand firm on the principle that the only way to be sure an article really will produce the promised chuckles is to read the completed piece. If you've ever seen a few people crack up while the rest of the group sits stony-faced or puzzled, you know how subjective humor can be. Avoid humor that has an edge of meanness or that pokes fun at short people, foreigners, blond women or members of other groups. Otherwise, go ahead and write the whole piece and send it in.

2. *Reader's columns.* For magazine or newspaper feature columns specifically set aside for contributions from readers, it's best to write and send the article. For instance, for years *The New York Times Magazine* alternated weeks for the "Hers" and "About Men" columns—personal essays on life experiences roughly related to the writer's gender. *Newsweek's* "My Turn" column runs stories that combine a political point with heartfelt personal perspective. Many magazines, like *Smithsonian* and *Field & Stream*, place this kind of feature on the back page. Word length must be right on target for these columns; if *Writer's Market* doesn't include that information, count up the words in a sample printed column and make sure your length matches.

3. *Killed pieces.* At least twice that I can recall, I sold articles that had been killed—rejected by the publication that had assigned them—to another publication by simply sending in the completed article with a cover letter that did not reveal the previous rejection. This can work because rejections occur for many reasons that have nothing to do with the quality of your work. I confessed to the editor of *New Realities* after he accepted my 3,000-word article on intuition that I had originally written it on assignment for *Cosmopolitan.* "Well, we *were* wondering, to tell you the truth," the editor confessed back. "But we're thrilled to have it."

4. *Short pieces*. For articles of 1,000 words or less, there's so little more beyond the query that you might as well complete the article and submit it in toto. Just be careful not to submit a short piece simultaneously to two competing publications. Although they really should ask your permission before setting your submission in type and sending it off to the printer, if they've got a hole in their next issue that your article conveniently fills, editors have been known to use your piece right away and let you know about it later. I heard of one case where that blew up in the writer's face. She had submitted a piece praised by her journalism professor to two magazines for journalists. Both wanted it, and one of the editors became livid when he saw her piece among the coming attractions listed in the back pages of his competition. It cost him considerable trouble to yank her piece from his upcoming issue, and he let the writer know he blamed her for the problem 100 percent.

5. *Timely pieces*. Write the whole thing and fax it in when you have something for a newspaper that would be appropriate tomorrow but not next week. Usually this would be an op-ed piece. Don't assume because millions are taking in world or national news that thousands are writing in today with your unique perspective on events. The person in charge of the editorial pages of *The New York Times* once told a group of National Writers Union members in Boston that when the Persian Gulf War broke out, they didn't have any variety in their commentaries on the goings-on in the Mideast. When an essay from a professor in the Midwest who wasn't pleased about his son fighting in the Gulf arrived in the editorial office, the staff became ecstatic, she said. The professor's piece appeared the next day, and he received his forty-five minutes of fame, because his point of view challenged what most people were thinking and feeling that week.

When sending in a completed manuscript, don't staple it or put it in any sort of a binder. Editors prefer paper clips holding manuscripts together. You don't need a separate cover page, either. On the first page, provide your name, address, phone and fax numbers, the number of words in the manuscript, the rights you are offering and your Social Security number, to facilitate payment. On later pages, use a header consisting of your last name and the page number.

Chapter Eight

Research and Interviewing

B eginning freelancers sometimes get overwhelmed by the prospect of research. Memories of high school and college papers bring on misleading visions of dreary hours in the library and endless stacks of note cards. Interviewing people can seem just as intimidating. What if the best sources don't want to talk to you? How do you even find the people who know what you want to know in the first place?

Most freelance writing involves some sort of information gathering, and once you understand how the pros quickly locate data, you'll know how to provide editors with the kind of fact-filled, up-to-date articles that sell. It's just as easy in most cases to line up people who are happy to serve as sources for your articles and to coax the details you need from them. You need only a tiny bit of nerve and some practice to execute the proven strategies that yield relevant quotes and expert commentary for your work.

FIRST, KNOW WHAT YOU'RE LOOKING FOR

Often in the first stage of research you know so little about a subject that you can't even formulate proper questions or know where to hunt for relevant material. B.J. Roche knew when she won an assignment from *Country Journal* to write about troublesome septic systems that her first imperative was to get up to speed on leach fields, wastewater and household sludge. She began by calling the agricultural extension service at the University of Massachusetts nearby, which sent her some very helpful texts written for the layperson. They also referred her to a local soil science professor who had studied waste disposal

systems all over the world. Talking to plumbers and tracking down a book called *Country Plumbing* from a small Vermont publisher helped too. "It took a couple of weeks for me to really understand how a septic tank works," she recalls.

To avoid asking distressingly ignorant questions of experts, it may be wise to orient yourself first through a private campaign of reading. Depending on the subject, you can get a quick mental map of your topic at the library by checking encyclopedias, books, databases of recent magazine and newspaper articles, or reference works like *Who's Who*. If technicalities feel initially above your head, look for children's books or textbooks, which may explain difficult concepts simply enough for you to make your way through more advanced discussions. If you're Internet-literate you might track down a relevant Frequently Asked Questions (FAQ) file about your topic. Don't get hung up on finding quotes to use from all these written sources, however. Unlike school term papers, for magazine and newspaper articles you'll rarely cite print references. Your reading merely serves as background so that you can hunker down for the nitty-gritty research and interviewing with suitably specific questions.

You can also quickly get your bearings in new territory by finding someone knowledgeable and taking them out to lunch. Ask them about the big picture, the background and context of your topic, and for suggestions of worthwhile people to talk to. In this preliminary stage I may not take the usual kind of notes, concentrating more on gaining an understanding of important areas to probe and coming up with good questions to ask when I get to the on-the-record interviews. When I researched sensitive topics like sexual abuse and people dissatisfied with college, I didn't even bring a pen along to my preparatory interviews, and assured the friends who had agreed to brief me that whatever they told me wouldn't be cited in the article. Immediately afterwards, I made notes on the general themes that came up, some of which I would not otherwise have recognized as relevant to the topic.

During this stage, you want to be sure you master any terminology necessary to demonstrate you've done your homework. For instance, many adults recovering from childhood sexual abuse prefer to be called "survivors" rather than "victims"; ad-

vertising professionals talk about "direct-response" or "direct-mail" marketing rather than the lay person's "junk mail."

THE BASICS OF FACT-HUNTING

The most timesaving, simplifying guideline for finding facts is this: Instead of trying to track down the information on your own, ask yourself "Who would know?" Three categories of sources provide avenues for quick, reliable research: organizations of various sorts; individual experts; and the greatest detectives alive, reference librarians.

I learned the number of pairs of sunglasses sold every year in the United States after first consulting a reference work you can find in most libraries, the *Encyclopedia of Associations*, a guide to thousands of professional and trade organizations, interest groups and other national associations. Looking up "sunglasses" I found the telephone number of the Sunglass Association of America. I left a message on the Association's machine identifying myself and describing the fact I was seeking, and in no time got a call back with the answer. This technique works because one basic purpose of such organizations is to make facts available to the media. In fact, I can't think of any time I turned to the *Encyclopedia of Associations* and struck out.

Suppose you wanted to find out the most popular musical instruments among elementary-school children in your area. National organizations usually don't collect such local data, so you need to go on to the second quick-research strategy. Among the individual experts who know the answer would be: any elementary-school music teacher in the area; the owner of a local store selling and renting instruments; and the local sales representative for an instrument company supplying the schools. With this kind of example, trying to find authoritative numbers wouldn't pay off as well as accepting inexact testimony from those in the best position to know. And of course before using information provided by either an individual or a group, you want to assess whether your source might have a bias or a skewed perspective.

For instance, I wouldn't take as gospel the rate of complications after cataract surgery from an ophthalmologist. I'd want to weigh it against figures provided by a consumer health-watch organization. With the kids' musical instruments example, I'd

need to understand how kids obtained their instruments and the prevalence of private lessons in the area to evaluate which of the three sources I named above would likely have the most reliable perspective.

As for reference librarians, the third avenue of appeal, they have saved me so much time and grief I wouldn't begin to know how to thank them. At most major public libraries and many smaller ones, you can call the reference desk to ask them to look up a fact for you. If they can locate the answer in five minutes or less, they happily go to work on the question while you hold on. In that amount of time, they've supplied me with what I needed to know on queries like these:

- What's the current population of the United States?
- How many books did Anthony Trollope write?
- What's the correct spelling of "cappuccino"? (My dictionary didn't say.)
- How can I contact the Federal Trade Commission?
- What's the name of France's equivalent to the CIA?

For more complicated inquiries, they might tell you to come to the library. Head right over to their desk and they'll point you in the right direction for a search that you have to perform on your own. Don't be afraid to ask off-the-wall questions. Never once have I had a librarian look at me askance and even give the appearance of thinking, "Why on earth do you want to know that?"

Another slightly less reliable method of tracking down facts is searching CD-ROM, online, printed or microfiche indexes of newspaper and magazine articles on your subject. I consider this method a bit less reliable because it puts you in the position of possibly repeating another reporter's mistakes. As anyone who's been interviewed numerous times can tell you, errors dot published accounts the way chocolate sprinkles accent a kid's ice cream cone. So long as you confirm any facts reported by other journalists, you'll save time by consulting magazine and newspaper indexes. I go that route mainly during the orientation phase, not for serious research.

If all else fails, invoke the principle "Who might know?" and post your question in an appropriate online venue. When I

wanted to confirm the exact wording of chapter three's Flannery O'Connor quote, which had lodged in my brain from who knows where and when, the Boston Public Library whizzes said that her name didn't turn up the quote, and that it was impossible to look through the thousands of quotes on writing all lumped together. I appealed for help in the "Writers & Editors" section of CompuServe's Working from Home online forum, and within hours another writer who'd read my message had pulled a book down from his bookshelf, located the quote and typed the whole passage out for me. Unbelievable? Actually, for me answers have turned up that way more often than not.

IDENTIFYING AND FINDING SOURCES

Much of the time, filling up an article pertinently requires that you locate experts, authorities or others with quotable comments, such as people who have experienced a certain problem or situation. I know from questions at my workshops that the prospect of finding people to interview terrifies some beginners. But when you learn a few standard methods of lining up sources, it becomes as easy as putting a noun together with a verb. Try these routes:

• *Professional, trade and hobby associations.* Groups like the American Psychological Association, the National Court Reporters Association and the Balloon Federation of America, all listed in the *Encyclopedia of Associations*, which I mentioned above, will happily refer you to authorities on topics concerning psychology, court reporting and hot-air ballooning. Ask to speak to the "Media Relations" or "Public Affairs" department of the organization, then identify yourself as a freelancer working on a story about X and looking for experts qualified and willing to discuss Y. Most larger groups maintain a database of members who have specifically volunteered to speak with the media; at smaller organizations the director or receptionist simply searches their personal memory and Rolodex file for someone appropriate.

• *College and adult education catalogs.* With any topic that might be taught, track down a teacher of it and you'll have an expert. For an article in *New Woman* on nonverbal

communication, I found communication consultant Laurie Schloff among the course listings of the Boston Center for Adult Education. For my *TWA Ambassador* article on cross-cultural relationships, I had heard that Lesley College in Cambridge had a program on the topic and called to ask who taught the relevant course. The public relations department of a university or school will refer you to the appropriate person if you don't have a name from a catalog. On a bigger scale, an organization called ProfNet (see Resources, p. 203) e-mails your inquiry to a national network of college public relations personnel.

• *Public relations departments of corporations.* If you're seeking someone to make predictions about future photographic technology, a call to PR people at Kodak or Polaroid should set you up with well-informed (though possibly biased toward their own company) high-tech pundits. Call Hasbro or Milton Bradley if you need comments on the age-appropriateness of children's toys.

• *Published books and articles.* I located another expert on cross-cultural relationships by pulling a book off my shelf, looking first at the biographical information and then at the author's preface to learn where the author lived. The former didn't provide telltale clues, but the latter ended with "Dugan Romano, Washington, DC." The District of Columbia directory information gave me her phone number. Next I would have tried calling the publisher. Many large publishers protect their authors with roundabout contact procedures, but smaller publishers usually give out phone numbers to reporters who call asking for an interview. I've also lined up folks to consult by reading published articles that quoted experts and stated where they lived. The more recent the book or articles, of course, the greater the odds for hints that help you sniff your way along.

• *Your grapevine.* Aside from professionals with credentials, you often have to turn up "civilians"—non-famous people who, say, have had an employee steal from them, have a stepchild older than themselves or are former cult members now living normal lives. Telling everyone you encounter about your search often bears fruit, as does asking everyone you know if they know anyone who might know a _____. I've even gotten results

by standing up at a relevant meeting, describing the kind of person I'm looking for and asking for leads.

• *Yellow Pages and other ads.* Seeking interior decorators outside of your area for a national article on decorating pitfalls? Head to a public library that carries telephone directories from all over the country and let your fingers walk through them. For my book *Six Steps to Free Publicity* I found several people to interview by browsing through listings in the National Speakers Association member directory, which I obtained free by calling the organization and identifying myself as someone wishing to interview members. A book called *Yearbook of Experts, Authorities and Spokespersons*, consisting of listings paid for by specialists who hope to be interviewed, is similarly free to working journalists (see Resources, p. 203).

• *Other interviewees.* At the end of every interview, ask if your source knows someone else who fits such-and-such a description. Some of your best leads will come about in this way.

• *Your mail and your files.* If you specialize in a topic area, pass your name around to companies and organizations that want to publicize related new developments. At no charge they'll add you to their distribution list for press releases, catalogs and other newsworthy announcements. Saving and filing such mail in case you need it could pay off.

• *Cyberspace.* Working on an assignment for *American Medical News* on part-time doctors who also pursue another career, Shirley Moskow had a devil of a time unearthing examples far from her home base in Lexington, Massachusetts. But when her son put up a notice for her on the Internet, within hours she had enough leads to complete her article.

Similarly, Jayne Hitchcock, a contributing writer for *Biblio* magazine, appealed to an Internet newsgroup—a special-interest electronic bulletin board—for sources on manga, Japanese comic books translated into English. Someone posted a note saying that *Hawaii* author James Michener was a manga enthusiast. How to find Michener? she asked back. He's associated with the University of Texas at Austin, the answer came. Hitchcock cruised online to the home page for the university, but didn't find Michener listed. She sent an e-mail to someone who looked to be an important person at the school's library

and bingo! That person's office was right across the hall from James Michener's assistant. Hitchcock soon arranged her interview with the distinguished author.

PREPARING FOR AN INTERVIEW

Once you've gathered names of people you'd like to speak with for an article, you confront two important decisions. The first is: Do you need to do the interview in person? You must if you're writing a profile or any other kind of article that requires you to watch, observe and describe the person whose words you're quoting. But for informational articles, where you focus on facts, opinions and perspectives, meeting your source in person is optional. The great majority of the more than six hundred people I would estimate I've interviewed, I met only over the telephone. But I do interviews in person when I'm fishing for an angle or researching a sensitive subject, such as childhood sexual abuse, which I once wrote on for *Cosmopolitan* magazine.

The second decision prompts some disagreement among professionals: Should you tape record interviews or just take notes? I once heard Nanci Donellan, ESPN's "Fabulous Sports Babe," admonish a hall full of newspaper reporters that without using a tape recorder, they couldn't possibly expect to get their source's words right. She based this view on countless instances where what she told a journalist had been distorted, sometimes beyond recognition. But the room erupted in violent disagreement. Reporter after reporter stood up to explain that their deadlines don't allow the extra time necessary for listening to a tape again, and that their long practice taking notes enables them to get it right on their notepads and in the copy they file. Yet, many magazine writers with longer deadlines would never dream of showing up at a subject's home or office without their little sound-capturing machine to set out on the desk. Otherwise they're too busy taking notes to listen carefully and ask questions, and a tape recorder distracts their source less than continual scribbling, they say.

The correct answer to this controversy, I believe, involves determining the method that enables you, with your idiosyncratic abilities and constraints, to get the story accurately, unobtrusively and without wasting too much time and energy. From all

too many years in school, I happen to be good at taking notes, and I distrust machines that can fail to work, so I never use a tape recorder for in-person interviews. I have a button on my answering machine that I can press to record while I'm speaking to a source, and I often turn it on as a backup during phone interviews, in case I find myself with someone who talks a mile a minute. Most of the time I record over the tape during my next interview, knowing that I have what I need in my notes. Try different options, although I have to warn that relying completely on the tape recorder is dangerous, as journalists who've found themselves with blank tapes after a fantastic session will attest. Also, rarely would you want to tape your interview, type the whole thing out at home and then use the transcript as a reference while writing up the article. This procedure simply takes too much time. If you do use a tape recorder over the phone, ask the other party's permission, since not doing so counts as "illegal wiretapping," a felony in many jurisdictions.

After making these two crucial decisions, contact your source to set up a time to meet or talk. Don't call or, even worse, show up without an appointment and expect to do the interview on the spot. Usually I call and introduce myself like this: "My name is Marcia Yudkin, and I'm a freelance writer working on an article for _____ magazine on _____, and I'd like to get your thoughts on _____ for the article. It shouldn't take more than twenty or twenty-five minutes. Can you tell me when would be a good time for us to talk?" Giving a time indicator reassures subjects that you're not demanding too much of them, and asking when the interview would be convenient for them encourages them to pull out their date book and find a time to fit you in. Occasionally someone says, "How about right now?" and once in a while someone who understands the writing business inquires whether you're on assignment, what your angle is and how quickly your deadline is coming up.

Beginning freelancers often express doubt about people's willingness to be interviewed and trepidation about asking for this favor. In my experience, unless you do confrontational journalism or tackle especially controversial issues, ordinary folks and experts alike enjoy being consulted. Someone who hasn't received media coverage usually feels flattered and excited about

the prospect of being interviewed, while a typical authority or business owner understands that his or her reputation and livelihood can grow with your publicity. Even as she was complaining about sloppy journalism, for example, Nanci Donellan made it clear that, as a prominent entertainment figure, she knows that part of her role involves cooperating with interview requests week in and week out. Over the course of sixteen years, I can recall fewer than five people who refused my request to interview them. Make sure that your words and tone of voice reflect confidence, because if you phrase your request like, "Um, I was wondering, well, I know you must be terribly busy, and I'm not Barbara Walters or Bob Woodward or anything like that . . .," you will encounter turndowns.

Just before a prearranged interview, I prepare a list of questions for the person I'm going to be speaking with. I never run through them all in order, but this exercise helps me focus on what I need to or would like to learn from that encounter. I'll keep the list available during the interview to glance at, and sometimes tell the source when I'm just about finished that I'd like to look back through my list of questions to see if there's anything I forgot to ask. Early on the first two questions on the list were always, "How do you spell your name?" and "How would you like to be identified?" By now I can remember always to ask those questions without a reminder, so although they don't show up on my lists, they do still always get asked.

THE INTERVIEW ITSELF

Think of an interview as a one-sided, focused conversation: conversation because of the semi-spontaneous flow you want to promote, focused because your aim is information that will make your article sparkle and one-sided because you should do less than 25 percent of the talking. Conversation flows when you allow answers from your interviewee to suggest your next question, rather than firing a preset series of interrogatories at a victim. You can't proceed totally spontaneously, though, because you don't want to veer off into a fascinating discussion of, say, street crime when the topic of your assignment is Boston's fashion designers. Once you toss the conversational ball into the air, most of your volleys will take the form of requests like "What

do you mean by _____?" "Can you give me an example?" "Why do you say that?" "When was that?" or "How many were there?" Remember that above all you'll need details such as specific names, dates, places, incidents, quirky metaphors and sensory descriptions to breathe vividness and life into your article.

Notice the difference between ineffective, choppy Interview A and the better flowing and more useful Interview B, because of poor listening in the former and thorough follow-up questions in the latter.

Interview A:

Q. Why do you think Boston's fashion industry has seen a revival in the last decade?

A. It has to do with the increased European presence in the city.

Q. Are the designers native Bostonians or transplants?

A. Mostly transplants.

Q. Where should people go to see what Boston designers are up to?

A. Shops on Newbury St.

Interview B:

Q. Why do you think Boston's fashion industry has seen a revival in the last decade?

A. It has to do with the increased European presence in the city.

Q. What brought that about?

A. Actually, a lot of factors—monetary exchange rates, the fact that Boston feels more European than other American cities, the increased percentage of foreign students at universities in the area and popular events like the Boston Marathon, which brings people in from all over the world.

Q. But Boston doesn't have a first-rate fashion design school.

A. Oh, right. It's not that design students are settling here after school so much as that the business, art, scientific and other students from Europe create a market for European styling.

Q. So are the new designers here American or European?

A. They're American, European and from Japan and Hong Kong, but Europe is the reference point.

Q. European—which countries are we talking about specifically?

A. Italy, France and, of all places, Sweden, not normally known as a hotbed of fashion.

Q. Who's from Sweden?

A. Sven Grundig and Alstrom Kroner. They're next door to each other on Newbury St.

Q. And how did each of them happen to come here?

And so on. If you can remember nothing else during your interviews than your responsibility to ask for more specifics, you'll find yourself gathering the kind of information that fascinates readers and gratifies your sources.

I'll never forget interviewing someone I knew slightly for an article *TWA Ambassador* had assigned on getting married abroad. Before we spoke, I knew only that she had had a marriage ceremony on a yacht in Monte Carlo. I was thinking that a description of the event might make a good lead for the piece, so I began by asking Jackie what her wedding was like. She offered a few helpful details, and by grabbing on to what she said and digging deeper and deeper, I gradually learned the rough weather conditions that week, how the harbor of Monte Carlo was shaped, the fact that the yacht, which I'd wrongly imagined as an especially nice two-bedroom boat, contained a heliport and that her guests had included former Beatle Ringo Starr and several counts and countesses. When I read my opening paragraph back to her over the telephone, she exclaimed, "Wow! It sounds like you were there." The authenticity derived as much from the way I'd questioned her as from my writing skill.

As for your 25-percent-or-less speaking role in this conversation, you have to remember that your own opinions and experiences deflect the focus of the interview, and make it less likely that you'll end up with usable material. Some interviewers write repeatedly in their notes, reminding themselves, "Shut up shut up shut up." Turn off any intense desire you have for your interviewee to like or even respect you. You need minimal rapport

with the person you're talking with, but beyond that your loyalty lies with your ultimate readers. You especially need to be willing to appear stupid by asking dumb questions like "How do you spell 'Smith'?" and "I'm sorry, but what's a 'gunwale'?" When I interviewed gardening writer Barbara Pleasant for this book, she used a phrase like "squash vine bores," and I had to ask her to repeat it three times because I couldn't settle the unfamiliar sounds in "vine bores" into words. I wrote it down, then later e-mailed to check the spelling, and learned that it should have been "vine borers." She was happy to help me get it right, but some people in her position might have found my persistence on the point annoying.

At a televised news conference, a spokesperson for the National Transportation Safety Board got a laugh from the room when he good-humoredly responded to a reporter, "I said one last question—that was three!" Avoid two- or three-part questions; they're confusing. Your source will usually respond to the last part and have forgotten the first part or two. Minimize yes-or-no questions too in favor of open-ended questions, which encourage fuller explanations. For example, instead of "Do you have any famous clients?" ask "Who are some of your clients that people might have heard of?" Even though you can always ask for amplification of a "yes" or "no," a monosyllabic answer tends to freeze the flow you're aiming for.

In contrast, open-ended questions can draw out things you would never dream of asking about. When B.J. Roche interviewed criminologist Richard Moran, she asked him what it was like growing up in his neighborhood and learned that he grew up down the street from the Boston Strangler! And don't shy away from silence. Waiting a few extra beats after an interesting answer can provoke rumination out loud on the part of your interviewee. Similarly, I've noticed that the questions that send someone into a cloud of thought often indicate that the person doesn't have an automatic response. Wait the silence out, and you'll get fresh reflections.

If a source asks to approve your article before it's published, offer to check the accuracy of your quotes and other information, but don't agree to show him the full article. The latter can raise a hornet's nest of dangers, such as your interviewee

nitpicking at irrelevant parts of your article or demanding that you remove quotes he really did say. I've found that reading back a source's quotes saves me from having misinterpreted what I heard, and sometimes elicits additional details that improve the article. When they hear a quote, rather than see it written out and surrounded by other people's thoughts, they're less likely to find fault with you and kick up trouble.

PROBLEM INTERVIEWS

Nerves can get the better of you when you find yourself conversing with someone famous. While working on an article on llamas, Jayne Hitchcock managed all the hurdles necessary to arrange an interview with actor Dennis Weaver, who co-owned a llama farm in Colorado. She contacted the Screen Actors Guild, then Weaver's agent, then his manager and finally learned that Weaver would call her to do the interview. "I was so excited!" she recalls. "When he called, I tried to 'kiss up' to him but named the wrong TV show he was famous for—I called it *Big Valley* when it was *Gunsmoke*. It was downhill from there. No matter what I asked, he answered in two or three syllables. Period. I finally got a little out of him, enough to include him in my article, but he had no sense of humor. I felt like I blew it having blurted out the wrong title at the beginning, even though I knew the correct one."

Shauna Roberts, a medical writer based in New Orleans, faced the problem of an uncooperative central source who almost sabotaged an assignment. For an article on the ethics of fetal tissue transplantation for *Diabetes Forecast*, she turned up only a few American researchers working in this controversial field. One not only refused to answer any questions but launched into a diatribe about why it was ethically wrong for Roberts to write the article. He claimed that reporting fetal tissue research, thought to be promising for people with diabetes, would inflame antiabortionists to picket his clinic. He also called the associate editor of *Diabetes Forecast* and tongue-lashed her on why they shouldn't publish the article. "Luckily, one of this man's colleagues spoke with me, so that I was able to complete the article. When the article ran, there were no bomb threats, no pickets, no subscription cancellations, just letters, both pro and con."

Roberts reflects that although you probably can't prevent this kind of obstacle, you can take steps to lessen its effect on your psyche and your article: Collect more interviewee names so that if some refuse to talk, you can still finish the article; be confident about your objectivity so that someone like that scientist won't throw you; and remind yourself that being a brilliant scientist doesn't mean that person has a grasp of the big picture.

Santa Monica, California, freelancer Kit Snedaker recalls having to redirect a few interviews that jumped the tracks. Once an interviewee got stuck on the topic of his sex life at the age of seven. Another time a famous actor became inquisitive about what kind of underwear she wore. "That problem I solved by answering 'the usual cotton things' and moving right on to another question," Snedaker says. "I've come to think of interviews, particularly with celebrities, as slightly dangerous. Here's the reporter smiling, being warm and friendly, and it's easy to mistake that for an overture. You have to be prepared to draw the line, for example by saying, 'I appreciate your interest, but I have a job to do right now.' To giggle or blush or act resentful sends a signal you don't want to send at that moment."

ELECTRONIC-AGE ALTERNATIVES

Some people whose experiences you are reading about in this book I never spoke with, either in person or by phone. Instead I elicited anecdotes by posting notes on the Internet or an online service describing what I was looking for, then requesting clarifications or additional details by e-mail from those who'd volunteered good stories. This technique shrinks your telephone expenses for interviewing and makes accessible for your articles people living on another coast or another continent. It's more suitable for quick illustrations when you already have a good grasp of the terrain than for exploratory or in-depth interviewing, since the back-and-forth proceeds slowly.

I experienced another technique that made a virtue out of the drawn-out pace of e-mail when Debbie Ridpath Ohi asked to interview me for her electronic newsletter for writers, *Inklings*. She proceeded by e-mailing me one question at a time, then at the end collecting her questions and my answers in a Q&A format. Answering one question at a time felt easy, whereas being faced

with a list of seven at once might have felt burdensome. If I hadn't given her succinct, articulate answers or hadn't checked my e-mail regularly, though, this procedure would not have worked.

A competing method of interviewing in cyberspace that I'd tried and then discarded is arranging a time to meet someone on CompuServe or America OnLine in a specific "conference room" where we can exchange questions and answers live by taking turns typing out questions and answers that both of us can see on our computer screens. The record of such a session might not look all that different from a transcript of a telephone interview, but the typing speed of the two parties constrains the rate at which this kind of electronic interviewing can take place. Compare 40 words per minute via typing with 180 words or more per minute in conversation, and you'll understand why I finished this online session with exhausted hands and a lot of frustration. For me, voice-to-voice interviewing still represents the standard to beat.

Chapter Nine

Structuring Your Article

O nce you've collected plenty of quotes, facts and examples, you face the challenge of disciplining that
scattered, disorderly mess into a shipshape article.
To do that quickly and skillfully, you need two sets
of tools: an understanding of the proper structure for articles
and techniques for organizing material.

ARTICLE STRUCTURE

Although most freelance work does not involve reporting news,
you should know how news articles get structured, so that you
don't become confused. News gets written up in a traditional
structure called the "inverted pyramid." In the first paragraph of
a news article, you present the "Five W's"—Who, What, When,
Where and Why (or how). The remainder of the news piece
elaborates on the Five W's in order of decreasing importance.
The news piece has no formal conclusion. Rather, the article can
be clipped off anywhere, even after the opening paragraph, to
fit available space in the newspaper. Also, paragraphs for news
articles might consist of only one sentence, in keeping with the
narrow columns of a newspaper. For example, here's how a news
article about a lighthouse might begin:

> *SEASIDE—For the fourth straight summer, on Monday
> environmental activists and preservationists in Seaside
> Harbor presented the state legislature with a petition
> designed to save the village's historic lighthouse from
> destruction.*

Subsequent paragraphs would probably discuss the fate

threatening the lighthouse, who the activists and preservationists were, what happened in the three previous summers, the response of legislative leaders, and so on. But the kernel of the story sits right up front in that opening paragraph.

News articles comprise the bailiwick of daily journalism, and if you work as a stringer (see chapter six) for a newspaper or a trade magazine, you might be called upon to write some. But otherwise, the freelance work you submit to newspapers and magazines takes the more graceful beginning/middle/end form of a *feature* article. Instead of starting off with the Five Ws, then trailing off to wherever the editor cuts your piece, the typical magazine article or feature article for a newspaper consists of four parts:

1. Lead
2. "Nut Graph"
3. Body
4. Conclusion

Without an attention-getting lead, no one reads your article. A good lead grabs the reader's attention and funnels it into the rest of the article. I'll spend the most time in this chapter discussing leads because where salability is concerned, they matter more than all the other parts of your article combined. Fortunately, they're also fun to write—unless you're under pressure to produce a blazingly original one in five minutes. I often arrive at the stage of writing an article knowing roughly what the lead will be. Once in a while it made its first appearance in my query letter; more often during the process of researching and interviewing I'll run across something and know "There's the lead!" Other times while rereading my notes a quote, an incident or a description waves a flag at me as an excellent way to start off. To help you out when you're stuck on a beginning, I've included below a typology of leads to prompt your rumination. Except for a very long article, which can support a proportionately longer opener, your lead usually takes up just one paragraph, sometimes two.

Whereas many attention-getting article openings could lead into more than one topic or focus, the next section of the article's structure makes it crystal clear exactly what this piece will and

will not concentrate on. Editors call the paragraph following the lead the "nut graph" because it concisely sets forth (as if in a nutshell) what the article is about, along with any background or context necessary for appreciating the rest of the piece. As we'll see, the challenge there is to communicate, without being crass or obvious, "This is an article about _____ and it matters because _____." If the lead functions as a wide funnel attracting reader interest, the nut graph serves as the constricted neck of the funnel, conducting that interest into the more spacious container of the article body. Ordinary readers don't admire skillful nut graphs, but editors do.

Next comes the longest section of your article, the body. Here you develop at length the issues you announced in the nut graph, weaving them together in a coherent, flowing fashion. The main challenge of this section is keeping the prose moving without allowing the reader to become bored or get lost.

Even good things come to an end, and articles usually end with a flourish—a final section that seals the whole package and creates a deliberate last impression. The conclusion represents your opportunity to reinforce your twist on the topic, both in terms of the content you place there and the verbal gesture you make as you close. No one reaches the end of an article that has a lousy lead, but when people finish reading, a strong ending tends to make the entire story linger in their mind, which rarely results from a great lead. Although typical magazine articles consist of all four sections, some articles lack conclusions. In special circumstances, described below, a piece just ends.

Let's go back through the four vital article elements now.

INVITING LEADS

Since a dull lead dooms your article, you must develop the skill of grabbing a reader's attention concisely, colorfully and relevantly at the outset. Professional writers sometimes brainstorm a handful of leads of different types before choosing the optimal one, so don't feel shy about using the upcoming list of lead types as a checklist when it's time for you to craft a lead. Generally the opener goes on no longer than one paragraph. Slim yours down if it bulges much bigger than that. Sometimes you'll find that a too-long lead actually consists of two leads one after

another—a phenomenon that writing teachers call "throat-clearing," in an analogy to warming up for speaking out loud. In that case, select the stronger one and delete the other. Probably several dozen valid ways to start articles exist, each with advantages and disadvantages. But after analyzing hundreds of articles in several different types of magazines, I've narrowed down the most prevalent types to the following twenty:

1. Anecdote. Storytelling has earned the attention of people since they crouched around a fire in prehistoric times. The human-interest factor involved and the compelling curiosity about "What happened next?" equally work magic on today's busy readers. In just one paragraph, a good anecdote contains a central character or two, conflict and at least some momentary suspense. Either the mini-story wraps up with a resolution right in the lead or does so later in the article. For instance, I led off my first article for *TWA Ambassador* like this:

> *Five years ago in Beijing, China, I caught the fever of love. In veiled letters to distant friends, I described the sudden sweetening of a harsh year, the thrilling dangers of clandestine meetings. My friends thought our adventure unbelievably romantic. But when my sister visited and met the tall, handsome Chinese man I was skulking about with, she sat me down for a stern warning. "You've lost touch with reality," she said. "You're living in a dream world." She thought she saw a fantasy relationship that could have no relationship with my life back home.*

I haven't seen many lousy anecdotal leads. Choose a dramatic tale, sprinkle in enough details to make it vivid, and almost any article gets off to a powerful start. My only cautions here are to make sure an anecdote doesn't take up too much space in a very short article, and that it remains in tune with the tone of the rest of the writing. A vivid story like mine wouldn't work attached to a dry survey of United States-China political vicissitudes in the 1990s.

2. Scene. Where an anecdote compresses a story line comprising several different moments, a scene vividly shows the reader

what occurred at just one time and place. A portrait of a fairly new business might start off with a scene like this:

Burnsides' debut winetasting went off brilliantly last May. Denver's best and brightest raised antique crystal goblets to one another as the scents of chardonnay and muscatel wafted amongst refined conversation. Even the sun cooperated, with a spectacular setting that drew exclamations from the men and women watching from the showroom's extravagantly sized, painstakingly polished picture windows.

Here the scene's theme of brilliance would aptly introduce a portrait of Burnsides as splendidly successful from the beginning or, perhaps, as financially shaky beneath a classy veneer. It could also segue into an article about openings as a marketing technique. Optimally the scene you portray in a lead reveals something important about your topic and doesn't function merely as window dressing.

3. Surprising fact. Here, without any "Did you know . . . ?" preamble, you smack the reader right between the eyes with an astonishing truth.

Distance runners in the Sri Chinmoy Marathon Team use yogic techniques to get through races of up to 1,300 miles.

—*Yoga Journal,* March/April 1995

What can you do for $5? Buy a sandwich for lunch. Get a paperback. Rent two videos. Or register your corporate jet with the feds.

—*Common Cause Magazine,* Spring 1994

These facts sure snapped me to attention. In both cases the writers tossed out their information in one quick burst and then drew back and waited for the inevitable "Wow" from the reader. If you can find tidbits this surprising, feature them right up front in your lead.

4. Huh? See if these two one-sentence leads provoke the "Huh?" for you that they did for me:

James Bond would probably be happy working at home today.
                    —*Working Woman*, September 1990

Wig shops are the kiss of death.
—Joel Garreau, *Inc. Magazine's The State of Small Business 1995*

Begin with a zinger that requires some explanation and you've got the reader's attention, at least until you resolve the perplexity. The remark about James Bond leads into a short item about neat gadgets available to work-at-homers, while the comment about wig shops steers the reader into a host of generalizations about the kinds of geographical settings most alive for business. These are the kind of leads that come to you in the shower or while driving, and if the Muse blesses you with one, try it out. If you can make the transition to your main points work, run with it.

5. Alert. I have just one of these in the collection of leads I've put together over the years, but I rather like it:

If you think OSHA is a small town in Wisconsin, you could be in trouble!
—Sharon Lynn Campbell, *Entrepreneurial Woman*, January/
February 1991

This resembles a "Huh?" lead, except that it makes a more direct connection with readers, motivating them to find out what trouble they might land in and how to avert it. With a dab of humor, an alert lead also lets the reader know this article won't go down like a grim lecture. Consider using this technique when you're writing to warn about a danger people don't ordinarily think about.

6. Accepted fact. Say something that people have already heard, and believe, and they'll wonder what you're getting at, since they're reading this not-new observation in a current magazine or newspaper. You've then slyly set readers up to learn from you that this is actually not the case. They'll be yours as you go on to reveal the real scoop.

As we all know, adventure sports like mountaineering and skydiving present the biggest perils of injury and death.

Stay at sea level, in contact with the earth, and fun will likely remain fun, without significant dangers.

Hardly anyone could read this without expecting you next to slip them the news that ordinary sports like hockey or marathon running actually place you in more jeopardy. The pace and timing for this lead require some skill to pull off, but it can't help but involve the reader—your primary goal in opening an article.

7. Juxtaposition. By placing two conflicting facts or two contrary descriptions side by side, you create a tension for readers that impels them to find out more.

From her author photo, Raquela Katz sends a simple, sweet smile at the reader. Her jet-black pompadour bun and high-necked white blouse add to the aura of a Victorian matron. Her prose would qualify for Shock of the Year awards, however, with its raw descriptions of gruesome knifings, brutal beatings and ferocious cruelty. Good does not triumph over evil in her books, either. In Rue Lapin, her latest, the pilot-villain escapes justice at the end of the book, free to wreak his twisted vengeance against innocent travelers once again.

Is Katz's benign appearance a marketing ploy? Will the article writer explain how such unmatronly visions live within such a nice-looking woman? Produce a strong contradiction for readers, and you've hooked them. As with all the other leads, of course, the remainder of the article must live up to such a powerful opener.

8. Then and now. As in a juxtaposition lead, you can create suspense for the reader by describing contrasting situations, first a long time ago, and then now.

In the 1970s Passaquiddock was a sleepy crossroads, with one convenience store, one gas pump, one part-time police officer and one elementary school. Past nine o'clock in the evening, the frogs and crickets dominated the soundscape. Since 1991, idling engines, horns and shouts clog the night, as traffic cops attempt to direct thousands of gamblers in and out of nine new parking lots. The casino has brought jobs, controversy and crowding to this corner

*of New England, where residents keep rubbing their eyes
and ears. "Is this what we really wanted?" asks the town's
weary school commissioner, Reggie Van Neele.*

For any kind of dramatic change, this sort of lead is a natural.

9. Fantasy. Paint a word picture that the reader knows
couldn't be true, and you may have created momentum for depicting the reality.

*In my next life, I'll have a clean desk. Before leaving the
office every day, I'll file away all my pending materials,
label all the stray diskettes, reshelve the books and place all
the pens, staplers and calculators in their ever-so-functional
holders. I'll prepare one sheet of paper for the following
morning—my goals for that day, that month, that year,
which I always fulfill. Never does a phone call go unre-
turned, an opportunity unpursued.*

The entertainment value of this lead can help to spice up what
might otherwise be a bland topic.

10. Generalization. You can begin with a sweeping statement
that few would disagree with. These three snippets illustrate the
approach:

It's tough to find loyal employees these days.
*Runners don't need bats, pools, goalposts, helmets or
teammates. But shoes—without well-designed, good-
fitting specialty shoes, serious runners don't last long.*
*Holy to three of the world's great religions, Jerusalem
holds unique treasures for mystics and history buffs.*

You'd better immediately get more specific, though, because
such broad observations quickly become boring. You want readers to be nodding "Yes, that's right" as you get to the more
interesting stuff, not protesting, "Geez, I already know that."

11. Quotation. Some friend probably shared this secret with
you during high school: Whenever you don't know how to start
an essay, just look the topic up in a quotation guide and lead
off with what Abraham Lincoln, or Croesus, or Beulah
Hinchcliff said. This might have taken you off the hook with
your English teacher, but it won't win you many friends among

today's editors. True, I inflicted one of these on you in chapter three, but I had already earned some good will, I presume, in chapters one and two. The risk that a quotation gets your article off to a weak beginning is high. Stay away from this one.

12. Quote. In contrast to the preserved, and usually over-pickled, phrases of a quotation, a quote uses the fresh words of someone you actually interviewed to engage the interest of the reader.

> *"My 1927 farmhouse functions fine. My 1978 Toyota Corolla still has several years of life in it yet. My 1989 home computer is just about obsolete, though," says Harry Winstead, the 34-year-old mayor of Newport, Iowa. "And that makes me mad."*

Like an anecdote, a well-chosen quote from someone named and described produces the effect of real life captured on the printed page. If you've done your interviewing well, you may have more than one great quote lurking within your notes.

13. Question. Tricky, these.

> *Did you ever wonder why the word "umpire" begins with a linguistic hiccup?*
> *Would you like to learn how to calm a nervous stomach?*
> *Do you buy a new computer every three years?*
> *Who is Teresa Nuncomb and why is her picture hanging in every room of the new Lights Out Inn on Cadwaller Boulevard?*

As an editor, I'd reject every one of these four lame excuses for leads. The last thing an article should do is turn away readers who might otherwise enjoy or profit from an article, and in allowing a "no" answer, the first three questions do exactly that. In addition, the first question, like almost every "Did you ever wonder?" attempt I've seen, comes off as incredibly weird. Instead of assuming your readers have had an unlikely thought, give them something to wonder about. The second topic would have a better chance after a lively description gets readers to recall the nervous-stomach sensations they have undoubtedly experienced from time to time. In the third situation, you'd include more readers by starting off more along the lines of "If you buy a new computer

every three years, you're right on schedule as far as the computer industry is concerned. If you don't, you may soon discover that. . . ." The fourth question doesn't prompt a "no" so much as "Umm, who cares?" You could provoke readers to care, though, by taking them around the new inn and revealing that one woman's photograph, which you describe, hangs in all the rooms. The question of who she is and what her connection with the inn might be then naturally arises along with momentum for this curiosity to become satisfied.

Avoid question leads unless you have reason to believe that every member of your target audience will answer in the way that keeps them reading on.

14. Hypothesis. Here you invite the reader to suppose something, or pose a "What if" scenario, as in these two examples.

> *One morning you look up from your newspaper and see that your two-year-old son, strapped into his high seat, isn't breathing. Do you know what to do first?*

> *It starts with personal letters arriving bearing an unfamiliar postmark. Then your spouse takes many more trips out of town than usual. Lovemaking cools—"too busy, too tired," run the excuses. The car-phone bills get rerouted to your spouse's office. Could anything else be happening besides an affair?*

So long as readers identify with your supposition, you've gotten the article off to good start.

15. "You." The second hypothesis lead above, about the possible affair, also qualifies as a "you" lead, which wriggles into the good will of readers by posing a situation they can identify with. It functions almost like an anecdote except that it doesn't concern a real incident.

16. "We." This one presents a general statement using "we" instead of third-person phraseology.

> *We either idolize or demonize our parents. In the former case, we see them as larger than life—even when we become taller, smarter or more successful. In the latter case, we view them as unredeemably evil, even when their worst offense was denying us that new red tricycle, breaking our heart.*

Like the "you" lead, this can establish common ground with your reader. Although neither the "we" nor the "you" lead will ever put you in the running for a Pulitzer, they do belong in your repertoire.

17. Description. I don't want to overlook the lure of a well-crafted verbal sketch of the sensory appearance of a person, place or thing. Had I continued in the following way, the Katz juxtaposition lead we pondered earlier would become a more straightforward but still effective description.

> *From her author photo, Raquela Katz sends a simple, sweet smile at the reader. Her jet-black pompadour bun and high-necked white blouse add to the aura of a Victorian matron. Somehow she finds the energy to run a household of seven in addition to penning two best-selling romance novels a year. She doesn't allow media people into her home, but while taking tea with a reporter in a hotel suite, she gives the impression of being the kind of hostess who knows exactly the proper angle at which to crook her little finger while lifting her cup.*

Conflict or contrast isn't necessary for an animated description lead.

18. Reminiscence. Pensively recounting something that happened to you in the past can jump-start your article, even if the piece concerns something very contemporary, like this one on Internet cafes:

> *When I was a kid, the cars changed every fall, but the restaurants were on a longer cycle. Lately, it's the other way around. All the Szechuan restaurants turned into Thai restaurants, and then all the French restaurants went Italian. Now every Tom, Dick and Giuseppe is switching to the espresso-bar format.*
> —Robert Nadeau, *Inc. Technology,* Summer 1995

Yes, this lead does have a nice transition to its non-nostalgic topic. Stay tuned!

19. Take-off on a current saying. If you like puns, you may enjoy scouring your memory bank for a jingle, slogan or common phrase that you can tinker with. For instance:

> *Uncle Sam wants you . . . to get involved in government procurement.*
> —Cynthia E. Griffin, *Entrepreneur*, August 1995

Beware, though: While some readers and editors like this sort of thing as much as you do, others find word play corny and tiresome.

20. Definition. The very weakest lead of all, this deserves total shunning from your repertoire.

> *Webster's defines "decorate" as "to furnish or adorn with something becoming or ornamental. . . ."*

Aren't you already on your way to Sleepyland?

THE "NUT GRAPH"

Your lead does not have to point unequivocally toward the focus of your article. The lead might appear to be headed in one direction and then settle legitimately on a less obvious course. For instance, the article with the hypothesis lead about the suspected affair might turn out to be about handling suspicions, rather than about unfaithful spouses. Immediately after the lead, the so-called nut graph narrows down all the directions in which the article might develop to one and only one. In addition to proclaiming the limited scope of your article, the nut graph presents necessary background and context for the topic at hand. Often, you'll load up the nut graph with dates, quantities and other fundamental facts that demonstrate the significance of the subject.

After the nostalgic lead in number eighteen above, for instance, the first sentence of the next paragraph announces the true subject of Robert Nadeau's article: "Next on the cutting edge is coffee and the Internet." Lead number fourteen, which gets the reader to imagine a two-year-old son turning blue, might continue along these lines:

> *Although more than 27 percent of children encounter breathing problems at some point before the age of 13, fewer than 15 percent of parents of small children have taken cardio-pulmonary resuscitation (CPR) training, according to the American Center for Choking Prevention.*

Last year slightly more than 750 children nationwide died from drowning, choking or various other breathing difficulties, says the Centers for Disease Control, which tracks all causes of untimely death. "Almost all of those 750 deaths were preventable," comments Mary Prinsla, a CDC staff epidemiologist.

Here the nut graph defines the scope of the problem, setting up the theme of prevention for the rest of the article.

If your article wanders all over creation, you may not have written a tightly defined nut graph, which should implicitly announce what the article will include and what it will leave out. For instance, I would expect that the paragraph just quoted would lead into a discussion of why so few parents learn CPR, where the reader can learn emergency techniques and what to remember if one's own child stops breathing. This nut graph rules out a discussion of adult rescues, child suicides, the causes of "911" delays and injuries due to falls from high chairs.

ORGANIZING THE BODY OF THE ARTICLE

Once you've proclaimed the focus of the article and set the context, the body of your article allows you to develop individual points at greater length one by one. Confronting a full notebook or a stack of notes, some novice writers get stuck. You can make order out of chaos painlessly with this method I've successfully taught to hundreds of people. Buy a pack of small index cards, or tear ordinary blank paper into two-inch squares. Looking at the research or brainstorming notes for your article, write down every topic from your notes on a separate card.

For instance, if you interviewed someone named McKeen who talked about a lighthouse's origin, its current financial problems and erosion at the beach, you could compose three cards: "lighthouse origin—McKeen"; "lighthouse fin. problems—McKeen" and "erosion at beach—McKeen." Adding "McKeen" will serve as a reminder of your source on the topic, but for a smallish pile of notes that may not be necessary. You should end up with anywhere from twelve to forty cards. Less than twelve, and you either haven't completed enough research or you're conceiving of topics too broadly for this method; more than forty and

you've either done way too much research for an article or are writing down individual facts rather than topics. That's step one.

Once you've finished notating your stack of cards, begin sorting them by putting together any two cards that seem to belong together. Let the pairs of cards evolve into piles as you continue matching up items that go together. You can do the sorting on a table, on the floor or on your lap. You should end up with four to eight groupings of cards. Don't worry if you're forced to make a "group" out of just one card that doesn't belong anywhere else. If you like, add a title to each stack of items, such as "Env. problems"; "History of the beach"; "History of the lighthouse"; "Activists get involved." You've now completed step two.

For step three in organizing your article, arrange the groups in the order in which they might appear in your piece. This gets easier when you have a firm grasp of article structure, which I'll explain in a moment, but even complete beginners to magazine writing usually have a good intuitive sense of how information might flow in an article. When you have placed the card groups in a possible order, you have organized your article! You have a tentative sequence for blocks of information to work from and modify as you plunge into the actual writing process. Often putting the groups of cards in order makes it clear to you that certain bits of lore won't fit in the article, or that you need more substance on certain topics. Depending on your deadline, either do additional research now to fill in the gaps, or get started writing and leave holes in the text to fill in later when you track down the missing material.

Two other organizing methods are worth mentioning. First, some word-processing programs include a module that facilitates outlining. This allows you to easily line up and move items, expand and contract the level of visible detail in an outline and create movable relationships among headings and items falling under them. I use an ancient shareware program like this called PC-Outline, which hooks into my word processor. One advantage of outlining on a computer screen is that you can grow the article right from the outline by expanding an entry here and then there into a paragraph. On the minus side, these outlining programs sometimes evoke memories of the rigid structures imposed on term papers in school, where Roman-numeral head-

ings need to be followed by at least two capital-letter headings, and so on. Organizing the contents of an article needs to be a fluid process.

Second, a "right-brained" or non-linear method of organizing material called "mindmapping" involves diagramming in visual form the relationship of the different aspects of a subject. To use mindmapping to organize an article, you'd write the overall topic within a circle in the center of a big sheet of paper, then draw offshoots representing the parts and subparts of the topic. When you had a complete mindmap resembling the one below, you'd still have decisions to make about how to wind your way in the article through the ingredients of the diagram, but you might find that task easier when you can see everything in front of you at once. Proponents of mindmapping recommend that you vitalize the picture with colors and little drawings. For example, you could draw a blue lighthouse under "Landpoint Lighthouse," a green "$$" beside "ownership," a rocky beach in red for "environmental issues," and so on. For more detailed instructions, see Joyce Wycoff's book, listed in Resources, p. 198.

Sample Mindmap for Lighthouse Article

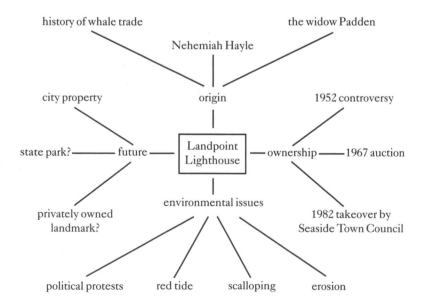

WRAPPING IT UP AT THE END

Nearly all of the lead types I described above can also serve as endings for articles. Because no explanations can follow the ending, however, you wouldn't want to leave the reader wondering with a "huh?" A hypothesis would likewise dangle weirdly in midair. I can't recall ever seeing an article end effectively with a question, either. Similarly, the "accepted fact" lead wouldn't work in a conclusion, since it sets the reader up to learn the opposite of the conventional wisdom. Probably the most common endings involve an anecdote or scene, a description, a quote from an interviewee, a generalization or a species we don't often find at the beginning of articles—a prediction. In choosing a conclusion for your article, decide first what impression you want to leave with readers. Do you want them remembering an overview of the issue? Feeling compassion or motivation to take action? Do you want to provide the enjoyment of an ironic twist? With a clear idea of what you'd like to accomplish at the end, you'll more easily choose and craft a conclusion.

Although I don't always do this, I enjoy rounding off an article with something that harks back to my lead. I call this an "echo ending," and I believe it works much on the level of sound, analogously to a melody or a variation on it repeating in music. Usually I'll use some of the very same words, to drive home the reverberation more than merely coming back to an idea stated at the beginning. I started off a business column, for example, with the sentence, "Here's a common lament from people promoting a small business: 'I just spent $700 on advertising and only got two responses. Help!'" I ended that column with the sentence, "Follow all of these guidelines and your new lament may be 'The phone is ringing off the hook. Help!'" Readers are more likely to notice the resemblance, and feel the circular sense of completion I intended to create, when I repeated the words "lament" and "Help!" than if I had written the second sentence as "Follow all of these guidelines and you may end up complaining about the phone ringing off the hook." To my ear, this alternative doesn't come anywhere close to the ring of the repetition.

Another favorite technique of mine is the split anecdote, which goes farther than an echo ending to tie together the lead and the conclusion. In a split anecdote, the lead tells the

beginning of a story, with the reader kept in suspense until the conclusion, which picks up the tale again and wraps it up. My *TWA Ambassador* article used this approach, with a middle that never mentioned my Beijing romance again up till the final paragraph of the article:

> *Back in Beijing five years ago, my sister would have been right to warn that working out the kinks with someone willing to leap into your culture isn't easy. My Chinese boyfriend eventually followed me to my home turf and we married. We've stumbled through confusing conflicts over food, time and jobs. He is still searching for his niche in business here; our American friends don't live up to his Chinese standards of loyalty. But even though every day hasn't been a holiday, I'd still recommend international love for incorrigible explorers. It's the surest way I know to bring the adventure of foreign travel permanently back home.*

I can count at least five echoed elements from lead number one (see p. 120). Can you find them?

As I mentioned earlier, articles without any conclusion exist. Very short, factual pieces sometimes just end, and how-to articles on a theme like "Twelve Ways to Cook Shark Meat" may simply halt after point number twelve. Even so, a skilled writer would choose the last point in a series to fit well as the terminal paragraph, and craft the concluding sentence to sound more like a finale than ordinarily.

WRITING TO LENGTH

Since almost every assigned magazine article carries a target length, it's wise to work some consciousness of size into your organizing process. The index-card method actually helps you gauge the relationship between your material and the length you're shooting at. If the editor assigned you 1,200 words, and you tend to write paragraphs of about 100 words each, you can figure the lead, nut graph and conclusion take up three paragraphs, or 300 words, leaving you 900 words for developing the story. With six groupings of index cards, that means you could devote two paragraphs to some topics, just one to others. If you

look at your groupings and find three or four major points or examples in each pile, you know before you begin tapping away at the computer that you can include only one or two of them, not all the fascinating stuff you've unearthed.

Cutting down a draft on which you've already lavished creativity and energy can be a heartbreaking, time-consuming exercise. If you're no more than 20 percent over the limit, you can often trim the article to size by pruning your sentences of every extra word and example. With a greater than 20-percent overrun, however, you'd probably have to slash whole paragraphs. Projecting from the tentative outline represented by the groups of index cards to the written article before you start fashioning paragraphs can save you a lot of mindwracking work later on.

SALESWORTHY SIDEBARS

Up to now I've written as if articles had just a start-to-finish flow. You also need to know a way to submit valuable outtakes that belong separately and together with your main article. Most magazines include what are called sidebars along with some of their articles—short accompanying pieces placed alongside the primary bylined story. For instance, destination pieces in travel magazines often include a boxed section containing the nitty-gritty details of where to stay, how much they charge and how to contact them. Some common contents for sidebars:

- Practical details, such as contact information and prices
- One especially illuminating anecdote or example that can stand on its own
- List of tips
- Glossary or definitions for terms some readers may know and others may not
- Q&A—questions and answers
- A historical sketch putting something or someone featured in the article in context
- A chart, quiz, recipes or other nonstandard kind of text

Editors like sidebars because they offer additional chances to involve and serve their readers, and to create an interestingly varied layout on the page. For writers, sidebars solve a common organizing problem. When you want to include something that

goes on for, say, four paragraphs, out of proportion to other topics that you treated and that can't be integrated easily into your text, the solution is a sidebar. They also work well for highlighting a kind of information that contrasts with the sort you focused on in the main document.

Sometimes an editor requests a specific sidebar when assigning the main article. In that case, make sure you know whether the word count for the assignment includes the sidebar, or whether the sidebar gets toted up separately. But if no sidebar came up in the conversation, and during the course of organizing your article you spot a perfect candidate, contact the editor to find out if a short related piece would be desirable. Some editors tack on extra pay if they tell you at this point to go ahead and pass in a sidebar in addition to the original assigned word count. It's better to present your idea about a sidebar to the editor as a possibility that might enhance the article rather than the remedy to a headache about how to fit everything in the piece you were assigned.

OTHER STRUCTURES

Not every article fits the general pattern described in this chapter. Madeleine Kane, a prize-winning humor columnist in Bayside, New York, has published numerous takeoffs such as funny contracts, comical memos, fictitious dialogues and monologues, parody question-and-answer interviews and humorous quizzes. In a more serious vein, articles might take on a diary or letter format, or the form of a freewheeling meditation. But unless there's an obvious reason for a creative structure, editors may look at your inventive organization and think that you just don't understand how to write. So for greatest salability, stick to the Lead-Nut Graph-Body-Conclusion outline most of the time.

Chapter Ten

Writing for the Reader

People who have written for their own pleasure for years face some rude shocks when they begin writing for public consumption. In my workshops I've seen this scene again and again and again: Someone whose work is being discussed hears that some point is confusing, missing or is being woefully misinterpreted. "What are you talking about?" the writer responds, his voice going shrill, his finger finding the exact place to stab at. "I explained that right here. How could it be any plainer?"

It's natural to feel indignant and betrayed when your ideas don't come across the way you intended. Unless you want your writing to keep piling up in your desk drawers, though, you must adopt the attitude that your customer—the reader—gets to say what you have and have not communicated. Your writing can't require mind reading. Not only must you pay respectful attention to feedback from your most consequential reader, the editor, you have to embrace writing habits that place readers in general, not yourself, on a pedestal. Certainly someone, even an editor, can read carelessly or make a dumb suggestion. But successfully writing for publication demands that in large and small matters of style you be oriented toward pleasing readers. This chapter contains lessons I've learned in a decade and a half of honing my own writing skills and those of students and consulting clients.

WANTED: VIVID, CONVERSATIONAL WRITING

If you come to article writing from the business world or from academe, or if you haven't written anything for evaluation since

school, you have to adjust your understanding of the dos and don'ts of writing to those characteristic of the magazine and newspaper marketplace. The measure of freelance prose isn't strict correctness so much as a natural, informal presentation of ideas. That is, proper grammar and usage matter, but some of the constricting rules enforced in other writing venues don't apply here. Where the ideal of a conversational tone comes into conflict with tradition, high propriety should bend.

For instance, forget about those schoolmarmish warnings never to begin a sentence with "But" or "And." Rarely will editors rap your knuckles for using the pronoun "I," or reproach you for using "who" where it sounds more fitting than a stilted "whom." You can usually end sentences with prepositions if they read better that way, split infinitives and spice up your text with sentence fragments. Really! Marathon-length sentences layered with semicolons don't go over well here, but contractions pass muster fine.

Along with a conversational tone, you'll have to master the art of specific, concrete writing. You can't get very far in the business with general, vague stuff like this:

> *Henricks grew up among a large brood of siblings who all turned out to be professionals of various sorts, he says. Except for a few years when he "dropped out" to find himself, he's been busily climbing every ladder in sight in his field, ever higher and higher.*

Nothing wrong with the tone there, but the airy texture leaves much to be desired. Too many questions go unanswered, too many opportunities to pin down the details passed by. How many siblings? Professionals like doctor, lawyer, accountant or like movie director, symphony violinist, museum curator? A few—how many? When he "dropped out," did he make a pilgrimage to India, do drugs on a houseboat in Key West or sit around reading comic books in a cloud of depression? What kind of ladders are we talking about here, and what field is this? Partly how well you name names goes back to the thoroughness of your research, but it also relates to the precision of your observations, the rigor of your thinking and the discipline to choose "doctor" over "professional," "Tom Cruise look-alike" over

"handsome" and "sun-baked" over "light-colored."

Learn to fill your articles with colorful, specific details, and you'll be the darling of editors. Give readers descriptions that their visual—and auditory, olfactory, gustatory and tactile—imaginations can go to town with. Instead of "For a decorator, Tessilini is surprisingly messy," paint a word picture like "Tesselini's desk is a jumble of yellowing correspondence and crumpled napkins with doughnut remains poking out." Break abstractions, especially enormous numbers, down into more familiar terms. Rather than "more than $160 billion," which most people can't fathom, try "$689 for each man, woman and child in the United States." Replace generalizations with examples. In place of "Sanford and Sanford fought often," write more along the lines of "Sanford and Sanford interviewed seven agents before finding one the other didn't hate, and they once had a break-the-dishes, screaming fight in front of dinner guests." The extra work on your part pays off big.

You'll probably need to acquire a knack for working in the quotes you gathered from your experts and other interview sources. In keeping with the informal tone and rapid pace of articles, you want to introduce your quotees quickly and accurately along with some striking bit of what they said. Don't show amateurism in straining for original substitutes for "she said" or "he says"; those old standbys do the job well, staying in the background of readers' consciousness the way commas and periods do. Intersperse summaries of the merely factual parts in your own words with the experts' best stuff the way they said it between quotation marks. Watch this before-and-after transformation, where the second, smoother version without extraneous information better highlights the expert's surprising judgment (which I made up).

BEFORE: *Allison Pepper, M.D., emeritus professor of dermatology at the University of Beachside, has studied the role of expectations in cosmetic surgery for more than 25 years. "In a 1975 study that we repeated in 1995, we found that 56 percent of women with moderate expectations for improvement from cosmetic surgery, pre-surgery, rated themselves 'moderately satisfied' post-surgery," she said.*

"Of those who had high expectations for improvement, pre-surgery, 74 percent rated themselves 'highly satisfied' post-surgery. There weren't enough low-expectation women to be statistically significant. If there were some kind of placebo surgery, like taking sugar pills, where the patient only thought the procedure was done, I'd predict the high-expectation group would be extremely happy with the 'results.' But that kind of test isn't possible."

AFTER: For Allison Pepper, M.D., emeritus professor of dermatology at the University of Beachside, satisfaction with cosmetic surgery has a strong relationship with how much a woman expects it to improve her appearance. Women whose pre-surgery questionnaires categorized them as having moderate expectations had moderate satisfaction afterwards, while those with high expectations expressed high post-surgery satisfaction. "If there were some kind of placebo surgery, like taking sugar pills, where the patient only thought the procedure was done, I'd predict the high-expectation group would be extremely happy with the results,' " she said.

More judicious selection of your source's exact words and summary of necessary but routine information strengthen your prose. Practice writing up quotes by having several skillfully written magazine articles at hand while you're drafting yours, and following their patterns of quotes, summaries and commentary.

Anecdotes are another element of magazine work that you may need to master. A compressed story, an anecdote retells an event either in the words of the person it happened to, your words or, usually, some combination. Chapters two and six of this book open with anecdotes. In magazine or newspaper articles, as in book chapters, anecdotes serve as illustrations of points you're making rather than the main focus. As with quotes, good anecdotes turn up in your research when you probe for them with questions like, "For example?" and "Can you tell me about a specific time when that happened?" When writing anecdotes into an article, you must treat them with the proper proportion. You have to provide enough detail for the reader to

believe, for the length of that half-paragraph, paragraph or two paragraphs, in what happened. But you normally shouldn't dwell on the event so long that readers keep thinking about it once you return to the main point or move on to another anecdote.

A *Cosmopolitan* editor once taught me the importance of closure with anecdotes—readers shouldn't be left wondering about the mini-story when you go on to the next thing. In an article on intuition, I mentioned a bicyclist in Central Park who suddenly got an image that there would be danger around the corner—and there was. An attacker was waiting for her, to knock her down and perform who knows what other kind of harm. I ended the story there. "So what happened? You left us up in the air," the editor objected. Oh, that's not relevant, I replied. The crucial point was that she'd had the image and the image was accurate. "No," the editor said. "Even though this isn't an article on rapes or muggings, readers need to know whether or not she was hurt. Was she?" I had to go back to my source to find out, and added a sentence that actually improved the anecdote, on how the split-second intuitive image gave her time to prepare and escape the attacker safely. (And by the way, this whole paragraph represents a nice, complete anecdote for you to study!)

WISE WORD CHOICE

Two words, if taken to heart, will generate greater improvement in your writing than anything else: STRONG VERBS! Try mightily to avoid the weakest verbs in the English language— "is," "are," "was," "were" and other forms of "to be." I doubt I can prove this principle any more powerfully than to confess that originally I wrote the preceding two sentences as follows:

> *The two words that, if taken to heart, will lead to greater improvement in your writing than anything else are: STRONG VERBS! The weakest verbs in the English language are "is," "are," "was," "were" and other forms of "to be."*

Notice the added zip when I thought again and eliminated the two "are's" and changed the anemic "lead to" to "generate"? Experiment yourself by pretending that some evil genie will blow

up your house if you allow an "is" or "are" or even worse, phrases such as "There is" or "There are" into your writing. You'll have no choice but to construct livelier sentences. Either you replace "to be" with a more dramatic action, or you recast your idea with a different sentence structure. Practice strengthening the following examples, then compare my answers in italics.

There is no finer artist in the history of art than Picasso. *(No artist has ever deserved more accolades than Picasso.)*

The Joneses were the first in Skyville to sign up. *(The Joneses set the tone for Skyville by signing up first.)*

Valerie was as rangy as a newborn doe and as elusive as Houdini. *(As rangy as a newborn doe, Valerie escaped notice for years in the streets of Monte Carlo.)*

The behind-the-scenes perpetrator was none other than Pamela Smart. *(Pamela Smart holds the real responsibility for her husband's death.)*

There were tears in his eyes as he delivered his son's eulogy. *(Tears pooled in his eyes as he delivered his son's eulogy.)*

The same goes for adverbs, which tend to weaken your prose. Ineffectual ones tied to adjectives include "really," "very" and "extremely," but even seemingly substantive qualifiers for verbs like "slowly" or "proudly" should prompt you to search instead for a more specific, punchier verb. For instance remove the adverbs in these sentences:

FROM: *She walked slowly up to the podium to accept her award.*

TO: *She plodded (or struggled, or lumbered) up to the podium to accept her award.*

FROM: *Her grandson smiled proudly.*

TO: *Her grandson beamed.*

A thesaurus, whether printed in book form or computerized, can expedite your search for the perfect word, so long as you use such lists as a memory jogger and not as a menu for exotic word sprinkles. You want words that nail your exact meaning to the reader's mind, not that attract attention to you as a writer.

As generations of writing teachers have noted, never use a long, oddball word to impress or provide variety.

Some beginning writers have the idea that they must avoid repeating a word within a sentence or a paragraph and set off on a solemn, neverending—and unnecessary—hunt for synonyms. In the preceding paragraph, for example, I used "word" four times in three sentences. Most likely, you didn't even notice, because the more familiar a repeated word, the less readers catch wind of it. Had I strained to insert "locution" or "verbalization" or both in a misguided attempt at variety, you would have become counterproductively aware of me fiddling with my tools. The same magician-fumbling-on-stage effect occurs when you use an uncommon word too often, because the less familiar any word you use is, the more it pulls readers out of the spell necessary for immersion in your message. Words like "succumb," "hypnotically" or "cryptic" can serve as an accent when they appear once but become a mannerism or a pest when they show up more frequently in an article.

Make sure that your adjectives add content, and that nouns genuinely need to be there. Empty modifiers such as "fabulous," "exciting," "special," "lovely" and "wonderful" have no meaning and inject your sentences with hot air. Along the same lines, business-writing expert Richard Lauchman coined the word "intruders" for nouns "that have nothing in particular to do and decide to crash the party." In these examples of his, find the intruders and toss them out for cleaner prose (answers in italics):

- High wind conditions *(High winds)*
- Intelligence-gathering effort *(Intelligence gathering)*
- Software error problems *(Software errors)*
- Deteriorating sales situation *(Deteriorating sales)*

Send off to oblivion, too, clichés and other types of conventional phrases that readers have encountered so many times that they could complete your sentences in their sleep. "Voters raised a hue and _____ when the incumbent, crazy as a _____, added insult to _____ and came to an untimely _____." I'll bet you couldn't help filling in those blanks as you read, with "cry," "loon," "injury" and "end."

Jargon—insider language that may obscure more than it illu-

minates—can present stickier problems. The following questions may help you decide whether you should use it, provide a gloss for noninitiated readers or expunge it from your work.

• *Who is your audience, and are you certain that all of them understand the terminology in question?* Professional speakers and meeting planners who hire them know what "faxable one-sheets" are, but people new to the business need to be told that these brochure alternatives convey someone's photo, topic, credentials and supporting quotes to someone at another fax machine. Similarly, in *Windows Developers* magazine, for programmers, you can pepper an article with "IS," "GB," "NTFS," "PIM," and "OLE" without explanations, but for *Family Computing* you'd better translate.

• *From the point of view of your audience, is the phrase designed to hide unpleasant circumstances?* Writing for corporate managers, you could use "downsizing" with impunity, but in a union magazine or one read mostly by employees, you should use straighter language like "layoffs," "firing" and "adding to the unemployment rolls."

• *Is it self-important, made-up, baffling language?* Eject ugly, bloated phrases like "revenue enhancement" (for taxes), "domestic engineering" (for housework) and "incendiary event" (for fire) permanently from your vocabulary.

Apart from all these guidelines, of course, your writing thrives and improves to the extent that you take a keen interest in words, your medium. Keep a dictionary close at hand and use it when you encounter unfamiliar expressions or when you find yourself tempted to use a word whose meaning is hazy for you. The other day I was thrilled to meet the word "galoot" and learn that it's slang for a clumsy or uncouth person; I would never insert a word like "factotum" in an article without checking its definition in the dictionary first. When you encounter writers whose style sings to you, go back and observe how the words they chose contribute to the overall effect of their article. As with music, which creates miracles out of a limited number of notes, you may find that you know every word used by a writer you admire. The art lies in which one ends up where.

LUCID SENTENCES

If words comprise the bricks of prose, with sentences you build thoughts by stacking bricks beside and atop one another. In some of my workshops, I start students on a sentence self-improvement program by teaching the four basic kinds of sentences:

1. Simple—one subject-verb unit: *The sun rises in the east.*

2. Compound—two or more subject-verb units, connected by a semicolon or conjunctions like "and" or "but": *The sun rises in the east, and it sets in the west.* Each segment of a compound sentence could stand on its own as a separate sentence. ("The sun rises and sets" would be a simple sentence with a compound verb.)

3. Complex—two or more subject-verb units, one of which could stand separately on its own, and the other not, because it is introduced by a word like "when," "before," "because," "who" or "which": *When all is working well, the sun rises in the east.*

4. Compound-complex—combination of compound and complex sentences, with at least two subject-verb units that could stand on their own, and at least one nonindependent subject-verb unit: *When all is working well, the sun rises in the east and it sets in the west.*

Although this may seem pedantic, many students find it illuminating to examine a piece of their writing to see what percentage they used of each type of sentence, and then compare with other students and with writers they admire. The use of too many simple and compound sentences compared with the number of complex and compound-complex ones can produce a juvenile or flat tone. Too many complex and compound-complex sentences vis-à-vis simple and compound can yield a slow pace and a dense, academic texture. I wouldn't venture to prescribe any ratio in particular, since this contributes to your distinctive style. But if you find you rarely use one of the four sentence types above, it's time to expand your repertoire.

Besides the four basic types outlined above, study your prose to see how great a variety of sentence patterns you use. Do you usually start your sentences with the subject? Do you go over-

board with sentences containing subject-verb units in series? Do you ever or often begin with a modifier or dependent clause? How frequently do you insert a question? Here you definitely want a substantial mixture of sentence patterns, without creating a mannerism or annoyance from leaning too heavily on one. This issue is not something you should think about once and never again. Becoming aware of ruts you may have fallen into and possibilities you haven't tried benefits even very experienced writers. A few years ago, my literary agent pointed out that in a book proposal I'd overused a triad arrangement—"meeny, miny or moe"; "hammers, screwdrivers and wrenches"; and so on. I made some needed changes. And as I was writing this chapter, I came across in a personal essay an interesting sentence type not in my collection: inversions, as in "Death I did not fear, only poverty" or "Never did I fear death, only poverty." Rarely have I used this pattern, but I rather like it.

Continue your sentence self-improvement program by assessing your characteristic sentence length. Some grammar-checking programs compile this data on a specific piece of writing for you. As I recall, they focus more on the average sentence length, which I don't find a useful benchmark, than on the extent of variation, which I believe is more worth looking at. Contrast in sentence length, not for the sake of wildness, but for stimulating rhythms, belongs in your stylistic bag of techniques.

Finally, fashion your sentences in accordance with the psychological laws of emphasis. You place the most emphasis on a word or idea when you place it at the end of a sentence—better yet at the end of a sentence that closes a paragraph. The second most emphatic position in a sentence is the beginning. Put an element of meaning in the middle of a sentence and you might as well have dumped a few feet of dirt over it. Halfway from both ends it retreats from the reader's notice. You can make great hay of this principle, by the way, in letter writing. If you have good news, get the greatest attention for it in either the first line or in the "P.S." If you must impart nasty news, pack it into the middle of a sentence smack in the middle of a paragraph, and it comes across cushioned rather than harsh.

These last three guidelines—vary sentence patterns, use different lengths, arrange for emphasis—have become second nature

to me because I'm an auditory writer. That is, hearing is my leading sense, and I instinctively rearrange things to sound good, even though I'm not really writing to be read aloud. I have a very hard time writing a clunky sentence, the way some visually oriented people almost feel physical pain looking at clashing colors. Even people who appear to lack this kind of musical sensitivity are, I believe, nevertheless influenced by the rhythm of writing. If you'd like to improve your perception and command of this dimension of writing, you can. Just regularly read your own work and that of others out loud, noticing what pleases your ear and what does not. For instance, here's how I might improve an auditorily repulsive sentence.

> *CLUNKY: The VW Golf GTI-VR6 offers convenience, room for groceries, great handling in snow, kicky horsepower and thus undeniable appeal for hatchback fanciers.*
>
> *EASIER ON THE EAR: For those who fancy a hatchback, the VW Golf GTI-VR6's convenience, room for groceries, great handling in snow and kicky horsepower have undeniable appeal.*

Consider conscious punctuation part of crafting your sentences. Commas, apostrophes, periods and other punctuation marks have to show up at certain places, but you still have a wide range of choices with respect to optional nuances and gestures. Compare these alternatives, for instance:

- The sun rises in the east. It bakes the plains at noon.
- The sun rises in the east; it bakes the plains at noon.
- The sun rises in the east, and it bakes the plains at noon.

Periods also go by the name of "full stops" because they impose the greatest space between ideas. A semicolon signals a shorter breather, and a comma just a pause. Because semicolons convey an egghead flavor, I stay away from them. And if I notice too many commas slowing down a sentence or paragraph, I'll reword or restructure to keep the pace moving. Beginning writers need to watch out for overusing exclamation marks. With some extra effort you can choose words that convey surprise or marvelment without the crutch of an explicit marker. With underlining, which becomes italics when typeset, a little similarly

goes a long way. *Always* question your initial impulse to visibly accentuate a word or phrase. Test this out by rereading the previous sentence after mentally removing the italics. With good writing, readers will (not: *will*) instinctively understand the emphasis you intended.

WELL-CRAFTED PARAGRAPHING

A paragraph presents and develops one central idea. If you use the index-card outlining method I described in chapter nine, you'll find paragraphing a breeze. A majority of the time, a card corresponds to a paragraph. Exceptions usually occur when an anecdote takes an inordinate amount of space to communicate, when you decide to include several examples of the same phenomenon or when, because of overall space limitations, you have to press several points together under a more general umbrella than you had originally planned. Also, readable dialogue may demand more dispersed paragraphing. My own general rule is not to include more than one person's words in quotes within one paragraph. Otherwise, readers can get lost and confused.

In the *Cosmopolitan* anecdote about the Central Park bicyclist earlier in this chapter, I kept the story in one unit without quoting two different parties by putting my side of the dialogue into indirect discourse. If I wanted to recreate a conversation with quotes from two parties, I would usually spread it out the way Laurie Schloff and I did in this anecdote about a New Englander stopping in a small-town store in Arkansas, from our book *Smart Speaking*:

> *"Do you have oil?"*
> *"Do we have what?"*
> *"Oil. Oil [pronounced* oyl*]."*
> *Blank look from the store owner.*
> *"Oil. You know, motor oil for my car?"*
> *"Oh,* erl. *Erl. Of course we got erl."*

Topic sentences are an under-appreciated device for making sure paragraphs do their job unobtrusively. As you may recall from English composition classes, a topic sentence, generally the first sentence in a paragraph, announces the overall subject of that paragraph. For instance, in the unit of prose you're reading

right now, the opening sentence, "Topic sentences are an under-appreciated device . . .," sums up what I'm telling you in this component of my piece. You can't go wrong structuring your articles so that every paragraph from the nut graph on begins with a lively summary statement that the rest of the paragraph develops. You need greater skill to leave out these topic sentences, the way you court greater risks when you drive with just one hand on the wheel. Yet when severe space limits send you on a slash-and-cut hunt for extra words, see how well your paragraphs can stay on track without topic sentences, depending on repetition of key words and context to keep your article flowing.

Paragraphs almost never get published in isolation, of course. Four kinds of transitions stitch them smoothly together. First, transitional words and phrases like "However," "Afterwards," "Along the same lines" and "Therefore" serve as signposts telling readers, respectively, "We're looking at the other side now," "We're moving ahead in time," "We're adding another example of the same type" and "We're drawing a conclusion." Don't be afraid to use these old workhorses! Like "says" and "the," they fade into the background as they perform their conventional function—preventing readers from getting lost. Second, keep readers on track by repeating key words from the end of one paragraph in the next. Third, keep the thread going with implicit repetition or echoes, where you repeat the idea but not the exact wording from one paragraph to the next. All three of these techniques, by the way, also help keep readers oriented within paragraphs, too. Finally, for longer articles in magazines that use the device, you can signal a switch from one topic to another with a subhead, a technique I use in my chapters in this book.

A more intuitive, less logical kind of paragraphing applies to some historical pieces, profiles that recount the reporter-subject encounter, many personal essays and much so-called creative nonfiction. In building the drama of a story, topic sentences can get in the way. And when telling a story you may want to end paragraphs and start new ones for effect, rather than to observe the one-central idea rule. Transitions matter just as much as ever, though, as with a quick "Later" or "On the other side of town" you keep readers right alongside the action. For extended narration, feel free to paragraph by ear.

TONE, VOICE, ATMOSPHERE

I've left the most ethereal aspects of article style for last. Editors, readers and critics talk about a writer's "voice," and yet almost no one can tell you exactly what it is. For nonfiction writing, I define it as the personality and set of attitudes that come across to the reader from your idiosyncratic selection of words and the particular way you pile up sentences. Independently of your topic, the points you made in an article and whether or not you shared personal information explicitly, readers form an impression of you. They may imagine you as, say, young or mature, tough or compassionate, or perhaps, an urban elitist, a country homebody, a nitpicky fussbudget, an adventurer, a blustery take-charge type. If you don't believe me, observe your reactions to these three passages on one subject, vegetarian cooking:

(A) Consider the democratic onion: It joins any stock pot without complaint, adds zest to humble and elegant dishes alike, and its papery wrappings make an exquisite addition to your compost pile. In "Aunt Millie's Soy Strudel" and "Turkish-tinged Stroganoff," this month's main-dish recipes, our basement-bin friend turns ordinary entrees into gloriously textured treats.

(B) Despite annual tsk-tsks from our doctors, the typical dinner-party menu of the late nineties reads like a cholesterol disaster zone. We resolve to reform, but we couldn't exactly serve watercress casseroles to the Agees and the Rockefoodles, could we? Hence I'm delighted to report having discovered CEO-worthy, low-fat vegetarian entrees that combine well with full-bodied cabernet and present beautifully on your best china.

(C) If you've ever wanted to puke at the sight of some unidentifiable lentil-and-tofu crud brought to a pot-luck supper by the diehard no-nukers in your neighborhood, the very word "vegetarian" can make you pick up the nearest empty beer can and get ready to throw it. This is misguided, guys. The "artificial meat" recipes I've put together are a snap to cook, get scarfed down by kids and can last for a whole week in the refrigerator without attracting scuzzy blue fuzz.

I imagine *A* as a bandana'd earth mother who wears sandals with socks in winter; *B* as a middle-aged male who spends hundreds of dollars a year searching for the perfect cappuccino machine; and *C* as a divorced, not-quite-domesticated father of three. Do you agree?

I'm exaggerating here, but only a little. My intention is to raise your consciousness about the extent to which style creates an image in the mind of a reader. As we know from the fact that I made up all three of the passages above, writers don't need to get stuck in whatever voice comes to them naturally. After thinking about or asking others what kind of impression comes across in your everyday article style, you may want to stretch and practice other voices, the way serious actors learn to play characters whose real lives they would never find themselves in. If you haven't settled into any consistent voice yet, such exercises can help you stumble across the style that feels just right. Write an article the way a black-clad, green-streaked teenager would; rewrite it pretending you're a Biblically well-informed, family values buff, and then again as a school-of-hard-knocks, chronically ill and always complaining grandmother. Or practice infusing the same facts with a different dominant feeling: outrage, compassion, fear, silliness, scorn, smugness.

Eventually you'll have refined your perception and your dexterity to the point where you can discern which magazines have a taste for writers with your characteristic tang, and where you know how to adjust your style in keeping with the preferences of an outlet where you'd very much like to be published. Just as chameleons can't match every color in the rainbow, though, you'll probably find some attitudes, personalities and identities you can't manage to put on.

Early in my career, I received an assignment to profile an educational program called The New England School for Nannies. The assigning editor told me the piece I turned in had a fatal flaw: it was "too earnest." I could hardly believe my ears. Did he want me to make fun of the nannies? He wouldn't put it quite that way, but basically the answer was yes. Making fun of well-meaning people just isn't in me, so I accepted a kill fee for that article and crossed that magazine off my list of prospects.

Besides an incompatibility of attitudes or values, you might

not be able to ventriloquize your way into a particular market because of subtle ignorance of its lifestyle. For all I know about wines, for example, I could have committed a deadly lapse when I made up the phrase "full-bodied cabernet" in example *B* above. And to tell you the truth, even though I haven't used words like "puke," "crud" and "scuzzy" in at least twenty years, I had the most fun composing example *C*. Maybe the mold at the back of my refrigerator can tell you why.

Chapter Eleven

Rewriting and Dealing With Editors

S uppose you've just had one of those rapturous writing experiences you've always dreamed of. The Muse popped in for a visit when you couldn't have needed her more. She whispered a terrific lead, then whole paragraphs in your ear, so that you had to do no more than transcribe your entire article fluidly from beginning to end. All you have left to do now is pull out an envelope, address it to the editor who made the assignment and head off to the post office, right?

Wrong. Wonderful as The Muse is, she can't eliminate the need for rewriting. She represents inspiration, not a fine-tuned consciousness of your audience, a critical editorial eye, accuracy of every detail or calibration of length—not to mention eventual collection of your fee. You still have several crucial writerly and business tasks to take care of once she's made her contribution. Keep that manuscript out of that envelope for a short while yet!

WRITING AND REWRITING

Completing a publishable article includes making sure that it fits the needs of the editor who assigned it, or the market for which you've designed it as an on-speculation piece. Set it aside once you believe it's finished, at least overnight. Then begin a fresh-eyed assessment of it by reviewing your contract, the relevant listings in *Writer's Market* or your notes on the conversation where the editor said, "Yes, we want it." Ask yourself first, what was to be the purpose of the article? And have you fulfilled that purpose with what you put down on paper? Quite often a writer gets carried in an unplanned direction during the research and writing process, which then needs to be matched back up with

the original purpose of, say, arguing that welfare reform is a sham or explaining why Australia's sheep shortage has no effect on this year's fashions. If you discover a discrepancy of purpose, usually you should adjust the flow of your article accordingly. Sometimes, though, after research and reflection you discover that your original intention for the piece doesn't fit the facts. When you therefore can't deliver what you promised, inform the editor before sending in the completed article. "Editors do not like surprises," warns veteran reporter Ann Monroe.

Also, remind yourself now of your audience, and examine whether or not you've tailored your language, content and style for that group of readers. For instance, for California readers you should generally use the word "freeway" rather than "highway," but vice versa for a national audience. For an electronics publication you could delve into the workings of ISDN connections much longer without provoking boredom than you could for the *Sunday Argosian*. For a highbrow readership you could get away with longer, more complicated sentences than you could for the circulation of *Boys' Life*.

And how about your voice? As I explained in chapter ten, you give the reader an impression of yourself in everything you write, whether you mean to or not, so you ought to consider whether or not you come off in an acceptable way. Try to read your article now as if you've never encountered those words before. How does its author come across—as you hoped? With voice and some of the other subtle elements of writing, you may get your most helpful input from friends and fellow writers who have not seen the piece in progress. I've found that to get the feedback I need prior to sending off an article, I have to prep my test readers with specific questions, such as, "Does the tone seem light?" "Did you lose interest anywhere?" or "Did you find anything confusing?"

You should submit your article no more than 10 percent shorter or longer than the agreed-upon length. If you're like most writers, you'll now have to go searching for sections, sentences and words to cut. Even your favorite anecdotes and phrases must pass the tests of relevance and necessity. They should stay only if the article would lose some essential nuance without them.

Finally, check the organization of your piece. Does it grab the

reader's attention quickly, state its focus and lead step by step to a memorable conclusion? When I've put a piece aside for even a short while, I'll often notice little "huh?"'s as I reread it, indicating spots which need some kind of rearranging, explanation or improved transitions.

When you do slip the article into the envelope, include a cover letter so that the person who opens the mail realizes that you are submitting it for publication. You also need that kind of preface if you've been asked to submit the piece by e-mail or fax. Some magazines require along with the manuscript a list of each of your interviewees and their telephone numbers. This goes to the fact-checking department, which I will explain shortly. In my cover letter, I always include a sentence to the effect that I would be happy to discuss any changes necessary in the article, which seems to have helped to prevent distressing unilateral rewrites by the editor. If you expect to be difficult to reach at any time in the next few weeks, provide alternate telephone or fax numbers, explain the dates you're most accessible or promise that you'll be checking messages faithfully. Editors can become frantic when Deadline Day looms and a writer needed to answer questions about the article appears to have gone AWOL.

Regardless of how perfectly you've crafted the article, expect the editor to have some questions, suggestions or changes for you. These may come in the form of general comments during a telephone conversation, a detailed written memo or questions written in red all over your manuscript. An editor may also have gone ahead and incorporated changes into your work and then show them to you as a courtesy. Try to swallow your inevitable defensive reactions here and view this as a legitimate crack at refurbishing your work for a showcase and audience the editor understands much better than you do. Swallow *very* hard if you have to, before complaining.

One writer bled about it this way to fellow scribblers on the Internet: "I just received the edited version of my article by fax today. I was feeling so great when I read, 'Hardly any changes at all. Wonderful job!' Then I took a look and . . . well, it's difficult to write about. I am mortally wounded. *Someone* wrote *all over* my nice pretty manuscript! Ouch!" Another writer ad-

vised, "Yeah, it hurts. Yeah, how dare they?! But let's face it; we're generally too close to our own work to be able to judge what needs improvement. Take all that red ink as a sincere attempt to help you." A few days later, the original writer had calmed down and realized that most of the changes were small and had kept her main points and her favorite passages intact.

Elsewhere online, a feistier gripe from a writer about editing attracted very little sympathy, though: "Most freelance writers hand in crap, which editors have to beat into shape. So freelancers who polish every word tend to get shredded in this machine. I'm a perfectionist and highly polish my copy, so I have a defense for each word choice. Editors find me abrasive and contentious—even though my tone is polite—because they're used to dealing with writers who don't care in the first place and shrug off changes."

Besides having insulted the craftsmanship of other writers, this fellow was taken to task for setting himself up as having the last word on the best way to say something. "Experienced pros know there is *always* another way to say something," one highly credentialed writer responded. Another questioned the wisdom of getting so attached to the original product. "Life is too short to worry that much about editors changing your stuff. Just keep on producing and collecting the clips and the money." I added my two cents that being viewed as abrasive and contentious rarely leads to repeat assignments, and the editor of a national magazine sent me a private e-mail saying that she indeed would never give this fellow any work, even though he appeared to have credentials in her area of interest. Editors do not get annoyed when you stick up for the facts or for an explainable nuance, only when you appear to be objecting to changes primarily because they're not what you originally wrote.

The general rule in the publishing industry is that the writer owes the editor one general rewrite for no additional charge. This doesn't mean becoming a total pushover, though, agreeing to modifications that you believe distort the facts or violate the English language. After I passed in an assigned article on the controversial topic of memories of sexual abuse, for instance, an editor asked me to give the opposite side of the issue more credence than I thought it deserved. This became one of just a

handful of instances where the editor and I weren't able to find a solution both of us could live with, and I received a kill fee for the assignment. You too should take a stand with editors rarely—when some major ethical principle, not merely aesthetics or your pride, is at stake. Whenever the editor insists on changes that make you squirm, you have the right to ask that your byline be dropped from the article—and still receive the check.

THE LITTLE STUFF

After negotiations between you and the editor over content, style and wording, your article's journey hasn't come to an end. Another editor specially trained to pick at nits, the copy editor, gets to work on the manuscript. This editor makes a lot of little changes in your writing so that your work conforms with standard usage and the magazine's idiosyncratic preferences with respect to capitalization, use of numerals versus words for numbers, word choices, paragraph lengths, punctuation options and much else. Don't bother squawking about these sorts of changes—they're not open to discussion. Once I didn't like the fact that "gelled," as I had written it, turned into "jelled" in the copy editor's hands. Too bad, the latter was "house style," I was told.

At many publications, the copy editor works in conjunction with another stickler for details, the fact checker. The fact checker ascertains that the profile subject actually graduated from the University of Southern Maine, not from the nonexistent Southern Maine University; that she is indeed the provost rather than the acting president; and that she did formerly win a national racquetball title, not a regional championship in squash. Thank your lucky stars when you have a fact checker. Careful as you are, bloopers can slip by to necessitate red-faced apologies, retractions and corrections later.

Freelancer Michael Smith recalls referring to the "cervical cortex" in a piece on a well-known brain researcher. "She phoned me up and asked me very politely where such an organ might be found, and only then did I realize what I had written. It should have been cerebral cortex, of course." Similarly, in the first draft of an earlier chapter I wrote "Winnipeg, Saskatchewan," and only when I thought I'd better check the spelling of "Saskatchewan" in my atlas did I discover that Winnipeg is actually in Manitoba.

I'd relied on memory—always a bad idea. A better policy: Look it up. Even if you're certain, look it up. And even if you'll have a fact checker, look it up! Lucy McCauley told me that in her thirteen years of editing and fact checking, an article had never come to her that did not contain at least one mistake. "They're not always the fault of the writer," she adds. "Prices might change, or a phone number."

Beyond copyediting and fact checking, your article might still be subject to changes because it has to fit into the allotted space in the publication. Last-minute shuffling of contents might mean that a version of your piece that you'd been led to believe was final needs to lose eight lines after all. Don't whine if this happens to you.

GETTING PAID

Ideally, you receive payment exactly when you and the editor had agreed you would. In the real world, mailboxes often fail to yield checks on time. Businesslike tactics get the best results. Follow these guidelines:

1. Always submit a formal invoice along with your assigned article. To prevent payment delays, the invoice should include the topic of your article, your name, address and Social Security number, the total amount owed and any breakdown between article fee and expenses, or fee for the article versus photos.

2. If the check does not arrive on schedule, call the editor to find out who you should speak to about your check. The editor may offer to straighten it out for you. Allow three weeks and call again. Do not act as if the delay is the editor's fault, as in many cases it is not. If you can make contact with the person who writes the checks, ask when you can expect to receive payment. If they have no record of you and need another copy of your invoice, fax it and ask when you can expect payment.

3. If repeated promises come to naught, or if the editor or accounting person stops returning your calls, you may need additional muscle to collect. Some writers' organizations, such as the National Writers Union, help members collect from magazines. To help you, they'll need a copy of your contract or letter of agreement and a log of the collection efforts you've made

up to that point. Don't assume this means you're burning your bridges with the publication. I had to sic the National Writers Union on a well-known women's magazine to obtain a check that was four months overdue, and then had no problem getting an additional assignment from them the next time I tried.

4. When the publication that owes you money has an office in the state where you reside, and the amount owed falls within Small Claims guidelines, for a minimal fee you can go to court to collect. Before resorting to court proceedings, however, give the publication a deadline by which to pay up. For more information, look for "Small Claims" in the telephone listings for the court system of your locality. I would take this step only after unmistakable and prolonged signs of foot-dragging.

Of the numerous times in my career that payment became a problem, two stick out especially. After I learned that the check from a Boston-based magazine bounced, its accounting department told me, "Oh, just redeposit it, it's good now." Instead I went to the magazine's own bank to cash it, only to watch the teller shake her head sadly and push the check back at me under the glass. An irate call back to the comptroller produced the advice to go see a particular teller at a particular out-of-the-way branch. Shaking my head dubiously, I did. To my astonishment, the teller made a telephone call and then counted out the correct number of hundreds and twenties for me—only an hour after her counterpart at the downtown branch had refused.

The other bizarre incident involved the editor of a political magazine calling me to tell me they were experiencing a financial crunch, and would I please donate my writing fee? I politely declined. I'd done the work expecting to be paid, and paid I was after I firmly reminded them that they had earlier made the commitment to pay me.

WHEN YOU THINK YOUR IDEA HAS BEEN "STOLEN"

Almost every time I present a workshop, someone asks how you can prevent editors from plucking your million-dollar article idea from your query letter and assigning it to someone they regularly dispense assignments to. I understand the question, but

I've struggled to find an adequately diplomatic way of explaining that this concern is a result of serious misconceptions about the writing business. Based on fifteen years of interactions with editors, and discussions with lawyers about copyright issues, here is the way I see these misconceptions. I am not a lawyer myself, however, so please consult a qualified attorney if you have further questions on this issue.

First, since ideas cannot be copyrighted or owned in any other way, the notion that you own the ideas in your query letter doesn't make sense. Only the specific expression of your idea, or any idea, in words qualifies as intellectual property. That is, you own the paragraphs in which you proposed an article on the wonder dog Dipty Do in your town, but by submitting that proposal to a magazine you have no legal claim to the idea of *an* article on Dipty Do. This may not seem fair to you, but this is what copyright law states. Legally, this makes your query letters fair game for editors looking for assignments to make to their regular stable of writers. Note that this same doctrine gives you perfect freedom to propose or write an article about topics you learned about in the works of other writers.

With that said, you need to understand next that while editors legally have the right to hand off an idea you thought up to a writer they already know and trust, this almost never occurs in the world of magazines and newspapers. Editors either just say no and go on to the next query when they read a freelancer's good idea badly executed, or on rare occasions pay the writer a nominal fee for the idea and then hand it over to someone they believe is more qualified to write about it.

And in any case, notes Gary Goettling, who spent 10 years editing alumni publications for Georgia Tech, "Ideas are the easy part. Give me ten minutes and I can come up with a hundred ideas, a thousand ideas, most of which have been thought by someone else. The work, the research is the hard part, what writers are really paid for and what separates people who want to be writers from people who are writers."

Why do so many beginning writers believe that what I'm saying almost never happens has victimized them? The third element of their misplaced fear and outrage is lack of understanding of the commonness of ideas. Newcomers to the writing world

have no notion that every week most magazines receive similar queries thought up independently by freelancers in different states. An article idea that came to you in a brainstorm and did not show up in that season's mail from anyone else represents the exception rather than the rule. Karen Thomas, a freelance writer as well as editor of *Windplayer* magazine, points out that one October, both *Ladies' Home Journal* and *Redbook* ran cover stories on breast cancer. "Not only that, the cover lines and focus of both were quite similar—Myths of Breast Cancer. Do these magazines have undercover spies sifting through each other's wastebaskets? Hardly. It's just that certain ideas seem to permeate the culture at certain times."

Even for an obscure topic, the editors may have learned about it exactly the way you did—by reading a small-circulation specialized or local publication. For instance, *Yankee* magazine subscribes to daily and weekly newspapers from many hamlets and towns throughout New England; *Entrepreneur* profiled a friend of mine because it received the newsletter of an organization she belonged to, which went out each month to only 350 people.

Finally, writers who believe their ideas have been stolen often show a misunderstanding of the time line of magazine publishing. "I queried them for a profile of Dipty Do the dog and two months later there he was in the magazine!" I'll hear. Logistically, two months before publication the finished copy of the magazine was probably already on its way to the printer. If a magazine had robbed you, the dastardly deed would have had to occur at least four months before publication.

The upshot, with respect to dealing with editors: Don't let suspicions run away with you and accuse editors of having swiped your ideas. In 99.9 percent of the cases one of the explanations above applies, and even if your case falls into the .1 percent, you have little legal recourse. To editors, these sorts of complaints put you in the "crank" category. Gary Goettling said he couldn't imagine what might prompt someone to make such an accusation "unless the writer were irrational." Karen Thomas said that if a freelancer accused her of stealing an idea, she'd burst into laughter. "I'm too busy with all the great ideas that I find just from picking up a newspaper or exploring an Internet site to need to steal some writer's topic."

While I don't know of a single provable case where this much-feared scenario of beginning writers has played out, I do know of another kind of article theft that definitely occurs. Several freelancers I know have spotted their work reprinted without their authorization. In one case, a major newspaper reprinted in a special supplement articles that it had previously bought and published in a section of the daily paper. No signed contracts with the writers entitled them to do that. Since the law states that in the absence of any written agreement to the contrary, a writer has sold just one-time rights, it did not take much for National Writers Union grievance officers to convince the paper that it had erred. The newspaper soon paid all the writers involved an extra fee for reuse of their work. In another case, I was teaching freshman English and noticed a friend's essay that I'd originally read in *The New York Times Magazine* in an anthology. "Congratulations!" I wrote him. "Hmm," he responded, "This is the first I've heard of this," and got his literary agent right on the tail of the anthology publisher and *The New York Times*.

If you hear about work which you originally sold for first serial rights appearing in a publication besides the one you dealt with originally, instead of leveling harsh accusations of theft, begin your inquiry with the knowledge that you're entitled to compensation for the reprint, and the assumption that it occurred inadvertently. For all you know, the editor of the second publication could have tried to send you a check and been unable to locate you. Large book publishers have employees who handle reprint requests as their sole job, but at magazines and newspapers such inquiries may fall between the cracks without any felonious intent. A polite, firm letter may get you results, but if not, see if you can arrange to have much the same message sent on the letterhead of a lawyer or a writers' organization.

In recent years, the scenario of unauthorized reprints on the Internet cropped up on such a wide scale that a number of writers undertook a lawsuit against *The New York Times*, the database service Lexis/Nexis and three other companies to seek redress and explicit rulings by the court that such appropriations were illegal.

OTHER TUSSLES WITH EDITORS

Ask a group of long-time freelance writers whether editors ever mistreat them, and you might have stories pouring into your ears for days. Besides botched or irrational rewrites and late pay, a common complaint is an assigned article disappearing into limbo. You submit it on time, and every so often when you ask the editor who requested it what happened with it, you learn that it's still sitting in the editor-in-chief's "in" pile. Or a newspaper or magazine that pays on publication says they like your piece and hope to publish it—and you wait, wait, wait, wait, wait, wait, wait. Unfortunately, you won't have much leverage in either situation. Complain too stridently and you'll get your manuscript back and have to start all over again elsewhere. "Sometimes I think publishers were put on this earth to teach us patience," says author Barbara Winter, who's experienced these sorts of frustration. The best course of action I can advise is pleasant persistence. Just keep checking in nicely to find out whether or not any new developments have occurred.

Naturally writers get distressed when articles get "killed"— rejected, especially when they feel they turned in a well-written piece that met the terms of the assignment or the go-ahead on speculation, and especially when the editor offers no explanation at all or baffling reasons for the rejection. If they invited you to submit or contracted with you for an article and then turned it down, they owe you something more specific than "Sorry, it just doesn't work for us." I'd call and ask for more information in a nonconfrontational way, such as "It would really help me out if you could be more specific about where I went wrong, or why the piece didn't match what you were looking for." But I wouldn't recommend arguing with their reasons. A decision is a decision.

I'll never forget one of my writing students holding up a negative response to his query and declaiming loudly, "This editor is stupid! He says my idea wouldn't work for *The Atlantic* because it's a local story, but I explained right here in the third paragraph how it was a national story. Can't he read?" This student failed to comprehend that, despite his argument, the editor had concluded otherwise and would not be swayed by a repetition of the unpersuasive evidence. In fact, years ago an

Atlantic editor told me that he had decided to compose vaguer rejection letters to forestall exactly this kind of tiresome and futile comeback.

Writers also sometimes grumble about unfair requests for updates. This occurs when an accepted piece gets held for a while, during which time something happens that renders your work inaccurate or incomplete. Or, a new editor comes on board and wants additional information inserted in an article you had been previously told was all set.

In either case you do have leverage when your work has been accepted and you've deposited the publication's check in your bank. Tell them that you'd be happy to provide supplemental copy for an additional fee, proportional to what you received originally. For example, if you passed in 2,500 words for $1,250, an extra sidebar or section of 500 words should earn you $250 more, particularly when it requires extra research. Fair's fair! Most editors won't argue with this request.

From the editor's point of view, however, misbehavior by writers has a way of mucking up the writer/editor relationship. Eavesdrop on a bunch of editors getting together and you might hear their gripes about writers go on and on. Elizabeth Hilts, senior editor of two weekly papers in Fairfield County, Connecticut, and Westchester County, New York, says she gets annoyed by writers who assume that editing is an easy job, and that an editor is a writer who couldn't make it. "Also, I have worked with, and continue to work with, some writers who consistently get all the right information, but put it together in a meandering, practically unreadable way. However, those writers rarely, if ever, complain about being edited heavily, and their research is usually so good I don't mind having to rework the piece." Nevertheless, when a writer goes so far as to refuse to make changes that she has requested, when given reasons why the changes were necessary, Hilts won't work with that writer again.

Similarly, Karen Thomas says she grits her teeth but puts up with some writers "who turn in sloppy copy—poorly phrased or replete with typos, misspellings, etcetera. I've had to remind a few that I don't take first drafts." She reached her limits of tolerance, though, with one fellow who tacked on voluminous and overly detailed footnotes at the end of his article that were

"distracting, unnecessary and unhelpful. He also wanted to see the finished article with my edits, which was fine, except that he proceeded to send me pages and pages of comments on what he agreed with and what he felt were unneeded. I took one look, noting the length and nitpicking quality of his comments and fired off a quick, polite and firm note that only where my edits changed accuracy would I make further changes. I won't be working with him again."

Like Thomas, Gary Goettling will put up with bad writing, rewriting it "because it is faster and easier to fix it myself." But for him, lazy writers fall beyond the pale. "I remember calling one to check on a person's job title, which didn't sound right to me. The writer gave me the guy's number and told me to call and get it. That fellow never wrote for me again." Also unforgivable in his eyes are writers who took on assignments despite knowing that they couldn't really handle the subject matter. "I couldn't trust those writers afterwards," he says. On the other hand, he praised freelancers who took extra time for background research that went beyond what was strictly necessary, who suggested questions and angles, and as he put it, "brought a lot of extra intelligence to the whole process."

Michael Romanello, editor of the *Observer*, a newspaper in Pittsburgh, Pennsylvania, told me that he won't stop doing business with a writer because of one screw-up, particularly with beginners, whom he'll often give an extra-early deadline so that there's breathing room in case of a late delivery. But repeated failures to meet deadlines, repeated factual errors and what he called "excessive prima donnaism" put a writer on his mental no-more-opportunities list. Trade magazine editor Amy Sitze also mentioned deadlines as a make-or-break issue with the writers she deals with. "When I give a writer five weeks to do a simple company profile (interviewing two people, writing 2,000 words), I don't expect the story one day past the deadline, I expect it on or before the deadline," she says. "I recently stopped working with a writer because he would consistently wait until the week before the story was due and then start making his calls to set up interviews. If the contact person happened to be on vacation, the story ended up two to three weeks late. His writing style was superb, but working with him was too much

of a hassle to make it worthwhile."

How can writers and editors best get along? Barb Freda writes regularly for a trade magazine on food, receiving assignments from an editor who always sends her articles to a food-specialist editor for approval of the content. Once Freda received one of her recipes back with a critical note attached from the food editor. "It implied that I didn't know what I was doing, and that sent me through the roof. I was a professional chef for ten years before going into writing. Soon I got a call from the food editor, apologizing for the misunderstanding and saying that she never doubted that the recipe worked. She had some legitimate points to make about the way the recipe was worded, and we parted on the friendliest of terms. It illustrates how easily feathers can be ruffled, and how little it can take—open direct communication—to smooth the feathers." I agree wholeheartedly with that sentiment. Try not to get your back up, and always look for constructive ways to settle disagreements.

Chapter Twelve

Building Your Freelance Writing Career

According to a recent survey of more than 1,200 writers by the National Writers Union, only 16 percent of full-time writers made more than $30,000 a year. By dividing the amount earned by the amount of time they reported spending on their writing, the surveyers calculated that these 1,200 writers made a median hourly wage of just $5.33. I don't tell you this to discourage you, only to make sure that you forge ahead understanding the economics of the territory of the freelance world. If you long to become a full-time freelance writer—one option among other honorable ones for writers—certain strategies will help you propel yourself into the ranks of those making enough for a car, a mortgage and occasional nights out. If you aim instead at making a publishing splash, or seeing your work enlighten and inform others, you can similarly profit from the wisdom of more experienced writers that I've collected here.

Don't expect to be able to plot out your future as in a formal business plan, however. Five years after first being published, few freelancers end up exactly where they had projected. Rotten luck, great luck and unforeseen opportunities are bound to crop up and combine for a path that would surprise, perhaps even shock, your earlier self. As you progress in the world of writing, you'll very likely adjust your preferences and ambitions, as well. But even if you do your work alone in your house, using no tool more dangerous than a telephone, you'll find yourself in for a rambunctious, exhilarating adventure. I guarantee that!

THE BOTTOM-UP STRATEGY

When I ask aspiring freelancers at a workshop whether they would rather hear about how to start from the bottom and work your way up or how to start at the top and work your way down, voices usually arise clamoring for each option.

The bottom-up strategy suits those who want to build up their confidence and skills before they approach big markets. Basically, it involves getting published somewhere, anywhere in order to collect clips, and then using those credentials to work up to assignments from ever more prestigious and better paying outlets.

K.D. Schutte of Hamilton, Ohio, describes her progress in freelancing as a gradual process of learning to spread her wings. When she was working as a proofreader for a daily paper, her hands shook the day she gathered the nerve to lay two book reviews she'd written on the desk of the editor. "These are good," the editor declared. "It's obvious you're a writer." After submitting book reviews, which made their way into the paper with only minor changes, Schutte ventured an article on a local woman who greenbroke horses, which was published as well. When that editor began calling her with assignments, Schutte felt she'd reached another milestone as a freelancer. "The confidence I gained from my writing spilled over into many other areas of my life"—and enabled her to keep moving ahead to the point where she now makes a living freelancing for local, regional and national publications, along with ghostwriting for various clients.

Similarly, one of the excited updates I've received from someone who'd taken several of my workshops came from Anne Fletcher Price, who filled me in on several recent coups. Price had taken a break from the novel she was completing when she spotted an ad in a local paper for a freelance writer. She rewrote an article on surviving breast cancer that she'd drafted a few years earlier and sent it in. *The Tab,* a Boston-area weekly, printed it and asked to see another article Price mentioned to the editor. Encouraged, Price called the editor of her hometown paper, the *Woburn Advocate,* to see if he had any interest in publishing the breast cancer article. He did, and requested two additional articles from her, publishing them during three

consecutive weeks. "I've just received my first check for a published article, made a copy for posterity, then cashed it. Now I really know I'm on my way," she said.

For Claire Tristram, a former sales manager at a computer company in California's Silicon Valley, the journey up from the bottom didn't take very long. Motorcycling on vacation in Death Valley, she had an accident that almost killed her and convinced her to make major changes in her life. "I wrote about the trip, received a really nice rejection letter from an editor at *Esquire*, and then quit my job," she says. Her first paid assignment ever, for a regional magazine, brought in 2½ cents a word for putting together its events calendar. Soon afterwards she received 10 cents a word from a regional business journal. Next, only three months after starting out, she started writing for *Open Computing* magazine at 75 cents a word, which soon rose to $1 a word. "When that magazine folded, it was the best thing that ever happened to me, because all the editors, whom I'd met, went to other magazines. From no contacts I had a lot of connections at different places." Two years after she launched her career, Tristram was averaging $1.56 a word in her magazine work and had a contract with a publisher for a book. "I think people overestimate how long you need to pay your dues," she says.

THE TOP-DOWN ROUTE

If grabbing the brass ring on your first or second try appeals to you, clues to this strategy have been sprinkled throughout the book. The key is coming up with a persuasive answer to this question: Why would an editor take a chance on you when you're unproven and inexperienced? Answers that work include the following:

1. Your unusual personal experience will interest readers.
2. The knowledge in your head puts you ahead of reporters with good research skills.
3. You have a unique slant in style or substance.
4. Because of who or where you are, you have insider access to a story they want.
5. You're the one who shows up at the right place and time.
6. You represent a low-risk option for acquiring content.

As I've already mentioned, I began my freelancing career with an essay in *The New York Times*. Looking back, I had four of the six factors above operating in my favor. Here's what happened. One day when I was getting ready to leave my job teaching at Smith College, I picked up the daily *New York Times*. For some unknown reason, my eye was drawn to the lower right-hand corner of page one, where a tiny notice announced that the *Times* was looking for advertisers for a new section on education scheduled for its first appearance in January. A little light bulb went off in my brain. If they're looking for advertisers they might be looking for articles, I thought, and education is a subject I have a lot to say about. In that pre-personal-computer era, I sat down at my typewriter and composed a query letter to the Education Editor of *The New York Times* offering to write an article for their upcoming new education supplement. Two days after I dropped the letter in the mailbox, I received a phone call inviting me to submit on speculation the piece I'd described. The Sunday *New York Times* published the piece I wrote in response to that invitation on January 4, 1981.

I didn't save a copy of my letter, but I remember the opening line running something like this: "In January I will be retiring from college teaching at the age of twenty-eight, and I'd like to write an article for your new educational supplement about what it has been like to be a professor, compared with the way I saw professors when I was a student." In that first sentence I accomplished several things. I promised an unusual story, since most aspiring professors hadn't finished their Ph.D. by age twenty-eight, let alone being ready to quit. I showed that the story would be told with style, since I didn't call it "quitting" but more provocatively, "retiring." And I had showed up at the right place and time. For their section debut, they did not have a huge stable of writers competing to gain entrance, hadn't reached the point of finalizing their lineup of contributors, and probably figured a new voice would add an excellent accent. Finally, I agreed to accept the risk of writing the piece on spec and got it in on time in good shape. They suggested only a few editorial changes, to which I consented.

Let's go back now through those six reasons and discuss them as practical strategies. Chapter two provided plenty of examples

of material magazines could get only from the mouth or the pen of those who had actually been through the experience. To pursue this route to breaking in at the top, case through your life's storehouse of experiences to single out the most noteworthy examples of things you've suffered or achieved that might offer a lesson of value to readers of a certain magazine or class of magazines. Then study the likely top markets and go after them. Much the same goes for reason number two, capitalizing on your insider's knowledge of, say, the real reasons for "pilot error," how kids benefit from day care, or five easy ways to fix your own PC. We talked about such possibilities in chapter three. Make a match between what you know and what readers of a specific magazine would enjoy learning, and the result could be checks and clips from major markets.

The unique slant of reason number three might take the form of fresh, clean humor, always in demand at most magazines. Or it might consist of your original writing style, an uplifting kind of passion or spark that the editor doesn't run across in the mail every day, particularly from the pros. If you believe something that runs counter to what most people are saying, you also can more readily rise above the pack. Alan Weiss, a management consultant in East Greenwich, Rhode Island, and author of *Our Emperors Have No Clothes*, has practically made a career out what he calls being "contrarian." When "total quality" was hot in corporate boardrooms, for instance, he wrote an opinion piece for *Training News* called "The Myth of Quality Circles." "They invited me to write a column that lasted for six years because of that iconoclastic article," Weiss recalls. Again, put your energy into the projects that will stand out at the top magazines, and over time that effort will pay off.

We talked about reason number four, taking advantage of your special access to people and events in the news, in chapters four and six. Have the confidence that because doors stand open to you that might slam in the faces of veteran reporters, you can seize an opportunity and run with it. Don't assume that because tens of thousands of people, of whom dozens must be freelance writers, are watching the same broadcasts or reading the same minor newspaper, others are rushing to their computers to dash out queries rivaling your idea to national periodicals. You may

be the only one on the ball.

As for reason number five, showing up at the right place and time, you can generate good luck by staying on the lookout for new publications, which haven't yet built up a stable of regular contributors. When Rick Friedman of Woburn, Massachusetts, went freelance after twenty-five years as an employed newspaper reporter and editor, he would scour the Sunday *Boston Globe* want ads for startup magazines and newspapers looking for staff writers. "I don't want you to hire me," he'd write the editor. "I'd prefer to write for you freelance. Here are some clips that show I can write on any subject, and have. I'll call about setting up a meeting for us to discuss story ideas." At least 10 percent of editors proved receptive to a meeting, Friedman says, and typically he'd walk out of the meeting with one or two firm initial assignments. Some of these contacts led to lucrative regular writing stints in areas like finance, technology and science that hadn't been strong suits for him before. Other ways to learn about new magazines include reading the trade magazines on publishing, like *Folio*, watching several newsstands closely, trading scuttlebutt with other writers and watching your so-called "junk mail" for premiere-issue solicitations.

Reason number six, presenting editors with a low-risk option might mean following in the path of writer Gregg Levoy, who broke into top magazines in his first year of freelancing by querying with ideas for newsbriefs, the 100- to 300-word items that usually appear in a section up front. The editor's risk was thereby lower than it would have been asking him to do a 2,000-word feature. Once editors got to know him, that often led to other things, Levoy says. I wouldn't recommend volunteering in a query to write on spec, but you should normally agree to it if the issue arises during a discussion with an editor tempted by your proposal but who expresses leeriness about your lack of clips. This likewise lets the editor test you out with minimal obligation.

Understanding what publications want and knowing how to write a compelling query letter increase your odds with all of the above strategies. However, keep in mind that you want to not only get a go-ahead from a magazine but also deliver an article that passes muster and that they buy and publish. As a

personal experience piece, my debut article for *The New York Times* didn't require any research or interviewing. Those skills I learned gradually over the next couple of years in articles for a local weekly paper. Judi Kesselman-Turkel won her first assignment ever from *Good Housekeeping*, but walked away from the experience with a kill fee rather than full payment and a clip. Years later, having become a nationally syndicated computer columnist, she wrote that what she had handed in was more like a term paper than a magazine piece. Chastened, she lowered her sights and aimed her next queries at less demanding markets. You wouldn't have to back down, though, if you had a teacher, writing coach or just a more experienced colleague on hand to talk you through the tangles of your first full-length assignment. Also, a journalism or freelance writing class can give you valuable practice researching and completing articles before you venture out soliciting top magazines.

FROM REJECTIONS TO RELATIONSHIPS

No matter how well you prepare, how gloriously you write, I promise that rejections will come your way. For survival in this business, you need the ability to withstand inevitable "no's." You also need to understand how, in a cordial and professional way, to turn rejections into stepping stones. This initially odd concept begins to make sense when you understand that editors turn down proposed articles for reasons that have nothing to do with the worth or relevance of your ideas, or with their assessment of your talents. They may just have assigned your topic to another writer, have covered something similar too recently, disliked a minor detail in your query or felt your suggestion was close to what they're looking for but just not striking enough to earn one of the very limited number of spaces in their publication. Consequently, when they say "no," you shouldn't interpret that as meaning, "Go away, you worthless turd." Instead, construe it as meaning simply, "We can't use your offer right now"— which sometimes is indeed what they tell you in the rejection letter. If it helps, compare yourself to baseball players, who know they'll strike out sometimes and hope for a batting average of .300 or better. They get more hits by orchestrating more chances at the plate, and so can you.

When an editor takes the time to add "Sorry" or "Try us again" to a form rejection letter, or writes you a letter from scratch explaining why they couldn't assign you the article, recognize that as an opportunity, not a calamity. Begin building a relationship by promptly sending along another idea, starting off with something like, "Thank you for your kind response to my previous query about _____. Here's another idea for your consideration." During my first few years of freelancing, I discovered that it might take as few as three such exchanges before the editor got to know me enough to call with the message, "We have to say no again, but we came up with something ourselves and we're looking for a writer on it. Are you interested?"

This happened to me early on with *New Woman*, the *Village Voice* and, almost, *Glamour*. Rona Cherry, executive editor of *Glamour*, called me to apologize for having to nix another query and added, "Why don't you come see me the next time you're in New York?" Grabbing my calendar, I flipped a few weeks ahead and seized some dates at random. "Gee, it so happens I'm going to be in the city February 20 and 21. Do you have any time then?" When I hung up the phone I had an appointment to stop by and discuss story ideas at the office of *Glamour*.

I've had what I call story conferences close to a dozen times since with various editors, and almost always they came about after an initial dance of rejections. Exchanges of "Would you like . . . ?" and "Not quite right for us" seem to function like small talk in the elevator with an appealing stranger who works elsewhere in the building. Each side gets to check the other side out, and if favorable impressions deepen, the editor gains confidence in the writer and issues or accepts an invitation. In the two cases I can remember where I went in to talk over ideas with an editor without having experienced this kind of dance in rejection letters, some other kind of informal contact had given us the chance to sniff each other out.

In a pattern that startled me at first, a story conference would typically begin with me suggesting idea after idea that the editor shot down. Rather than being kicked out when I reached the end of my prepared list, I'd then have a wandering conversation

with the editor during which some new idea surfaced, for which I got an assignment. This can happen only after you've established a bond of trust, I believe. In the sequence I experienced time after time, the trust came about because of clips and credentials that the editor saw, the persistence and interests that emerged in the series of query letters, and the personal rapport that developed during the in-person session.

By developing relationships with editors, you cut down on unremunerated marketing time immensely. Several highly paid freelance journalists told me they rarely write query letters any more. Some just pick up the phone and run possibilities by editors they're tight with until they get their next OK. Others say editors regularly call them with a set topic for their next assignment.

If you hope to build a flourishing freelance career, you must have the long-term picture in mind from your very first assignment. The trust I just spoke of compounds when editors know they can count on you for clean, well-researched copy on time in a style that works for their publication. "With most of the magazines I work for, it's a question not of will I do another story, but what will I do next," says Brooklyn-based journalist Ann Monroe. "I know how to get to the nub of a story, figure it out and write it up intelligently and clearly. And I always, always file on time. I get the feeling that I'm among the more reliable people at most of the magazines I work for. One editor told me about a writer who had done one story for them, and then had been in touch with them all along on the second, but at the last minute said he was sick and just dropped the whole thing. I can't understand someone doing that."

PART-TIME OR FULL-TIME?

When it comes to determining the ideal place of freelance writing in your work life, many alternatives exist beyond the two obvious ones of part-time or full-time. Perhaps you'll be happiest making only occasional forays of writing articles for publication and pay. A psychotherapist I know was thrilled to sell a self-help piece to a bridal magazine, then told me a year later when I asked her "What's next?" that she'd realized she wanted to devote all her energy to her primary career. Similarly, a school

reformer who had worked very hard to get some op-ed pieces published told me, when I hadn't seen him for quite a while, that those articles had satisfied him and he'd stopped writing and sending around editorials. "I have other creative outlets," he said. "And I'm enjoying playing with my grandchildren."

But if the writing bug has bitten you badly, your first byline will probably only increase your itch for more. Some writers told me that they couldn't wait to rev up their publication successes to the point where they could quit the "real job" they love much less. Here financial factors, access to health benefits, your family situation and your own attitude toward risk and entrepreneurship will undoubtedly swirl around amidst your strategizing. "I'm a part-time freelancer with a full-time job," says Kathy Beaver, a mother of four in Northern Virginia. "I find writing interesting and easy money compared to my day job. I can write anytime, anywhere and still be accessible to my family. But unfortunately, I'm not much of a businessperson or marketeer for my work. To go full-time with my writing I would need to become aggressive in marketing and in my writing, and I'm not ready for that in my life."

Another key consideration in finding your optimal proportion of freelancing is whether or not you can do justice to the writing assignments you enjoy while also fulfilling your responsibilities to an employer. Jack Germain, who writes for numerous computer magazines and also teaches English and journalism at a high school, hasn't found this a problem. "It seems that I am always working, but my deadlines are flexible enough that I can teach, get my writing assignments done and still be looking for choice new outlets for my work," he says.

But the scheduling freedom that accompanies being a full-time freelancer served as a decisive factor in R.G. Schmidt's retirement from working for a utility company in order to spend more than part-time on his writing. "In the outdoor field, which makes up 75 percent of my writing, photos to accompany a story are an absolute must. Now I can take off any time I choose to ram around Florida or the southeastern U.S. for photos. There's just no way I could do that before with a day here, three days there. Same thing with my op-ed column. Now with plenty of time for research, fact verification, I can tackle allegations about

public figures, which I formerly had to let slide, as I didn't have the time to research them thoroughly." On the down side, Schmidt noted an increased pressure to sell that accompanied his switch to full-time writing.

Toronto journalist and photographer Jack Kohane decided to try for an opposite move, however—from full-time freelance to full-time employment. As he neared a decade out on his own, he began to want to belong to a news organization. "Working freelance means you're outside the loop of regular day-to-day happenings at the media you're always striving to reach," he says. "A freelancer must work hard to build up rapport and confidence with an editor, but if that editor then leaves, you have to begin the process over again with a new person, who often brings the work in-house. Over the years, many of my markets have dried up. I decided to get a journalism degree as my best hope of landing a full-time journalism job." Other writers told me that employment lured them away from freelancing because they wanted a respite from juggling deadlines and hustling to collect money, or because a magazine they often wrote for made a job offer they couldn't refuse.

Whatever your situation and longings, keep in mind that with solid writing skills and experience, you're rarely locked in forever to the part-time/full-time situation you have now. I realized a few years into my freedom as a full-time writer that, while I enjoyed not having to report regularly to a boss, the isolation of staying home all day most days writing bothered me. Leavening writing with teaching adult-education classes and coaching other writers felt better. Once in a while, when my finances got dicey, I'd teach English composition part-time at some nearby college. Unlike conventional employers, editors and publishers don't look down on writers who zigzag in and out of freelancing. They may have that kind of history themselves! In 1996 I enjoyed seeing three editors I had formerly written for hit the best-seller list with their books—Thulani Davis, once editor of the *Village Voice* with the novel *Maker of Saints*; Jonathan Harr, once editor of the *Valley Advocate* with his nonfiction work *A Civil Action*; and Dan Goleman, once editor at *Psychology Today* with his *Emotional Intelligence*.

SHOULD YOU SPECIALIZE?

Many writers in the $30,000-a-year-or-more category told me that having a specialty makes it much easier to keep the article checks streaming in. "A specialty gets you into a smaller club," says Catherine Dold of Boulder, Colorado, who concentrates on environmental and health topics. "You get to know the people in the field, and particularly where science is concerned, editors perceive that if you're not scared of that kind of stuff, you must be good at reporting it. Also, I find it easier to come up with ideas because I specialize. I know where to cruise around on the Internet to see what people are talking about, what are the issues with the big environmental groups, and what to listen for on the news. I'd hate to have to pluck ideas out of thin air."

With specializing comes credibility, adds Joanne Cleaver, who focuses on business reporting and family travel. "When I tell editors that I've written for *Crain's Chicago Business* every week for fifteen years, it impresses the hell out of them. 'Wow—fifteen years': their tone of voice changes," she says. "They tell me it's hard to find people who understand business and have a track record as a writer. I'm not a name-brand writer, but after I wrote for *Small Business Computing*, the editor there referred me to another editor, who in turn referred me to someone else. I get tons of assignments by phone, and the cash flow is pretty good."

But to Kurt Repanshek, a former Associated Press reporter now hustling on his own, specializing doesn't offer enough opportunity for someone who has to cobble together a decent living quickly. "It takes too long to gain a reputation as a specialist, one who can command big bucks per article," he says. "You could starve before that happens. When I left a secure job with the AP I had to take just about any assignment so I could pay my bills. I had figured my fourteen-year career with the AP would open doors to magazine assignments, but it didn't. A few years later, my articles range from travel to business to ski industry to public lands to general assignment items for a major metropolitan paper. While some of my clients pay a buck a word plus expenses, most are in the 25-to-50-cents per word category. That's not great, but if you pack enough of them together while continuing to crack the major markets, you can get by."

For Ann Monroe, who spent fifteen years in finance writing,

sticking to one field represents a trap she is trying mightily to wriggle out of. "Finance isn't what I care about in my personal life," she says. "Because it paid more than other specialties, I went after a job at a financial newsletter which had such a high turnover it would hire anyone who could breathe. I learned on the job there, then worked for *The Wall Street Journal* for four and a half years as a corporate finance reporter, then left to freelance. Now I'd like to be more visible, to get my work into magazines on the newsstand." Monroe finds querying a trial after having finance editors who know her calling her to suggest assignments. But she is slowly piling up nonbusiness credits.

Yet Los Angeles-based Lydia Boyle hasn't had much trouble switching specialties four times during her thirty-year career as a sometimes employed, sometimes freelance journalist. In her early twenties she focused on fashion and beauty when she wrote for a small beauty magazine a friend of her father had invested in. In the late 1970s, the handicraft field flourished, and she wrote on weaving, knitting, quilting and similar hobbies she had long taken an interest in. By the 1980s, though, women had turned their attention to health and fitness, and Boyle followed suit. A transition to celebrity and entertainment journalism came about after Boyle got to know a lot of stars who figured in fitness stories she was working on. Throughout the Menendez and Simpson trials, she milked her Hollywood contacts as an off-camera researcher for *Prime Time Live*, *NBC Nightly News* and *Dateline NBC*, as well as for print media. Finally she decided to move into the field of true crime. "Things go out of fashion," she says. "The amount of work in a specialty can dry up. Unless you flow with the tide you won't be able to continue making a good living. I could never have switched to sports, though. I chose my specialties according to what I knew about and cared about."

LAUNCHING A COLUMN

Do you dream of following in the footsteps of nationally syndicated columnists Abigail Van Buren, Dave Barry, Ellen Goodman or Bob Greene? *Writer's Market* lists more than fifty syndicates that distribute bylined columns like clockwork to newspapers and magazines around the world. But as in many

arenas involving fame, a catch stands in the way of budding columnists: unless you already have a huge readership, syndicates are unlikely to take you on. Jim Pawlak of Rochester Hills, Michigan, conceived a column called "Career Moves" and launched it in the *Detroit Free Press*, one of the fifteen largest newspapers in the United States. All the syndicates he contacted rejected the concept. "They're like banks that only want to lend money to people who already have it," Pawlak says. "I can only imagine how much more daunting it would be for someone who did not have their column running in any major paper."

Pawlak did not give up, however. While continuing to publish his weekly 650 words in the *Detroit Free Press*, he mailed solicitation packets on his own to business editors at the top 153 metropolitan newspapers, and called each to follow up. This strategy, called self-syndication, yielded a second customer for his column only after his three-hundredth telephone call. Almost four years after he established the column, he had 28 papers lined up, and received an average of $40 a week per paper. It takes him about one day a week to write his column, which might highlight a success story, present job-search strategies, review a book or answer reader questions, and another two-thirds of a day each week to handle the paperwork of self-syndication and deal with the 100 to 150 letters that he receives from readers. The feedback he receives, including a lot of "thank-you" notes, is part of the satisfaction Pawlak takes in the column.

Alabama writer Barbara Pleasant tried the self-syndication route as well, and managed to line up a few papers here and there for a weekly question-and-answer column on gardening. She decided that the paperwork, like creating and mailing invoices and duplicating articles, outweighed the remuneration, though, and dropped all the customers except her local paper, the Huntsville *Times*. Pleasant had pursued the *Times* for years and was delighted when a new editor finally okayed her column. It takes her less than an hour each week to take reader questions, jazz them up to make them more entertaining, answer them and send them off. She encourages other writers to propose a column to their local paper.

"Editors love columns in all kinds of fields from someone local who is a professional writer, who gives them copy at the

right length that they can plug into the paper without even read-ing it," she says. "That's exactly why self-syndication didn't work well for me outside of my area. Editors know that if readers want national stuff they'll watch TV and read *USA Today*."

MOVING ON TO BOOKS

Like many freelancers, you might discover that writing short pieces naturally leads you to the ultimate long piece—a book. Perhaps you collected much too much material to fit into a few articles. Maybe you yearn to write something that lasts a little longer than the newsstand shelf time. Or as happened to soft-ware engineer Steve Heller, a book editor might get in touch after reading an article of yours he liked. Heller was gratified to receive a letter from an editor at Academic Press who praised an article of his in *Dr. Dobb's Journal*, a computer magazine, and asked if he'd be interested in writing a book. "Sure, why not?" Heller replied, and completed three, not one, computer books for that publisher within four years. "When I write a book I have virtually total control over the content," he says. "And as far as I can determine, it's more feasible to make a living writing books than writing articles." With books, sales and hence income can go on and on for years, while with articles the fee is the fee, Heller explains.

Joanne Cleaver and a few other veteran freelancers I spoke with pointed out, though, that hardly any book writers receive $1.50 or more per word, making magazine work the more lucra-tive pursuit. Nevertheless, her four books, and especially one called *Doing Children's Museums*, have attracted requests for magazine excerpts and assignments from editors that represent almost effortless additional income. "I just cannot drive a stake through the heart of my children's museums book," Cleaver says. It started with a 1984 feature story on the Chicago Children's Museum, after which she soon published half a dozen spinoff stories with other angles in different magazines. Seven years after her book on the subject, with a national scope, ap-peared, *Parents Magazine* called to ask if she would give them 500 words on the topic. "This happened more times than I can count. My best hit was *Family Fun* asking me to put together parts of different chapters into an article. It took me an hour

and a half and I got $900," she says.

For me, book writing has proved such a pleasure that I haven't had time for much magazine work in the last few years. I like the long, single deadline and being able to concentrate on a project where an equivalent to kill fees is practically unknown. The book editors I've worked with have rarely imposed some agenda contrary to mine, as happened a tad too often for my liking with magazines. I've also enjoyed the spinoff income opportunities like public speaking and consulting that authorship makes possible. More than a decade of intensive work for newspapers and magazines gave me a solid foundation of skills so that I could complete a full-length book efficiently, cleanly and responsibly. Yet I found three significant differences between magazine and book writing that I wasn't quite prepared for during several of my first few rounds with book proposals.

First, a book isn't really a 3,000-word article expanded 25 times and divided into chapters. Unless you have a sturdy organizational structure for a book from the outset, the huge scale of research necessary to fill up that much space will bury you. My first book, a project assigned by a publisher I worked for in China, presented writing challenges that, despite the dozens of articles I'd completed up to then, nearly stumped me. Second, with magazine and newspaper work, the editor looking at your proposals considers mainly, "Can this person do the job?" With books, the editor also ponders, "Is this person a promotable authority?" As a freelance writer, you might be trusted with almost any subject you can responsibly report. But to publish a book on, say, health or finance or car mechanics, you usually need non-journalistic credentials in those fields. Third, magazine and newspaper editors commission articles that they believe their readers will enjoy and benefit from. But they don't ask you to convince them that your article will increase subscription rates or sell more copies of that issue from the newsstand. For books, whether or not editors believe people will go out and purchase your volume often seals or ruins the deal.

OTHER BUSINESS-BUILDING TIPS

A few other strategies help to move you out of the starving-artist category into the ranks of those who can afford to relax about

their income. One crucial underpinning of financial success in freelancing is simply thinking of yourself as carrying on a business. Taking this step means that, in addition to the pleasure you take in writing, you understand yourself as being in the business of supplying publishers with content that enables them in turn to satisfy their subscribers, advertisers and investors with a coherent, appealing, profitable publication. As a businessperson you have every right to engage in practices common in business the world over, such as negotiating, holding the other side to payment promises, maximizing your income and protecting your intellectual property from exploitation. I don't say this to encourage you to become a rapacious cutthroat in your dealings with magazines (which wouldn't go over well in any case), but because I so often hear writers ask in a timid voice whether it could maybe possibly be okay to ask for a little raise in pay after seven years. Once you've proved your value to editors, asking for more does you no harm. And as someone running a business, you should devote some thought to ways to reduce your risks, lower your ratio of effort to payoff and maximize your income from each project.

Diversification keeps at bay the disastrous possibility of depending too much on one source of work or one type of writing. Establishing yourself as indispensable to just one or two periodicals leaves you vulnerable if those one or two periodicals go bankrupt, get sold or undergo major policy or personnel changes. As grandparents and schoolteachers would put it, don't put all your eggs in one basket. The same applies to overly narrow specialization. Although computer magazines now pay extremely well, if the computer industry went into a tailspin and you'd never written about anything except computers, it might take you a while to make new contacts, collect new credentials and restabilize your income.

Even from this hardnosed business perspective, don't focus too much on the amount of pay per article. Four thousand dollars may sound unbelievably lucrative for a magazine article, but if it requires three months of in-depth research and one month of rewriting, you wouldn't be faring so well financially. More relevant than how much the work pays is the relationship of the compensation offered to the amount of effort required to do the

job. Four hundred dollars for an article you can whip off in two hours is far more profitable than four thousand for that investigative piece that takes you five hundred hours to complete. Of course, if the investigative piece enables you to contribute to world peace or justice, or to resolve a quandary that has troubled you for decades, certainly take that into account in planning how to distribute your writing time and effort.

Sometimes writers have a low effort-to-payoff ratio not because their work really demands so much time and hair-pulling, but because they over-research, write much too much so that they then have to cut, or dawdle around the house for days at a time instead of writing. Those with perfectionist tendencies that keep them polishing way beyond any noticeable improvements may similarly be holding back their overall earnings. These problems have cures; see David Fryxell's *How to Write Fast (While Writing Well)*; my audiotape, "Become a More Productive Writer"; or Neil Fiore's *The Now Habit*, all listed in the Resources section, pp. 196-197.

From a business point of view, you'll make more with less exertion if you make it a habit to recycle your research and resell your articles. The former means that every time before you file away your notes for a completed assignment, you ask yourself whether any facts and insights that you turned up suggest another article with a different angle for a different audience. A habit of reselling means that whenever you receive copies of just-published work to which you've sold first serial rights, you send your fingers walking through *Writer's Market* in search of publications that buy second serial or reprint rights (see chapter seven). Some writers I know confess that they fail at this process because after they wrap up an assignment, they can't bear the thought of revisiting old territory. They'd rather chase after the next challenge. I can't come down too hard on such people, because I fall into this category myself!

In addition, writers, like other successful businesspeople, must stay attuned to developments in their industry. You can satisfy that imperative by joining writers' organizations, attending events for writers, reading magazines that cover publishing and participating in online interchanges with experienced writers. You will never outgrow this need. When I speak at writers'

conferences, I usually take away as much new information from the others as I've given—especially fresh perspectives and anecdotes from editors and ideas from writers whose focus and strategies differ from mine.

Finally, keep it all in perspective by remembering the values and goals that matter most to you and that can make writing a source of vitality and satisfaction for you, not a drain or an unending chore.

Former veterinarian Brad Swift was initially pleased early in his freelancing career when an editor at *USAir Magazine* who had liked his queries called to ask him if he'd do articles on topics like trends in office suites. "I kept saying 'yes' even though each topic was progressively less interesting to me. My writing suffered, and they told me the pieces were flat. I realized that I have to be enthusiastic or passionate about a subject to come up with a winner," he says. Swift then came up with something he calls Project Purpose—a goal of publishing at least one hundred articles about people whose lives are dedicated to a bold and inspiring purpose.

Since I keep seeing Swift's byline in magazines that I subscribe to, I know that his project excites editors as much as it continues to propel his career forward. "When you write about what you really care about," he says, "it comes through in the query letter so that editors know they'll get what they're willing to pay for. Through my articles, I'm able to encourage people to pursue what turns them on. And when thousands of people read those articles, I'm making a much bigger contribution to the world than I was as a vet cleaning their dogs' ears."

Resources

RECOMMENDED BOOKS AND OTHER RESOURCES

Resources on Style

Cheney, Theodore A. Rees, *Getting the Words Right: How to Rewrite, Edit and Revise*. Cincinnati, Writer's Digest Books, 1983. Worth reading and rereading to absorb lessons on self-editing from a master wordsmith.

Lauchman, Richard, *Plain Style: Techniques for Simple, Concise, Emphatic Business Writing*. New York, Amacom, 1993. A first-rate tutorial in crafting vigorous prose.

Paulos, John Allen, *A Mathematician Reads the Newspaper*. New York, Anchor Books, 1995. This provocative commentary on journalistic pitfalls and fallacies from an expert in quantitative reasoning can get you thinking about how to use numbers and statistics responsibly in your work.

Queneau, Raymond, *Exercises in Style*. New York, New Directions, 1981. One of the most amazing books I've ever encountered: French virtuoso Queneau tells the same anecdote in ninety-nine writing styles, for which translator Barbara Wright managed to find English equivalents. Study it for inspiration on different voices you might try out in your writing.

Strunk, William, Jr., and E.B. White, *The Elements of Style*, third edition. Needham Heights, MA, Allyn & Bacon, 1979. Avoid muddy prose by reading and rereading this classic guide to clear and concise writing.

Waddell, Marie L., Robert M. Esch and Roberta R. Walker, *The Art of Styling Sentences: 20 Patterns for Success*, third edition. Hauppauge, NY, Barron's, 1993. A superb reference for any sentence self-improvement program.

The Inner Writer

Ballenger, Bruce and Barry Lane, *Discovering the Writer Within: 40 Days to More Imaginative Writing*. Cincinnati, OH, Writer's Digest Books, 1989. Substantive, informative, entertaining exercises to get that pen or computer keyboard moving.

Cameron, Julia, *The Artist's Way: A Spiritual Path to Higher Creativity*. New York, Putnam, 1992. This popular book offers a twelve-week program for getting you into the habit of writing, along the way coaxing you past common blocks and obstacles.

Cook, Marshall J., *Freeing Your Creativity: A Writer's Guide*. Cincinnati, OH, Writer's Digest Books, 1992. Filled with genial anecdotes and suggestions for gearing up to do your best writing.

Fiore, Neil, Ph.D., *The Now Habit*. Los Angeles, Jeremy Tarcher, 1989. A psychologist's sensible recommendations for overcoming procrastination and getting things done—important for freelance writers.

Fryxell, David, *How to Write Fast (While Writing Well)*. Cincinnati, OH, Writer's Digest Books, 1992. Unless the very words "discipline" and "organization" make you choke, you'll find lots of smart suggestions here for getting more writing done in less time.

Goldberg, Natalie, *Writing Down the Bones: Freeing the Writer Within*. Boston, Shambhala, 1986. A Zen-inspired guide to unlearning your way to freer, truer writing.

Keyes, Ralph, *The Courage to Write*. New York, Henry Holt, 1995. If you think taking a look at writers' dark sides—terror, jealousy, revenge, eccentricities—might help, this is the book for you.

Lamott, Anne, *Bird by Bird: Some Instructions on Writing and Life*. New York, Anchor Books, 1994. Reading this book is like having a funny, wise, unfailingly honest writing friend on the line. Save it for when you most need encouragement, inspiration or perspective on the writer's life.

Shaughnessy, Susan, *Walking on Alligators: A Book of Meditations for Writers*. San Francisco, HarperSanFrancisco, 1993. Written to be read in one-page chunks; each passage has a quote from a well-known writer, a discussion of the theme raised therein and an affirmation for the day.

Ueland, Brenda, *If You Want to Write: A Book About Art, Independence and Spirit*. St. Paul, MN, Graywolf Press, 1987.

A spirited pep talk for writers, as relevant today as when first published in 1938.

Wycoff, Joyce, *Mindmapping: Your Personal Guide to Exploring Creativity & Problem-Solving.* New York, Berkley, 1991. A fast course in a popular method of visual outlining.

Yudkin, Marcia, *Become a More Productive Writer.* P.O. Box 1310, Boston, MA 02117, 1992. Sixty-minute audiotape explaining how to get good pages piling up on your desk by balancing discipline with inspiration. Includes self-awareness exercises.

Market Guides

Bacon's: Newspaper/Magazine Directory. Chicago, Bacon's Information, Inc., annual. A good number of libraries contain this directory, designed mainly for public relations purposes. Use it as a supplement to *Writer's Market* for specialized publications, or to look up section editors of newspapers in the United States and Canada.

Gale Directory of Publications and Broadcast Media. Detroit, Gale Research Co., annual. Most libraries carry these volumes, whose listings contain minimal information for writers beyond a publication's contact information and name of the editor.

The International Directory of Little Magazines & Small Presses. Paradise, CA, Dustbooks, annual. Hundreds of offbeat paying markets, with submission information and fees, along with listings of specialized and small book publishers.

Literary Market Place. New York, R.R. Bowker, annual. Mostly, a reference for the world of book publishing, but it does contain comprehensive, up-to-date listings for writers' conferences, fellowships and grants, writing contests and writers' organizations.

Standard Rate & Data Service. Skokie, IL, Standard Rate & Data Service. This company publishes several periodical volumes that provide information targeted to potential advertisers, including a magazine's focus, circulation, ad rates, contact information and editors. Good though expensive resource for finding specialty publications; try borrowing copies from a public relations or advertising agency.

Travel Marketing Sources. 5337 College Ave., Suite 258, Oakland, CA 94618, annually updated. The Compilation on disk for IBMs or Macs of almost 600 magazines and 200 newspaper sections that buy travel articles from freelancers. Also available from the same publisher: editorial calendars for almost four dozen publications—who's planning to use what kind of travel piece when.

Writers' and Artists' Yearbook. London, A&C Black, Ltd., annual. The British equivalent to *Writer's Market,* including 100 pages on newspapers and magazines in the United Kingdom, New Zealand, Australia, Canada and South Africa, along with many more resources for the serious writer.

The Writer's Handbook. Boston, The Writer, Inc., annual. Briefer market listings and many fewer than *Writer's Market;* contains many more instructional articles, though.

Writer's Market. Cincinnati, Writer's Digest Books, annual. If you can buy only one more book to help you get published, make this the one. Half the volume profiles thousands of paying magazines you have probably never heard of, with just about all the information for each you'd need to send off a query and know what to expect in response time, pay, rights purchased and much more. You can buy the searchable CD-ROM version in addition to or instead of the book version.

Periodicals

Byline. P.O. Box 130596, Edmond, OK 73013-0001; phone and fax (405) 348-5591; e-mail Bylinemp@aol.com. Monthly magazine containing inspirational and practical articles for new writers.

Folio. P.O. Box 4949, Stamford, CT 06907-0949; phone (203) 358-9900; fax (203) 357-9014. The trade magazine for those who publish magazines, this can clue you in to the inside scoop on new, projected and in-trouble magazines. Look for it at a good business library.

Freelance Success: The Marketing and Management Guide for Experienced Journalists. 801 NE 70th St., Miami, FL

33138-5713; (305) 757-8854; fax (305) 757-8857; e-mail 102627.3467@compuserve.com. Subscribers get this newsletter weekly by e-mail or monthly by old-fashioned mail. The sample issues I saw included specialized how-to articles, portraits of high-paying markets, resources for writers and short items about changes in the magazine and newspaper world. Expensive but valuable.

New Writer's Magazine. P.O. Box 5976, Sarasota, FL 34277-5976; (941) 953-7903. Bimonthly magazine offering features, columns, stories and poems that orient you to the opportunities and realities of the writing world.

Poets & Writers Magazine. 72 Spring St., 3rd floor, New York, NY 10012; phone (212) 226-3586; fax (212) 226-3963. If you have literary as well as journalistic leanings, you can learn a lot about the writing life and publishing realities from this especially well-written publication. Includes listings of small magazines and anthologies seeking submissions.

Travelwriter Marketletter. The Waldorf Astoria, 301 Park Ave., Suite 1850, New York, NY 10022. Monthly. Indispensable for travel writers, helpful for others. Packed with details on upcoming press trips, thumbnail book reviews, announcements of interest to travel writers and a whopping average of fifty-five updates or mini-profiles on markets for travel pieces per issue.

Utne Reader. 1624 Harmon Place, Suite 330, Minneapolis, MN 55403; http://www.utne.com. Designed for readers more than for writers, but this *Reader's Digest* for the Hip Crowd can alert you to unorthodox, obscure publications that may welcome equally unorthodox work.

The Writer. 120 Boylston St., Boston, MA 02116-4615; phone (617) 423-3157; fax (617) 423-2168. Monthly magazine with articles on fiction and nonfiction writing, market profiles and prize competitions open to writers.

Writer's Digest. 1507 Dana Ave., Cincinnati, OH 45207; phone (513) 531-2222; fax (513) 531-1843. If this magazine sold lifetime subscriptions, I'd buy one. Each monthly issue contains

money-making writing tips and advice, market listings, resources and perspective for both new and experienced writers.

Approaching Editors

Beckwith, Barbara and Barbara Mende, *From Idea to Article: Twelve Freelancers Tell How They Broke Into Smithsonian, Cosmopolitan, The New York Times and Other Major Publications*. National Writers Union, Boston Local, P.O. Box 381073, Harvard Square Station, Cambridge, MA 02238, 1996. Twelve charming case studies explaining step by step how these writers won the interest of an editor, wrote an acceptable article and worked with the editor to produce the final published version.

Cool, Lisa Collier, *How to Write Irresistible Query Letters*. Cincinnati, Writer's Digest Books, 1987. Extensive tips on transforming a so-so article idea into a tantalizing query letter, along with more than a dozen successful samples.

Gage, Diane and Marcia Coppess, *Get Published: 100 Top Magazine Editors Tell You How*. New York, Henry Holt, 1994. Primarily this book presents needs, readership, payment and preferences of big glossy magazines like *Ladies' Home Journal* and *Popular Science*. Periodically revised; don't rely on its specifics if the revision date is more than two years ago.

Mandell, Judy, *Magazine Editors Talk to Writers*. New York, John Wiley & Sons, 1996. An outstanding resource revealing how editors think and the pressures under which they work. *Q & A* format, with outstanding *Q*'s and illuminating *A*'s from editors at magazines ranging from *Redbook* and *Parade* to *AutoWeek* and *Arthritis Today*.

Special-Interest Writing

Hartford Courant staff, *The Straight Scoop: An Expert Guide to Great Community Journalism*. Hartford, Connecticut, *The Hartford Courant*, 1996. Excellent compendium of articles on basic and specialized skills of newspaper reporting, from using Freedom of Information laws to covering banks, utilities and schools.

Murray, John A., *The Sierra Club Nature Writing Handbook.* San Francisco, Sierra Club Books, 1995. Nice introduction to getting your love of the outdoors down on paper, though it's geared more to those who aim to follow in the footsteps of Annie Dillard and Edward Abbey than those who hope to sell to *Outside, National Wildlife* or *Florida Sportsman.*

O'Neil, L. Peat, *Travel Writing: A Guide to Research, Writing and Selling.* Cincinnati, Writer's Digest Books, 1996. Useful overview of the field of travel writing; especially good ideas on keeping a travel journal.

Trillin, Calvin, *Deadline Poet: My Life as a Doggerelist.* New York, Warner, 1994. "Could there be anyone else who was inspired to write poetry by the presence of John Sununu?" So begins this hilarious account of Trillin's stint as a poetry columnist for *The Nation.* Probably there couldn't be space in this genre for anyone else, but this book might inspire you to create your own category of freelancing.

Whitman, Joan and Dolores Simon, *Recipes into Type: A Handbook for Cookbook Writers and Editors.* New York, HarperCollins, 1993. So you want to be a food writer? Get this book to learn the excruciatingly detailed do's and don'ts of publishable recipe writing.

Important Reference Resources

The Associated Press Stylebook and Libel Manual, 6th trade edition. Reading, MA, Addison-Wesley, 1996. From "a, an" through "ZIP codes," includes the AP's suggestions for proper capitalization, abbreviations, spelling and word use. The primer on libel can help you understand your obligations and liabilities with respect to what you state in print.

Berkman, Robert I., *Find it Fast: How to Uncover Expert Information on Any Subject,* third edition. New York, HarperCollins, 1994. Even better than its profiles of sources for researching specialized information are this book's sample searches and tips on research strategies.

Encyclopedia of Associations. Detroit, Gale Research Inc.,

annual. This guide to more than 20,000 organizations, from the Aaron Burr Association to the ZZ Top International Fan Club, serves as an invaluable source of leads on experts to interview.

Grammar Hotline Directory. Annually updated guide to numbers and hours of telephone hotlines that answer questions like "Should it be 'who' or 'whom'?" "Militant" or "combative"? Available by sending a self-addressed stamped envelope to: Writing Center Grammar Hotline Directory, Tidewater Community College, 1700 College Crescent, Virginia Beach, VA 23456.

ProfNet. An organization that forwards queries from journalists seeking academic experts by e-mail three times daily to public information officers at more than 900 institutions, mainly colleges and universities. For information, call (800) 776-3638, fax (516) 689-1425 or send e-mail to profnet@profnet.com.

Urdang, Laurence, Nancy Laroche and J.I. Rodale, *The Synonym Finder*. New York, Warner, 1991. More contemporary and comprehensive than any *Roget's Thesaurus* I've seen. Belongs on every writer's bookshelf beside the dictionary.

Venolia, Jan, *Rewrite Right! How to Revise Your Way to Better Writing*. Berkeley, Ten Speed Press, 1987. A sprightly, useful handbook to turn to when you need help on dilemmas like, "i.e." or "e.g."? comma or semicolon? "Vice-President" or "vice-president"? Also explains the process of editing and how to avoid sexist prose.

Yearbook of Experts, Authorities & Spokespersons. Washington, DC, Broadcast Interview Source, annual. Call (202) 333-4904 or visit http://www.yearbooknews.com on the World Wide Web for a directory of more than 1,500 well-categorized organizations and individuals eager to speak to the media on their special area of interest.

The Business of Writing

Copyright Basics. Washington, DC, Library of Congress. Well-organized, clearly written explanation of the who, what, when, where and how much of copyright protection for your work.

Available free by calling (202) 707-9100 or visiting http://lcweb. loc.gov/copyright on the World Wide Web.

Crawford, Tad and Tony Lyons, *The Writer's Legal Guide,* revised edition. New York, Allworth Press, 1996. Comprehensive, readable, electronic-era guide to legal issues affecting writers, including copyright, contracts, rights, taxes, wills, the Freedom of Information Act, privacy issues and libel. Highly recommended.

Fishman, Stephen, *The Copyright Handbook: How to Protect and Use Written Works,* third edition. Berkeley, Nolo Press, 1996. If you already have a grip on the basics of copyright and want to look up a particular question, this is a handy resource. If you don't understand the concept of intellectual property rights, the Crawford and Lyons book, above, or the free pamphlet from the Library of Congress, also above, provide a better starting point. Includes actual forms for copyrighting material.

National Writers Union, *Guide to Freelance Rates & Standard Practice.* National Writers Union, 113 University Pl., 6th Floor, New York, NY 10003, 1995. Eye-opening, empowering reference on existing and optimal working conditions and pay for journalistic, technical, academic, literary and other kinds of writers. Includes discussion of collaboration, contracts, censorshop and electronic rights.

Winter, Barbara J., *Making a Living Without a Job.* New York, Bantam, 1993. As a freelance writer, you're inevitably an entrepreneur. This guide to thriving while "joyfully jobless" will help you tune into hidden business assets and find original ways to multiply your income streams.

Tax Guide for College Teachers. Academic Information Service, Inc., P.O. Box 929, College Park, MD 20741. Designed for college professors, this clearly written guide to filing U.S. taxes explains just about everything writers need to know about deducting travel, educational, home-office and other business expenses. Contains sample filled-out tax forms and relevant tax-court case narratives.

Tax Guide for Small Businesses. Reasonably understandable to non-accountants, this official U.S. Internal Revenue Service guide to deducting business expenses is available free by calling (800) 829-3676 or visiting http://www.irs.ustreas.gov on the World Wide Web.

Writers' Organizations

Both *Literary Market Place* and *Writer's Market* list dozens of specialized writers' organizations; for general professional support, I especially recommend these four.

American Society of Journalists and Authors, Inc., 1501 Broadway, Suite 302, New York, NY 10036; (212) 997-0947; e-mail 75227.1650@compuserve.com. Stringent qualifications restrict membership to prolifically publishing writers, but ASJA's valuable "Contract Watch" e-mail newsletter and annual conference in New York City are open to nonmembers.

Authors Guild, 330 W. 42nd St., New York, NY 10036; (212) 563-5904; e-mail staff@authorsguild.org. For published writers only. Dispenses advice on contracts and other legal matters; lobbies Congress on issues relevant to writers; publishes enlightening quarterly publication.

International Women's Writing Guild, Box 810, Gracie Station, New York, NY 10028; (212) 737-7536; e-mail iwwg@iwwg.com. Supportive networking organization for women writers at all levels of professionalism. Workshops, newsletter, semiannual "meet the agents" program; events are open to men as well.

National Writers Union, 113 University Pl, 6th Floor, New York, NY 10003; (212) 254-0279; e-mail nwu@netcom.com. Membership open to serious working writers, whether published or not. Activist organization devoted to improving working conditions for writers in all genres. Especially good handling of grievances.

Software Resources

The Working Writer. Dolphin Software Solutions, 1917 W. 4th Ave., Suite 256, Vancouver, BC V6J 1M7, Canada; (604) 739-1336; e-mail diarmani@axionet.com. A specially designed

database program for Windows into which you can load information about markets, your submissions, upcoming deadlines, follow-up dates and payments, and generate reports such as submission histories, all accepted work, all unpaid work, etc.

WriteTrak. Grossman Development Company, P.O. Box 85732, Seattle, WA 98145-1732; (800) 891-0962; e-mail gdc@earthlink .net. A Windows or Mac program that makes it easy to keep track of article submissions, income and expenses, and to construct a list of all your publications.

Resources In or About Cyberspace

Gach, Gary, *Writers.Net*. Rocklin, CA, Prima Publishing, 1997. Offers thousands of annotated Internet addresses for finding online resources of interest to writers of fiction, poetry, plays, screenplays and journalism.

Groves, Dawn, *The Writer's Guide to the Internet*. Wilsonville, OR, Franklin, Beedle & Associates, 1997. Includes seventeen useful pages of Internet addresses of writers' mailing lists, newsgroups and World Wide Web sites. Most of the rest of the book concerns the technicalities of self-publishing your work online.

Rose, Lance, *Netlaw: Your Rights in the Online World*. Berkeley, CA, Osborne McGraw-Hill, 1995. Curious about how cyberspace affects writers and publishers? This highly readable work explains the operative legal principles, with illuminating case studies.

Yudkin, Marcia, *Marketing Online*. New York, Plume/Penguin, 1995. Several of the chapters here provide dos and don'ts for using the Internet and online services to "schmooze" and find editors who may be interested in your work.

Although addresses for online venues change rapidly and often, the following valuable resources will probably continue to remain available for years to come:

- Internet newsgroups: Check out misc.writing, alt.journa lism.freelance.
- Online services: Each of the major online services has at

least one large discussion area for writers. CompuServe has a Journalism Forum, the Writers and Literary Forums and the "Writers and Editors" section of the Working from Home Forum; America OnLine, the Writers Club; Prodigy, the Books & Writers Bulletin Board.

- The Freelance Writing Frequently Asked Questions (FAQ) File: Latest version available by sending any e-mail message to FL@yudkin.com

GLOSSARY

all rights—When a writer sells "all rights" to a publication, he or she agrees to have no further monetary or legal claim with respect to that piece of writing; generally, this represents an unfair deal for the writer.

angle—A specific aspect of a topic, which serves as a focus for an article.

assignment—An agreement between you and a publication that you will write a particular article by a certain date for a certain sum of money.

as told to—In a byline, this phrase indicates that the first party named provided the information to the second party named, who wrote it up.

bio or bio note—One sentence or two about the author of an article. In a publication, usually positioned either on the bottom of the first page of the article or at the end.

byline—A phrase like "by Jane Author" that signals who wrote an article.

cliché—A predictable, tiresome combination of words.

clips—Photocopies of your published articles.

column—A series of pieces by the same author appearing regularly in the same publication. Or, a *department piece* (see below).

consumer magazine—Magazine oriented toward the general public or some demographic subset thereof, narrowed by geography, age, special interests, etc. Contrasts with *trade magazine*, below.

contract—Agreement signed by two parties, enforceable through the legal system.

copyediting—Detailed editing for consistency and correctness of punctuation, spelling, usage, titles, etc.

copyright—Legal ownership of a piece of writing. Unless a freelance writer signs something to the contrary, a piece of writing belongs legally to the writer, not a publication that prints it.

cover letter—Letter included along with a completed article. Should always be addressed to a specific person.

deadline—Day by which the writer must submit an assigned article, without fail.

department piece—One of a grouping of shorter articles usually placed toward the front of a magazine, in topic areas that tend to be the same issue after issue. Contrasts with *feature article*, below.

editor—Person responsible for collecting and/or polishing the content for a periodical.

electronic rights—Right to include a writer's work in online, CD-ROM or similar computer-based compilations.

fact checkers—Personnel at better magazines charged with the task of checking the accuracy of names and facts in articles prior to publication.

feature article—For a newspaper, an article constructed in magazine style, with a lead, nut graph, body and conclusion. For a magazine, a longer article on a subject not treated in every issue; contrasts with *department piece*, above.

first serial rights—Right to publish a work for the first time in any periodical. Often modified by a geographical adjective, such as "first *North American* serial rights."

forum—Online, a special-interest discussion group that proceeds by people posting public messages over a series of days or weeks.

freelance writer—In contrast to a staff writer, someone who writes on a per-article basis for various publications.

ghostwriting—Where a writer produces work using someone else's expertise or experiences, to appear under the other person's byline or with a joint byline.

house style—A periodical's idiosyncratic rules about how to treat numbers, capital letters, spelling, etc.

Internet—An international network of computers that can communicate with each other.

kill fee—Fee that a writer may receive after an assigned article is rejected. Stated as a percentage of the normal fee, ranging from 10 to 100 percent.

lead—Introductory paragraph or paragraphs of an article.

lead time—The typical length of time at a periodical between submission of an idea and publication of the article stemming from that idea. For a monthly magazine, lead time ranges from four months to one year.

letter of agreement—Summary in letter form of the terms of an agreement; when signed by both parties, it functions as a contract.

literary agent—Person who represents authors vis-à-vis book publishers.

mailing list—Online, a special-interest discussion group that proceeds by people posting messages that get sent automatically to all members of the list.

masthead—List of who's who at a magazine; usually a vertical column of titles and names near the beginning of each issue.

microfiche—Information system which stores the pages of old newspapers and magazines in miniature, readable on special machines in libraries.

modem—Device which sends data over phone lines from one computer to another.

multiple submissions—Sending a completed article simultaneously to more than one potential outlet. Not recommended, although *multiple queries* (see below) are usually safe.

multiple queries—Simultaneously sending essentially the same query to more than one publication. See *query*, below.

news article—An article, usually in a newspaper, which recounts events, with all the main points at the very beginning of the article. In contrast to a *feature article* (see above).

news hook—*Lead* (see above) that uses current events or concerns to introduce a topic.

news peg—Same as *news hook*, above.

newsgroup—Internet discussion group focused on a specific subject. Similar to *forum*, above.

nut graph—The section of a magazine article just after a lead, whose function is to lay out the focus of the piece and, often, background or perspective on the topic.

on assignment—See *assignment*, above.

on spec—Short for on speculation. Arrangement where the publication isn't promising to buy a piece, only to give the completed article a serious look. Contrasts with *on assignment*.

one-time rights—The non-exclusive right to publish a work once, without regard for being first or later. A writer can sell one-time rights for the same piece to many publications, which is not the case for *first serial rights*, above.

op-ed piece—The sort of short opinion piece that gets published on or opposite the editorial page of a newspaper. Can also appear in a magazine.

payment on acceptance—Policy whereby the writer receives an article fee shortly after the completed piece is accepted for publication.

payment on publication—Policy whereby the writer does not receive the article fee until shortly after the piece is published.

profile—Article that provides a well-rounded picture of one person.

Q&A—Format for reproducing the back-and-forth of an interview.

query or query letter—Article proposal, usually one page, in letter format.

quotation—Saying of a famous person.

quote—Use of a person's exact words, within quotation marks, in an article.

reprint rights—Same as *second serial rights*, below.

rights—The collective name for the different ways in which writers can authorize publication of their work. See *first serial rights, second serial rights, reprint rights, one-time rights, all rights* and *electronic rights*.

roundup—Type of article consisting of comments or stories from several people on the same topic, joined together with a brief introduction.

royalties—Semi-annual payments made to an author by a publisher for book sales.

SASE—Self-addressed stamped envelope. It's customary to enclose one with your query letters or submissions to magazines.

second serial rights—The right to publish, one time, a piece that has already been sold or published elsewhere. The counting stops at second, so that if a piece has appeared fifteen times, the writer is still selling second serial rights.

serial—Librarians' word for periodical.

self-syndication—Arranging on one's own the regular sale of a newspaper column to a number of papers.

sidebar—Shorter article accompanying a longer one, often boxed and bylined separately.

slant—Equivalent to *angle*, above.

slush pile—The mountains of unsolicited manuscripts from people unknown to the editors.

spec or speculation—See *on spec* above.

staff writer—A writer employed at a magazine or newspaper, receiving a salary and benefits.

story—A term used by editors, a story can denote a nonfiction article as well as a fictional short story.

stringer—Non-employee of a periodical who covers events for it.

subheads—Subtitles within an article.

Sunday supplement—Magazine distributed as part of a Sunday newspaper.

syndicate—Organization that distribute articles to newspapers and collect fees, a percentage of which goes to the writer.

syndication—Distributing articles through a *syndicate* (see above). See also *self-syndication*.

topic—General subject of an article. Broader and vaguer than an angle or slant.

trade magazine—Magazine oriented toward a particular industry, profession or business, designed to inform and advise on business-related developments in that field. Generally not on newsstands.

transitions—Words and phrases that link one paragraph or one sentence to another.

World Wide Web—A portion of the *Internet* (see above) where individuals and companies post information for general access.

work for hire—A legal term designed to refer to the fact that an employee's work generally belongs to the employer. As with *all rights*, above, freelancers who sign contracts designating their articles work for hire thereby give up all further legal and monetary claim to their work.

writer's guidelines—Set of information available from a magazine that describes its needs, payment, policies, contact information, etc.

INDEX